Political Parties and Democracy in Central America

Political Parties and Democracy in Central America

EDITED BY
Louis W. Goodman,
William M. LeoGrande,
and Johanna Mendelson Forman

Westview Press
BOULDER • SAN FRANCISCO • OXFORD

Cover photograph: Guatemala, 1990, courtesy of Bill Garrett

Copyright © 1992 by Louis W. Goodman, William M. LeoGrande, and Johanna Mendelson Forman

Published in 1992 in the United States of America by Westview Press, Inc., 5500 Central Avenue, Boulder, Colorado 80301-2877, and in the United Kingdom by Westview Press, 36 Lonsdale Road, Summertown, Oxford OX2 7EW

Library of Congress Cataloging-in-Publication Data
Political parties and democracy in Central America / edited by Louis
    W. Goodman, William M. LeoGrande, and Johanna Mendelson Forman.
        p.   cm.
    Includes index.
    ISBN 0-8133-8242-4. — ISBN 0-8133-8243-2 (pbk.)
    1. Political parties—Central America.   2. Central America—
Politics and government.   I. Goodman, Louis Wolf.   II. LeoGrande,
William M.   III. Forman, Johanna Mendelson.
JL1419.A45P65   1992
324.2728—dc20   92-21060
                                                                         CIP

Printed and bound in the United States of America

The paper used in this publication meets the requirements
of the American National Standard for Permanence of Paper
for Printed Library Materials Z39.48-1984.

10   9   8   7   6   5   4   3   2   1

On November 16, 1989, six Jesuit priests and two women at El Salvador's Central American University were murdered. Two of the slain Jesuits, Father Ignacio Ellacuria and Father Segundo Montes, participated in the conferences that led to the creation of this work. We dedicate this book to the memory of those slain in El Salvador and to the courageous work they performed in promoting a more just and equitable future for El Salvador and for the region.

Contents

PART TWO
Political Parties and Their International Connections

Preface

Fortunately, contemporary Central American politics has changed since this project began in 1987. This book is a result of a four-year effort to describe and analyze the evolution of political parties in Central America. Today democracy is accepted as the organizing principle of the region's political systems. No longer is the primary regional concern the role of external actors in internal political events. Central American political leaders are working together to resolve some of the most thorny regional problems, most salient among them the need to continue the consolidation of democratic politics, which remain at risk despite the gains of recent years.

In 1987, two great powers were at loggerheads in the battle to win the "hearts and minds" of the Nicaraguan people. A military strongman was terrorizing a broad coalition of civilian forces in Panama. A Costa Rican president was trying his own brand of shuttle diplomacy in an effort to peacefully resolve regional disorder. And a Salvadoran president was steadily losing the battle against a growing shift from the center to the right in public reaction to the ongoing civil war.

There was also hope. Guatemala in 1986 had held a fair election, and the first freely elected civilian president in over thirty years had renewed the struggle for political space. Belize also demonstrated new directions as a free state, with emerging political parties and the attendant problems of a postcolonial government all coming to bear on its fragile democratic system. Hondurans, torn by loyalties to support its military, also bore the brunt of hostilities as that nation served as a buffer for the international political struggle that raged next door in Nicaragua.

The American University joined forces with the *Centro Interamericano de Asesoría y Promoción Electoral* (CAPEL), a Costa Rican organization concerned with electoral reform and training, and in 1987 scholarly teams began to explore political party development in Central America. A group of U.S., European, and Central American scholars began a journey of collaboration that started in Guatemala City and ended in Washington, D.C.

In June 1988 project scholars met in the capital of Guatemala to review early drafts of papers that would form the core of the chapters in this volume. Because of the subject matter of the project, scholars were enlisted to suggest political leaders who would comment on their work and attend an international forum on political party development. That forum, a Washington conference of Central American political leaders, took place in April 1989. The event was unique because it brought together scholars with key politicians of the region. The April 1989 conference brought together *Sandinista* officials with party leaders of what eventually became known as the UNO coalition in Nicaragua. It brought to Washington the renowned Jesuit Father Ignacio Ellacuria, who spoke eloquently about the efforts to promote a dialogue with the FMLN guerrillas. We will all miss the compassion and skill at mediation he brought to his work before his untimely death in 1989. Also among the conference participants were political leaders from Belize, Costa Rica, Honduras, and Guatemala. Panama was represented only by a spokesperson for the Noriega regime; that government enjoined the participation of any opposition leader. Reflecting on the proceedings of that conference, it is now clear that many signals of recent events were already evident.

After the conference others entered the dialogue, so that by 1990 we had commissioned essays not only from the core group of participants but also from scholars in the Soviet Union and Mexico. Many of the essays reflect recent events that have affected political party development in the region.

Although the conference in Washington marked an important point in the public dialogue about political issues that affect party development in Central America, the publication of a volume that explores the evolution of political parties in the region affords a wider forum for examining the roots of Central American civic culture. The process of commissioning, editing, and revising these essays has brought us into close contact with a special group of scholars and Central American leaders and has created a vital network that endures with the publication of this book.

No project is possible with the work of editors and authors alone. This book is the product of a team based in the Democracy Projects at The American University. The initial translation and organization of this book was carried out by Michael Gold, associate director of the Democracy Projects. Staff associate Maria Gil Montero and staff assistant Tricia Juhn played key roles in the early days of the project. Steven Pierce served as rapporteur and translator and assisted in the preparation of essays for this volume. Elizabeth Arias facilitated the publication of this book. Patricia Loo assisted throughout this project; without her help many parts of this work would be incomplete. Maria Dávila assisted in the final editing. Her painstaking work with the final manuscript and her ability to check original Spanish text against the English translation are reflected in the text and documents in this volume. Ana Centeno, James McDonald, Graciela Canedo, Betty Sitka, and Cathy Kreyche also provided important assistance.

Conference work in Central America was carried out in collaboration with the staff of CAPEL. Jorge Mario Garcia Laguardia, CAPEL Director, and his capable assistant, Cecilia Cortes, made the early phases of the project possible and provided the basis for this important collaborative effort. The 1989 Washington conference was the work of Cynthia Arnson, currently associate director of the Washington, D.C., office of Americas Watch. Her guidance and energy made it possible to bring together some of the most diverse political talent from the region. She also coauthored a chapter in this volume.

No endeavor of this kind is possible without financial support. The United States Agency for International Development (AID), Office of Democratic Initiatives, Latin America and the Caribbean, provided the principal funding for this project. Program Officer Roma Knee assisted the project at every step of the way. Her guidance and willingness to find solutions to a variety of problems are most appreciated. We are also deeply grateful to Dr. Norma Parker, director of AID's Office of Democratic Initiatives during the life of the project; to her successor, Mr. William Schoux; and to Latin American and Caribbean AID deputy administrator, Ambassador James Michel. The United States Department of State, Office of Policy Planning, American Regional Area, under the leadership of Luigi Einaudi, provided important support for our Washington conference. That office helped encourage dialogue among the diverse political leaders who participated in our project.

Other major financial support for this project came from the Ford Foundation's Mexico City office. Stephen Cox and Christopher Welna, respectively director and program officer of the foundation's office in Mexico City, lent vital assistance, including bringing to the dialogue political leaders from Nicaragua, Cuba, and the Soviet Union. The American University's continued support helped make the project a reality. Special thanks go to University Provost Milton Greenberg and to Frederic Jacobs, dean of faculties.

The chapters in this volume reflect a complex process of collaboration and revision, but, as with any book, the final responsibility lies with the editors alone.

Louis W. Goodman
William M. LeoGrande
Johanna Mendelson Forman

Introduction

1

Political Parties
and the Political Systems
of Central America

Louis W. Goodman

Before the late 1970s, Central America was a subject of little concern for scholars, policymakers, or the general public in the United States. Few citizens could name any of the seven countries of the region; for policymakers major issues included keeping the Panama Canal free of silt and the price of bananas low; few scholars had researched the politics or societies of the region. As a result, when the Salvadoran dictator Gen. Carlos Humberto Romero was overthrown in 1979 by a group led by progressive junior officers and when the government of Anastasio Somoza in Nicaragua was ousted through civil war led by the *Sandinista* Front, a huge reassessment began. Central America became news. U.S. citizens started to read about the region on the front pages of their newspapers; policymakers evaluated the meaning of these changes for global political strategy; scholars began to build an inventory of research focusing on the region.

By the 1980s, the seven countries on the isthmus between Mexico and South America had become central to American foreign policy. The United States saw itself locked in a struggle with its giant rival, the Soviet Union, for control of the political systems of the countries of Central America—Belize, Guatemala, El Salvador, Honduras, Nicaragua, Costa Rica, and Panama. Civil wars in Guatemala, El Salvador, and Nicaragua pitted U.S.-backed forces against those supported by the Soviet Union and its Western Hemisphere ally, Cuba. Honduras and Panama were victims of political instability in the 1980s with the Honduran military asserting the need to protect itself from its neighbors'

3

civil wars and from purported home-bred insurgence. Panama's political system was dominated by the Panamanian Defense Force led by Manuel Antonio Noriega until December 20, 1989, when U.S. troops invaded Panama and established a civilian government.

Government policymakers quickly concluded that Central America was an area of "regional conflict"—a small stage on which the global rivalry between the United States and the Soviet Union (with its "surrogate" Cuba) was being played out. Other analysts argued that the upheavals reflected the massive political, economic, and social inequality of the region and that U.S. interests would be better served by ameliorating these inequities and focusing less on the Soviet threat.[1] In this heated atmosphere, all new knowledge about the region presented to policymakers or scholars became contentious. Information was immediately seized on and used to sustain one policy position or another. Advocates created images of Central America that had more to do with their own political agendas than with the social and political realities of the region.

The 1990s has been heralded as the decade that will usher in the "end of history."[2] What is hoped for is the consolidation of democratic political systems worldwide, now that the rivalry between communism and democracy, the Soviet Union and the United States, has subsided. Whether such hope is realized depends on the complexities of international relations and national politics. With the onset of the "new thinking" in the former Soviet Union, Central America has ceased to be viewed as a theater for superpower rivalry. Policymakers are less concerned with advocating positions and more focused on improving prospects for democratic pluralism in the region. They have discovered that little knowledge is available about Central America, especially in the United States and especially about the region's political systems.

Central America is now experiencing competition in the shaping of its political systems, unprecedented since the wars of independence from Spain in the early 1800s. Although civil wars still rage in El Salvador and Guatemala, all sides now concede that the region's future lies with democracy.

The most widely accepted definition of democracy is a political system with three essential characteristics: (1) meaningful and extensive competition among individuals and organized groups for effective positions of government power at regular intervals that exclude the use of force; (2) a high level of political participation in the selection of leaders, at least through regular and fair elections, such that no major group is excluded; and (3) a level of civil and political liberties—freedom of expression, press, association, assembly—sufficient to ensure the integrity of political competition and participation.[3] Like all definitions, this describes an ideal type, not something one would expect to encounter perfectly represented in day-to-day life. Even long-established democracies such as the United Kingdom, the United States, and Switzerland have political practices that substantially deviate from the ideal of full participation, perfect competition, and complete civil liberties.

How democracy will be shaped in the countries of Central America depends on the nature of the political system of each country in the region. The evolution of the major institutions of these systems—principal among them political parties—will be crucial to the ultimate form of democratic consolidation.

In what political parties theorist Maurice Duverger calls "true democracy," political parties provide a dual link between a nation's people and their government.[4] They aggregate the diverse interests of individual citizens and make policy choices possible by posing feasible alternatives. Political parties do this by performing four important functions for a nation's political system: (1) nominating candidates for election to public office under the name of the party, (2) structuring the voting choice in elections, (3) proposing alternative government programs, and (4) coordinating the actions of government officials. Unfortunately most political parties in Central America do not carry out these functions efficiently. Many lack the coherence, party discipline, or resources to do so.

The significance of political parties for the political systems of Central America varies widely. In McDonald and Ruhl's analysis of the significance of political parties in Central American politics between 1968 and 1988, they concluded that parties were "marginal actors" in Panama; "secondary actors" in El Salvador, Guatemala and Honduras; "primary actors" in Nicaragua; and "dominant" in the political system of Costa Rica.[5] Although they did not include Belize in their analysis, the strength of its parties would surely place it in the latter category.

Much of the weakness of political parties in nations in which they are "marginal" or "secondary" can be attributed to parties' relations with other institutions in their political system. In most Central American nations the armed forces, either separately or in league with private-sector interest groups, have dominated national political systems for more than one hundred fifty years. Although the role of the armed forces in Central American politics has changed in important ways in the twentieth century, the history described by Richard L. Millett in this volume documents repeated suspension of democratic political party activities when the armed forces have judged their interests threatened. The result is weak political parties that can often be characterized as elitist, plagued by factionalism, personalistic, poorly organized, and without consistent bases of mass support.

Despite these circumstances, all seven countries of the region have elected civilian presidents since 1985, and all, with the exception of Panama, have seen a president of one political party voluntarily relinquish power to an elected successor of a rival party. Although this is a highly positive sign, to assume that this is an indicator of untrammelled political participation, competition, and broad respect for civil liberties would be what Terry Karl has called "the fallacy of electoralism."[6] Yet as Duverger indicates in his 1951 classic *Les Partis Politiques,* such activities, permitting the development of new elites, are crucial for the deepening of democracy.[7] Although there is always a danger that parties can become closed and authoritarian, Duverger argues that elections, by requiring parties to be involved in "organizing the masses and recruiting leaders...protect(s) democracy against the toxins that it secretes within itself in the course of its development."[8] Thus, while the political parties and political systems described in this volume may have grave imperfections, many incompatible with strict concepts of democracy, the recent history of Central American political parties points to institutions beginning a process of consolidation and, most important, a process of developing political leaders with stronger ties to the mass of the region's citizens.

Just as the individual political parties of Central American countries are experiencing change, so too are the national political party systems they comprise. In 1988 McDonald and Ruhl described Nicaragua as having a single-party system; Costa Rica and Honduras as having two-party systems; and El Salvador, Guatemala, and Panama as "emerging multiparty" systems.[9] Belize, more clearly than any other nation in the region, has a strong two-party system.

While comparative political theorists once believed that two-party systems consolidate democracy in national political systems, recent writings by Lijphart and others have shown that characteristics such as party polarization are more important for democratic stability.[10] The experiences of Switzerland, the Netherlands, and Italy show the compatibility of multiparty systems with the consolidation of democracy. The long history of two-party rivalry in Argentina, Colombia, and Honduras indicates that two-party rule can coexist with military-authoritarian rule and extreme political elitism.

The debate about the virtues of two-party and multiparty systems has not been present in scholarly discussions of single-party political systems. Although Sartori has pointed to a variety of single-party systems, there is wide agreement that single-party political systems impede the development of open and free political competition so essential for the deepening of democracy.[11] Thus the confirmation in Nicaragua of broad-based party competition with the *Sandinista* Popular Front can only be seen as a positive sign for that nation's politics.

Two key characteristics of Central American political party systems are fragmentation and polarization. For example, in Guatemala the presentation of presidential candidates by eight political parties in the 1985 elections and twelve political parties in its 1990 election reflected a highly fragmented political system. Furthermore, only six of the parties presenting candidates in 1990 had also presented candidates in 1986. This reflected a severe lack of party continuity, even in the course of four years. Jorge Serrano, the 1990 victor, had been in 1985 a member of the party of his principal 1990 rival Jorge Carpio Nicole's National Civic Union. Although such lack of coherence is present in a number of Central American countries, this instability is particularly severe if accompanied by political polarization. Although South American political systems such as those of Chile and Uruguay had long histories of democratic competition among established parties, deep-seated hatred fueled by strong reactions to ideological differences opened these countries to years of authoritarian military rule in the 1970s and 1980s. Similarly, while only briefly abandoning the facade of democratically contested elections between 1953 and 1958, profound enmity between Colombia's political parties slowed its consolidation of democracy such that only in the 1990s are political parties with broader representation taking their places in that country's political system.

With the passing of the cold war an important ideological basis for political polarization has been removed. Both conservative and progressive political parties are eschewing utopian solutions to national dilemmas. Efforts at reconciliation in Nicaragua after the triumph of the Violeta Chamorro-led UNO coalition over the *Sandinista* Front and other more modest indications of interparty cooperation elsewhere are important, positive signs.

How we judge whether Central American political parties enhance prospects for democracy in their countries depends on knowledge of the evolution of the politics of each country over time and of the effects of international influences on its politics. This book, which provides information to assess this situation, is divided into two parts. The first part discusses the roles of political parties in the national political systems of Central America. The second part examines the principal international influences that have affected the region's political systems and its political parties. The authors of the twelve chapters of Part One have studied the political systems of the seven Central American nations for most of their scholarly careers. In fact, seven of the eight authors of chapters 5–12, which treat specific Central American countries, are citizens of those countries. Each brings many years of experience analyzing, and sometimes participating in, his or her nation's politics.

The first part begins with four chapters that provide an overview of the role of political parties in the national political systems of Central America. In "Colonial Heritage, External Domination, and Political Systems in Central America," Rodolfo Cerdas Cruz updates the discussion of how the historic legacy of Central America has affected its national political systems. Cerdas Cruz traces the dynamics of Central American politics from the colonial times of the *Capitania,* dominated by Guatemala City, with cross-border family politics. He demonstrates the present-day interplay of these historic forces within the context of rapid social and economic change and intense external interests—both economic and political.

In their chapter, "The Transitions to "Electoral" and Democratic Politics in Central America," Morris J. Blachman and Kenneth E. Sharpe examine the role of political parties in the region. They argue that, although elections indicate progress from military-dominated authoritarian rule, a transition to democracy is far from complete. Using the cogent analysis of history-based political science, they discuss the importance the limited roles political parties can play in furthering this transition in the region.

Richard L. Millett's chapter, "Politicized Warriors," provides an overview of the role the military as an institution has played in Central American politics since the nineteenth century. Although Millett indicates considerable variation in the structure of the armed forces from country to country, he describes an important process of transition: The firm alliance that existed between the military and local oligarchies at the beginning of the twentieth century broke down when military leaders concluded that they were being manipulated by national economic interests. This led to a seeming professionalization of many military institutions in the region and, more important, an escalation in the levels of arms and violence. Millett traces the evolution of Central American military relations to the present day, when some military institutions have concluded that their repressive domination of local politics can only result in societies in which violence is counterproductive, even for the military as institution. Millett concludes by tracing the efforts of Central American military institutions to transfer power to civilians and the halting response of civilian political leaders inured to decades of military repression of politics.

An understanding of law supports an understanding of history, political structure, and civil-military relations in setting a context for understanding political systems. Jorge Mario García Laguardia, in "Constitutional Framework for Political Parties in Central America," describes how the rule of law has evolved from a mechanism that excluded political parties from operating in the personalistic politics of the region to the present day, where national constitutional regimes are being restructured to facilitate political parties as leading actors in national political systems. Although the rule of law cannot guarantee that political systems function in a manner consistent with democratic principles, it nevertheless constitutes an important parameter for possible political action. Understanding the evolution of Central America's legal system and constitutional regimes is crucial for understanding the alternatives available to the region's political parties.

The final eight chapters in Part One comment on the history and structure of a single national political system and the role of political parties within it. They begin with Guatemala and continue down the isthmus to Panama. In the first chapter, "Parties, Transitions, and the Political System in Guatemala," Héctor Rosada Granados describes a political system that in 1991 celebrated the first transfer of power in its modern history between freely elected civilians of different political parties. This transition from Christian Democrat Marco Vinicio Cerezo to conservative businessman Jorge Serrano was cause for hope in a country whose political system, as described by Rosada Granados, has been a tragedy of authoritarian rule and failed transitions for many decades. Guatemala, as clearly as any other country, indicates that when the military relinquishes the presidency to an elected civilian, it relinquishes far less than 100 percent of political power. In fact, when Cerezo took office in 1986 he declared that he held 30 percent of the power in Guatemala's political system, while the armed forces retained 70 percent. A key question for analysts of political systems in Central America is whether Cerezo's election was a high point for democracy in Guatemala, prefacing a new decline into violence and authoritarian rule, or whether his regime and those that will follow will describe halting steps to consolidate justice and democracy in a political system wracked by civil war and decades of brutal authoritarian rule.

Party politics in Belize, described by Assad Shoman in his chapter of the same name, is distinct in most respects from that of its six Central American neighbors. Recently emerging from British colonial rule, Belize has adopted the Westminster political system and has a prime minister elected by parliament as its chief executive officer. In the past decade Belize has successfully weathered the first years of independence as well as alternation of power between the traditionally dominant Peoples' Unification Party to a newly resurgent United Democratic Party. Shoman provides a fascinating analysis of the transition from colonial rule to independence and asks whether political liberties associated with pluralist democracy have been respected in Belize's early years of independence. This is a significant question, not only for Belize but also for its Central American neighbors. In the future this question may need to be addressed in Belize in terms similar to those of its neighbors. Increasing numbers of Spanish-speaking immigrants are settling in this sparsely populated English-speaking country wedged between Mexico and Guatemala on the Caribbean coast, and Belizian per-capita income has fallen substantially since 1980.

In "Parties, Programs, and Politics in El Salvador," Cristina Eguizábal describes the struggles of disparate political interests to consolidate their positions after decades of authoritarian military rule. With a fragmented political system and political parties representing interests as diverse as a landed oligarchs and committed socialists, El Salvador has experienced ten years of disastrous, bloody civil war. At the same time political leaders have attempted to knit together a democratic political system. The murder of Father Ignacio Ellacuria, a principal participant in this project's 1989 Washington conference, and his colleagues bears tragic witness to the distance El Salvador must travel to end its violence and to create a political system in which citizens can be confident that justice will be done and interests fairly represented.

Ernesto Paz Aguilar, in his chapter, "The Origin and Development of Political Parties in Honduras," describes a nation in which political groups based in century-old conservative and liberal political movements have struggled for power in a relatively unconsolidated political system. The great fear in recent decades in Honduras has been that the military would impose itself and that bloodshed comparable to that of its neighbors would result. Honduras has not been exempt from political tragedy. This is, in part, due to its own deployment of its military as a buffer against violence in neighboring countries, in part because of its political parties' inability to clearly establish civilian control. Less clear has been the impact of a massive presence of U.S. troops, which has led some to call the nation "Battleship Honduras." Paz Aguilar's chapter gives readers the opportunity to judge for themselves the prospects for the consolidation of pluralist democracy in Honduras.

"Nicaragua, 1944–84" was written by Virgilio Godoy Reyes, elected in 1990 to serve as vice president of the government of Nicaragua. (The 1990 elections transferred political power from the *Sandinista* Front to the coalition of political parties led by Violeta Chamorro.) Both a well-known scholar and an active participant in Nicaraguan politics, Godoy describes the historical role of liberal and conservative party groupings in Nicaraguan politics, the background of Nicaragua's political system during the authoritarian rule of the Somoza family, and the transformation of Nicaragua's political system during the first five years of rule by the *Sandinista* Front. Godoy describes a system in which the roles of political parties in power and political parties in opposition are far from fully defined. Although the transfer of power in 1990 indicated greater maturity in Nicaragua's political system than some observers had anticipated, the potential for instability in Nicaragua is evident in the description provided in this chapter. In "Political Parties and Postrevolutionary Politics in Nicaragua," William M. LeoGrande complements Godoy's history and brings it up to 1992. LeoGrande not only discusses Nicaragua's recent political party history, but also foreign influences on it throughout elections which brought the UNO coalition to power and into the first year of Violetta Chammorro's government.

Costa Rica is frequently described as the "success story" of Central America. Its pluralist democratic government, born in a civil war that ended in 1946, effected the formal elimination of the Costa Rican military institution. The depth, coherence, and extent of this "success" is analyzed by José Luis Vega Carballo in "Political Parties, Party Systems, and Democracy in Costa Rica." Despite Costa Rica's success, Vega Carballo's chapter shows that struggle and contestation are critical for sustaining pluralist democracy in Costa Rica.

With the installation of the government headed by civilian Guillermo Endara as a result of U.S.-backed "Operation Just Cause" on December 20, 1990, David A. Smith's political-historical analysis in "Panama: Political Parties, Social Crisis, and Democracy in the 1980s" has gained immediacy. Smith describes the history of a weak political system, long dominated by narrow political interests. He describes the change in that system when military strongmen Omar Torrijos and his successor Manuel Noriega attempted to insert populism through military rule. The removal of General Noriega by U.S. troops and the dismantling of the Panamanian Defense Force by the Endara government has created an opportunity for political architects to design new political institutions. Whether the edifice of Panama's political system will be new authoritarianism with increased social and economic stratification or a pluralist democracy with broad and deep representation of the interests of the 1.8 million citizens of this strategically located nation is a question whose answer can be informed by Smith's chapter.

The second part of this book focuses on the international connections of political parties. During Central America's long national histories of inward-looking authoritarian rule, a variety of international forces struggled to influence the transformation of the region's political systems. The seven chapters of the second part of this book describe the efforts of the most important international forces that attempted to gain such influence: the United States, the Soviet Union, Cuba, the Catholic church, international groupings of political parties, and other Latin American countries.

The complex efforts of the United States to influence national politics in Central America are described by Cynthia J. Arnson and Johanna Mendelson Forman in their chapter, "Projecting Democracy in Central America: Old Wine, New Bottles?" Through interviews with U.S. and Central American officials, as well as detailed analyses of the public record and scholarly literature, Arnson and Mendelson Forman allow the reader to judge the extent to which efforts by the United States have enhanced prospects for consolidated pluralist democratic political systems. While rejecting the conclusion that electoral assistance was merely a fig leaf for doing battle with Soviet and Cuban-based forces, they raise important questions about the coincidence of U.S. and Central American political objectives.

In "Esquipulas: Politicians in Command," William Goodfellow and James Morrell describe the process through which Central American politicians created an environment in which it became possible to strengthen the fragile democratic elements of their political systems. Their chapter complements that of Arnson and Mendelson Forman by describing the evolution of "an ideological confrontation between Washington and Managua" into a transformed regional context for political party politics.

More questions about the interests of a superpower and its allies in the region are raised by Wayne S. Smith in "The Soviet Union and Cuba in Central America: Guardians Against Democracy?" Smith describes how the Soviet Union and Cuba attempted to pursue their political interests in the region, both jointly and separately, through the 1980s. Smith suggests that, although these nations were pursuing interests different from those of the United States, to suggest that they were merely promoting antidemocratic political objectives is an oversimplification. Smith analyzes these more complex objectives and the Central American and U.S. response.

In "The Communist Party of the Soviet Union and the Communist Movement in Central America," Sergo Mikoyan complements Wayne Smith's analysis. Mikoyan, long-time editor of the Soviet National Academy of Sciences publication *Latinskaya Amerika,* argues that relations between Soviet and Latin American Communist parties had a life of its own, often irrelevant to the politics of the region. Mikoyan describes Soviet practice, which ignored the political conditions of the region and was largely designed to affect the careers of a small number of Soviet and Central American party officials. This chapter questions the nature of the "Soviet threat" in the region prior to *glasnost.* It also suggests that the Soviet Union will have little capacity to have an impact on politics in Central America while it is struggling to put its own political house in order.

In "The Official Party of Mexico and the Country's Diplomacy in Central America," Adolfo Aguilar Zinser describes the actions of another political system long dominated by a single party but undergoing its own *perestroika*. Mexico's political struggles have been focused on establishing positive relations with its neighbors in Central America while maintaining autonomy from the "Giant of the North," which has often been seen as a threat to its own political autonomy. Thus the actions of the long-time official party of Mexico—the *Partido Revolucionario Institucional* (PRI)—have had important impacts on Mexican diplomatic efforts to strengthen allegiances with political interests in Central America. These actions likely will continue to be important as both Mexico and nations of Central America struggle to make their political systems more democratic and pluralist.

The political actor with the longest consistent record of influence in the region is the Catholic church. In her chapter, "Religion and Democratization in Central America," Margaret E. Crahan describes the efforts of the Catholic church and its Protestant rivals to influence politics in the region. Crahan describes the struggles between liberal-minded priests who sought to disassociate their institution from the alliance with oligarchic forces that had characterized it since colonial days. Crahan's comparative political historical analysis indicates how the church can be driven to play a political role when its constituents are abused by secular political institutions. Similarly, in noting the activities of Protestant ministries in Central America, Crahan provides readers with insights into contestations for the "hearts and minds" of Central American citizens in the realm of the sacred.

The final chapter of this book's second section describes the activities of transnational political parties. In "The Party Internationals and Democracy in Central America," Wolf Grabendorff describes the role of European-based political parties in the region. Grabendorff shows how these activities are firmly rooted in the domestic political dynamics of their host European countries. He explains the dynamics that result in internationals having greater influence during times of opposition, especially to authoritarian governments.

This book contains a comprehensive scholarly description of Central America's political systems, the political parties that shape these systems, and international influences that have affected them. Since publicly available information on the region's political systems is in such short supply, this book aims both to improve the quality of knowledge about political systems of Central America and to fill gaps in the scholarly literature. The information and perspectives of regional scholarly research can enhance the capacities of policymakers to make sound judgments that strengthen the region's political systems. The chapters in this book do so by focusing on political parties—the key institutions in the political systems of the region for consolidating democracy. The rich detail about both the national political systems of the region and the international forces that affect these systems and their political parties is essential for understanding the region's political future and the separate futures of each of its seven nations.

Finally, and most important, this book is a collaborative effort of a multinational team of scholars: eight of the volume's twenty chapters are written by Central Americans, nine by United States citizens, one by a Mexican, one by a German, and one by a Russian. Their views provide a fresh approach to a region where new ideas are crucial for understanding the core issues of its political future.

Notes

1. See, for example, Morris J. Blachman, William M. LeoGrande, and Kenneth Sharpe, eds. *Confronting Revolution: Security Through Diplomacy in Central America* (New York: Pantheon, 1986).

2. See Frances Fukuyama, "The End of History," *The National Interest* (Summer 1989):3–8.

3. Adapted from Larry Diamond, Juan J. Linz, and Seymour Martin Lipset, eds., *Politics in Developing Countries: Comparing Experiences With Democracy* (Boulder, Colo.: Lynne Rienner, 1990).

4. See Maurice Duverger, *Les Partis Politique* (Paris: Armand Colin, 1951; English ed., New York: John Wiley and Sons, 1954).

5. Ronald H. McDonald and J. Mark Ruhl, *Party Politics and Elections in Latin America* (Boulder, Colo.: Westview Press, 1989), p. 2.

6. For a discussion of how certain elections can "impede democratization," see Terry Karl, "Imposing Consent: Electoralism vs. Democratization in El Salvador," in Paul Drake and Eduardo Silva, eds., *Elections and Democratization in Latin America, 1980–1985* (La Jolla, Calif.: Center for Iberian and Latin American Studies, University of California at San Diego, 1986).

7. Duverger, *Les Partis Politiques*.

8. Ibid., p. 425.

9. McDonald and Ruhl, *Party Politics and Elections*, p. 9.

10. Arend Lijphart, *Democracies: Patterns of Majoritarian and Consensus Government in Twenty-One Countries* (New Haven: Yale University Press, 1984).

11. Giovanni Sartori, *Parties and Party Systems: A Framework for Analysis* (Cambridge: Cambridge University Press, 1976), chap. 7.

PART ONE

The Role of Political Parties in National Political Systems

2

Colonial Heritage, External Domination, and Political Systems in Central America

Rodolfo Cerdas Cruz

Viewing Central America as a unified entity with a single history may be politically or intellectually convenient, but it is an artificial construction. As such it ignores the highly differentiated experiences that have variously shaped the political systems of the countries in this region.[1] This chapter will eschew a unified approach. Instead it will examine the dynamic interaction between external and internal factors in terms of the many contexts created by the historical experiences of conquest and colonialism. Understanding this interaction will not only help explain the variety of political systems currently found in the countries of Central America, but it will also provide a way to evaluate the prospects for democracy within these countries during the coming decade.

Historical Antecedents

The nature of the conquest had important implications for the development of Central American societies.[2] Fundamentally, the conquest produced a new elite that exercised dominion over lands, material resources, and indigenous peoples.[3] The competition for wealth and power among the conquistadors created bitter rivalries over conflicting claims and interests. Through the expropriation of indigenous lands and the awarding of estates (*encomiendas*) by the Spanish Crown, each conquistador and his followers would attempt to stake a claim on territory over which he could exercise exclusive authority and power. As

17

in the Middle Ages, these territorial fiefdoms were expanded by marriage as well as by warfare. Marriage and sexual relations between the Spanish and Indians were also determinants of social organization within colonies.[4] These territorial aggrandizements and familial claims eventually determined the "limits of the modern nations" of Central America.[5]

Diverse methods of domination and different social structures developed according to the conditions faced by each group of conquistadors. Variations in both topography and demography produced different solutions to the problems of political control and economic production. Generally speaking, the further south one travels in Central America, the more scarce become land, material resources, and indigenous labor. Temperate, low-lying, and more productive land is found in Guatemala and Chiapas (then part of Guatemala). Land on the Caribbean coast is poorer for agriculture than that on the Pacific side, with the exception of the Petén region and the Izbul Lake area in Guatemala and Trujillo in Honduras.

In terms of capital, mining played an important role in the nations where precious metals abounded. Sickness and abuse drastically reduced the indigenous population, however, and mining declined during the sixteenth century and for the next century existed primarily in the center of Honduras and New Segovia. The 1700s produced a "new expansive phase," which peaked toward mid-century.[6]

Labor was decisive in constituting the economic, ideological, social, and political universe of colonial society. The *encomienda* became the cornerstone of the colonial economy.[7] The *encomenderos* in America sought privileges usually denied them in Spain. Their existence was based on the exploitation of the Indian. Human labor, not land, was the fundamental value. The forced labor system continued undiminished in Guatemala and El Salvador throughout the changes in production, and new sectors developed in the economy—whether cochineal replaced indigo or coffee replaced cochineal. *Encomiendas*, seasonal *repartimientos*, and *mandamientos* put laborers in debt and served to justify their detention and forcible relocation to the estates. Indians were also forced to labor in public works.

The social and political consequences of this economic system were devastating and long-lasting. The denial of human rights and the disenfranchisement of the vast majority of the population were a far cry from the tenets of a democratic political system. Olive B. Thomas's comment to Elizabeth Hoyt regarding fifty Guatemalan coffee estates during the mid-1940s could have been written in any of the preceding three centuries. It speaks eloquently of the enduring legacy of colonialism.

Social and cultural difference between the bosses and the laborers in the coffee estates [that] is greater than that existing in feudal times....the total or partial absenteeism of the owners, observed in more than 50 percent of the farms, has contributed to widening this cultural distance between the owner and his peons.[8]

The *encomienda* system in Guatemala, for example, created a complex feudal social structure. In 1600, eighteen indigo processing plants existed from Guazacapán to Jalpatagua. The prospect of indigo profits motivated the Guatemalan *encomenderos* to harness sufficient indigenous labor to the plantations and processing plants, particularly on the coast of Escuintla. Despite variations, from the beginning of the colonization until the introduction of coffee, involuntary servitude characterized the social and economic situation of the Indian. Efforts to modify the system, urged by Father Bartolomé de las Casas, were unsuccessful.[9] By 1665 Guatemala had seventy-two *encomiendas* producing 80,000 ducats per year.

In Costa Rica on the other hand, Indians, indigo, processing plants, *encomiendas*, and wealth were less significant. Although there were a few *encomiendas* and some *repartimientos* of Indians in the sixteenth century,[10] the relative absence of indigenous peoples and profitable holdings reduced the degree of exploitation suffered by the Indians.[11]

In El Salvador, the population was racially mixed (*mestiza*). In the rural areas, however, Indian social organization and language survived well into the nineteenth century. Yet the abolition of the Indians' economic structure during the Liberal Reform through increased repression wiped out their cultural legacies. The *mestizo* population was largely unaffected.[12]

Thus, we can discern three structural variants of the political systems in colonial Central America.

- In Guatemala, El Salvador, and parts of Nicaragua there was a strong system derived in large part from the interaction between a small cadre of capitalist landowners and a large indigenous population. The desire of the landowner to exploit the labor potential of the indigenous population and the accompanying need to control it politically and socially are the salient determinants of this variant.
- In Honduras and eastern Nicaragua (New Segovia) there was a relatively weak system designed to support the mining industry and related commercial activity. Although a capitalist and landowning elite composed the nucleus of the political system, the decline of mining and lack of other suitable alternatives kept this system weak and unformed.

- In Costa Rica and part of Nicaragua there was a relatively egalitarian system derived from commensurate levels of wealth and social status. These were thinly populated areas where subsistence farming predominated. The scarcity of capital and labor made efforts to produce tropical export products, such as cacao and tobacco, unsuccessful.

Independence did not change the system of exploitation. Although the domination of Spain was broken, the essential internal elements of colonial domination remained intact. The power of the landowning class grew, land holdings were increased and consolidated, and the exploitation of the indigenous masses continued. The introduction of new products for export did not by itself change the overall structure. The new means of production were adapted to internal realities, and, though modified, the essence of the labor exploitation system remained.

With the introduction of coffee for export and the further development of commerce, however, the old dominant class was transformed. Various groups expanded, and the labor force was redistributed according to the new production demands. The Liberal Reform at the end of the nineteenth century was instituted by the new estate owners, who largely represented an emerging creole class.

In El Salvador the Liberal Reform eliminated communal lands and forced the Indians into an accelerated proletarianization. The coffee plantations maintained the colonial class structure and expanded it into the new coffee-growing sectors.[13] This was not the case in Costa Rica. From colonial times through independence the social and economic organization favored free labor and land ownership. The absence of an Indian population and the emphasis on agricultural production for local use established the context for the later production of coffee. The development of coffee launched a new era of capitalist relations in agriculture.

It is useful to contrast the situations in Guatemala and Costa Rica. In Guatemala a captive labor force reinforced a rigidly hierarchical society with a clearly repressive tendency. In Costa Rica free labor and a different system of land ownership contributed to the formation of a more open society with egalitarian and substantially less repressive tendencies. In both countries a dominant class appeared, heir to the same conquering elite yet broadened by new sectors assimilated during the social and economic evolution of the country. In each country social and political attitudes differed, and these differences were reflected in their labor sectors and political systems. Diverse combinations of social and economic elements resulted in different systems.

External Conditions and the Political Systems

External market factors consolidated and reinforced colonial structures. Exploitation of the Indian intensified—in the indigo factories, the mines, and the coffee *mandamientos*. In El Salvador, the speed and energy involved in the expropriation of communal (*ejido*) lands and the formation of a labor market are notable. Within fifteen years all of the *ejido* communities disappeared.[14] Community lands in Guatemala, however, remained for many years, and in Nicaragua and Honduras they continue to exist.[15]

Another mechanism of labor exploitation was indentured servitude. Workers agreed to remain on a plantation for life in exchange for the satisfaction of their debts. In some cases, families remained for generations. This system affected the children of *mestizaje* as well.

The development of coffee also took various turns. In Costa Rica it produced a democratic society. Following a period of dictatorial tendencies from 1860 to 1871, Costa Rica moved toward a democratic system during the administration of Cleto González and Ricardo Jiménez.[16] In northern Central America, however, the development of coffee strengthened the repressive and authoritarian trends of the political system. The colonial heritage endured during the production of indigo and the introduction of coffee. The new coffee oligarchies in El Salvador and Guatemala continued the domination of the Indian. Coffee forced changes in a structure previously favoring the producers of indigo. The so-called Liberal Reform became the mechanism for opening the political structure.

The arrival of the banana companies in Guatemala, far from strengthening the emergence of free labor and furthering the liquidation of servile relations, produced a symbiosis with the local system. Although the development of banana plantations speeded modernization and the integration of domestic economies into the international market, it also reinforced traditional class relations, worsening the exploitation of the general population of the country. In Costa Rica, however, where the same banana company tried to link itself with the military and the oligarchs, it encountered resistance both from within Costa Rica and from the U.S. government.[17] The symbiotic relationship between the banana companies and the local power structure demonstrates that the impact of foreign investment can be understood only through an appreciation of internal political culture. It was foreign capital that adapted to domestic structures and not vice versa. Foreign capital thus served strategic interests as well. Whereas the commercial connection with the world market and the presence of foreign investment strengthened the inherited colonial structure in Guatemala, in El Salvador a more independent oligarchy was able to develop. Salvadorans directed their export efforts toward Europe, particularly Germany. In Costa Rica, the infusion of foreign capital exporters sowed the seeds for the development of a workers' movement and the Communist Party. In Honduras, foreign investment captivated the national elite in a way that hampered the formation of a strong, independent state. Foreign capital transformed Nicaragua into a center of regional influence.

The importance of foreign influence cannot be dismissed for any of these countries, particularly following World War II. But its impact on the societies and political systems of Central America varied substantially. In Costa Rica social reform prevailed, even though a representative of the United Fruit Company had to "read the program of the Labor Code with smelling salts in his hand."[18] This was not the case elsewhere, where traditional structures would prove more resistant to efforts at social transformation.[19]

Honduras and Nicaragua represent intermediate cases, geographically and politically. In Honduras the importance of foreign capital is incontrovertible.[20] The Honduran oligarchy was limited to a small number of merchants in San Pedro Sula and Tegucigalpa and a few hundred estate owners still raising cattle and producing tobacco and lumber. They possessed a great deal of autonomy in their own territory but lacked the means to undertake a broad national program. Honduras had an inherently weak elite, and foreign capital made substantial inroads in domestic politics.[21]

The banana companies established themselves in the lowlands of northern Honduras. Because this area was infested with malaria, it was sparsely populated and large numbers of peasants were not displaced. The companies populated the area and built railroads, ports, and towns. They wrote the laws and dominated local governments. A series of strikes between 1916 and 1934 was systematically repressed. The dictatorship of Tiburcio Carías (1933–48) was decisive in quieting labor unrest through the liquidation of the labor organizations. Labor unions were not formally recognized until the strike of 1954.

The landowning Honduran elite was replaced by the armed forces. Although a swelling of the military's ranks did not occur as in Guatemala and El Salvador,[22] the military became the preferred diplomatic channel within the country and now appears to be one of Honduras's political liabilities. The fragmentation of Honduran society, including the armed forces, serves as a barrier to national development and full participation in international relations.

Unlike the Honduran elite, the elite in Nicaragua had sufficient latitude to develop economically. But like in Honduras, external factors were salient in the formation of the political system.

In this way, northern Central America, possessing relatively abundant resources, crystallized the colonial modalities of labor relations. In southern Central America the relative lack of resources encouraged the development of a free labor market. In Costa Rica relations between dominant and dominated sectors were more balanced. The opening of new agricultural frontiers sped the process of modernization in labor relations and in social relations in general. In the center of the region the relative weakness of the elite encouraged a foreign presence, a situation that had social, economic, and political repercussions.

Different Political Systems in Central America

The social and economic environments of the different countries in Central America greatly affected the development of their political systems. In the north, the need to guarantee the forced labor of the Indians resulted in a closed system. An agrarian oligarchy of colonial origin incorporated modern capitalist methods to develop industry, banking, and commerce. In Guatemala "the grower assumed the responsibility of maintaining law and order; had established certain rules for the sale and consumption of alcohol; and frequently owned a prison to punish the transgressors."[23] Thus, the contemporary political system was merged with the heritage of colonial domination.

A primary function of the Guatemalan state was to guarantee labor for the coffee estates.[24] Thus its ideological grounding becomes ineluctably clear: the Indian had to be perceived as an object, not a subject, of society. Here racism—like illiteracy— was not an accidental result of social marginalization but, rather, an instrument of domination and exploitation of 60 percent of the population. Characterizing Indians as infantile, lazy, ignorant, and treacherous is the ideological justification that permits arbitrariness and violence, even death, to keep them subjugated.[25] This attitude not only permeates the oligarchy and the army, but even all of society, a society that rests on the peculiar social position of the Indian as cretinous and despised.

The emphasis on racial differentiation in contemporary Guatemalan society contrasts with the stronger dynamic of assimilation at work during the colonial period. Sociologically a creole oligarchy existed in Guatemala until recently. The consciousness of the creole class was already apparent in the first colonial years, and until 1944 creoles were indisputably the dominant class in the country. Creolism is still alive in the thinking of powerful groups.[26]

In El Salvador, important changes accompanied the development of coffee. The oligarchic domination of the Meléndez and Quiñones families supported by the military after 1932 marked the beginning of a closed political system for El Salvador. In El Salvador the coffee grower had not only an economic role, but a social and political one as well. The coffee producer had the police and National Guard at his disposal.

These repressive tendencies, directed first against the indigenous population and later against the laborers and peasants, also have their roots in the colonial period and the time of the Liberal Reform.[27] The forms of expression varied. Martínez Peláez distinguished three principal ones in Guatemala: the smothering of individual expressions of rebellion, the maintenance of a sector of prehispanic Indian nobility in local authority, and, most important, the ample and impudent tolerance of violations of the Indian's rights.[28] Terror was thus essential in the colonial domination of the Indian. It became a political tool, sanctioned by centuries of use, that would continue to be employed throughout the twentieth century.

The dominant elite tended to delegate the exercise of public power to the military. The elite preferred to reserve for itself the economic and financial activities of the nation. It did so by ensuring civilian control of two government portfolios, the ministries of economics and foreign relations, which control the value of the currency and the connections with the world market.[29]

This situation gives the political system a characteristic instability. Héctor Rosada Granados observed that of the ten presidents elected between 1944 and 1985 in Guatemala, seven were military officers and only three were civilians. The two provisional and one designated president, as well as the two chiefs of state, were military officers. Of twenty junta government members, nineteen were active duty military officers.[30]

In El Salvador, as Rafael Guidos Béjar noted, from 1944 to 1984 there were four new constitutions adopted, five successful coups d'état and five failed ones, four provisional presidents, ten modifications of juntas governing as a result of coups, and eight constitutionally elected presidents.[31] This makes a total of twenty-seven changes of government at the highest executive level—a change every 1.6 years.[32] Of the twelve Salvadoran rulers, nine were from the military and three were civilian. Eleven members of juntas originating from coups d'état were military officers and thirteen were civilians.[33]

A related phenomenon is the growing institutional autonomy of the armed forces.[34] In Guatemala the military has acquired independent power within the political system. It has also gained considerable economic power because the officers at the highest levels have appropriated lands and resources. In this way the military has become part of the ruling elite.

This also occurred in El Salvador. There the armed forces strengthened their position relative to the oligarchy. The military expanded its role and the direct participation of its members in economic functions.[35] As a result, tensions within the political system, the loss of confidence in it, and rising demands from the poorest sectors produced indescribable repression. Such repression has marked El Salvador's political system for a long time.[36]

External influences helped shape the new role of the armed forces. The cold war and the doctrine of national security influenced the character of the militaries and their role within their respective societies. As one observer noted, the last stages of the "militarism of Central America can only be found within the context of the cold war and the anticommunist policy of the governments in Washington."[37] The political system functions to satisfy the demands of the elite for "social peace."

Every authoritarian political system maintains itself not by popular appeal but through efficient mechanisms of social control. Such closed political systems are prone to periodic political crises, such as coups d'état, palace conspiracies, guerrilla activities, and popular insurrections. When popular demands are rejected, the feedback mechanism that invigorates a political system is destroyed. The legitimating aspect of the "demand-response" dynamic is interrupted. The electoral process does not fulfill the dual democratic functions of constituting and legitimating power. Political power is concentrated in the military, whose accountability lies outside of the electoral process. Elections only fulfill a ritual function geared to improving the country's image internationally.

In the long run authoritarian political systems produce a crisis in all social sectors. Society in general becomes alienated from the political system by the consistent exclusion of its demands. The armed forces are altered, gradually changing their status from guardians of the elite to full members of a new economic and political elite. Through the expropriation of land and participation in agriculture, banking, industry, and commerce, the military becomes a powerful, autonomous institution that impinges on all other aspects of the society. This process appears to be different from that taking place in other Latin American countries.

In contrast, conditions in Costa Rica created a limited economic role for the elite. Elites quickly moved on to other interests, particularly politics and the liberal professions. Unlike in northern Central America, the struggle for political power did not occur within the military. In the south the struggle was among factions of the economic elite, some among them even belonging to the same families. Discerning who held the title to power was made more difficult by this intrafamily rivalry. Initially the battles between members of elite families included violent means. Gradually, however, more refined instruments of social and political control were used.

A broadening of the political base occurred as aspiring politicians looked for support outside of their own class. Later, new participants emerged from previously excluded sectors, bringing with them a different set of interests. Pressure from the new sectors to be taken seriously was especially strong. New rules of the game evolved that regulated the selection process for candidates for offices, including those of the presidency, the ministries, and the legislative assembly. These new rules were modified over time to allow for the expansion of the social base of the system. The legal framework for electoral processes in Costa Rica also developed. These changes fostered the creation of peaceful and legal mechanisms to resolve political disputes.

A system that required the support of other social strata of the population readily opened itself to their demands. These demands were answered in various ways. Some responses generated new demands. Out of this give and take the Costa Rican political system became open and democratic.

The process was not easy or straightforward. In the beginning the system was limited, excluding the participation of those who had no property, capital, or liberal profession.[38] Later, when coffee had enriched the lower social strata and they had become active participants in the system, the requirements for suffrage were changed to once again exclude them. Literacy became a condition to vote and serve in elected office. But in a move only apparently paradoxical, the most prominent sons of the conservative oligarchy modified the constitution and instituted compulsory primary education paid by the state. In this way the members of the least favored elites could count on their own social base to negotiate with the oligarchy itself. Suffrage became universal, secret, and direct in 1901.

In northern Central America the political system emerged in a weak form because it was closed and systematically ignored the principal demands of the population. In the south the system was also weak. The growing distance between popular expectations and the material, institutional, and political capacity to satisfy them undermined the legitimacy of the system.

The case of the central states of the region is different and more complex. In Honduras the absence of a hegemonic elite and the asphyxiating presence of foreign capital created political diffusion that adversely affected the process of nation-building. In Nicaragua, U.S. intervention at the beginning of the twentieth century reinforced the country's colonial heritage. The elite concentrated on economic development but was divided along liberal-conservative lines.

The military interventions of the United States in the 1920s had the strange virtue of exacerbating the liberal-conservative conflict. The resistance movement of Augusto Sandino recruited new social sectors with fresh demands.[39] The U.S.-assisted effort to build a national guard with Anastasio Somoza Garcia as its head began a chapter without parallel in Central American history.[40]

Whereas in other countries the dictatorships became assimilated into repressive governments, in Nicaragua the situation was different. Only the dictatorship of Jorge Ubico in Guatemala invites comparison, not only because of the degree of repression but also because the dictator came from the dominant economic elite. Somoza was not simply a tyrant. He brought together elements that created the most solid dictatorship in Central America. With regard to repression and human rights, Somoza was hardly benevolent, but his regime was substantial from a social and political perspective.

Through the political power of the National Guard, Somoza soon became the president, a move that gave him political power with a military base. Then he married Salvadorita Debayle, who was from a colonial family from among the Nicaraguan elite. Somoza thus controlled three key elements—military, political, and socioeconomic—a feat other dictators had not achieved.

He also added a fourth. With singular mastery Somoza made himself the most trustworthy interlocutor in the region with the North Americans, whose interests he came to understand and represent so well.[41] That he could do this successfully shows that the general was not simply a puppet of the United States. His local power base gave him sufficient autonomy to confront the North Americans while retaining a significant role in the region.[42]

Somoza became the axis of power for all of the Central American region. More than guardians of a dynasty, Somoza and his National Guard formed a dynasty of guardians for North American interests as well as those of the local oligarchies. The privileged situation of the Somoza regime strengthened its ability to concentrate power in a patrimonial-familial state. In the end it constituted a closed political system, by virtue of both internal and external circumstances.

Final Considerations

Based on the conclusions of this overview of the region, carrying out a policy of social and legal engineering to consolidate democratic institutions in the isthmus seems impossible. Political systems cannot be constructed by the adoption of models or the ritual celebration of elections, both of which have loomed large in the political life of the different Central American political systems. In addition, elections often only cover over the blemishes of a deeper, more complex reality that eventually will surface.

Today the Central American countries live in a state of profound crisis. This crisis encompasses not only their different political systems but also their social and economic structures. The dominant classes have lost significant power; their legitimacy is being questioned by the popular sectors, the armed forces, and even their allies abroad.

The future of the region will thus be affected by internal political adjustments as well as by new relationships with external actors. Certainly the shift of global power calls for a rethinking of the region's role in the world. It also challenges the emerging political leaders to redefine their roles in the context of a new international environment. But primarily the coming decade will be a time when the opportunities and pressures for deep, lasting political change from within will bring old elites and new sectors to fundamentally reassess their history and the forces that have shaped their present societies.

Notes

1. See, for example, Ralph L. Woodward, Jr., *Central America: A Nation Divided* (New York: Oxford University Press, 1976); Edelberto Torres-Rivas, *Interpretación del Desarrollo Social Centroamericano* (San José: EDUCA, 1981); and Héctor Pérez Brignoli, *Breve Historia de Centroamerica* (Madrid: Alianza Editorial, 1985).

2. Severo Martínez Peláez writes: "The colonial reality is our deepest reality." *La Patria del Criollo: Ensayo de Interpretación de la Realidad Colonial Guatemalteca* (Guatemala City: Editorial Universitaria, 1973), esp. pp. 574–75, 584.

3. Samuel Stone, *El Surgimiento de los Que Mandan: Tierra, Capital y Trabajo en la Forja de las Sociedades Centroamericanos* (San José: Estudios del CIAP, 1980), p. 14.

4. See, for example, Magnus Mörner, *La Mezcla de Razas en la Historia de América Latina* (Buenos Aires: Editorial Paidós, 1969); Daisy Rípodas Ardemaz, *El Matrimonio en Indias* (Buenos Aires: Consejo Nacional de Investigaciones Científicas y Técnicas, 1977); and Alejandro Lipschutz, *El Problema Racial de la Conquista de América* (Mexico City: Editorial Siglo XX, 1975).

5. Ciro F. S. Cardoso and Héctor Pérez Brignoli, *Centro América y la Economía Occidental, 1520–1930* (San José: Universidad de Costa Rica, 1983), p. 63.

6. Ibid.

7. Martínez Peláez, *La Patria del Criollo*, pp. 112–20.

8. Elizabeth E. Hoyt and Olive B. Thomas, "El Trabajador Indígena en las Fincas de Café de Guatemala," in *Economía de Guatemala*, n.a. (Guatemala City: Ministerio de Educación Pública, 1958), p. 296. For his part, John Parke Young wrote in 1925,

> The work on the plantations is principally done by Indians following the system of peonage, which, in effect, is similar to the system of slavery and is open to serious abuses....The life of the Indian is harsh; his conditions of life are crude; he is undernourished and mistreated and, as can be supposed, lacks efficiency.

"La Moneda y las Finanzas Centroamericanas" in *Economía de Guatemala*, pp. 139–40.

9. Ibid., p. 68.

10. The *repartimientos* of Perafán de Rivera are well established in the documents appearing in León Fernández, *Documentos Para la Historia de Costa Rica* (San José: Imprenta Nacional, 1881), 1:170, 207, and passim; also ibid., 2:154 and passim.

11. Cf. Claudia Quirós Vargas and Margarita Bolaños Arquín, "El Mestizaje en el Siglo XVII: Consideraciones Para Comprender la Génesis del Campesinado Criollo del Valle Central," paper presented at the Symposium on Colonial Society in Meso-America and the Caribbean, San José, December 1986.

12. Cf. Lisa North, *Bitter Grounds: Roots of Revolution in El Salvador* (Toronto: Between the Lines, 1985), p. 17; and James Dunkerley, *Power in the Isthmus: A Political History of Modern Central America* (London: Verso, 1988), p. 7 and passim. Cardoso and Brignoli, *Central America*, p. 73.

13. See Rodolfo Cerdas, *Farabundo Martí: La Internacional Comunista y la Insurrección Salvadoreña de 1932* (San José: Estudios del CIAPA, 1982), p. 16 and passim; Dunkerley, *Power in the Isthmus*, p. 96 and passim; Alastair White, *El Salvador: Nation of the Modern World* (London: Ernest Benn, 1973), p. 10; David Browning, *El Salvador: Landscape and Society* (Oxford: Clarendon Press, 1971), pp. 177–78; and Rafael Menjívar, *Acumulación Originaria y Desarrollo del Capitalismo en El Salvador* (San José: EDUCA, 1980), p. 87 and passim.

14. One arrives at this figure by using the Law of the Extinction of Communities as a benchmark.

15. Cardoso and Brignoli, *Centro América*, pp. 61–62.

16. Rodolfo Cerdas, *La Crisis de la Democracia Liberal en Costa Rica* (San José: EDUCA, 1972); Samuel Stone, *La Dinastía de los Conquistadores* (San José: EDUCA), 1975; and José Luis Vega Carballo, *Hacia Una Interpretación del Desarrollo Costarricense: Ensayo Sociológico* (San José: Editorial Porvenir, 1980).

17. Cf. Armando Ruiz Rodríguez, *La Administración Gonzálo Flores* (San José: Editorial Universidad de Costa Rica, 1968); Eduardo Oconitrillo García, *Los Tinoco, 1917–1919* (San José: Costa Rica, 1980); and Hugo Murillo Jiménez, *Tinoco y los Estados Unidos: Génesis y Caída de un Régimen* (San José: Editorial EUNED, 1981).

18. Jacobo Schifter, *Las Alianzas Conflictivas* (San José: Editorial Libro Libre, 1986).

19. Cf. Mario Montefiore Toledo, *Centro América*, 2:130.

20. James W. Wilkie and Adam Parkal, eds., *Statistical Abstract of Latin America* (Los Angeles: UCLA Latin American Center Publications, 1985), 24:37.

21. See Dunkerley, *Power in the Isthmus*, pp. 34–35. These conditions would explain Walter LaFeber's affirmation that Honduras was probably the country that gave "banana republic" its meaning of a country dependent on foreigners, characterized by general corruption, whose economy is based on only one export product; *The Inevitable Revolutions: The U.S. in Central America* (New York: W. W. Norton, 1983), p. 42. Also, Mario Posas, *Las Luchas del Movimiento Obrero Hondureño* (San José: EDUCA, 1981).

22. Cf. José Luis Cruz Salazar, "El Ejército Como Una Fuerza Política," (n.p., n.d) mimeographed; Toledo, *Centro América*, vol. 2; North, *Bitter Grounds*, p. 58; and Dunkerley, *Power in the Isthmus*, p. 34.

23. Hoyt and Thomas, "El Trabajador Indígena," p. 295.

24. Populating the new coffee zones had to be forced because the Indians lived in the high zones of the country. Cf. Valentín Solórzano F., "Evolución Económica de Guatemala," in *Seminario de Integración Social Guatemalteca*, ed. José Pineda Ibarra (Guatemala City: Ministerio de Educación Pública, 1963), pp. 362–63; and Sanford, "Economía Cafetalera," pp. 172–73, note 19.

25. Prejudice against the Indian was, thus, part of a deliberate, not casual, social attitude. The latifund and exploitative class that used semifree or cheap labor...has necessarily opposed anything that implies technologizing production (Solorzano F., "Evolución Económica," p. 587).

26. Ibid., pp. 112–13.

27. Mario Solórzano Martínez, *Guatemala: Autoritarismo y Democracia* (San José: EDUCA, 1987), p. 43 and passim.

28. Martínez Peláez, *La Patria*, p. 520.

29. Stone, *Las Convulciones*, p. 18.

30. Ibid., p. 86, Table 6.

31. Ibid., p. 22. If we consider the connection between political power and the family trees of the conquistadors, the following picture emerges: none of the descendants of Jorge de Alvarado Contreras, the conqueror of Guatemala and El Salvador, became president in Guatemala, one did in Honduras, two did in El Salvador, one did in Nicaragua, and nineteen did in Costa Rica; of the descendants of Juan Vásquez de Coronado Anaya, conqueror of Costa Rica, none became president in Honduras, Guatemala, or El Salvador, whereas eleven did in Nicaragua and twenty-two did in Costa Rica. In the same work, Stone provides an inventory of the principal families of Central America and the number of presidents coming from each one. The numbers confirm these families' trend of allowing other social sectors, particularly the military, to exercise titular power and reserve the economic sphere for themselves. The case of Costa Rica is different. Ibid., p. 19, Table 1.

32. "La Enigmática Dinámica del Sistema de Partidos en El Salvador," working paper of the CAPEL project on System and Political Parties in Central America (Mexico City and San José, 1986), p. 16, Table 1.

33. Ibid., p. 17, Table 2.

34. Cf. Monteforte Toledo, *Centro América*, 2:179, and Cruz Salazar, "El Ejército," p. 75. Both authors agree that the army is born in Guatemala with the Revolution of 1871 as a permanent, professional, and technical institution. Also, Cruz Salazar, "El Ejército," pp. 88-89 and passim.

35. North, *Bitter Grounds*, p. 58.

36. Cruz Salazar writes, "Under the government of Peralta the state of siege was made into a principle of government, and individual protection, exhibition, and guarantees were suppressed. When Méndez Montenegro won the presidency in 1965, he reached an agreement with the military circle of Peralta. From those years dates the calvary of terror and violence that have been contributing factors for the substitution of political parties and organized groups, by the armed forces, for conducting national policy" ("El Ejército," p. 96).

37. Monteforte Toledo, *Centro América*, 2:185.

38. Stone, *La Dinastía*, p. 264 and passim.

39. Rodolfo Cerdas, *La Hoz y El Machete: La Internacional Comunista, América Latina y La Revolución en Centro América* (San José: EUNED, 1986), p. 206 and passim.

40. See LaFeber, *Inevitable Revolutions*, pp. 69–82.

41. LaFeber says: "And then the United States created and supported the Somoza family dynasty (1934–79). The country played a key role in the diplomacy of Washington, due to the Somozas' willingness to act as instruments of the United States, and also because the natural waterways made of it an ideal place for a possible inter-oceanic canal" (*Inevitable Revolutions*, pp. 11, 49).

42. Cf. Rodolfo Cerdas, "Costa Rica: Fifty Years of Political History," in *Cambridge History of Central America* (Cambridge: Cambridge University Press, forthcoming), in this article I examine the role Somoza played in the 1948 crisis, his policy facing nonrecognition by the United States, and the Central American policy that threatened him. See also Stone, *Las Convulciones*, p. 42 and passim; and Rodolfo Cerdas, "Nicaragua: One Step Forward, Two Steps Back," in *The Central American Impasse*, eds. G. Dipalma and L. Whitehead (London: Croom Helm, 1986), p. 175 and passim.

3

The Transitions to "Electoral" and Democratic Politics in Central America: Assessing the Role of Political Parties

Morris J. Blachman and Kenneth E. Sharpe

As the 1990s opened, the only country in Central America that could claim to hold periodic free and fair elections was Costa Rica. El Salvador, Guatemala, Honduras, and Nicaragua all had held elections, but this inchoate "electoral politics" still fell considerably short of democratic politics. In general, there was little effective participation or broad-based representation and little political accountability between the elected officials and their supporters, and elected officials had limited power vis-à-vis a still-dominant military and, in some cases, a still-powerful oligarchy.

After colonial times in Guatemala, El Salvador, Nicaragua, and Honduras powerful, entrenched classes led by landed interests (but also including commercial and financial elites) and powerful military institutions opposed, often brutally, groups that sought to create democratic political institutions. Following World War II, however, the defense of the existing land tenure system, of related economic interests, and of military power and privilege became more difficult, as important

We would like to thank Elisabeth Escalante for her comments and assistance. We also want to thank Rodrigo Carazo, William M. LeoGrande, and the other members of the conference for their comments.

national and international changes created new social forces that demanded reform and democracy. When change failed to occur, many turned to revolution. As the structural conditions of the old system, what some have called "reactionary despotism," broke down, the landed and military elites reacted with a mixture of repression and largely cosmetic reforms in an effort to restore order and maintain their power and privilege.[1] The "electoral politics" of the 1980s was part of this response.[2] Only in Costa Rica, where the post–World War II transformations had an impact on political and class structure, was the pattern different.

In Central America we find three categories of electoral politics: pseudo, limited, and democratic. In pseudo electoral politics, there is a pretense of electoral democracy. The casting of ballots is conducted in a relatively free and fair manner, as is much of the counting of them. But certain segments of the population—particularly those on the left—are systematically excluded from participation (for example, in El Salvador in 1982). The electoral process is truncated by limited and unequal access to the media and the public. Those in power use intimidation and coercion to maintain control. Outcomes are also closely monitored so that ruling groups do not lose control over the political system or major policy decisions. The leadership is not accountable to the citizenry at large. To the extent accountability exists within the system, it does so among factions of the ruling groups.

In limited electoral politics, most groups in the society are permitted to participate. The casting and counting of ballots is conducted in a relatively free and fair manner. Candidates and parties have considerably greater access to the media and to the public. Intimidation and coercion have significantly diminished, but this reduction resulted from a political decision by the ruling groups; that decision, therefore, could be reversed at any time. Outcomes are respected, but the power of those elected to make significant changes in important policy areas is severely restricted. Those who hold office may have little power, and fundamental control of the system is not up for grabs (for example, in Honduras). Accountability of leadership to the citizenry is weakly maintained. Principal accountability is to the ruling groups.

Democratic electoral politics involves open participation in a free and fair electoral process. Voting and tallying the ballots is fair and free. Access to the media and to the public is not hampered by either overt nor tacit political restriction, nor is it limited by intimidation or coercion. Outcomes are respected, and control over the political system and its agenda is up for grabs at election time. The leadership is accountable to the electorate through the regularized periodic holding of elections.[3]

The Pre–World War II Structure:
Reactionary Despotism

Baloyra uses the term *reactionary despotism* to describe the regimes of Central America that were based on landed interest and opposed to political and social modernization—that is, democracy and social reform. At the heart of reactionary despotism was what Weeks describes as a "system of land tenure and labor coercion that emerged during the nineteenth century, itself predicated upon authoritarianism."[4]

It was not the concentration of land that was critical to this system but the coercive use of labor, which developed particularly in Guatemala, El Salvador, and, to a lesser extent, in Nicaragua. The landed oligarchies (concentrated particularly on large estates in Guatemala and El Salvador) relied on the state to ensure the large labor supply they needed in two ways. The state dispossessed peasants from the prime coffee lands, often using liberal land reform laws, which turned inalienable communal lands into private property. This not only provided the coffee growers with prime land, but also with a large, underemployed labor force. Second, the state created various coercive labor systems: debt peonage, labor contracts, and, later, vagrancy laws, as well as the *colono* system, in which landowners assigned plots to families in exchange for field labor when required.[5]

Thus, coffee production for the world market expanded, yet the commercialization of agriculture did not result in modern capitalist labor relations. Instead it resulted in coercive, often feudal, methods of labor control, and the landed interests depended heavily on a necessarily antidemocratic state and military to maintain these systems.

If recalcitrance to reform and democracy among Central American elites was shaped by the perceived need to maintain a coercive labor system supported by state repression, it was also reinforced by two other factors: the growth of a military with institutional interests of its own and U.S. intervention in the area. In El Salvador and Nicaragua, the military played a major role much earlier than in Guatemala or Honduras. El Salvador's oligarchy ceded considerable power to the military for decades following the 1932 massacre. In Guatemala and Honduras, the militaries did not take on a life or interests independent of economic elites until later. But officers in the high commands did assume economic and political interests that were not those of the oligarchies. They became involved in corruption and often practiced or condoned brutality. As a result, many of them developed suspicion, distrust, even fear of democratic reformers who might challenge their position or punish their actions.

The United States often mediated or intervened in intra-elite disputes. Yet

> because Washington demonstrated a willingness to use force to keep
> certain groups in power (having put them there in the first place in some
> cases), the ruling elites felt little pressure to accommodate the demands of
> the middle and lower classes for reform or even nominal political participa-
> tion.[6]

Post–World War II:
Repression, Revolution, and "Electoral Politics"

Central America entered the post–World War II period with no country experiencing regular, free, and fair elections, let alone democracy. With the exception of Costa Rica, the economic and military elites had at best little interest in democratic reforms (Honduras) and at worst were willing to use force and state repression against those who sought political or social reform (El Salvador, Nicaragua). In addition, aside from Costa Rica, the particular form of economic development they experienced had not created an independent small farmer class, an economically strong or viable urban middle class, or an industrial/entrepreneurial group that might have organized to demand a political voice and social reform.

Yet important internal and world system changes beginning in the late 1940s and early 1950s created a new historical conjuncture. With it came pressures for political and social change from new groups demanding social reform and political democracy. The different reactions of the military and economic elites in each country generated patterns of repression, reform, and insurrection out of which emerged the forms of electoral politics present in the 1980s and early 1990s.

Four interrelated moments can be found in this conjuncture.

1. Transformation of the internal economic and class structure as a response to a changed relationship with the world capitalist system. In the 1950s, 1960s, and 1970s Central American military and economic elites used state power to change important relations of production. There was a diversification out of coffee and bananas into cotton, sugar, and cattle. The commercialization of agriculture favored those with access to capital or credit; thus, thousands of smallholders, squatters, and tenant farmers were forced from their lands. Concentration of landholding increased in El Salvador, Guatemala, and Nicaragua as commercial agriculture worsened the problem of land scarcity.[7]

The creation of the Central American Common Market (CACM) in the early 1960s stimulated industrial growth without the major reforms necessary to redistribute income and create adequate markets in each individual country. CACM helped spur industrialization and growth, and trade among the five skyrocketed from $32 million in 1960 to $260 million in 1969.[8] Such efforts to stimulate growth were pushed along by U.S. economic assistance under the Alliance for Progress. The structural reforms urged by the Alliance, however, were largely ignored.

Light industrialization created jobs but not in sufficient number to counteract rural dislocation and rapid population growth. Thus, years of rapid GNP growth were also paradoxically years of increasing inequality and joblessness.[9] These economic transformations put forward new social forces. The middle class expanded. The urban labor force grew. Displaced peasants were forced to seek scarce work for low wages and swelled the numbers of underemployed rural wage laborers. Others moved to urban slums.

These new social forces were organized into new associations. Centrist and leftist political parties organized and demanded reforms and civilian government. Sometimes the military and the oligarchy responded with reactionary counterorganizations as they sought to create official parties or rule through existing parties. But in no country except Costa Rica did the reformist parties have the organization and power to play a major role in creating a transition to democratic electoral politics. In fact, it often fell to nonparty associations to organize the new social forces: labor unions, peasant organizations, and popular organizations, often building on *comunidades de base,* Christian base communities.

2. Transformation of the Catholic church. These base communities grew out of a revitalization of the church that began in the early 1960s with Vatican II and was reinforced by the conference of Latin American bishops at Medellín, Colombia, in 1968. The bishops denounced communism and capitalism as equal threats to human dignity and located causes for the region's misery and hunger in a social and economic structure dominated by the rich and powerful. Some factions in the church began to weld the poor and dispossessed into a new social force, organizing base communities, and called for a "preferential option for the poor."[10]

3. Short-term cyclical economic trends in the early 1980s. Beginning in 1979, economic decline engulfed the region. The causes were not limited to the inequalities, joblessness, exhaustion of the import substitution models, and uneven growth generated by the structural problems discussed above. More immediate short-term factors also worsened economic conditions and created severe internal pressures. One was the effect of the civil wars that wreaked havoc in El Salvador, Guatemala, and Nicaragua. A second was regional disintegration, much of it spurred by the civil wars that undermined regional trade and the growth it had promoted. Finally there were a series of external shocks: "a sharp deterioration in the terms of trade, declines in export volumes, and suddenly rising interest rates on international debt."[11]

4. Changing U.S. geopolitical concerns. Although U.S. hegemony in the international political and economic system has been declining, U.S. policy is still guided by a hegemonic strategic vision. The United States has been, at best, suspicious and, at worst, openly hostile to the popular organizations and parties of the left, driving forces for reform and change without which no large-scale democratic reform would have been possible. As a consequence, the United States neither supports these groups nor helps protect them from repression. At times, the United States even encouraged the forces of repression on the grounds that reformist groups and parties represented the opening wedge of communism. These policies often served to strengthen the very militaries whose opposition to reform blocked democracy in the first place. But there was a contradictory effect as well: the price of getting U.S. military and economic assistance was that the military had to allow some political opening.

Reactionary Despotism to "Electoral Politics"

The impact of these structural conditions depended on the reaction of landed and military elites in each country. There were two basic patterns. In Costa Rica and, to a lesser extent, Honduras the state was less coercive and the economic and military elites less powerful, less reactionary, and more open to elections, reform, and, especially in Costa Rica, democratic electoral politics. In El Salvador, Guatemala, and Nicaragua powerful and recalcitrant economic elites, backed by increasingly strong militaries and coercive states, met efforts at reform with brutal repression. The result was the outbreak of insurgencies and revolutions. In El Salvador and Guatemala the transition to pseudo electoral politics was part of the military's and the oligarchy's response to the problems created by civil wars (armed insurrections). In Nicaragua, the failure to respond with a transition to some form of electoral politics fanned the flames of revolution.

Pseudo or Limited Electoral Politics

The transition to democratic electoral politics in Costa Rica came in the late 1940s. It involved dismantling the military and establishing a broadly representative and reformist democratic welfare state. But in the other countries the potential transition, the opening for transition, appeared to come only in the early 1980s and was restricted to pseudo or, at best, limited electoral politics. This highly circumscribed transition resulted from internal pressure by parties and groups who sought full democracy but lacked the power to force such change. It also resulted from external pressures by the United States that shaped the "willingness" of the military and authoritarian governments to allow the modest change.

In El Salvador the repression of reform efforts in 1979 and 1980 led to full-scale revolution, which the military then had difficulty containing. But the military's continuing desire for U.S. assistance led it to accept limited political changes, pseudo electoral politics, to show enough movement to overcome U.S. congressional reluctance to provide that aid. The role of the United States in creating this alternative was much more direct in El Salvador than in Guatemala.

In Guatemala the military was institutionalized, skilled, efficient, and not personalistic like Somoza's National Guard. It relied on brutal repression to destroy both reformers and mass organizations as well as to bring insurgents under control in the countryside. When order was restored and a military-authoritarian system institutionalized in the countryside, the military was willing to move toward pseudo electoral politics to resolve the severe economic difficulties created by its own policies and worsened by international isolation. Military leaders correctly thought that holding elections would overcome congressional refusal to provide economic or military assistance and gain them a certain legitimacy in Europe and Central America.

In Honduras the transition occurred without great organization or pressure from mass organizations. Parties played a more important role, but the military yielded primarily because of pressure from the Carter administration. In Nicaragua, the Somoza regime refused to yield to internal and external pressures for democratic reform. The consequence was a broad-based revolution. The transition to electoral politics in Nicaragua began in a postrevolutionary context.

With the exception of Costa Rica, one clear pattern emerged amid these variations: the reluctance of the military to allow a transition except as a way to get needed U.S. support, and then only under controlled circumstances that assure its continued dominance. The military allows the aperture because it is worried about its ability to handle increasing pressure from below, from social movements. At the same time it seeks to maintain an economic model that promises growth, legitimizes its rule, and does not disturb its allies among the economic elites. This in turn often demands external economic and military support. If the military's lack of international legitimacy threatens its ability to sustain its political and economic model or if its ability to control emerging social movements seems to be weakening, then it is likely to turn toward some form of electoral politics so as to avoid greater pressure, which might threaten it as an institution.

Once the military decides to allow an electoral process and civilian government, it seeks to control and limit the transition process. The kind of control it seeks and its ability to achieve that control vary depending on the country's history, but we can make some broad generalizations about its intentions.

- The military will seek to exclude from the range of opposition parties any organizations that seek broad or rapid socioeconomic change or that are perceived as wanting to challenge the power and prerogatives of the military. The military will seek to work with those who seek legal-political changes, not structural ones.
- It will favor partial, interim changes—elections for a constituent assembly, elections for an interim president, and a vote on the constitution—rather sweeping reforms that include the election of a president or parliament.[12]
- It will seek to limit the control of elected civilian regimes over the military, such as the power to punish military officers for past human rights abuses, to tame corruption, to end military sinecures, to control military budgets, or to determine military policy. They may do this by making pacts or agreements with those parties they will allow to take office.

In short, there is a pattern in the electoral strategies of the military. The military will define as "democratic" and "legitimate" those parties that do not threaten mass mobilization, demand structural transformation, or challenge military prerogatives. This excludes parties that would want to incorporate or organize the popular sectors and mass organizations and may even exclude democratic socialists. The military may use techniques to exclude these other groups such as refusal to grant them protection, repression (death squads, arrests, harassment, intimidation, disappearance, torture), and limited access to the media. The military will try to control the electoral calendar and slow, delay, or reverse the process if things seem to be getting out of control.[13] The military might also try to control the balloting.

This permits us to suggest two hypotheses concerning the role of political parties in the transition process.

- Parties do not play a major role in creating the conditions for an electoral transition. But once the military and economic elites decide to allow the transition to take place, certain parties, especially moderate and centrist ones, can play an important role in organizing the electoral process and the transition.
- Because of the restrictions placed on the transition process by the military and dominant groups, parties are severely limited in their ability (1) to articulate a reform program that challenges the

power of the military or threatens the basic socioeconomic structure, and (2) to establish effective working alliances with center-left or left parties or with mass organizations whose support might later be necessary to bring about major structural reforms. This puts the moderate parties in a vulnerable position on taking office. The political compromises these centrist parties must make to be able to participate in the process limits their power and, perhaps, their will to undertake the major socioeconomic changes needed to move to democratic electoral politics.[14]

The Transition to Democratic Electoral Politics

In Costa Rica democratic electoral politics had already become firmly rooted in the years following the 1948 Revolution. The transition to pseudo or limited electoral politics in the other four countries in the 1980s thrust reformist, modernizing political parties into new prominence after decades of exclusion and, often, repression. But the transitions left those electoral systems still far from democratic. Further, the parties in Guatemala, El Salvador, and Honduras lacked the power and authority to grapple with the dilemmas they confronted, and even the much more powerful National Liberation Party in Costa Rica and the *Sandinistas* in Nicaragua faced severe constraints.

The traditional yardstick for measuring progress toward democracy emphasizes the processes and procedures of Western democracies—political parties, competitive elections, and a certain consensus about the rules of the game. The absence of these criteria show the serious defects in electoral politics in El Salvador, Guatemala, and Honduras. The problem has generally not been a lack of opposition parties to compete in elections but a failure on their part to aggregate emergent new interests. This leaves wide sectors among the peasantry, the unemployed, urban workers, and slum dwellers under- or unrepresented.

One reason opposition parties have been unable to represent labor unions, peasant organizations, or other popular organizations is that the parties have been denied the opportunity to develop public support from these groups. The parties have not had adequate access to the press, and their members' ability to assemble, speak, and organize has too often been threatened by unwarranted arrest, torture, assassination, and disappearance.[15]

Worse, parties sometimes make pacts with those who have traditionally monopolized power—the military and economic elites—thereby ensuring the continued exclusion of important sectors of the population. These pacts, whether unwritten or written, decide the distribution of power—who gets what, when, and how. The pact between El Salvador's Christian Democrats and the military immediately following José Napoleón Duarte's election as president is one such example.

Electoral politics is further weakened by the personalism and factionalism so prevalent in many parties in the region. In the Central American context, this "reinforces the tendency toward internal competition and conflict resolution, rather than on purpose and problem solving. In this context, payoffs (political favors, jobs, unequal access to limited resources such as foreign exchange) are related back to groups competing for power, not forward to their consequences to society."[16]

Although the elections in Guatemala, El Salvador, and Honduras did lead the military to step down from governmental office, it continues to rule behind the scenes in El Salvador and Guatemala and remains the major force in Honduras.[17]

Thus, the elected officials in these three countries are to a great extent figureheads; they are accountable to the military and, to some extent, the oligarchies and economic elites but not to the citizenry at large. Elected officials hold office but little power. They lack the power to carry out land reform or to tax and are often limited in their power to protect the basic freedoms of speech, assembly, and the press necessary for democratic practices. They cannot punish officers who have been involved in crimes; they cannot investigate and have difficulty stopping disappearances, torture, and assassinations. They cannot end military corruption or bring the military under civilian control. The exceptions are Costa Rica, where there is no military, and Nicaragua, where the ruling *Sandinista* National Liberation Front (FSLN) controlled the military before the 1990 election.

A hidden dynamic, however, is built into the present situation. The ability of the parties to sustain their status, let alone be the impetus for a transition toward electoral democracy, is shaped by their capacity to handle demands of their own supporters, who view the transition to pseudo or limited electoral politics not simply as a good in and of itself but as a mechanism for achieving reform. In each country there are demands for land reform, labor reform, and economic recovery. In El Salvador, Guatemala, and Honduras, there are demands to lift restrictions on civil liberties, to end human rights violations, and to bring the military under civilian control. In El Salvador and Guatemala there are also calls to find negotiated solutions to the armed conflicts. In Nicaragua conservatives have been demanding the military be freed from the control of the FSLN.

But the parties all face serious internal constraints in dealing with these often contradictory demands. At the same time the elections in Guatemala, Honduras, and El Salvador have only given the parties office, not power, they have also created political openings that have enabled popular associations to organize and put forward their demands outside of narrow electoral channels. The parties are constrained in meeting those demands not only by the continued power of the military, but also by the limits the capitalist economy places on state action: failure to ensure an appropriate investment climate will lead to disinvestment and economic deterioration.

In Nicaragua the constraints on the *Sandinista* government were shaped by both the *Contra* War and the need to deliver on reforms. Reforms were difficult to finance and were opposed by economically powerful opposition groups. The Chamorro government, victor in the 1990 elections, is no longer constrained by the *Contra* War, but it is severely limited by economic devastation, created in large measure by that war and by the powerful demands for economic relief by the FSLN and popular organizations.

In addition, there are serious external constraints. Service payments on foreign debt drain much-needed foreign exchange. Restrictions on economic policy placed by the international banks, the IMF, or the U.S. embassy as the condition for more loans force austerity and devaluations, which makes needed reform and growth difficult. The geopolitical strategies of the United States have also imposed serious external constraints on the region. In El Salvador, the U.S. embassy for years vetoed a negotiated solution to the war in favor of continuing the counterinsurgency program. The United States also opposed any significant opening of political space for many popular organizations and the left. In Honduras, U.S. policy was designed to make Honduras a forward base for U.S. strategy against Nicaragua.

Managing demands for reform in the face of such internal and external constraints would be a severe test even for strong, stable Western democracies. The "elected" governments in Central America do not have the remotest ability to handle such difficulties unless they generate the power and authority that only a transition toward greater democracy and more popular support could give them. What then are the prospects for such a transition, and what role might parties play in it?

If we judge electoral politics in Central America using formal procedural criteria drawn from Western European and North American electoral and party systems, we conclude that all countries except Costa Rica and to some extent Nicaragua are far from democratic. Further, the prospects for democracy are not good. Some critics are harsher. They brand elections like those in El Salvador as merely "demonstration elections"[18] and describe Central America as a region of "facade democracies" *(democracias de fachada).*[19]

Without question Central American social reality constitutes a harsh environment for the development of democracy. But if our criteria are based on a less formal, less Western European model, the prospects for democracy, while still difficult, appear more promising. We can define democracy in terms of the relationship between citizens and their leaders without specifying a goal or purpose. It is a system in which informed citizens can participate actively and effectively in making decisions that shape their lives and in which they can hold their leaders politically accountable to themselves and to laws made with the effective participation of the citizenry.[20] Further, it is a system in which there is an underlying consensus about who is a citizen and who can participate in politics, about the rules of the game for participation and accountability, and some rough consensus on which areas of life can be legislated and which are beyond the authority of the state.[21] Approaching democracy this way incorporates the concern of the two other major approaches toward democracy: the formal approach, which focuses on having adequate procedures for setting the rules of the game for democracy, and the substantive approach, which recognizes the necessity for citizens to have the capacity to enter and play the game using the same set of rules.

Within our approach, we focus on three key criteria to assess the role of political parties in the transition to electoral democracy: *effective participation, civic virtue,* and *accountability.*[22] Competitive elections are, therefore, not synonymous with democratic politics. Rather, a country is more democratic the more it allows and encourages such participation, the more widespread the underlying consensus on rules of the game and limits of authority, and the more it fosters accountability. Judged by these criteria, the countries of Central America look varied, from democratic in Costa Rica to much less so in El Salvador or Guatemala.

In this transition to electoral politics, political parties could play a far more significant role than mere participation in competitive elections. To assess their prospects in a transition process to electoral democracy, the student of parties should address the following key questions.

I. How Can Parties Help Create Conditions That Might Enhance Effective Participation?

Effective political participation requires that people be allowed the freedom to assemble and speak, to organize associations, to formulate and press their demands, and to have the freedom of the press necessary to gain and disseminate information. It also requires institutions through which these demands can be heard and considered. Necessary as well is a minimal level of economic resources—money and time—to allow the parties to make use of the freedom to organize and to utilize effectively the institutional channels for articulating their demands.

Elections are only one such institution, and parties only one kind of organization for effective political participation. Other associations include labor unions, peasant organizations, cooperatives, Christian base community groups, neighborhood groups, women's, students', and teacher and professional organizations—what are often called "popular" organizations in the Central American context. Nonelectoral institutions for effective participation may include legally sanctioned collective bargaining, local development projects directed by local organizations, and self-government of universities.

Honduras and especially Costa Rica have been relatively open to such nonparty modes of participation and have allowed freedom of assembly, speech, the press, and association without much fear of repression. But the social and economic resources to facilitate such participation are often not available to a large majority of the population.

In El Salvador, Guatemala, and Somoza's Nicaragua such popular organizations did, at times, form, but in each case, by the late 1970s, they had been severely repressed and there was little effective political participation. One consequence of the transition to electoral politics in El Salvador and Guatemala and of the revolution in Nicaragua, has been the creation of improved conditions—however limited—for such political participation. In El Salvador and Guatemala the military's willingness to allow a transition to pseudo electoral politics was in large part the result of a broader effort to gain international legitimacy, particularly within the U.S. Congress. This required a reduction in some of the most brutal forms of repression—death squad killings, assassinations, disappearances—and the lifting of certain restrictions on the press, on the freedom to demonstrate, and on the right to strike. This created a political opening that not only allowed party activity but also the reemergence of participation by popular organizations. This participation is still limited and could be closed down again. Nevertheless the growing effectiveness of participation is evident in cooperatives, slum communities, refugee camps, and even prisons.

In Nicaragua, the revolution increased the ability of some popular organizations to participate and limited the effectiveness for others. Many of these were organized before the *Sandinista* party came to power and thus maintained an independence of the party organization; new ones were formed subsequent to the revolution. Still others, mostly on the right, ceased to exist. Organizations of small peasants and producers (UNAG), of growers (like the rice growers association), and of women (like ANMALAE), originally closely directed by the FSLN, grew increasingly independent and often participated effectively in decisions that affected the lives of their members. Other groups (both the communist and noncommunist opposition unions) were allowed to organize, but until the 1990 election their participation was limited by such actions as government efforts to prevent strikes and the state of emergency imposed during the *Contra* War.

Given the importance of such nonparty participation in democratic politics, it is important to ask how parties have helped expand conditions for effective participation? Parties face two different tasks in this respect: first, incorporating new groupings into the political system and, second, expanding the political space for themselves and others to create a well-functioning system. It is important to examine the role parties play in bringing popular organizations and mass movements. Do these relationships provide for representation of the interests of these groups, or are they cooptive and controlling like Mexico's ruling Revolutionary Institutional Party (PRI) or Argentina under Perón?

Trying to incorporate emerging sectors into the ongoing political fabric is difficult. With the exception of the *Sandinistas*, few parties have had the skill or the wherewithal to mobilize large groups of people.[23] As we pointed out earlier, some of the parties, including "modernizing" ones like the Christian Democratic Party (PDC) in El Salvador, have been willing to accommodate other dominant power groups at the cost of excluding these newly emerging sectors.

Moreover, some members of society are significantly restrained from effective participation as a result of the structures, values, and behavior prevalent in other societal institutions—family, religion, and so on—that carry over into the political system. Class analysis will address some aspects of this problem, but attention should also be paid to the ways the society incapacitates social groupings such as women in their ability to participate, to overcome the institutionalized biases that may inhibit or prevent these social groupings from participating effectively.[24] Are the parties even exploring these issues? Do they have programs to address them?

What role do the parties play in helping expand the necessary conditions of effective participation—ensuring freedom of assembly, organization, and the press; taming the military and death squad abuses of human rights; ensuring access to the media and the safety of persons who want to organize; overcoming institutionalization biases? Although it is important to examine how parties seek to make it possible to establish broad center-left coalitions that could bring excluded leftist parties into the political system, it is also important to note their contribution to the establishment of a system in which opposition and dissenting parties and coalitions are, at minimum, permitted.

In El Salvador in late 1980 attempts were made to broker an agreement between the *Frente Democrática Revolucionario* (FDR) and PDC, but these collapsed when the military assassinated the FDR leaders in November of that year. In 1981, Washington sought to promote a PDC-ARENA *(Alianza Republicana Nacionalista)* coalition to modernize the right-wing/death squad oligarchy and ally its party with the Christian Democrats. More recently, the *Convergencia Democrática* has tried to bring together center-left parties and popular organizations in a united front to push for reforms and a negotiated solution to the war. In Nicaragua, the FSLN helped mobilize the involvement of formally excluded groups in politics. It will be interesting to see how the *Unión Nacional Oposición* and its constituent parties will function under current conditions.

Finally, the parties must work to expand the base of empowered participants. This requires releasing the tight grip on leadership positions and changing the old, ineffective rules of the game. Parties must develop mechanisms for recruiting and training followers and leaders.

II. How Effectively Do Parties Foster Values and Attitudes Supportive of Democratic Civic Virtues?

A key facet of the transition to electoral democracy is the promotion of values and attitudes that sustain and expand democratic institutions and practices. Among them are the creation of a climate of trust and honesty, respect for the rule of law, tolerance of opposing views, and reliance on peaceful means for resolving political conflict, especially the use of negotiation and compromise.[25] A student of political parties must explore the contribution parties might make to fostering such democratic civic virtue.

Honesty is essential to promoting effective participation and accountability. As Kalman Silvert wrote,

> Lying is the most nefarious political offense....Untruths....destroy the possibility of creating common perceptions of political events, and therefore can fracture a political community at all levels of participation....Political falsehoods create many social events out of one empirical occurrence, threaten community cohesion by opening up the possibility of value conflicts...tend to produce erratic politics, and this...impoverishes individuals and societies.[26]

To what degree do political parties promote honesty in both their own behavior and in that of other politically relevant actors? In a situation where the government or ruling class elite lies to the citizenry, political parties can provide a reliable alternative source of information, giving the public a way to judge the validity of what they are told. Further, by encouraging honesty and integrity in the system and among their own members, they can help pass these values on to party members and to the rest of the society.

The events of the past two decades in Latin America have led to a renewed commitment to the rule of law by those who seek to move away from authoritarianism toward a democratic order. Arbitrariness and inequity in the application of power and the great difficulty of stopping military and vigilante forces from regularly taking the law into their own hands underline the importance of an effective legal system for electoral democracy.[27]

The law sets the rules defining the nature of legitimate participation and the mechanisms through which leadership can be held accountable. To what degree do the political parties actively support the rule of law, even in the face of strong opposition or a losing decision? To what degree do they demonstrate their commitment and support for the rule of law by their behavior within the party itself? How do the parties seek to transmit this value to their own adherents as well as to other members of the nation?

In democratic electoral politics diversity and dissent are to be celebrated, not suppressed. As Kalman Silvert argues, democratic politics "should be seen not as the art of guiding the use of legitimized force, but as the art of promoting and synthesizing difference."[28] Dissent not only permits the consideration of alternative policy options, it can also provide correction in the system for inaccurate or misleading information—whether the inaccuracies or misinformation were purposeful or not. In this latter sense, dissent is important to accountability. In the former sense it is a key to effective participation. In both cases, the valuing of dissent is a critical civic virtue.

To what degree then are parties supporting the presentation of dissenting views? To what degree do they encourage this within the deliberations of the party itself? How, if at all, are they attempting to pass on the importance of tolerating, if not encouraging, dissent?

Conflict among differing ideas is essential to accountability. Indeed, conflict is a normal part of democratic processes. What is important about conflict is not that it occurs, but that it is bounded by an acceptance of the rules of the game, which require settling disputes peacefully, through the political process. Many Chileans learned this lesson during the Pinochet years. Members of parties that had engaged in conflict with other parties to the point of political homicide began to realize that although the struggle was important, having an arena in which such conflicts could take place was even more important than the outcome of a particular fight.[29]

Respect for the rights of others to hold different views and to seek different policies means accepting victory without trying to destroy the opposition and accepting defeat knowing that other opportunities to compete will not be denied. The presence of an arena for the resolution of political conflict through negotiation and compromise must be more highly valued than victory on any specific issue.[30] Students of parties need to examine the efforts parties make to stimulate the peaceful resolution of conflicts; to support a process of negotiation and compromise as opposed to arbitrary rule, the use of force, or the political extinction of opposition; and to promote the use of an open political process to resolve disputes within the party.

III. How Can Parties Help Create Conditions That Enhance Political Accountability?

Accountability is more difficult for political parties to effect than is participation or the promotion of civic virtue. Nonetheless, political parties are central actors in political life and their role is a crucial one. Throughout much of Central America's history, governments have either been the province of the relatively few privileged members of society or caretakers accountable "to either the military, the oligarchy, the private external financial interests with investments in the country, or some combination of these groups."[31]

Attempting to hold regimes accountable in the Central American context may be not only dangerous, but in some cases may also be futile. The "lack of internal structures for promoting and fostering open discussions about political issues" has been a persistent problem. "Few of the region's countries have allowed for ongoing debate and discussion among moderates and the non-revolutionary left."[32] In some cases political actors have turned to the international arena to bolster their efforts to hold regimes accountable.[33]

Finally, the issue of accountability cannot be resolved without considering the role of the United States. As the preeminent, most powerful external actor in the region, the United States has had a profound impact in each of the Central American nations.[34] Traditionally the U.S. embassy has been such a major player that it has, all too often, inhibited the development of internal political accountability of the government to the local citizenry and nation. As Rosenberg observes,

> In Central America, the United States has unrivaled political power and resources and represents one of the largest economic enterprises in each country....The U.S. ambassador is one of the most studied figures in each country. The embassy itself, its staff, programs, and aid activities, are

analyzed, scrutinized, and then hustled by locals who specialize in "working" the U.S. institution....National politicians and military officials inevitably spend as much time cultivating U.S. embassy clientele and visiting dignitaries as they do with their own nationals. [35]

To maintain the integrity of a nation's electoral democracy, accountability to the United States must be substantially subordinated to accountability to the citizens of the country.

Conclusion

We have endeavored to accomplish two tasks in this chapter: first, to show the significant changes that have taken place in the context in which political parties operate in Central America in the past several decades and, second, to provide a framework and series of questions by which one can assess the role parties can play in a transition from pseudo or limited electoral politics to more fully democratic politics. Answers to the three overarching questions—concerning effective participation, civic virtue, and accountability—will help us understand that phenomenon.

As the transition from pseudo to limited to democratic politics occurs, greater numbers of individuals and groups participate and accountability grows. Therefore, the closer one comes to democratic electoral politics, the more social forces there are with which to compete, and all political participants, including political parties, become more empowered.

Any reasonable assessment of the role of political parties in promoting a transition to democracy must recognize the limited impact they can have. Parties are only one of many actors, and they are not autonomous and are composed of a relatively small number of adherents. Finally, their power to act in the system is also circumscribed by the broader, external socioeconomic and political context, which includes actors such as the United States.

Notes

1. Enrique A. Baloyra, "Reactionary Despotism in Central America," *Journal of Latin American Studies* 15, 2 (November 1983). Much of the following analysis draws from John Weeks, "The Central American Crisis," *Latin American Research Review* 21, 3 (1986):31–53.

2. Although we are emphasizing the domestic conditions and responses to change inside Central America, we are aware of the tremendous importance international pressures played in shaping the response of the elites to the demands emanating from the broader publics. In particular, the policies of the United States affected the use of some form of "electoral politics" by these regimes to allow them to generate external legitimacy while maintaining internal control.

3. One could argue that there is a fourth category. That would be a system in which elections are held but in which opposition is simply not permitted and the outcome is a foregone conclusion well before any balloting. In this system there is little pretense that the process is a democratic one. Such was the case, for example, in the 1976 presidential election in El Salvador. This was essentially the situation in El Salvador, Guatemala, and Nicaragua at the end of the 1970s. See Mario Solorzano, "Centroamerica: Democracias de Fachada," *Polemica* 12 (November–December 1983).

4. Weeks, "Central American Crisis," p. 35.

5. For a fuller discussion, see Weeks, "Central American Crisis," pp. 38–39, and the analysts he cites. See also John A. Booth, *The End and the Beginning* (Boulder, Colo.: Westview Press, 1982), for the Nicaraguan case.

6. Weeks, "Central American Crisis," p. 35.

7. Richard Newfarmer, "The Economics of Strife," in *Confronting Revolution: Security Through Diplomacy in Central America*, ed. Morris J. Blachman, William M. LeoGrande, and Kenneth E. Sharpe (New York: Pantheon, 1986), pp. 209–12.

8. Peter Smith, "The Origins of the Crisis," in *Confronting Revolution*, p. 9.

9. Newfarmer, "Economics of Strife," p. 214.

10. Smith, "Origins of the Crisis," p. 12.

11. Newfarmer, "Economics of Strife," p. 215.

12. James Petras, "The Redemocratization Process," *Contemporary Marxism* 14 (Fall 1986):1.

13. See a similar discussion of electoral strategies in Petras, "Redemocratization Crisis," pp. 8–9.

14. Note that Petras makes a similar point in describing the different situations of transition in Peru, Bolivia, and Argentina. See ibid., pp. 10–14.

15. For two case studies that emphasize these obstacles to party organization, see Frank Brodhead and Edward Herman, *Demonstration Elections* (Boston: South End Press, 1985); and Martin Diskin and Kenneth Sharpe, "El Salvador," in *Confronting Revolution*.

16. Mark Rosenberg, "Obstacles to Democracy in Central America," in *Authoritarianism and Democrats: Regime Transition in Latin America* (Pittsburgh: University of Pittsburgh Press, 1987), p. 204.

17. The impact of U.S. policy bolstered the power of the military with respect to all other institutions in the society. See, for example, Phillip Sheppard, "Honduras," in *Confronting Revolution*.

18. See Brodhead and Herman, *Demonstration Elections*.

19. Solorzano, "Centroamerica."

20. For one recent discussion of effective participation and political account-ability as constitutive of democracy, see Richard Fagen's article in Richard Fagen, et al., eds., *The Politics of Transition* (New York: Monthly Review Press, 1986). Also see Kalman H. Silvert, *Man's Power: A Biased Guide to Political Thought and Action* (New York: Viking, 1970).

21. Robert Dahl emphasized this point, though perhaps a bit too narrowly, when he wrote:

What we ordinarily describe as democratic "politics" is merely the chaff. Prior to politics...is the underlying consensus on policy that usually exists in a society among a predominant portion of politically active members.

Preface to Democratic Theory (Chicago: University of Chicago Press, 1956), pp. 132–33.

22. We have chosen to focus on these three criteria because we believe they provide an adequate way of examining the role of parties in the construction of democracy—its institutions, practices, and values. We are not suggesting that these three constitute a full explication of a theory of democracy.

23. Rosenberg, "Obstacles to Democracy," p. 205.

24. Morris J. Blachman, *Eve in a Democracy: The Politics of Women in Brazil*, Ph.D. diss., New York University, 1976.

25. Silvert, *Man's Power*.

26. Ibid.

27. For a solid and important treatment of this issue, see Tom J. Farer, "Democracy in Latin America: Notes Toward an Appropriate Legal Framework" (a revised version of a paper originally delivered at the conference on "Transition from Military to Civilian Rule in South America" at the University of South Carolina, Columbia, S.C., in March 1987).

28. Silvert, *Man's Power*, p. 162.

29. This point was forcefully made by some Chilean political party leaders at the conference on "Transition from Military to Civilian Rule in South America" at the University of South Carolina in March 1987.

30. "Power should shed its meaning related to the imposition of will, and assume the broader meaning of having to do with increasing man's ability to control the consequences of choice." Silvert, *Man's Power*, p. 162.

31. "Only in Costa Rica has some tradition of accountability been established, largely through the electoral system, and to a lesser extent through the courts." Rosenberg, "Obstacles to Democracy," p. 208.

32. Ibid., p. 199.

33. Ibid.

34. See Blachman, LeoGrande, and Sharpe, eds. *Confronting Revolution*.

35. Rosenberg, "Obstacles to Democracy," pp. 197–98.

4

Politicized Warriors: The Military and Central American Politics

Richard L. Millett

In his classic 1832 study, *On War*, Karl von Clausewitz observed, "War is not merely a political act, but also a political instrument, a continuation of political relations, a carrying out of the same by other means." Throughout their history, the armed forces of Central America have inverted this famous dictum. They have repeatedly made politics an extension of military power and conflict. In the process they have become the final arbiters of political power. Of the five Central American nations, only Costa Rica has managed to escape this trend for most of its history. Although not historically part of Central America, Panama too fell into this pattern from the 1960s through the 1980s.

The methods used by the officer corps have become more sophisticated in recent years, the process of interaction between military and civilians more complex, but in El Salvador, Guatemala, Honduras, and Panama it is still impossible to understand the political process without an appreciation of the central and, when they choose to exercise their power, decisive role played by the armed forces.

The contemporary political role played by Central America's armed forces, especially those in El Salvador, Guatemala, and Honduras, is a product of three major factors: the Latin American tradition of military involvement in politics; the influence of the United States, which has shaped both military and civil institutions in Central America; and the ongoing regional political and economic crisis that began with the 1978–79 Nicaraguan Revolution against the Somoza dynasty.

From Spain, Central America's military inherited the concept of the *fuero militar*, the exemption of officers from the jurisdiction of civil courts and their elevation to the status of a privileged class. Lyle McAlister wrote that the military was "a class apart and so regarded itself. The possession of special privileges enhanced its sense of uniqueness and superiority, and at the same time rendered it virtually immune from civil authority."[1]

Military forces had been weak in colonial Central America, but their importance increased rapidly with independence. The short-lived Federation of Central America was wracked by constant civil strife. In Guatemala, Chief of State Mariano Galvez divided that province into four *comandancias*, each commanded by a general. This set a pattern for military government, and the federation's leaders soon "resorted to martial solutions in regulating the morality of the inhabitants, suppressing criticism of their own policies, and persecuting their enemies."[2]

Conservative opponents of Galvez turned to force to attain power. Rafael Carrera, a lower class *ladino*, became their leader, raising an army of 4,000 and seizing Guatemala City in 1838. He occupied it again in 1839 and, in the following year, overthrew the vestiges of federation government, formalizing the division of Central America into five independent states. Carrera ruled Guatemala until 1865, thus setting a pattern of long-term rule by military strongmen. Military force determined who held power in most of the region during this period.

Although politics were militarized in Central America, before the 1870s it was difficult to speak of a military caste separate from the political leadership. The rise of "Liberal" dictators in Guatemala, El Salvador, and Nicaragua led to initial efforts to create a professional officer corps in the 1860s. Then in 1873 Guatemala's military academy, the *Escuela Politecnica*, was founded. With assistance from foreign instructors, it, and a similar institution in El Salvador, began training professional junior officers.[3] Drawn principally from urban backgrounds and more sympathetic to the ideas of the Liberal than the Conservative Party, these officers began to introduce professionalism into the military structure, thereby reducing prospects for successful revolts. The rise of coffee as a dominant crop, especially in El Salvador, also increased stability. Revolutions became less frequent, and by early in the twentieth century there were civilian presidents in El Salvador and Guatemala.

In Nicaragua, President José Santos Zelaya attempted similar reforms, but these efforts did not survive his overthrow in 1909.[4] Costa Rica's military remained small, and, especially after 1889, that nation developed a tradition of civilian rule and political stability. Only Honduras remained outside the regional trend toward political and military modernization, in part because of its neighbors' continuous armed intervention in its internal affairs.

The U.S. decision to build a canal through Panama opened a new chapter in the political and military history of Central America. Washington now believed that its increased security interest in the region required greater internal political stability in each nation and an end to the constant conflicts among the Central American republics. Key elements of this policy included promoting free elections, reducing the strength of national armies, and making the military less political and more professional.

Only in Nicaragua, following U.S. armed intervention in the 1920s, and in Panama, which was virtually an American protectorate, was the United States able to impose its model on the military. But related changes were occurring elsewhere. In El Salvador a separate national guard, trained by Spanish officers, and a national police were created early in the twentieth century. Both were staffed by officers graduating from the military academy.[5] Thus, while the army gained control over internal security, it was relieved from most of the daily police tasks associated with this responsibility.

U.S. pressure also helped produce a virtual end to international conflicts in the region and a notable decline in successful revolutions. But there was a price to pay for this. Deprived of their traditional roles of fighting neighboring nations or defending the government against its political opponents, the military officers began to play a new political role. Civilian political factions began to see the support of the military as the most certain way to reach and maintain power. They began to select officers as candidates for president or vice president. At the same time the post of war or defense minister changed. In the nineteenth century this post was usually filled either by the most notable military *caudillo* of the ruling party or by a trusted subordinate or relative, if the *caudillo* himself held the presidency. Now, however, those who filled the post functioned as either the voice of the officer corps in the councils of government, concerned increasingly with maintaining the military's privileges and power, or as an ambassador from the government to the officers.

The U.S. creation of the *Guardia Nacional* in Nicaragua furthered the trend of separating the army from the traditional political parties without, however, producing any subordination of military to civil authority or any clear guidelines for relations between the two. Thus the professional armed forces that emerged in the first third of the twentieth century, while less inclined to invade their neighbors, were more capable of defeating the armed political partisans of the traditional parties. This imbalance set the stage for the takeover of politics by the officers. All they was needed was an opportunity. That came in the 1930s. The Depression undermined support for existing governments, and the United States, under the rubric of the "Good Neighbor Policy," relaxed its opposition to coups, providing such changes of government did not threaten U.S. security interests and reduced internal disorder and instability. The result was the establishment of long-term military dictatorships in El Salvador, Guatemala, Honduras, and Nicaragua.[6]

The establishment of these dictatorships, headed by generals and dependent on the military for their survival, signaled a fundamental change in the politics of Central America. Never again would the region be dominated by traditional contests between Liberal and Conservative parties. Never again would the armed supporters of such parties defeat the armed forces and place their own partisans in power. From 1930 until the 1979 Nicaraguan Revolution, with but two exceptions, every violent, extraconstitutional change of government in Central America required acquiescence, if not participation, of the existing military establishment. Fighting, when it occurred, was often between factions of the military. If the faction in power lost the support of the officer corps, the faction's leaders would usually be exiled for a limited time or simply sent home in involuntary retirement. Even when leaders were assassinated, as in Panama in 1955, Nicaragua in 1956, and Guatemala in 1957, it was the military that determined who succeeded to power.

The two exceptions to this rule were Costa Rica and Guatemala. In Costa Rica the victory of the revolutionaries in 1948 was facilitated by violation of the nation's tradition of honest elections by the party in power and by the weakness of the Costa Rican army. One of the first actions taken by the revolutionary junta was to abolish the army altogether.[7]

The other exception was the 1954 revolution in Guatemala, which succeeded because the United States supported the revolutionaries and because the military was already disenchanted with the government of President Jacobo Arbenz and was unwilling to risk the institution to defend the regime. The final settlement was worked out, in part, by direct negotiations between the U.S. embassy and the Guatemalan military.[8]

Regional military institutions underwent fundamental changes from 1930 until 1979. Many of these changes reflected the extent to which Central American institutions have been influenced by external forces, particularly during World War II and the cold war. The impact of U.S. security concerns on the nature and political role of regional armed forces became clear even before the United States formally entered World War II. In 1941 the United States urged the Panamanian Police, the predecessors of the present-day Panamanian Defense Forces (PDF), to oust President Arnulfo Arias, who was balking at granting Washington ninety-nine-year leases on additional military bases and sites outside the Canal Zone.[9] The police were more than willing to oblige and launched the first of three coups against Arias. This episode not only marked a major upsurge in military involvement in Panamanian politics, it also signaled the reversal of the earlier U.S. policy of seeking to prevent all coups in the region. Instead, Washington had become the instigator of coups. Loyalty to American policies in international conflicts had replaced democracy and regional stability as prime policy goals.

After the attack on Pearl Harbor, the Central American nations quickly declared war on the Axis powers. Washington established a few small military bases in the region, greatly increased its training efforts, and made equipment available under the Lend-Lease Program. The result was growth in the size, strength, and professionalism of regional armies. Younger officers and many educated civilians also absorbed the constant messages about being part of the war for democracy and against tyranny. Given the nature of their own governments, the contradiction in this message was readily apparent. The result was the growth of both military reformism and civilian pressures for greater democracy, resulting in the overthrow of long-term dictators in El Salvador and Guatemala in 1944. In both nations this precipitated a prolonged period of political conflict within the military that involved both ideology and personal loyalties. In El Salvador, traditional forces ultimately reasserted control, but in Guatemala a reformist government was installed. Disputes over the presidential succession and over the extent to which Guatemala should continue to move to the left led to violent conflicts within the military in 1949. The leader of the conservative faction, Col. Francisco Arana, was assassinated, an attempted coup was crushed after heavy fighting in the capital, and Col. Jacobo Arbenz, leader of the leftist faction, became Guatemala's president.[10] In 1954 he was overthrown by a CIA-sponsored uprising that divided the army. Following the coup, the army leadership became increasingly identified with far-right elements in the nation. Factionalism, however, persisted. After 1954 the army became the decisive political force in the nation. The outcome of internal military disputes and the results of efforts by civilian political factions to gain military support became more important than elections in determining Guatemalan politics.

In Honduras and El Salvador a similar pattern of praetorian politics developed. The 1956 Honduran coup that ousted President Julio Lozano Diaz marked the first institutional involvement of the military in internal politics. A junta was set up, with a promise to restore constitutional order as soon as possible. Elections were held the following year. A proclamation issued the day before the elections laid out the high command's views on the political role of the armed forces. Declaring that they could not simply go along with whatever occurred in the "institutional life of the country," they claimed that they would always serve as "permanent guardian of the national institutions."[11] It soon became clear that the institution they were most interested in guarding was the military. Pressured by right-wing elements opposed to the social reforms being instituted by the government of President Ramon Villeda Morales and alarmed by probable victory of his Liberal Party in upcoming elections, the military overthrew the government in October 1963. The issue that united the armed forces was Villeda Morales's plan to create a civil guard separate from the armed forces and controlled by the president.[12]

Armed Forces Commander Col. Osvaldo Lopez Arellano installed himself as president. An alliance was created with the minority National Party, which gave the government a civilian, constitutional facade and effectively excluded the Liberals from power.[13] This represented a new phase of military involvement in politics. A traditional party retained a good deal of independence, especially in internal party affairs, but allied itself with the armed forces, agreeing to a form of power-sharing in order to exclude its rivals from power. This was a marriage of convenience that would be frequently disrupted and ultimately terminated. Like many marriages, it was not a union of equals. When interests diverged it was clear the military would have the power to impose its solutions.

Divergence came following the 1969 war with El Salvador. The government of Lopez Arellano had become increasingly unpopular, and pressures for reform were building. The poor performance of the army in the conflict forced the military to agree to a restoration of civilian government. The two parties agreed to a degree of power-sharing. Elections resulted in a victory for the National Party candidate, thanks in good part to military backing. But twenty months later the military ousted the government and once again installed Lopez Arellano in the presidency.

Under Lopez Arellano and, to a lesser extent, the regime of his successor, Gen. Juan Alberto Melgar Castro, Honduras experienced a period of limited social reform. An agrarian reform was instituted, the government took control of forestry resources, and labor and peasant unions grew rapidly. At the same time the military began to develop an institutional leadership separate from the power of the officer who served as president. As a result, in 1975 and again in 1978 the military ousted military presidents, replacing them with the officer next in line.[14] At the same time the pace of reform slowed and then virtually

stopped as growing political turmoil in Nicaragua and El Salvador came to dominate the concerns of the military.

El Salvador too experienced military reformism during this period. The colonels who ruled the nation during the 1950s had become increasingly corrupt and unpopular. On October 25, 1960, a coup toppled President (and Colonel) José Maria Lemus and installed a civilian-military junta that leaned to the left. Although few officers were unhappy to see Lemus go, the composition and orientation of the new government raised concerns. The greatest fear was not of reform but of a lessening of the army's role in government, which in turn could lead to civilian involvement in promotions and assignments.[15] Washington was also concerned because one member of the junta expressed open admiration for the Cuban Revolution.

These concerns produced a countercoup in January 1961. A military junta was installed, and the following year, with the civilian opposition boycotting the process, the junta's leader, Col. Julio Rivera, was "elected" president. The junta and the Rivera government enacted a program of reform, including a new labor code, a limited program of social welfare, and even a rudimentary income tax. To promote and consolidate their power, the ruling officers created the *Partido de Conciliacion Nacional* (PCN), which provided a facade for military rule.[16] As time passed, the military's interest in reform waned in response to right-wing pressure. The election of Col. Fidel Sanchez Hernandez as president in 1968 confirmed this shift.

At first the new government allowed a limited political opening. But the frustrations of the 1969 war with Honduras, growing pressures from the right, and the military's fear of losing power changed all that. By 1972 the army was willing to do whatever was necessary to retain its hold on power.

The nation's conservative elite, the legendary fourteen families, blocked further reforms and kept parties like the Christian Democrats out of power by gaining and maintaining the support of the military. Their controlled press constantly reiterated the danger of communism, which was identified with virtually any change in the status quo. Bribery, flattery, and threats were all employed to influence individual officers. Some officers were even allowed to marry into elite families.[17] While seeking to influence the army and its political vehicle, the PCN, the right also formed its own political parties, giving it both an option and an instrument of pressure. These parties were frequently personal vehicles for ambitious officers who lost out in the fight for control of the PCN. A notable example was Gen. José Alberto Medrano who led the United Democratic Front (FUDI) and ran against the official candidate, Col. Arturo Molina, in the 1972 elections.[18]

Despite intense government pressure and electoral fraud, the PCN candidate, Colonel Molina, was unable to win a majority of the votes in 1972. Yet, over opposition protests, the Legislative Assembly chose Molina as the nation's next president. The government also proceeded to rig the next month's Legislative Assembly elections to ensure that it would control all branches of the government. This divided the military and led to a bloody coup attempt in March 1972. The effort failed, and the government used the uprising to justify the arrest and exile of the Christian Democratic Party (PDC) presidential candidate, José Napoleón Duarte.[19] A similar fate befell those officers who supported the uprising.

The events of 1972 undermined the support and credibility of the government. In an effort to strengthen his position, Molina attempted to initiate limited reforms, including a mild agrarian reform. But pressure, bribes, and threats from the right combined with growing fears of the radical left caused him to abort this program.[20] In 1977 the regime moved even further right when the officer corps chose Gen. Carlos Humberto Romero, identified with a 1975 massacre of students, as the PCN's presidential candidate. With Duarte in exile, the moderate opposition nominated retired Col. Ernesto Claramount, hoping this selection would be acceptable to the military. It was not. Fraud and repression produced a victory for Romero, further discrediting electoral solutions and increasing support for the left, which was turning to violence as a political tactic.[21]

In Guatemala from the mid-1950s through the 1970s the military played a dominant, but not always consistent, political role. Col. Castillo Armas, leader of the CIA-sponsored exile invasion, assumed the presidency in 1954 but was assassinated in 1957. After months of conflict and confusion Gen. Miguel Ydigoras Fuentes was elected president. Despite his military background, he had constant conflicts with elements of the officer corps, some of whom supported the far-right National Liberation Movement (MLN). Others resented the government's allowing the United States to train Cuban exiles in Guatemala. U.S. support helped defeat an uprising by the latter group, but dissident officers then created a guerrilla movement with ties to the Guatemalan Communist Party (PGT).[22]

Ydigoras survived the 1960 uprising, but his position was weakened. New disturbances and another foiled coup, this one from the right, undermined what remained of his authority. He was forced to militarize his cabinet, and the minister of defense, Gen. Enrique Peralta Azurdia, exercised real political power. In March 1963, to block the candidacy of former President Juan José Arevalo in upcoming elections, the military ousted Ydigoras and installed General Peralta as "chief of state."[23]

The military government scheduled elections for 1966. There were two military candidates, former Defense Minister Col. Miguel Angel Ponciano of the MLN and Col. Juan de Dios Aguilar of the Institutional Democratic Party (PID). The PID had been created by Peralta to serve as the party of the armed forces. The lone civilian candidate was Julio Cesar Mendez Montenegro of the Revolutionary Party (PR). To the surprise of the military, Mendez Montenegro won. He was allowed to take office, in part because, along with the other candidates, he had earlier signed an agreement not to interfere in army matters, to virtually give the armed forces a free hand in dealing with insurgents, to accept as defense minister the individual nominated by the high command, to guarantee officials of the Peralta administration immunity from future prosecution, to bar anyone suspected of communist sympathies from government office, and to refrain from negotiations with guerrilla groups.[24]

Under these circumstances, although Mendez Montenegro held office, the military continued to hold power. There is a popular, probably apocryphal, story that the president complained that throughout his term of office that Guatemala had two presidents, himself and the minister of defense, and the latter kept threatening him with a machine gun. The defense minister, Col. Carlos Arana Osorio, supported by right-wing private armies and death squads, conducted a ruthless counterinsurgency campaign that decimated guerrilla strength in rural areas at the cost of the lives of thousands of innocent Guatemalans.[25] Eventually Mendez Montenegro was able to replace Arana, sending him as ambassador to Somoza's Nicaragua, but he was never able to control the armed forces.

In 1970 the MLN and PID united to support Arana's presidential candidacy. He won in a relatively honest election. During his term most important posts were filled by officers who had taken part in his earlier counterinsurgency campaigns. While militarizing the government, Arana also tried to destroy the political influence of such groups as labor unions, university students and faculty, and rural cooperatives.[26] As president he also extended to urban areas the antiguerrilla terror he had previously applied against rural insurgents.

In 1974 the PID, MLN, and Arana's own political party, the Organized Aranista Center (CAO—later renamed the Authentic National Center, CAN), supported the candidacy of Gen. Kjell Laugerud Garcia. The Guatemalan Christian Democrats (DCG), who had replaced the PR as the leading moderate party, nominated another general, Efraín Ríos Montt, in the hope that the military would allow a relatively honest election. Their effort failed; massive fraud resulted in the election of Laugerud. Ríos Montt, demonstrating that he valued institutional unity more than electoral honesty, refused to contest the result and went into diplomatic exile as ambassador to Spain.[27]

Four years later, the military divided over selecting the next president. Three major candidates emerged. The MLN ran former Chief of State Peralta Azurdia; the PID, CAO, and PR supported Gen. Romeo Lucas Garcia; and a moderate coalition, including the DCG, ran Col. Ricardo Peralta Mendez. With no candidate receiving a majority of votes, the election went to the government-controlled Congress, which selected Lucas.[28] Backed by the bulk of the officer corps, the new president was soon to reveal both an incapacity and an unwillingness to maintain power at any cost.

In Nicaragua the *Guardia Nacional* never evolved into an independent political actor. It remained dominated by the Somoza family throughout its existence. When General Somoza Garcia was assassinated in 1956, the guard ensured that Somoza's sons inherited his power. In the process, it became an increasingly corrupt, subservient organization. The Liberal Party too was reduced to little more than an appendage of Somoza rule. Elections were a guard-controlled farce. Opposition parties were frequently coopted, divided, and, when necessary, persecuted. By 1978 the isolation of the *Guardia Nacional* and the Somozas from Nicaraguan society was relatively complete, and increasing numbers of Nicaraguans were ready to believe that only violence could change the system.[29]

While in El Salvador, Guatemala, Honduras, and Nicaragua the tendency from the mid-1960s through much of the 1970s was toward a military increasingly separate from the bulk of the population, Panama was undergoing a different type of evolution. Under the leadership of Gen. Omar Torrijos, the Panamanian National Guard, reorganized in the early 1980s into the Panamanian Defense Forces, was practicing a form of military populism. Although the National Guard's influence over politics grew from 1940 on, it had been used largely at the behest of various civilian political groups or simply to remove from power the guard's chief nemesis, populist political leader Arnulfo Arias Madrid. But following yet another ouster of Arias from office in 1968, this pattern changed. General Torrijos defeated opponents within the guard, then suspended existing political parties. Ruling through civilian figureheads, Torrijos began a program of populist reform that produced growing conflict between the military and the traditional elites but won him support among the lower classes.

Ultimately, in part because of U.S. pressure during negotiation and ratification of the new Canal treaties, steps were taken to reinstate traditional politics. The guard created its own political party, the Revolutionary Democratic Party (PRD), which included an amazing variety of politicians on the left and center, government bureaucrats, and opportunistic businessmen. A new constitution was adopted and plans were made for presidential and legislative elections to be held in 1984.

The 1978–79 Nicaraguan civil war, which led to the destruction of the *Guardia Nacional* at the hands of the Marxist-oriented Sandinista National Liberation Front (FSLN), shook the military-dominated regimes in Guatemala, El Salvador, and Honduras. During the conflict, the *Sandinistas* received support from Costa Rica and from the reformist-military regime of Gen. Omar Torrijos in Panama. Although Guatemala provided limited support to Somoza, the trio of military regimes played a marginal role in the conflict, in part because of their own dislike of Somoza and in part because of U.S. pressure. The situation of these governments was further complicated by a deteriorating relationship with the administration of President Jimmy Carter. Pressure for improvement in human rights led El Salvador and Guatemala to abrogate military assistance pacts with the United States. Honduras, weaker and fearful of both developments in Nicaragua and its unresolved border issues with El Salvador, could not afford this luxury. Instead, its government responded to U.S. pressure by replacing the Melgar government with collective military leadership led by Gen. Policarpo Paz Garcia and by moving toward a return to civilian government, if not civilian rule.

Despite increasingly brutal repression in both El Salvador and Guatemala, the success of the *Sandinistas* emboldened forces on the left and contributed to a resurgence of guerrilla activities. Disorders were greatest in El Salvador. There, on October 15, 1979, a group of junior officers, with at least tacit U.S. support, overthrew the Romero government and installed a reformist civilian-military junta.

The Honduran military, pressured by the United States and increasingly frightened by events on its borders, continued to turn the government back to civilians. A new constitution was drafted, and in 1981 the Liberal Party candidate, Roberto Suazo Cordova, was elected president.

In Guatemala, the Lucas regime managed to hold on longer. Violence increased, guerrilla strength grew, and the nation's international isolation hurt the economy and the combat capability of the military. In 1982, following the fraud-marked election of Lucas's hand-picked successor, Gen. Angel Anibal Guevara, the junior officers revolted. Lucas was exiled, and a junta headed by General Ríos Montt was installed.

The coups in El Salvador and Guatemala and the return of civilian government in Honduras represented a failure of the traditional model of military rule in Central America. In Guatemala and El Salvador these coups also demonstrated a growing political gap between junior and senior officers, created in part by the realization that left-wing insurgencies threatened the existence of the military institution. The fear of radical-left revolutions was shared by moderate as well as right-wing political parties, providing a basis for political cooperation. In each nation, the change in regime produced a crisis in relations between the armed forces and the far right, a crisis that would play a major role in subsequent political developments.

In each of these nations, the change in regime found the military internally divided on the issue of its political role and on future patterns of civil-military relations. These divisions also reflected the fact that these military institutions differed markedly in character and composition from those that had existed before World War II.

In Honduras and Nicaragua, and to an extent in Guatemala and El Salvador, the military had acted as a predatory force, with little institutional concern beyond ensuring its own survival. In 1964 an authority on Latin American armed forces could contend that Honduran officers were "by education and profession incapable of thinking in the abstract" and displayed "few nationalistic tendencies."[30] They exercised a "fundamental and dominant role" in these societies and served to maintain the "closed and authoritarian character of these political regimes" and the "concentrated and restrictive" nature of the social and economic order.[31]

From 1941 until the early 1980s, however, these traditional forces underwent considerable change. They were modernized, professionalized, and institutionalized. Modernization involved the acquisition of new weapons and skills and the creation of air forces and even small naval units. Professionalization included expanded programs of officer education, frequently involving study abroad. Such experiences contributed to making an officer a career professional. Institutionalization, the most important change, involved the transference of loyalty from individuals to the military institution and the development of collective leadership concerned with maintenance of the institution's power and privileges.[32]

As these tendencies developed, the nature and behavior of Central America's armed forces began to resemble that of the larger, more developed forces in South America. Amos Perlmutter, a specialist on the political role of the military, described the nature of such forces as follows:

> In Latin America the military are a ruling class....The defense of corporate professionalism and the expansion of civilian and military bureaucracies are the military's chief priorities....Development, modernization, and political stability...are therefore limited by the military perception of the

contribution that participation could make to the resiliency of the military organization.[33]

These developments reduced the ability of any individual, military or civilian, to dominate the armed forces. Officers who became presidents discovered that they could not assume they would receive the loyalty of the armed forces and realized they had to negotiate with the officer corps to maintain their position. In Honduras the collective military leadership was institutionalized in the Superior Council of the Armed Forces (CONSUFFAA), in other nations it operated somewhat less formally, and in Somozas's Nicaragua it never existed at all. In the post–World War II period the armed forces, except in Panama, have been at least as likely to overthrow a military government as they were to replace a civilian regime.

The reduced tendency of the officer corps to give its loyalty to a single individual contributed to divisions within the corps. This, in turn, led those outside the military to compete for its support and those within the officer corps to seek alliances with external forces. This produced military-dominated political parties, nomination of officers by civilian-dominated political parties, and efforts by elite sectors to pressure the military into opposing social and economic reforms, efforts that on occasion involved the promotion of coups by one military faction against another. The United States was also drawn into this process. It increasingly attempted to promote favored factions within the officer corps; in turn, factions strove to gain Washington's support or at least to deny such support to rivals.

The situation in Central America was further complicated by the modernization of other institutions and the proliferation of external actors involved in regional politics. For decades the military, in part because of its own nature and in part because of U.S. assistance, had been the strongest, most modernized, and most cohesive force in society. Although it retained that position in the 1980s, the gap between the military and other institutions, including political parties, labor unions, economic interest groups, and the Roman Catholic Church, was narrowing. One cause was an increased flow of external assistance to these other organizations, but this change also reflected the incorporation of a larger percentage of the population into the national economic and political life.[34]

Political parties were greatly affected by these changes. Increasingly they reflected ideological orientations and were allied with similar parties in other nations. This was clearest in the rise of Christian Democratic, Social Democratic, and Communist parties. Liberal parties also began to establish ties with the Liberal International. Even extreme right-wing parties established such contacts, notably between parties in Guatemala and their counterparts in El Salvador.

All of this made coups harder to justify. In addition, the growing opposition of the United States, especially in the Congress, to military coups and the rising tide of violence within the region raised the costs and increased the risks involved in attempting to overthrow a government. During the 1980s the military's role in politics came under increased criticism.

This has forced the military to seek new alliances and formulate new methods of exercising its power and defending its corporate interests. Except in pre-1990 Panama, the military has found it increasingly difficult to either govern on its own or through parties created and controlled by the military. The effort continued in Panama until the U.S. invasion in December 1989, but at a tremendous cost.

The Central American experience confirms the more general observation that parties created by the military generally fail to maintain support because

> the coalition essential to maintain the working of the polity at any level does not permit regenerative changes to be made....The military regime fails because it can neither hold together the disparate and hostile social forces it has had to harness nor maintain the mass support that, through organizational analogy, it might otherwise have held.[35]

Although the political role played by the military and the nature of other forces contending for political power has fundamentally changed, the values and attitudes toward civilian authority held by the officer corps have not. Officers are still suspicious of politicians in general and of those on the left in particular. They remain unwilling to concede control over military affairs to civilian authorities or to submit the actions of officers to the judgment of civilian courts. At the same time they continue to believe that they have a right, indeed a duty, to supervise the actions of civilian governments, preventing or reversing actions that go against their concept of the national interest or that impinge on the powers and privileges of the armed forces. The officers are also determined to retain the ability to oust or prevent from coming to power any regime they believe represents a threat to the military.

All of this has created dilemmas for the region's armed forces. Old methods of political behavior are no longer safe or effective, but there is no consensus as to what strategies and tactics will advance military interests. This is evident in the experiences of each army.

In Guatemala, the Ríos Montt coup ended the traditional pattern of military rule but created new problems. The ongoing military dominance of politics kept Guatemala isolated and provided justification for the ongoing insurgency. The disruption of the system of military hierarchy represented by the coup was resented by many officers, creating an additional source of friction within the officer corps. Ríos Montt's efforts to create new forms of political authority, notably his abortive Council of State, further alienated existing political parties while providing little concrete support. All of this set the stage for the August 1983 coup led by Gen. Oscar Humberto Mejia Victores, the minister of defense.

The new government kept its pledge to restore civilian government. In 1984 a constituent assembly was elected as the first stage of this process. The results of the election showed extreme political factionalism, a broad base of support for moderate, centrist parties, and a high degree of skepticism about politics, reflected in the 26.5 percent of ballots that were invalidated, cast blank, or unused.[36] Also apparent was the rejection of parties, such as the PID and PR, associated with previous military regimes.

The victory by the DCG in the 1985 presidential and legislative elections presented the military with a dilemma. The outcome was difficult to accept because of the long history of hostility between the military and the Christian Democrats, coupled with the unacceptability of that party to the army's traditional political allies on the right. Prior to the election, the armed forces evidently considered supporting a new, more conservative party, the National Center Union (UCN), but it was clear that public perception of military backing for any party would only decrease its popular support. Any effort to prolong military rule risked further international isolation and a dangerous increase in internal military divisions. Under such circumstances, the military refused to intervene in the process, producing outraged cries of betrayal from the far right.[37]

Although DCG candidate Vinicio Cerezo was allowed to win the 1985 election and take office as president, he was still subject to numerous restrictions on his power by the military. By his own estimate, he entered office with 30 percent of the power, a figure he hoped to increase to 70 percent by 1989.[38] He made it clear that he would not interfere in internal military affairs and that the defense minister would be selected by the military. In addition, he accepted amnesty for officers whose actions were decreed by the military government shortly before it left power.

Yet the tension was constant, and there were numerous plots against the government. For example, when the Cerezo administration, in conformity with the Esquipulas II agreement of the Central American presidents, opened talks in Madrid with representatives of the Guatemalan guerrillas, the acting defense minister publicly admitted that many officers were unhappy. At the end of 1987 a military spokesman declared that the armed forces had "advised" the president not to hold a second round of talks with what were characterized as "terrorists, robbers, and highwaymen."[39] To no one's surprise this round of talks then ended and no new talks were held until 1990.

In May 1988 a small group of officers, encouraged and supported by elements of the far right, attempted to mount a coup. The effort failed, largely because of the opposition of the defense minister, Gen. Hector Gramajo, who denounced those responsible for the coup and reiterated military support for the Cerezo administration. But his greatest concern seemed to be that the attempt represented a break in military unity and discipline. It is worth noting that although some officers involved were subjected to civil court proceedings, they were discharged or reassigned, not imprisoned.

Following the failed coup, attacks by the far right on General Gramajo increased. One officer reportedly accused the general of "being at the service of the Christian Democratic Party instead of protecting the interests of the armed forces."[40] Rumors of additional coup attempts were constant, but by early 1989 both Gramajo and Cerezo appeared to be consolidating their positions. The president was going out of his way to avoid criticizing the military. He described the army as a "professional institution that supports democracy and the institutional process," adding that the military's thinking had changed, and "it now guarantees constitutional order."[41]

Despite efforts by Cerezo and Gramajo, civil-military tensions continue amid rumors of plots and attempted coups. Neither the military nor the politicians have separately reached consensuses as to the future role of the military in politics, making it impossible to even attempt a joint consensus.

A similar situation prevails in El Salvador. Conflicts within the military; officers' distrust of politicians associated with the left; demonstrations, demands, and occasional violence from the left; and efforts by the extreme right to reestablish its traditional alliance with the armed forces all doomed the junta installed in October 1979. When the military refused demands by a group of cabinet ministers, Supreme Court justices, and directors of state agencies that it submit to the junta's authority, the junta and cabinet dissolved, and most of its members on the left joined the opposition.[42]

U.S. pressure helped constitute a new junta and fend off a coup by the extreme right, but it could not end repression, restore order, or curb the activities of right-wing death squads. In March Archbishop Oscar Romero was assassinated by the right, and shortly thereafter several members of the second junta resigned. Only Duarte's agreement to join a new junta kept the government from collapse. However, a steady drift to the right continued. In November a group of opposition political leaders were massacred. In December 1980, Col. Adolfo Majano, representing the less traditional, reform-minded junior officers, was dropped from the junta, leaving a conservative, Col. Guillermo Garcia, as the dominant military figure. Also in December, elements of the military were involved in the murders of American churchwomen and agricultural advisors. The following month the military managed to defeat an abortive offensive by the guerrillas, now united into the Farabundo Marti National Liberation Front (FMLN).

For a time it appeared the alliance between the far right and the military might be recreated. The right, led by retired Maj. Roberto D'Aubuisson, formed a new political party, the Nationalist Republican Alliance (ARENA), which finished second to the PDC in the 1982 election of a constituent assembly. ARENA and the PCN, the traditional military party, controlled a majority of the delegates. U.S. pressure kept the Assembly from electing D'Aubuisson as interim president or ending the program for agrarian reform. A visit by Vice President Bush helped convince the army that its survival depended on curbing death squads and allowing an honest presidential election in 1984.[43] That election was won by the individual the military had prevented from taking power in 1972, José Napoleón Duarte.

Duarte's experience in office was similar to that of Cerezo. The military maintained his government in power, kept the activities of right-wing death squads under control, at least until late in his administration and allowed limited reforms. But Duarte was never able to gain control over the military, deal effectively with the nation's economic and social problems, or find a way to end the brutal civil conflict. The military itself remained divided on political questions, and within it was considerable internal opposition to attempts at social and economic reforms, curbing death squads, and any negotiations with the insurgents. Duarte's inability to control the armed forces is illustrated by the case of Col. Roberto Staben. Despite being implicated in a kidnapping ring and openly attacking government policies, the colonel retained and strengthened his position in the armed forces. Another right-wing officer, Col. Sigfredo Ochoa, was forced to retire, in part because he publicly criticized the military high command as well as the civilian government.[44]

By 1988 growing corruption among the Christian Democrats, a revival of insurgent strength and death squad activities, and the collapse of Duarte's health all threatened the military-PDC alliance. Yet to the surprise of many the military did not block the signing of the 1988 Esquipulas II agreements or the 1989 Central American president's accord in El Salvador. It allowed exiled left-wing leaders, including

Guillermo Ungo and Ruben Zamora of the Democratic Revolutionary Front (FDR), the political arm of the FMLN, to return, create a political party, and run in the 1989 elections. At the same time the military did nothing to discourage the growing strength of ARENA, which won those elections.

The ARENA victory, the continuance of the war, the strength of right-wing elements within the military, and the transition to a new generation of military leadership keep the future role of the armed forces in Salvadoran politics an open question. All of this is further complicated by evident military involvement in the murder of several prominent Jesuit educators in late 1989, murders that underscored the lack of effective civilian controls over the military and have jeopardized the continuance of U.S. assistance.

As a result, both the military and ARENA, the political party now most closely identified with the military, face critical decisions. Pressures are mounting both for a political solution to the civil conflict, something probably not possible without restructuring the armed forces, and punishment of those officers involved in the Jesuits' murders. Although agreeing to either would jeopardize the military's traditional role and immunities, failure to make progress in these areas could lead to loss of external assistance and risk the institution's very survival. The officer corps is clearly the strongest political force in the nation. It has the final say on death squad activity, on any peace negotiations, and on the power and programs of the civilian government. Many officers now recognize that a military solution to the national crisis is impossible. But these same officers adamantly oppose any negotiated settlement that does not force the insurgents to disarm and accept the legitimacy of existing military and political structures.[45] The old pattern of military participation in and dominance of politics has been largely destroyed in the flames of civil conflict. The virtual collapse of the PCN in the 1989 elections underlined this fact. But, as in Guatemala, no definitive new pattern has yet emerged.

On the surface, events in Honduras have been much less complicated. The civilian government of President Roberto Suazo Cordova completed its term and in 1986 was replaced by another Liberal administration, this one headed by José Azcona Hoyo. Elections were scheduled for November 1989 and were likely to have been held on time with a minimum of military interference. But appearances are deceiving. During much of the Suazo administration, real power was exercised by the commander-in-chief of the armed forces, Gen. Gustavo Alvarez Martinez. The autonomy of the armed forces was ensured by the Honduran Constitution, which gave the president and the Congress almost no control over military appointments, operations, or budgets.

The only check on the commander's power is that exercised by the Superior CONSUFFAA, a body of senior military officers created to voice institutional interests.[46]

Alvarez used his position to dominate many aspects of foreign policy as well as internal security concerns. He negotiated directly with the United States on matters concerning the *Contras*, the training of Salvadoran troops on Honduran soil, and the presence of U.S. forces in Honduras. He also created the Association for the Progress of Honduras (APROH), which helped forge ties between conservative business groups and the military.[47] Meanwhile, human rights violations increased, the size and power of the military grew, and the possibility of war with Nicaragua seemed to be steadily increasing.

To the surprise of most observers, including President Suazo and the U.S. embassy, a March 1984 internal military coup ousted and exiled Alvarez. He was replaced by the air force commander, Gen. Walter Lopez Reyes. The coup represented an odd alliance between officers concerned over Alvarez's mounting political ambitions, his ignoring of CONSUFFAA, and the deteriorating human rights situation, on the one hand, and corrupt, inefficient officers whom Alvarez was attempting to purge, on the other hand.[48]

With Alvarez ousted, President Suazo attempted to manipulate the 1985 electoral process in order to prolong his term or to at least ensure the election of a successor he could dominate. The new commander-in-chief moved to block this, forging an alliance with labor, peasant, and business groups to force the president to accept a complicated system of simultaneous primary and general elections and to renounce his ambitions for reelection. The result was the election of José Azcona, a bitter rival of Suazo's within the Liberal Party.[49]

Shortly after Azcona's inauguration, Lopez Reyes was ousted in another internal military coup. The new president was not informed of developments until the ouster was complete and then was forced to accept CONSUFFAA's choice of Gen. Humberto Regalado Hernandez as the new commander-in-chief. All of this demonstrated the weakness of the new chief executive and the autonomy of the military.[50]

Further infighting wracked the armed forces in the months that followed. Azcona's prestige sank steadily. In foreign affairs the military seemed to be playing its own role, even sending a long telegram to the U.S. Congress on the eve of a 1988 *Contra* aid vote.[51] Problems with human rights violations continued, although well below the levels of those in Guatemala or El Salvador, and rumors of military involvement in narcotics trafficking increased. Although the government had no effective control over the armed forces, it was allowed considerable freedom in other areas. The 1988 primary elections in both the Liberal and National parties seemed free of military interference. Economic, social, and even important elements of foreign affairs apparently are left in civilian hands. But when a member of Congress suggested that the military draft could be ended, the reaction of the officers was swift, negative, and almost threatening, making it clear how sensitive they remain to any perceived civilian infringement on their prerogatives. How long the current uneasy division of power will endure is unclear. Military criticism of civilian officials and civilian criticism of military policies and corruption has mounted steadily in recent years. Like its neighbors to the North, Honduras too seems to have left behind much of the old pattern of military participation in politics without developing any consistent, effective new pattern.

In Panama the military's attempt to forge its own political party and to manipulate or undermine others produced an ongoing conflict that intensified in the 1980s. The leading military party, the PRD, was never able to forge an identity separate from that of the military. Instead it became increasingly the tool of the individual who dominated the military. Even with the military manipulating the results, the PRD was forced to form coalitions with other parties to give a semblance of legitimacy to its claimed victories. And those parties that allied with the PRD found their own legitimacy severely undermined. Efforts of the military, especially during the de facto rule of Gen. Manuel Antonio Noriega, to divide and manipulate opposition parties proved unsuccessful. Instead, all this manipulation of the political process destroyed what little legitimacy the PRD had, and it suffered an overwhelming defeat in the 1989 elections. Noriega's annulment of those elections set the stage for the U.S. intervention and the destruction of Panama's military institution, along with much of what remained of the PRD.

In Nicaragua the *Sandinistas* created a military controlled by the *Sandinista* Party, much in the way the military is an instrument of the Communist Party in Cuba. But the Cubans eliminated opposition parties, something Nicaragua never did. Instead the opposition parties survived, and in 1990 mounting external pressures and internal economic chaos led the *Sandinistas* to risk their control of power in relatively free elections. When, much to their surprise, they lost, they turned over much of the government to their opponents but retained their dominance of the military. This has produced a peculiar situation in which the military is for the most part controlled by the largest opposition party. How this anomalous situation will resolve itself remains unclear.

The military's role in Central American politics remains a matter of debate, uncertainty, and confusion both within and without the region. As long as high levels of violence persist, this situation is likely to continue. Only in Costa Rica, where civilian control is firmly established, do issues seem resolved.

In Nicaragua and Panama new civilian governments struggle with the heritage of military institutions that had opposed them for years. The question in Nicaragua is how to control the institution; in Panama it is whether to even have a military. In Honduras, El Salvador, and Guatemala, the struggle for power, both inside the military and between military and civilian institutions, is likely to continue for years. A restoration of peace would strengthen civil institutions, but it could also remove many of the elements that currently inhibit military coups. Even without peace, coups remain possible, especially in Guatemala. What is likely, however, is continued, uneasy power-sharing and, over time, a reduction in the military's sphere of influence. What is unlikely in the near future is an end to the military's role as the ultimate arbiter of regional politics.

Notes

1. Lyle McAlister, *The Fuero Militar in New Spain* (Gainesville: University of Florida Press, 1957), p. 15.

2. Ralph Lee Woodward, Jr., *Central America: A Nation Divided*, 2nd ed. (New York: Oxford University Press, 1985), pp. 103–4.

3. Pedro Zamora Castellanos, *Vida Militar de Centro América*, 2nd ed. (Guatemala City: Editorial del Ejercito, 1967), 2:297–304.

4. Richard Millett, *Guardians of the Dynasty* (Maryknoll, N.Y.: Orbis Books, 1977), pp. 21–22.

5. Robert Varney Elam, "Appeal to Arms: The Army and Politics in El Salvador, 1931–1964" (Ph.D. diss., University of New Mexico, 1968), pp. 9–10.

6. The dictators were Generals Maximiliano Hernandez Martinez in El Salvador, Jorge Ubico in Guatemala, Tiburcio Carias Andino in Honduras, and Anastasio Somoza Garcia in Nicaragua. Somoza was more of a politician than a military officer, but he had been placed in command of the U.S.-created *Guardia Nacional* and used that force to gain and hold power.

7. For a description of this conflict and its aftermath see John Patrick Bell, *Crisis in Costa Rica: The Revolution of 1948* (Austin: University of Texas Press, 1971).

8. For descriptions of this episode, see Richard H. Immerman, *The CIA in Guatemala* (Austin: University of Texas Press, 1982); and Stephen Schlesinger and Stephen Kinzer, *Bitter Fruit* (New York: Doubleday, 1982).

9. J. Conte Porras, *Arnulfo Arias Madrid* (Panama City: Impresora Panama, 1980), pp. 95–107.

10. Immerman, *CIA in Guatemala*, pp. 59–61.

11. Leticia Salomon, *Militarismo y Reformismo en Honduras* (Tegucigalpa, D.C.: Editorial Guaymas, 1982), pp. 32–34.

12. Salomon, *Militarismo y Reformismo*, pp. 38–39.

13. Richard Millett, "Historical Setting," in *Honduras: A Country Study*, ed. James D. Rudolph (Washington, D.C.: Department of the Army, 1984), p. 39.

14. Thomas P. Anderson, *Politics in Central America* (New York: Praeger, 1982), pp. 116–20; Salomon, *Militarismo y Reformismo*, pp. 73–160.

15. Elam, "Appeal to Arms," pp. 156–57.

16. Edwin Lieuwen, *Generals vs. Presidents* (New York: Praeger, 1964), pp. 92–93.

17. Interviews in El Salvador with both civilian and military officials, 1977 and 1978.

18. Stephen Weber, *Jose Napoleon Duarte and the Democratic Party in Salvadoran Politics, 1960–1972* (Baton Rouge: Louisiana State University), pp. 158–63.

19. Ibid., pp. 168–80.

20. Interviews with Lt. Col. José Guillermo Garcia and with former minister of agriculture Atilio Vietez, El Salvador, 1977 and 1978.

21. Weber, *Jose Napoleon Duarte*, pp. 196–98.

22. Eugene K. Keefe, "National Security," in *Guatemala: A Country Study*, ed. Richard F. Nyrop (Washington, D.C.: Department of the Army, 1983), pp. 206–7.

23. Richard N. Adams, *Crucifixion by Power* (Austin: University of Texas Press, 1970), p. 275; Gordon L. Bowen, "U.S. Policy Toward Guatemala, 1954 to 1963," *Armed Forces and Society* 10 (Winter 1984):181–83.

24. Anderson, *Politics in Central America*, p. 29; Michael McClintock, *The American Connection*, vol. 2, *State Terror and Popular Resistance in Guatemala* (London: Zed Books, 1985), pp. 77–78.

25. Kenneth F. Johnson, "On the Guatemalan Political Violence," *Politics and Society* (Fall 1973):70–72.

26. James D. Rudolph, "Government and Politics," in *Guatemala: A Country Study*, p. 133.

27. Jan Knippers Black and Martin Needler, "Historical Setting," in *Guatemala: A Country Study*, pp. 34–35; Donald L. Etchison, *The United States and Militarism in Central America* (New York: Praeger, 1975), p. 19.

28. Anderson, *Politics in Central America*, pp. 30–33.

29. For details see Millett, *Guardians of the Dynasty*, pp. 223–61.

30. John J. Johnson, *The Military and Society in Latin America* (Stanford, Calif.: Stanford University Press, 1964), pp. 141–42.

31. Gabriel Aguilera, "La Dimension Militar en la Crisis de Centroamérica," in *Anuario de Estudios Centroamericanos* (San José: University of Costa Rica, 1986), pp. 27, 32.

32. Ronald H. McDonald, "Civil-Military Relations in Central America: The Dilemmas of Political Institutionalization," in *Rift and Revolution: The Central American Imbroglio*, ed. Howard Wiarda (Washington, D.C.: American Enterprise Institute, 1984), pp. 131–32.

33. Amos Perlmutter, *The Military and Politics in Modern Times* (New Haven: Yale University Press, 1977), p. 198.

34. Factors that contributed to this trend included the growth of urban centers, which made Central America nearly 50 percent urban by 1989, and the expanded influence of the media. The latter factor was fueled by increased literacy and by the spread of television, but the most important single factor was the introduction of cheap transistor radios, which spread that form of communication to the most remote corners of the region.

35. Edward Feit, *The Armed Bureaucrats* (Boston: Houghton Mifflin, 1973), p. 19.

36. *Central America Report* (Guatemala), July 6, 1984, p. 201.

37. For details on this period, see Richard Millett, "Guatemala's Painful Progress," *Current History* (December 1986):413–15.

38. Remarks by President-elect Vinicio Cerezo Arevalo at December 17, 1985, press conference, Carnegie Endowment, Washington, D.C.

39. Foreign Broadcast Information Service, *Latin America: Daily Report*, December 31, 1987, p. 32. [Hereafter, FBIS.]

40. FBIS, September 14, 1988, p. 12.

41. FBIS, December 19, 1988, p. 18.

42. Enrique Baloyra, *El Salvador in Transition* (Chapel Hill: University of North Carolina Press, 1982), pp. 93–98.

43. Max G. Manwaring and Court Prisk, *El Salvador at War: An Oral History* (Washington, D.C.: National Defense University Press, 1988), pp. 189–91, 212–15.

44. *Central America Report*, August 21, 1987, pp. 252–54; Manwaring and Prisk, *El Salvador at War*, pp. 453–54.

45. Interviews with numerous Salvadoran officers in 1987 and 1988.

46. Steve C. Ropp, "National Security," in *Honduras: A Country Study*, ed. James Rudolph (Washington, D.C.: Department of the Army, 1984), pp. 215–20.

47. Thomas P. Anderson, "Honduras in Transition," *Current History* (March 1985):114–17.

48. Interviews with Honduran officers, 1984 and 1985.

49. Mark B. Rosenberg, "Honduras: The Reluctant Democracy," *Current History* (December 1986):419.

50. Victor Meza, "La Caida de Walter Lopez: Significado y Ensenanzas," *Boletín Informativo Honduras* 58 (February 1986):1–2.

51. A copy of this telegram is in the possession of the author.

5

Constitutional Framework for Political Parties in Central America: From Exclusion to Participation

Jorge Mario García Laguardia

Since independence, Central America has formally been a liberal democracy. The constitutions promulgated in the region have, in general, recognized that their systems of government are republican and democratically representative. Constitutions, as well as secondary systems of laws, have adopted the fundamental elements of liberal democracy: universal suffrage; popular representation based on free elections; recognition of individual social, economic, and cultural rights; division of powers guaranteeing control of government by a congress; a system of checks and balances between powers; and a hierarchy of legal norms, with the constitution as the fundamental law of the land and the principle of legality. Constitutions of Costa Rica (1949), Honduras (1982), El Salvador (1983), and Guatemala (1985) include these democratic elements. Another basic element of political systems is the political party. Political parties, preferably in a multiparty system, are institutions essential to liberal democracy.

Legal Framework of Political Parties

Political parties are social phenomena; they exist prior to being recognized and regulated by law. In this chapter, I analyze how the constitution, as the highest law of the land, recognizes the political party. The legal perspective is especially relevant if we consider the role of parties in a pluralist framework. Here they act as intermediaries between the electoral body and government. Political parties are, as Paolo Barile has said, "the political skeleton of the people."[1]

In the Central American constitutional system, the political party is a group of citizens that meets to influence public decisions, act in public life, attain and exercise power, and exert pressure over the government through mechanisms established by law. It is a stable organization inspired by ideology and a political program. The political party is furthermore recognized as an institution by public or private law, based as it is on a contractual relationship established among its members.

Constitutional Recognition of Political Parties

The political parties of Central America have gone through the same stages as world constitutionalism.

> After a rigid phase of opposition to them...and after another one of absolute agnosticism with respect to the modern, liberally oriented state of the nineteenth century, we have now passed to a phase where they have become progressively regulated by law.[2]

In the first phase, constituents and legislators, mirroring the attitude of the classic European and North American liberals they followed, rigidly opposed the recognition of political parties. They distrusted them as intermediaries that stood between the state and the citizens. Pedro Molina, one of the most important deputies of the first Central American Constituent Congress of 1823–24, referring to Rousseau's *Social Contract*, affirmed this view: "I speak of parties, or better, factions, as always pernicious in a free state."[3] Another eminent deputy to the same congress, Juan Lindo—later president of Honduras and El Salvador—in the same vein proposed that "no citizen, association, or corporation may represent the assembly, supreme government, or other courts, taking the sacred voice of the people, under the threat of incurring the same penalties indicated for those who disturb the public order."[4] Along with harboring a deep mistrust of political parties, many found the constitution and political parties fundamentally incompatible.

Yet in the second half of the nineteenth century the increased number of legal rights adopted in the liberal constitutions included the right to associate for political purposes. This initiated the second phase in the development of political parties in Central America—that of accepting yet ignoring their existence. Based on this constitutional protection, the traditional Liberal and Conservative parties and other more ephemeral groups that appeared at elections came to survive owing to the benevolence of public authority.

In the third phase, political party activities were legally and constitutionally regulated. This was a response to the enrichment of political life that occurred in the late nineteenth and early twentieth centuries. Throughout the nineteenth century the right to vote was progressively granted. Some countries even sanctioned universal suffrage. In legislative assemblies, groups formed parliamentary blocs, hybrids of pressure groups and party directorates. Political clubs outside of the assemblies became more permanent, local political bosses shaped their clientele and manipulated elections, and the 1920s saw the first Marxist parties, which pretended to represent the interests of an almost nonexistent working class.

Recognition of political parties was first indirect and then later direct. The state initially began to accept partisan activities at the parliamentary and electoral levels. Political parties were considered in regulations drafted by congresses and in electoral laws. Constitutions, however, did not immediately recognize the existence of political parties. Regulations alluded to parliamentary blocs in congress as expressions of political parties. Electoral laws regulated partisan involvement in elections, parties' behavior during the electoral process, and their support of candidates. Later, with the increase in influence of political parties came control of their activities. Political parties, at first subject to limited regulation, came under extensive legal control. They entered the legal system through the back door, by indirect recognition.

Buscaretti mentions three procedures for such control,[5] all of which can be found in Central American law: (1) external or negative, (2) ideological or programmatic, and (3) structural or related to their internal function. The first, external or negative control, is geared toward framing political party activities within the established liberal democratic order. Legislation included sanctions for those groups that attempted to oppose democratic values. Nonetheless, most Central American constitutions recognized the right of assembly.

As the experience of Italy, Germany, and Russia demonstrated, using the liberties granted to them, elected extremist parties could destroy the democratic order. As a result, many Central American states enacted sophisticated legislation against political extremes. Prohibition of communist or anarchist parties provided a negative recognition of their existence.

In 1931, President Jorge Ubico's rise to power in Guatemala inaugurated a long dictatorial period. Political parties were constitutionally recognized, but those parties believed to threaten the liberal democratic system were banned. Article 25 of the 1879 text, which guaranteed the right of assembly, was revised to exclude "organizations or individuals whose doctrines seek to undermine established social and political institutions through violence." The commission that proposed the amendment clearly affirmed that it refers to "activities of a communist or anarchist nature."[6]

This is the first reference in a Central American constitution to the Communist Party as such. Yet prior to this, anticommunism was used as a pretext to persecute the political opposition. In March 1920, a law directed against the conservative Unionist Party yet curiously called "anti-Bolshevik" was submitted to Guatemala's Legislative Assembly.

Similarly the Nicaraguan Constitution of 1939 established that individuals who publicly express "opinions contrary to the public order, to the fundamental institutions of the State, to the Republican and Democratic form of government, and to the established social order" would be punished by law. It also prohibited parties with ties to "international organizations" and excluded their members from public service.

The Nicaraguan Constitution of 1948 was even more explicit. It indicated that the state did not recognize the legal existence of either political parties with international organizations or communist and fascist parties, except those that, "not being communist or totalitarian," promote the union of Central America. Because the only extant political party referred to was the Communist Party, the target of the prohibition was clear.

In this way a new type of control, ideological in nature, appeared. Although pretending to incorporate political parties into representative and constitutional democracy, regulations were directed against certain ideologies and political programs. A gradual transition was thus made from limited to extensive control of the party system. This was a transition to a concealed form of authoritarianism, a kind of constitutional and legal manipulation. Required was the reporting of party affiliation, recognition, activities, programs, history of the party leadership, and financial affairs. This covert prohibition of parties was left in the hands of the central government, which ultimately determined the scope of party activities and parties' very existence. In many countries, especially in Guatemala, Nicaragua, and El Salvador, a constitutional and legal framework was established to control partisan activities and to maintain a restricted pluralist system. This has prevented free and open opposition and has polarized political life and provoked violence and radicalism.

As part of the effort to preserve the system and contain adversarial groups, a prohibition against Marxist organizations was established in the Constitution. This restriction was the central aim of some reforms, such as those of 1956 in Guatemala. Similar measures were adopted in the region, amending all Central American constitutions beginning in the 1950s. Article 68 of the Guatemalan Constitution of 1965 recognized the right of assembly but also prohibited the "organization of groups that act in accordance with, or are subordinated to, international entities that propose the communist ideology or any other totalitarian system." It guaranteed the existence of political parties while prohibiting the "formation of political parties propounding the communist ideology or tending through their doctrine to promote violent action against the sovereignty of the State or the democratic organization of Guatemala."

The 1962 Salvadoran Constitution, while recognizing the right of assembly, prohibited the functioning of "international or foreign political organizations," unless they pursued through "democratic means" the union of Central America or "continental or universal cooperation." Even though the Constitution did not outlaw political parties, as Guatemala's did, it forbade "the propaganda of anarchic doctrines or those contrary to democracy" (Article 158, Paragraph 2). On this basis the Electoral Council denied the registration of the Communist Party.[7]

In Honduras, the Constitution of 1965 forbade "the formation, registration, and functioning of political parties that proclaim or practice doctrines contrary to the democratic spirit of the Honduran people" (Article 39). The Nicaraguan Constitution of 1955 expressly banned Communist Party activities "and those that sustain similar ideologies, along with any other party having an international organization." Even in Costa Rica, a country with a classic constitutional democracy and a flexible political system, the Constitution of 1949 prohibited the formation or functioning of parties that, "through their ideological programs, activities, or international ties, attempt to destroy the fundamental values of Costa Rica's democracy, or jeopardize the country's sovereignty." This prohibition was annulled in June 1975 by Law 5698.

Abusive interpretation and use of the judicial system persistently blocked the political participation of the opposition. Not only has the far left been obstructed, but moderate groups from the center to the left have been as well. In some situations these limitations have been used to control election returns. In 1974 a secret memorandum was leaked to the press. The memorandum, endorsed by the leader of the right-wing parties, who at that time was president of Congress, clearly described the crude method used to prevent registration of the Social Democratic party, the *Unidad Revolucionária Democratica* (URD), a party founded in 1961 by intellectuals and workers of the center-right.

For the past few months, in discussions held at high government levels, the president and almost all of the executive branch upheld the decision not to grant the URD a permit for functioning as a political party. My arguments for granting such a permit were finally accepted. My plan was first to analyze the strength of Manuel Colóm Argueta [the most important leader of the URD]; second, to encourage division among the left, because the URD would have to obtain its affiliation with the leftist parties, taking people away from the Christian Democrats and the Revolutionary Party; third, publicly to find out who belongs to that group; fourth, to make them spend money and effort; and, fifth, even if they did obtain the minimum of 50,000 [registered members] in the required six months, have the Electoral Registry set up permanent obstacles to their registration. For these and other reasons, my opinion prevailed. President Arana [Gen. Carlos Arana Osorio, 1970–74] carefully considered my arguments. I see him having greater political sense than before.[8]

This document is particularly disturbing because all of the members of the Central Committee of the Communist Party of Guatemala disappeared when the police broke up a clandestine meeting. Also, Colóm Argueta—the charismatic, popular leader of the Social Democrats and a strong presidential candidate—was assassinated in March 1979, one week after having registered the party *(Frente Unido de la Revolución)* following a long struggle.

Recognition of political parties first began with the Guatemalan Constitution of 1945, which inaugurated the cycle of social constitutionalism and was a product of the civil-military revolution that overthrew the dictator Ubico in 1944. The provisional governmental junta included in Decree 17 constitutional recognition of political parties and the representation of minorities, affirmed in Article 33 of the Constitution.

Article 32 prohibited the establishment of monastic institutions and associations, along with those political organizations having "an international or foreign character." Interviews with congressmen indicated that this prohibition was directed against rightist groups. Nonetheless, imprecise language in the article permitted in later years those opposed to reformist governments to give it an anticommunist bent, particularly after President Jacobo Arbenz authorized the Communist Party in 1952.

From then on all countries in the region recognized political parties in their constitutions. In general, laws were not repealed. They continued to include the right of assembly, under which the political parties operated until they achieved constitutional recognition after the Second World War.

The Current Constitutional Order

Central America has the dubious honor of having the most constitutional texts and of having developed the greatest number of frustrated constitutional projects in Latin America. Constitutional instability has been characteristic of Central American political life. Most of the constitutions currently in force are recent: Costa Rica, 1949, with various reforms; Honduras, 1982; El Salvador, 1983; Guatemala, 1985. In Nicaragua, a new text was being discussed in 1989, even though a "Fundamental Statute" was dictated in 1979. Electoral and political party laws are also recent: Guatemala's were issued in 1985; El Salvador's in 1984; Nicaragua's in 1984 and 1983, respectively; Honduras's in 1981; and Costa Rica's dates back to 1952.

Recognition

As I have indicated, all current constitutions organize their countries as liberal democracies with a republican system of government. The constitutions recognize free exchange of opinions and open competition for political power. Within this scheme, political associations play an essential role. They serve as intermediaries between public power and the organized population in the electoral body. Political parties are made up of citizens exercising their political rights who group themselves under the same ideological flags in a permanent manner—subject to legal statute—to influence politics.

Political parties are now recognized in the constitutions of most Central American countries. Article 98 of Costa Rica's Constitution states that "all citizens have the right to organize themselves into parties to intervene in politics, provided they commit themselves, in their programs, to respect the constitutional system of the Republic." The Constitution of El Salvador in Article 72 speaks of one of the political rights of the citizen as that of "associating to constitute political parties according to the law and of becoming a member of those already established." According to the Constitution of Guatemala, Article 223, the state "guarantees the establishment and functioning of political organizations, which will be limited only by the Constitution and by law." Article 47 of the Honduran Constitution affirms that "political parties legally registered are institutions of public law, whose existence and free functioning is guaranteed in order to achieve the effective political participation of all citizens." The Fundamental Statute of Nicaragua states that all citizens have the right to "organize or belong to political parties or associations." All constitutions therefore set the guidelines for political parties, but laws regulate them.[9]

Prohibitions

The political exclusion established by previous constitutions did not lead to the disappearance of "inconvenient" opposition. Instead, it fueled extremist opposition groups, prevented the development of a political center, and was one reason for the emergence of armed struggle in the region, which began in Guatemala in 1960. New constitutions have been more careful to limit controls on parties and encourage political participation.

In Article 98 of Costa Rica's current Constitution, party activity is recognized, with only one limitation—that parties "commit themselves in their programs to respect the constitutional order of the Republic." El Salvador's Constitution is silent on this point, and Honduras's only prohibits political parties from attempting to act against "the Republican, Democratic, and Representative system of government" (Article 48). The Fundamental Statute of Nicaragua also recognizes freedom of "political organization" and only establishes limits "that emanate from the constitutional rights and guarantees of Nicaraguans." Nonetheless, the Law of Political Parties of August 17, 1983—although it authorizes the free organization of political parties "without any ideological restrictions"—does impose on them vague "duties." These are to "promote and support the patriotic unity of the nation, to complete the tasks of reconstruction and development of the nation," and "defend the Revolution against any internal or external threat that pretends to install a regime of oppression and exploitation on the Nicaraguan People." Finally, it prohibits the groups or parties that promote the return "to *Somocismo* or propound the establishment of a similar political system."[10]

The most recent electoral law of the region, the Constitutional Law of Guatemala of December 1985, does not specifically limit political parties. To register, political parties are required to submit their "Declaration of Principles," which must include the obligation to respect existing legislation; their ideological platform; and the "economic, political, social, and cultural postulates they propose to accomplish." Additionally, they must take two oaths, one referring to the development of their programs through "peaceful, democratic means, respecting the rights of other organizations within a pluralist spirit" and another declaring that they will respect "democratic manifestations, particularly those produced internally for selection of their own leaders and candidates." When this bill was being considered, a proposal was made to include parties' obligation to outline the democratic character of the ideas they promoted. The trend toward more open systems may have prevented this from becoming a part of the final bill and thus made easier the registration of new parties.

Privileges

The recognition and registration of political parties involve a series of privileges, outlined below.

Proportional Representation. Representation of political minorities, which benefits parties defeated in elections, has been a right recognized at the constitutional level in Central America.[11]

Nomination of Candidates. This privilege carries with it the danger that the system will develop into a "partiocracy," in which political power is controlled by party oligarchies. In Central America, political parties have strengthened their monopoly of the nomination process and only allow nomination of independent candidates at the local level. Sentiment against party leadership and the ruling political classes who control activity, common throughout Latin America, led to the formation of interest groups that promote independent candidates.

Financing. The Constitution of Costa Rica, the oldest in the region, was the first to acknowledge the need for state contribution to parties' expenses in presidential and legislative elections. Recent constitutions in El Salvador, Honduras, and Guatemala have followed Costa Rica's example.

Electoral Administration and Justice. The administrative and judicial control of elections began after the Second World War as a response to abuses by dictatorial governments.[12] In El Salvador and Honduras political parties form part of the electoral organizations that oversee elections. Nicaraguan law establishes a mixed system of appointment: five members are designated by the Supreme Court of Justice, three elected directly by the court, and the other two selected from a list submitted by the National Assembly of Political Parties.[13]

Legal Nature of Political Parties. In Central America political parties are effective auxiliary organizations of the state in that, even if their activities are geared to satisfying their own needs, their actions become part of the liberal-democratic organization of the state. Indeed, political parties engage in public functions and activities that benefit the state and the community by inserting themselves into the power structure and legal framework of the state.

Functions of Political Parties. Political parties establish standards for the expression of popular will. They collaborate with the government's mechanism for succession by monopolizing the right to nominate candidates. They also participate in control of the electoral process. Finally, they help shape public opinion, contribute to the development of government programs, create political platforms, and help shape the political beliefs of citizens. Constitutions determine the operation of political parties by defining citizenship requirements, conditions for suffrage, organization of the electoral body, and the designation of rulers.

Democracy and Pluralism

Constitutions of Central America currently include norms that, to some extent, have produced exclusive political systems. There has been an effort to create a legal framework for political parties and to regulate the electoral system. Recognition of the classic functions of political parties regarding the articulation of social demands, as well as the subsequent responsible representation and mediation of these demands, is central to this effort. The effort to attain authentic political pluralism must be pursued so that different forces within society can freely express themselves. The social structure is by its very nature heterogeneous, the product of economic, social, professional, and ethnic realities that may at times generate conflicting interests. As Seymour Lipset has noted, a moderate level of conflict is natural to legitimate democratic systems.[14] Pluralism requires recognizing this diversity and channeling this expression through intermediary institutions. Recognition that conflict is legitimate and the delineation of clear rules of the game that govern conflict establishes a truly democratic system. Democracy accepts conflict, recognizes political and social pluralism, establishes channels for conciliation and consensus, and provides instruments for popular mobilization and participation. Without that what prevails is an atmosphere of distrust and noncompliance; citizens become divided into "friends" and "enemies"; and ultimately this polarization leads to violence. These conditions have characterized Central America for many years. Denying political parties their role blocks the expression of conflicting interest in an openly competitive system and produces a system that excludes democratic participation and leads to authoritarian regimes. For this reason political parties are a necessary element of democratic life.

Extremists oppose political parties and political activity in general, but only political parties can peacefully ensure a democracy. Hans Kelsen has affirmed that political parties are the basis of modern democracy and that a democracy sustains itself without them only by fraud.[15] Political parties are the instruments through which the fundamental values of pluralist democracy are expressed.

Notes

1. Paolo Barile, *Corso di Diritto Costituzionale*, 2nd ed. (Padua: Editrice Dott. Antonio Milani, 1964), p. 249.
2. Paolo Buscaretti di Ruffia, *Derecho Constitucional* (Madrid: n.p., 1975), p. 720.
3. *El Editor Constitucional*, No. 16, Folio 199 (Guatemala City), October 16, 1820.
4. "Mociones de Octubre de 1823: Asamblea Constituyente de Centroamérica," *Archivo General de Centroamérica*, Guatemala City, B6.2, Record 2456, Sheaf 91.
5. Buscaretti, *Derecho Constitucional*.
6. *Reforma Constitucional de 1936: Antecedentes; Texto Taquigráfico de los Debates Sostenidos en la Comisión de la Constituyente Que Abrió Dictámen Sobre la Materia* (Guatemala City: Tipografía Nacional, 1935), p. 14.
7. *Resoluciones del Consejo Central de Elecciones, 1965-1968* (San Salvador: Imprenta Nacional, n.d.), n.p.
8. *Diario la Hora*, July 21, 1973. Bracketed notations are those of the author.
9. In the case of Guatemala, this law has constitutional status. Reference to "ordinary law" is made in the following articles of each country's constitution: Costa Rica, Article 96, Paragraph E; El Salvador, Article 72, Paragraphs 2 and 210; Honduras, Articles 47 and 49; and Guatemala, Article 223 and Article 17 of Title VIII, Transitory and Final Dispositions, which establishes that laws regulating all that concerns such organizations must be constitutional.
10. See Walter Antillón Montealegre, "El Sistema Electoral Nicaraguense," in *Legislación Electoral Comparada: Colombia, México, Panama, Venezuela y Centroamérica* (San José: Centro Interamericano de Asesoría Electoral e Instituto de Investigaciones Jurídicas de la Universidad de México, 1986).
11. Representation is guaranteed in Costa Rica by Article 95; El Salvador by Article 70; Honduras, Article 46; Guatemala, Article 203 of the Constitutional Electoral and Political Parties Law; and Nicaragua, Article 122 of the Electoral Law.
12. The following institutions were authorized to organize and supervise elections: Costa Rica, Supreme Electoral Court; El Salvador, Central Electoral Council; Honduras, National Electoral Court; Guatemala, Supreme Electoral Court; and Nicaragua, which is considering a "Supreme Electoral Council."
13. Nicaragua's council is an atypical organization that is a "consultative" party to the council (Article 8).
14. See his *Party Systems and Voter Alignment: Cross-National Perspectives* (New York: Free Press, 1967).
15. See his *General Theory of Law and the State* (Cambridge, Mass.: Harvard University Press, 1945).

6

Parties, Transitions, and the Political System in Guatemala

Héctor Rosada Granados

From the October Revolution in 1944 until 1954, an effort was made in Guatemala to build a new hegemony founded on a broad alliance of classes. This alliance operated in a political climate favorable to the expansion of democratic practices. For the first time in Guatemala's national history a genuine party system emerged. With political parties acting as intermediaries, it was possible to channel social pressures and demands to influence the development of a political process.

The blocking of the 1944 revolutionary program, which included the reversal of the majority political decisions, was particularly directed against organized popular participation. The result was a closing of political space and the exhaustion of the leadership's legitimacy. A structural crisis generated by the breakdown of the economic growth model, the failure of party mediation, the maturation of an insurgency, and a crisis within the ruling bloc gave rise to a new military activism that made the army the most relevant force in the power structure. The loss of restraint within the armed forces has been manifested through its expansion into sectors traditionally controlled by the dominant political classes. The military's position in the state bureaucracy permitted the enrichment of some high-ranking officers, who later were incorporated into the small sector of large landowners.

The coups of March 23, 1982, and August 8, 1983, the elections for the National Constituent Assembly in July 1984, and the general elections of 1985 consolidated a new military program. The achievement of a new constitutional framework marked the transition from a military and authoritarian government to a civil and representative one, even though the internal power structure remained the same. The transfer of electoral loyalties in favor of more progressive options, diminishing the electoral impact of the more conservative, traditional sectors of society, was evident. Those parties that agreed to participate in the system—subordinated to a restricted ideological framework—gradually distanced themselves from the popular sectors of society, thus diminishing their role as intermediaries in the conflicts that disrupt Guatemalan society.

The future of political parties in Guatemala is intimately linked to the future of the political transition. If the transition fails, the parties will lose their raison d'être. In an environment characterized by the militarization of politics and the politicization of the military, party fragmentation does not guarantee the feasibility of transition, especially when this transition is unable to interpret the interests of the majority and remains distanced from the most acute problems of the nation. What type of consensus can be expected within a moderate ideological pluralism that does not represent the political community of the country?

The crisis of the existing social structure has placed Guatemala at the threshold of change. At present, Guatemalans must answer the questions "transition to what?" and "transition for what?" The transition must be a lasting and peaceful effort to build a new legitimacy based on a new developmental model. Otherwise, the internal contradictions of Guatemalan society will force the transition to include challenging the social structures themselves.

Historical Context of Party Participation

1944–54

During the ten years of the October Revolution (1944–54),[1] there was an effort to overturn the dominant order of the oligarchy-landowners and clear the way for the capitalist development of the country. Development was to be achieved through the modernization of the nation's economic institutions and through the stimulation of grass-roots and popular organizations. The basis for transforming Guatemalan society came from popular support of a revolutionary program. This revolutionary movement marked the beginning of contemporary Guatemalan political history. The most important structural changes that account for the present political reality can be traced to that period. In this chapter, I present Guatemala's political history, emphasizing the presence or absence of an authentic system of political parties.

The attempt to construct a new ruling order was based on a broad coalition of social groups who defined themselves by progressive tendencies—displaced landowners, representatives of the great commercial capital, some artisans and workers, and members of the urban middle class. This last group, in particular, took charge of the direction and administration of the nascent political reforms.

The new Constitution of 1945 initiated the expansion of democratic practices. It outlawed state repression, codified respect for political liberties, and acknowledged ideological pluralism. The spirit of the new Constitution expanded the process of popular participation, manifested by the emergence of organized political parties. The Constitution also underwrote a respect for university autonomy.

Between 1944 and 1954 political parties acted as mass organizations that channeled diverse social pressures. In this way they fulfilled their roles as intermediaries between the government and a wide range of social groups. For the first time, popular discontent could be expressed through the political party structure. Many Guatemalans received a civic and political education. A new political generation was born. Characterized by collective leadership, this generation came to replace traditional individual leaders.

In the previous period, 1871–1944, parties operated within an elitist framework. They acted as the standard-bearers of the interests of the landowners. They functioned as a chorus in the pseudo-democratic electoral processes that "legitimized" various dictatorships and other efforts at authoritarian rule.[2] In contrast to the parties that supported the 1944 revolutionary program, whose leadership was in the hands of the urban middle class and whose popular bases included peasants and workers, opposition parties were identified with the interests of the displaced oligarchies, the nascent and ascendant capitalist class, and some sectors of the urban middle classes tied to the economic modernization. The contradictions between old and new political parties were defined early on. Based on the first actions of the reform government, the opposition parties denounced the moves as a manifestation of Communist infiltration into the country. The first anticommunist movement, the *Acción Cívica de Defensa* (ACDCC), became a political party in 1948.

Political polarization became evident with the call for presidential elections in 1950. The revolutionary movement organized the popular sectors (workers and peasants) and the radicalized elements of the middle class. The anticommunist opposition consolidated its party organization, and the moderate elements of the first revolutionary coalition stepped forward as a middle option.

The electoral triumph of 1950 favored the revolutionary movement, thus beginning a second period of government characterized by intensified nationalist development.[3] The opposition became belligerent in its denunciations; it also conspired clandestinely. For the first time in national history, a solid class alliance took shape. It included members of the emerging revolutionary bourgeoisie, sectors oriented toward social democracy, key members of the Central Committee of the Communist Party, and the Guatemalan Workers Party (PGT). Their multiparty political action platform gave priority to agrarian reform programs and with it the expropriation of idle land, the organization and mobilization of the peasantry, public investment in infrastructure to further industrialization, and the creation of a broad-based internal consumption market. With the emergence of a party system, in accordance with the criteria established by Giovanni Sartori,[4] this period can be classified as one of ideologically moderate pluralism evolving toward ideologically polarized pluralism.

These actions, especially the expropriation of part of the substantial landholdings of a foreign corporation, provoked international reaction. The armed invasion of Guatemalan territory by the United States, coupled with a military conspiracy within the country, led to the destabilization of the constitutional regime and the resignation of President Jacobo Arbenz Guzmán on June 27, 1954. These actions left Guatemala with a series of de facto rather than de jure regimes.[5]

1954–63

The overthrow of Arbenz marked a reversal of the political gains of 1944–54 for labor and peasantry, gains that have yet to be recovered. From 1954 to 1963 political parties disappeared, and movements tied to the 1944 Revolution were outlawed. Prohibition of certain parties went hand in hand with growing persecution and repression of individuals associated with them. Some political organizations, such as the PGT, continued to exist through extralegal means and clandestine activities.

For almost nine years, various parties emerged, all of them anticommunist. They operated within a severely restricted legal framework. The expression of political viewpoints was limited, and conditions limiting free party participation were established. All of this hampered the process of political development initiated during the previous period. The dominant classes had difficulty establishing stable government alliances. One president was assassinated, two interim presidents were named, five government juntas were formed, one election was annulled, one presidential election was repeated, and one president elected through the mechanism of a coup d'état was deposed (see Tables 6.1 and 6.2).

TABLE 6.1 Political Changes in Guatemala, 1944–85

Period	New Constitutions[a]	Coups[b]	Provisional Presidents or Chiefs of State[c]	Juntas[d]	Plebiscites[e]	Elections Presidential[f]
1944–54	1	1	1	1	1	2
1954–63	1	3	3	5	2	2
1963–82	1	1	–	1	1	5
1982–85	1	1	2	–	1	2
Total	4	6	6	7	5	11

[a]1944, 1956, 1965, and 1985.
[b]June 27, 1954; July 27, 1957; October 24, 1957; March 31, 1963; March 23, 1982; and August 8, 1983.
[c]These include Carlos Enrique Diaz (1954), Ríos Montt (1957), and Oscar Megía Victores (1983).
[d]October 20, 1944; October 24, 1957; and March 23, 1982.
[e]Includes a plebiscite held in 1954 and the elections for integrating the National Constitutional Assembly in 1944, 1956, and 1985.
[f]General elections were held in 1945, 1951, 1957, 1958, 1966, 1970, 1974, 1978, and November and December 1985.

TABLE 6.2 Guatemalan Authorities per Sector of Origin, 1944–85

Authority	Military	Civilian	Total
Presidents, Elected	7	3	10
Presidents, Provisional[a]	2	–	2
Presidents, Designated[b]	1	–	1
Chiefs of State[c]	2	–	2
Members of Governing Juntas	19	1	20
Total	31	4	35

[a]Luis A. Gonzales L. (1957) and Guillermo Flores A. (1957).
[b]Efraín Ríos Montt (1982).
[c]Enrique Peralta Azurdia (1963) and Oscar Mejia V. (1983).

TABLE 6.3 Results of Guatemala's Presidential Elections, 1970–85

Year	Total Votes	Winner	Second	Third	Fourth
1970	640.7	251.1 39% (MLN-PID)	202.2 32% (PR)	126.0 20% (DGC-URD)	N/A
1974	727.2	299.0* 41% (MLN-PID-CAO)	228.1 31% (DGC-FURD-PRA)	143.0 20% (PR)	N/A
1978	652.1	263.0* 40% (PR-PID-CAN)	221.1 34% (MLN-FUN)	167.9 26% (DCG-FUR)	N/A
1982	1074.4	377.8* 35% (PR-PID-FUN)	274.2 26% (MLN)	220.2 21% (DCG-PNR)	98.7 9% (CAN)
1985 (11/3)	1907.8	648.8 34% (DCG)	339.7 18% (UCN)	231.4 12% (PDCN-PR)	211.0 11% (MLN-PID)
1985	1800.3	1133.5 63% (DCG)	524.3 29% (UCN)	N/A	N/A

* Results apparently obtained by fraud. After the coup of March 23, 1982, the elections of that year were annulled.

Note: Percentages do not add up to 100 because parties finishing lower than fourth in the elections are not included in this table. Votes are in thousands; N/A = not available. See Appendix, Guatemala, for political parties and their acronyms.

The party organizations that developed during this period, even if they manifested anticommunist leanings, distanced themselves from each other, for they represented a wide range of ideologies within the anticommunist movement. Three of the most important contemporary parties to emerge were the Christian Democratic Party of Guatemala (DCG), the Revolutionary Party (PR), and the National Liberation Movement (MLN) (see Table 6.3). In January 1958, as a result of general elections, a new government replaced the one elected the previous year; the earlier election had been annulled because of apparent election fraud.

At the end of 1960 a group of military officers discontented with the government and the level of U.S. military involvement during the training of the mercenary forces used for the attempted invasion of Cuba in 1961 initiated a rebellion.[6] This insurrection failed under circumstances that even today are not clear, but the uprising became the germ of an armed opposition movement to the regime. In 1962 the insurrectionary movement, radicalized, became a guerrilla group seeking to take power through violent means.[7] To control the popular uprisings of March and April 1962, the government was forced to appeal to the existing structures of political party mediation and name military officers to all cabinet positions. The decision to use political parties as mediators influenced the appearance of various parties identified with the ideological tradition initiated during the revolutionary period 1944–54. It led to the candidacy of ex-president Juan José Arévalo Bermejo. Arévalo threatened the military high command, whose members deposed the president of the republic on March 31, 1963. This was the fourth coup d'état of this period.[8]

Between 1954 and 1963 the party system withdrew to a new limited party pluralism, defined by almost imperceptible ideological differences. Yet by the end of this period the party system had evolved toward extreme pluralism. The popular movement and the revolutionary tradition fragmented as a result of the December 18, 1958, purge in the Revolutionary Party. From this schism new political groupings, such as the National Revolutionary Party (PNR), the Authentic Revolutionary Party (PRA), the Democratic Revolutionary Union (URD), and the Revolutionary Unification Party (PUR) emerged. The PUR was the political ally and ideological vanguard of the insurgent guerrilla movement, the Armed Revolutionary Forces (FAR).

1963–82

The nineteen years between the coups of March 30, 1963, and March 23, 1982, marked the consolidation and institutionalization of the army as an authoritarian political force. This was a direct result of the deepening structural crisis within Guatemalan society, a crisis intensified by the failure of the economic development model, the erosion of political party mediation, the maturation of the insurgency, and the structural crisis within the ruling bloc. Radically conservative positions emerged within the political party system and displaced reformist views. Paralleling this was the development of popular clandestine revolutionary organizations.

The origin of the military's consolidation of power was the reorganization of the armed forces under the 1945 Constitution. That document guaranteed the armed forces relative autonomy from the executive. As originally conceived, it sought to prevent the armed forces from using their power to support authoritarian regimes. Article 165 established the Supreme Council of National Defense. It also established the position of chief of the armed forces, thus generating an interdependent relationship between the military and the council. This relationship led to serious internal conflicts and the virtual nullification of the executive's power to intervene in military affairs. The chief of the armed forces had the sole right to name all the leaders of the armed forces. He was also obliged to guarantee the "empire of democracy, the defense of the duly enacted laws, and the social and political institutions of the country."[9] Military autonomy excluded the president from any military decision and established a precedent for military competence over political issues that encroached on presidential powers. This would later define military activities in the political sphere.

In 1962 the first military cabinet was legally formed. It ensured civilian subordination to the military and established conditions for the coup d'état of 1963. That coup signaled the military's intention to become a dominant force in politics. In addition to its defense functions, the military had developed a political agenda.[10] The coup of 1963 also eliminated electoral opportunities for the democratic opposition. Thus, the first step toward a massive national counterinsurgency operation was underway. During the three years of the military government (1963–66), Guatemalans were shaken by frequent political assassinations, illegal detentions, and other repressive operations by the state against the civil population. A new wave of terror began that was far more horrendous than that suffered during the months after the July 1954 coup.[11] The Assembly was dissolved, political parties suspended, union activities made illegal, and a state of siege existed for twenty months.

One of the first objectives of the new military regime was the consolidation of a single-party system. The military's formation of the Institutional Democratic Party (PID) allowed the military to penetrate the dominant classes as a broker for their interests. This party was openly supported by the de facto government. Progressive and reformist forces soon joined the ranks of the URD and the PRA. During the next few years these parties operated in exile, secretly, or through political alliances with legal, registered parties.

In this repressive atmosphere insurgency groups increased guerrilla activity, and the most important opposition leaders became disillusioned with the prospects for change through the existing political structure. The Central Committee of the PGT decided to recognize armed struggle as the fundamental form of class struggle. Between 1966 and 1970 almost ten thousand Guatemalans died as a result of armed struggle and state repression. Thus, the party winning the elections of 1966 was subordinated to the armed forces. From the military's perspective political parties were not only ineffective, they were unnecessary instruments of political stability.

The military initiated the consolidation of its counterinsurgency program by restricting the participation of political parties. In 1963 the party system was oriented toward limited pluralism, with three legally registered political parties participating. By 1965, when a new Constitution and a new electoral law were drafted, legal participation in the political system further restricted party development at the national level. The military set conditions governing the political space of the party winning the 1966 elections and expanded military influence into strategic areas of public administration. It entrenched itself further by establishing its right to shared governance with the winning conservative coalition in the 1970 elections.

During the 1970s, a result of the rampant political repression by the military government was the assassination of three of the most important leaders of these exiled parties in the capital of the country (Adolfo Mijangos, Manuel Colóm Argueta, and Alberto Fuentes Mohr). At the same time, the traditional party of the conservatives, the MLN, died out and three new parties emerged. The PID, CAN, and FUN were linked to the accommodation experienced among the governing groups and the consolidation of the counterinsurgency program.

The complete subordination of civilians to the military was clearest in the presidential candidacy of the ministers of defense between 1970 and 1978. The military now had absolute control over public power. Those self-defined "opposition parties," to play by the same rules, presented military candidates for the presidency of the republic during the elections of 1970, 1974, and 1978. Beginning with the 1974 elections, structural conditions within Guatemala changed considerably. On the one hand, the leading classes were unable to create a political party that would legitimate, through elections, the hegemony of the military. On the other hand, the army had become an accomplice in massive electoral fraud by validating the supposed triumph of the official party, negating the apparent success of the National Opposition Front.

The earthquake that devastated the country in 1976 further undermined the Guatemalan social structure. Hoping to legitimize a fraudulent mandate, the government of Gen. Kjell Eugenio Laugard Garcia permitted some popular mobilization and expression. Although selective repression of leading opposition figures continued, the government sought to decrease systematic and indiscriminate violence. Opening the political space to organized participation by certain opposition groups made possible both the emergence of new levels of political expression and the development of class consciousness among the popular sector.

The expansion of military activity into economic and political sectors traditionally controlled by the elites permitted their incorporation into the narrow sector of great landowners. Personal enrichment, facilitated by the presence of military officers in the state bureaucracy, became a certain path to wealth.[12]

The earthquake of 1976 marked the emergence of a series of popular movements and revealed the degree to which the popular sector had been previously stifled and political parties had been unable to channel demands and protests. During this period workplaces and educational institutions were mobilized and strikes were successful, massive public marches took place, and solidarity networks developed among the leadership of labor, peasant, student, and neighborhood unions. The culmination of these new protests were the demonstrations of September and October 1978. The trigger for these events was an increase in public transportation fares.

The change of government in 1978 came about by open and impudent electoral fraud. This prolonged the military's political domination. In early 1978 an internal split in the power bloc occurred as a result of the virtual isolation of the upper classes from the state bureaucracy, the principal protagonists in a series of fraudulent maneuvers and supporters of a policy of institutionalized corruption. From this point on, state terrorism was systematically used against the popular and democratic civilian leaders. Repression succeeded in reducing public demonstrations and resulted in the almost complete disappearance of any union or peasant leadership.

The massacre at the Spanish embassy on January 31, 1980, and the collective kidnapping of the leadership of the labor unions from the headquarters of the National Workers Central (CNT) and the Emaus buildings (on June 21 and August 17) marked the closure of the limited democratic opening and the end of popular protest.[13] With the means of expression of popular discontent shut down, the social bases for the insurgency movements grew and subversive activities increased. The military high command stepped up its counterinsurgency program.

Notwithstanding the acute military confrontation involving seventeen of the twenty-two departments of the republic, general elections were called and carried out in March 1982. Armed struggle was compounded by the virtual exhaustion of the power of party mediation and by international pressures advocating respect for human rights. During the fraudulent process, the presidency was awarded to the general officer next in succession in the hierarchical order. His designation marked the decisive rupture of the bloc in power.

During this period ideological diversity within the party system was limited and the political space restricted. Furthermore, the legal parties distanced themselves from the social conflicts ravaging the country. Opposition parties immediately denounced the electoral fraud. For the first time in years a successful public protest was held, headed by the leadership of the losing parties. The catalyst for action was a press conference held by the minister of defense and the chief of the staff of the Defense Department in which both defended the purity of the elections and denied the possibility of fraud.

1982–85

On the morning of March 23, 1982, Gen. Fernando Romeo Lucas García was deposed by a coup d'état led by high-ranking military officers. The coup leaders argued that "because fraudulent manipulations of the elections...undermined the faith of Guatemalans in democratic institutions, the situation demanded...the birth of a government legitimately constituted and based on genuine popular support."[14] The armed forces further argued that the country was experiencing a split of democratic forces. The disorder and corruption of public administration warranted drastic measures. The Constitution was suspended, the March 7 elections annulled, the assembly dissolved, and political party activities suspended.

On June 9, 1982, the military high command named Gen. Efraín Ríos Montt president. He had been chief of the government junta. This action set up a situation where the new president and some of the most important social forces of the nation were at loggerheads. The new power structure altered the counterinsurgency programs, which included an ideological and strategic reorganization of the armed forces. The Ríos Montt government generated a new political program to control the structural crisis of the country. It also sought to begin the process of political party development. Military activity began with the formation of special tribunals, the naming of a council of state with consultative powers, and the introduction of a plan to combat corruption and build a new image for the country internationally.[15]

Facing pressures from the private sector and its party representatives, a new Fundamental Statute of Government was decreed. In 1983 the government announced a democratic opening of the country. Three laws were promulgated to govern the future electoral process: the Law of the Supreme Electoral Tribunal, the Law of the Registration of Citizens and the Registration of Population, and the Law of Political Organizations. The provisional registration of political party committees occurred shortly thereafter. Thirty-six such committees and three civic committees registered before a special election was called to elect the National Assembly to draft a new Constitution. During the elections of July 1984, seventeen committees that sought the formation of political parties and three civic committees participated. Under these circumstances an apparently pluralistic system emerged. In reality, however, the political system was fragmented. There was neither ideological differentiation among the registered parties nor a dominant party, as the results of the July 1984 election demonstrate.

On the morning of August 8, 1983, by decision of the army's high command, General Ríos Montt was removed. The former minister of defense, Gen. Oscar Mejia Victores, was named chief of state, "according to an internal decision to introduce a change in the leadership, to reestablish hierarchy, subordination, and discipline, and the separation between church and state."[16]

The first measures taken by the new government were directed toward continuing the counterinsurgency, strengthening popular organization through civilian self-defense, suppressing the Special Tribunals, declaring respect for human rights, standardizing the electoral process, supporting gradual democratic change, revising the recent tax reform, and implementing formulas for understanding to prevent the worsening of the crisis or an eventual military confrontation in Central America. New elections were called for in the National Assembly; an electoral campaign characterized by aggressiveness and a lack of concrete proposals by contending parties and committees followed. The elections themselves were peaceful. Citizen participation was unusually high. The military government kept its promise not to intervene in politics. For the first time in fourteen years the elections reflected the will of the citizens.

Legal and institutional conditions were now considered that would let the election results serve as a springboard for opening the political space. The legitimacy of the election was a necessary preface to drafting a new Constitution that would guarantee both the ideological and legal redefinition of the power structure. The elections themselves were evidence of the most transcendent political event of the military's political program; they legitimized the democratic process. The viability of this new military program gave the armed forces a new base that was relatively autonomous from the ruling elites because the military possessed an unquestionable capacity to reconstitute its control of the political environment.

The 1985 Constitution preserved the interests of the existing political structure. It was oriented toward legitimizing and legalizing the ideological and juridical order of the ruling classes and their political allies. The heart of the Constitution-drafting project was the expected return to the rule of law and the reassembly of the governmental machinery. Although the new constitutional framework sought to facilitate the transition from a military and authoritarian government to a civilian and representative government, the power structure itself would be only slightly modified.

Despite the constitutional efforts to bring Guatemala under civilian governance, the political crisis continued to intensify at all levels. A climate of violence continued to prevail, preventing Guatemalans from living normal lives. Kidnappings, disappearances, and assassinations increased; bodies with torture marks were found each day.[17] The 1984 elections came when political party alliances were weak. Respect for human rights did not exist. The economy was in an ongoing crisis. The de facto regime was extremely fragile. The territory of the republic and its most important economic, social, and political activities were subordinated to the supervision and control of the armed forces.

Many analysts have suggested that this scheme would perpetuate military domination of civilian life, even after the government was transferred to legitimately elected civilian authorities. The armed forces' role in the new government was uncertain because it was difficult to conceive of eliminating military control of the civilian population without affecting the military's national security plans.

At the end of the electoral campaign of 1985 the party platforms had not come to grips with the national crisis. There were no options between the parties; the proposals presented were characterized by ambiguity and abstraction. The electorate did not understand what the parties had to offer at a time when clear and precise political answers were needed. The election was won by the candidates of the Guatemalan Christian Democratic Party. This result may have been a reaction against violence, authoritarianism, and militarization. The Episcopal Conference of Guatemala's support for the Christian Democrats, along with the critical nature of the national situation, undoubtedly influenced the voters.

The current activities of the political parties point toward establishment of a new party system characterized by moderate pluralism, with no ideological differentiation. The voters' acceptance of progressive, nontraditional sectors (DCG-AD-FCD-UCN) was noticeable, as was the distancing from traditional party options representing the interests of conservative groups (MLN-PID-PR-CAN-PNR) (see Table 6.4).

Internal Structure of the Political Parties

The antecedents of the present party system are rooted in the counter-revolutionary period.[18] They coincide with the closure of the democratic

TABLE 6.4 Results of Guatemala's Presidential Elections, 1944–66

Year	Total Votes	Winner	Second	Third	Fourth
1944	302.5	255.7	21.0	11.1	8.2
		85%	7%	4%	3%
		(FPL-RN)	(FND-PDC)	(PT)	(PSD)
1950	407.7	266.8	76.2	28.9	15.7
		65%	19%	7%	4%
		(PAR-PRG-PCG)	(UPA)	(PP)	(FPL)
1957*	N/A	N/A	N/A	N/A	N/A
		(RPN-PDN-PLN-PLA)	(RN-PLA-PIACO)	(DCG)	
1958	492.3	191.0	138.5	132.8	
		39%	28%	27%	N/A
		(RDN-PDN-PLN-PLA)	(PR)	(PR)	
1966	531.3	209.2	148.0	110.0	
		39%	28%	21%	N/A
		(PR)	(PID)	(MLN)	

*Elections were annulled on October 24 (data unavailable).

Note: Percentages do not add up to 100 because parties finishing lower than fourth in the elections are not included in this table. Votes are in thousands; N/A = not available. See Appendix, Guatemala, for political parties and their acronyms.

space, a situation that has encouraged the persistence of an ideologically moderate center.

All of the political groups considered in this section fulfill the minimum legal requirements. The composition of the National Assembly and the integration of the National Executive Committee are set up to guarantee the representation of minorities and the formation of a democratic consensus. In the everyday life of the nation, however, these prescriptions have been formal only; the practice of democracy has often been denied inside the party structures themselves. In Guatemala the parties have more of an electoral than a representative character. Party activity is not a constant force in politics.

Those parties that have labored to produce a program and an ideological base have made important efforts to form consulting and planning groups. They have tried to influence the voters through information campaigns, overwhelming publicity campaigns that attempt to sell a face and a slogan. Yet once the election campaign is over, promises are forgotten and programs are discarded.

Ideologies are no longer useful when the parties attain authority and power, sharing in a system of domination that already has its own ideology. The leadership of political parties that obtain an electoral majority, legitimately or fraudulently, helps define earlier compromises with the social forces most interested in the perpetuation and maintenance of a particular political project.

In Guatemala it has been impossible to establish an effective party system that will result in a more dynamic and democratic political system. Political parties are unable to effectively mediate social demands and are themselves ideologically ambivalent. Party leaders are unable to represent either the social composition of their supporters or the number of their sympathizers or voters, although they have some knowledge of the target population they want to reach and some idea of its relationship to financial support received. The movement of individuals—rank and file members and leaders—from one party to another is almost constant. The lack of ideological barriers encourages the change of party affiliation.

When interviewed, the representatives of political parties considered in this essay indicated that they have a collective and democratic leadership and a permanent, active process of recruitment. In practice this is not so. The leadership of each party gravitates toward an individual, usually someone associated with the creation of the party. Changes at the top occur with little consultation of the party base, much less consideration of the base's opinions. The recruitment process is different for every party. There are clear examples of proselytizing, especially at the time of the elections, but no evidence of a permanent, active process to increase party membership. During electoral campaigns, local and regional individuals are more effective in increasing the number of ballots cast.

Outside of the electoral process the presence of political parties in political life is almost imperceptible. Once a campaign ends, there is no evidence of mediation by the political party in the formation of the new government. Popular demands and social pressures are expressed in other ways. Parties in power have been more concerned about the distribution of political appointments in the state bureaucracy than in the fulfillment of campaign promises or the implementation of a new program.[19]

Practically speaking, party opposition is almost nonexistent. The exception is the image campaign run by some leader seeking to position himself for a future election. These operations, with their accords and alliances, are far removed from social bases and completely disconnected from the popular demands political parties normally channel.

The Dynamic of the Power Structure

Since 1954, and especially with the coup of 1963, Guatemalan politics can be characterized by a growing lack of legitimacy. Forceful actions by the military became evident. This situation resulted in a hegemonic crisis within the existing power structure and the subsequent consolidation of the military as a political force. This hegemonic crisis was symptomatic of the country's greater failure, its inability to create a genuine civic culture. The period between 1963 and 1982 saw competing economic interests unable to develop a common political program. This situation fostered the armed forces' relative autonomy from the ruling power bloc and the state itself and made them the only political force within the system that demonstrated the capacity to govern.

The relative autonomy of the military implied a change in the ideas of some within the high command. Traditional anticommunism was supplanted by a new doctrine of national security. The counterinsurgency program was reevaluated. The result was a new ideological perspective more favorable to economic development, which was supported without regard for the social problems of the country. The military's program of "institutional construction" (1984) was to become the axis for a new political structure.[20] The years of institutional reconstruction (1984–85) displayed a remarkable process of ideological maturation within the armed forces. This process led to the adoption by some leading military figures of positions that make social transformation possible. It also prevented the armed forces from losing political power. The military fashioned a new image at the national level; civilians were involved in the transition project, thus diverting some of the social pressures and demands generated by the country's crisis.

In the capitalist sector of society little change is evident. The crisis of the dominant oligarchy could not be resolved in the 1944–54 period. The oligarchy now views its problems as part of a crisis of national autonomy. The presence of large amounts of transnational capital drains the nation's resources and drowns the country in payment of external debt. The evolution of dependent capitalism under conditions of underdevelopment has made consolidating a national capitalist sector impossible. No social group has developed a political program that will raise the standard of living of the majority of the population. The nation's reconstruction and the recuperation of national sovereignty have not yet been politically conceived.

Political Parties and Democratic Transition

In Guatemala, political participation is restricted. Electoral fraud, terrorism, and the military domination of state and society have been the fundamental political strategies of its leaders. The party system has little credibility. As political options dwindled, violence became the main response both from inside and outside the system. What had transpired was the militarization of the political and the politicization of the military.

The minimal institutionalization of democratic practices in Guatemalan society has prevented the rise of political parties from the social and economic interests of the political community. Rather, parties emerge from crisis and the urgency to return the country to stability. Since 1954 the political realm has not been where accords are defined and solutions sought to the fundamental problems of the nation. Rafael Guido Bejar states that political decisions are made in other places and at other levels.[21] The ruling authority negotiates directly with special interests and establishes political accords with them. Thus, the power dynamic of personal authority has replaced the power of the political party. Parties merely bless decisions already made in the political black market, decisions made beyond any legal authority or regulatory process.

The fragmentation of the political party system does not guarantee the feasibility of the democratic transition. Because parties have been unresponsive to the problems of the people, what kind of consensus can be expected from this ideologically restricted pluralism? The absence of an authentic process of legitimation within society has fostered the indiscriminate use of force as a strategy of government. It has also entrenched repressive practices, which in times of crisis have amounted to nothing less than terrorist politics.[22]

At the structural level, the strategies of economic development have reproduced a system that has generated poverty for eight out of every ten Guatemalans. They have also made it impossible to establish an effective economic and social democracy that can help the poorest classes of society.

The closure of political, economic, and social space has forced the emergence of divergent modes of expressing popular discontent, ranging from spontaneous public protest to organized union mobilization and, ultimately, armed confrontation of the system. Viewed over the long run, the political programs of 1944–88 typify the internal development of the political crisis: Guatemala has moved from antidictatorial and anti-oligarchic governments to anticommunist and counterinsurgency. All of these programs are characterized by an oligarchical social structure that is ever more exclusive and dominating.

On the surface, some of the lost legitimacy and legality has been regained. The results of the elections of 1984 and 1985 testified to the presence of social movements that now have opted for participatory forms of expression to demonstrate their frustration and uncertainty. The dynamic of its social structure places Guatemala at a crossroads where the central questions are "transition to what?" and "transition for what?" The former question seeks to determine the effects of the transition on the political system and the party system. This is particularly important because the political parties have to choose whether to be participants or observers in the process. The second question asks if this last peaceful attempt at building a new legitimacy is based on a new model of development.[23] If this effort addresses the historical internal contradictions of Guatemalan society, then a dramatic structural change can be expected.

For the transition from military to civilian leadership to take place, the political system needs to become civilian controlled. The armed forces must relinquish part of their hegemony, without, however, losing the power to participate in or influence the national decision-making process. In fact, in the new constitutional order the military occupies a separate chapter, confirming its relative autonomy from the executive power. This autonomy has practically made it into a fourth branch of government.[24]

Two coup attempts, one in May 1988 and the other in July 1989, failed, but they weakened the civilian end of the pact that had been negotiated between the armed forces and political leaders in 1985. The resumption of indiscriminate killings and violence marked the final year of the Cerezo administration. International pressure to end the abuses did not mitigate the further weakening of civil society's ability to handle the transition. Thus, on the eve of the presidential elections of 1990 there was trepidation about the outcome, doubt about the ability of civilian leaders to keep the military from intervening, and a sense that Guatemala was retreating from its commitment to democratic reforms rather than moving forward with this agenda. For example, the New York Times described the November elections with this headline: "Guatemalans Vote, but Seem Disenchanted."

One troubling factor throughout the electoral process was the candidacy of former military leader Gen. Efraín Ríos Montt, who had become president of Guatemala in 1982 after a military coup ousted General Lucas García, another military strongman. Ríos Montt's candidacy was not only a test of the legal system created by the 1986 Constitution, which opened the way for elections and civilian rule, it was also symptomatic of perceptions of insecurity that many Guatemalans manifested through their support of a Ríos Montt candidacy. At issue was whether Article 186 of the Guatemalan Constitution, which prohibited anyone who had taken office as the result of a coup d'état from running again, would be upheld.

In what could be deemed a cliffhanger, Ríos Montt, his lawyers, and his followers (under the banner of the NOVENTA movement, a play on words that means both the '90s and "Don't Sell Out") waged an ultimately unsuccessful battle to include Ríos Montt in the roster of candidates on the final November ballot. As late as October, Ríos Montt had been allowed to register his candidacy and was awaiting the final decision of the Court of Constitutionality. On October 12, 1990, just one month before the election, the court decided in favor of a retroactive interpretation of the Constitution, thus eliminating the general from the roster.

Twelve political parties, two of which formed a coalition, ran presidential candidates in 1990. The *Union del Centro* (UNC), the *Movimiento de Acción Solidaria* (MAS) and the *Democracia Cristiana Guatemalteca* (DCG), and the *Partido de Avanzada Nacional* (PAN) were the three highest vote-getters in the November 11 election. Because no candidate won a majority of votes in the November election, a runoff was scheduled for January 6, 1991, between the UNC candidate Jorge Carpio Nicolle and MAS candidate Jorge Serrano Elias. Serrano won the runoff with 68 percent of the vote to Carpio's 32 percent. Turnout during the runoff was 42.9 percent of the registered voters, the lowest ever recorded.

This sideshow of the 1990 election campaign further destabilized the entire process, already rife with rumors of possible coups and the reality of increasing violence. Although Ríos Montt reluctantly complied with the court ruling and withdrew himself from the presidential race, he also instructed his followers to abstain from the process he considered so flawed.

Decisive for consolidating transition in Guatemala is respect for human rights. When Vinicio Cerezo was elected in 1985, Guatemala had experienced more than thirty years of direct or indirect military rule. The transition from authoritarian state to electoral democracy was marked by hopes of curtailing the human rights abuses that had long been characteristic of daily life in Guatemala and reaching the goal of restoring civilian state authority through the judicial system and more open political processes.

The present government of Jorge Serrano can guarantee the legal existence of human rights, but it cannot guarantee that respect for human rights will be enforced. There is, indeed, little expectation that the investigation of past human rights violations, much less the punishment of the responsible individuals, will occur. As long as the conditions exist that fuel the insurgents and counterinsurgency movements, respect for human rights is not feasible. In any case, the future must see a Guatemala without exploitation, without oppression, and without misery. It must be a future based on a genuine democratic order and built on the progressive opening of democratic spaces. Only time will tell whether such a democratic transition makes headway following forty-five years of instability and repression.

Notes

1. The revolutionary period extends from October 20, 1944, until the end of June 1954. This period corresponds to the governments of Dr. Juan José Arévalo Bermejo (1945–50) and Col. Jacobo Arbenz Guzmán (1951–54). See Robert Trudeau and Lars Schoultz, "Guatemala," in *Confronting Revolution: Security Through Diplomacy in Central America*, ed. Morris Blachman, William LeoGrande, and Kenneth Sharpe (New York: Pantheon Books, 1986).

2. The reelections of Manuel Estrada Cabrere (1898–1920) and Jorge Ubico Castañeda (1931–44) are examples of this process.

3. See 1950 in Table 5.1.

4. Giovanni Sartori, *Partidos y Sistemas de Partidos* (Madrid: Alianza Editorial, 1950), 1:151–54.

5. This refers to the expropriation of idle agrarian patrimony belonging to the United Fruit Company. This led to the formation of the so-called *Ejército de Liberación Nacional* (National Liberation Army) and the invasion of Guatemalan territory, supported by the government of the United States.

6. In the international context transcendent events occurred, such as the revolutionary triumph in Cuba and the immediate reaction of the U.S. government. This reaction is exemplified in the Alliance for Progress and the formulation and imposition of the national security doctrine.

7. On this subject see Gen. Ricardo Peralta Méndez, "El Alzamiento Militar del 13 de Noviembre," *Diario la Hora*, November 13, 1989, pp. 2, 29.

8. See Richard N. Adams, *Crucifixion by Power* (Austin: University of Texas Press, 1970).

9. José Luis Cruz Salazar, *Guatemala: Análisis Estructural de la Realidad Política*, nos. 1–2 (Guatemala: Asociación de Investigación y Estudios Sociales, ASIES, 1984), pp. 7–8.

10. Ibid., p. 9.

11. To establish these extremes, it is enough to review the press from March 1963 to June 1966.

12. The enrichment of some high-ranking officers of the armed forces begins in the period 1970–74 through a political strategy that located these individuals in alliances with the landowning, agricultural exporting, and industrial sectors in the field of social communication. Sociologists René Poitevín Dardón and Rocael Cardona have written on this subject.

13. Miguel Angel Reyes, Gabriel Aguilera, and Vinicio González, *Guatemala Crisis y Opciones: Informe Final* (San José: CADIS, 1986), pp. 7–11.

14. Héctor Rosada-Granados, "Guatemala 1984, Elecciones Para Asamblea Nacional Constituyente," *Cuadernos de CAPEL*, no. 2 (July 1985):7–11.

15. In the case of the Special Tribunals, characterized by the summary nature of their procedures, little is known because they operated in absolute anonymity and under what could be considered a state of military exception. The Council of State was constituted by the military government and made up of representatives of different sectors of Guatemalan society. The archives of the working sessions of the council can be found in the Congress of the Republic.

16. Rosada-Granados, "Guatemala 1984," p. 21.

17. See reports of Americas Watch, Amnesty International, and other human rights groups that document this trend.

18. See Héctor Rosada-Granados, *Partidos Políticos en Guatemala* (Guatemala City: Asociacíon de Investigación y Estudios Sociales, ASIES, 1987).

19. The only exceptions to this are the "official parties," which in an overt or covert form receive important financial and technical support from the power structure itself. In this way the "official parties" are able to generate ideological campaigns and proselytize. They can also develop the internal structure parties need to guarantee the perpetuation of the power structure and their place in it.

20. See the publications of the Army of Guatemala on the campaign of Victory '82, Firmness '83, and Institutional Reencounter '84.

21. Rafael Guido Bejar, *La Enigmática Dinámica del Sistema de Partidos en El Salvador*, Proyecto CAPEL, Guía de Partidos Políticos de Centro América (San José: n.p., 1986), p. 6.

22. In this regard, see the works of sociologists Gabriel Aguilera Peralta and Carlos Figueroa Ibarra.

23. An important majority of Guatemalan intellectuals agree on this point. It appears as if this line of future political work should be oriented toward the definition of a new model of development. In this regard the work of sociologists Mario Solórzano Martínez, René Poitevín Dardón, Carlos Sarti Castañeda, and Edelberto Torres Rivas is important.

24. In the text of the new Political Constitution, effective since May 1985, the armed forces occupy a separate chapter, located apart from the executive, where it had historically been located—this despite the formal recognition of the chief of the executive as commander of the armed forces.

7

Party Politics in Belize

Assad Shoman

The Colonial Legacy

Belize, because of its colonial history, has a different political culture and different constitutional, legal, and political structures than those of the other Central American states. Although the territory was occupied by the British with only brief interruptions since the middle of the seventeenth century, not until 1862 was it formally declared a colony by Britain. This was because its territory was carved out of a Central America under Spain's rule, which was recognized by Britain until well into the nineteenth century. Indeed, treaties between the two European powers in the second half of the eighteenth century limited the use of the territory by the British settlers and specifically forbade commercial agriculture, thereby confining the territory to its original colonial purpose, the export of timber.

This chapter describes and analyzes the political system of Belize, beginning with a historical sketch of the economic, social, and cultural underpinnings of the evolving political structures. The second section describes the formation, structure, membership, leadership, and ideology of the two political parties in Belize, analyzing the difficulties encountered in building democratic practice within them. The chapter ends with a consideration of prospects for democracy in Belize.

When the British settled coastal Belize, the indigenous Maya population was dispersed into the interior. Only when the focus of production shifted from logwood to mahogany after 1770 and the British penetrated the interior did the British meet with the Maya, who retreated further inland. At that time too the number of Africans imported as slaves into the settlement increased to meet the greater demand for labor for the cutting and export of mahogany. The slave mode of production was as firmly rooted in Belize as in other British Caribbean colonies, but the conditions of work differed. Unlike slaves on the sugar plantations, who were brought together in large numbers in single estates, the mahogany gangs worked in isolation in the interior and were composed of only between ten and fifty slaves. The small and dispersed nature of these gangs made it difficult for the slaves to combine to fight against their masters, and the location of the settlement allowed slaves to escape to neighboring jurisdictions. Nonetheless several slave revolts still occurred. When necessary, the local settlers were able to call on the imperial power to quell a revolt, revealing their dependence on the empire for survival.

Because of the ambiguous state of sovereignty—with the British acknowledging Spanish sovereignty but still fighting to maintain exclusive possession—state institutions were underdeveloped, and the settlers and the colonial representatives were in continuous conflict over power. By 1765 a few wealthy settlers had established a rudimentary system of government and enacted laws that reinforced their monopolization of power and land. Because of the dispersal and retreat of the indigenous Maya, the British were able to create a society in Belize from scratch. They subjugated the Africans who were brought in and attempted to suppress all elements of their culture. Those who entered the political economy of the settlement thereafter, such as the Garifuna, who came at the beginning of the nineteenth century, were forced to submit to the dominant colonial structures.

In 1838, when slaves became legally free, the colonial policy of making free grants of land was stopped and the land was priced such that it was beyond the reach of the newly freed men. Other mechanisms also helped maintain a cheap supply of labor.

In the British sugar colonies of the Caribbean, ownership and control of many estates had passed from local settlers to metropolitan hands by the time of abolition. In Belize this did not occur until the mahogany trade collapsed in 1847. As local firms collapsed, their assets were taken over by London merchants, to whom they were indebted. The monolithic nature of the small settler elite was also being eroded by the growth of a new commercial sector. After the independence of Central America opened a significant entrepôt trade with that area, commercial houses from England, independent of the old settler class, were established and gradually gained an important place in the settlement's power structure.

In 1848 thousands of refugees from the Caste War in Yucatan more than doubled the population of the settlement and introduced a large number of *mestizos* and Maya, who had a different culture and language and a history of agricultural activity. The immigrants settled in northern

Belize, establishing there the first villages of small independent cultivators of rice, corn, vegetables, tobacco, and, of course, sugar. In 1857 the first shipment of locally grown sugar was exported.

In 1850 and 1856, treaties between Britain and the United States called on Britain to evacuate areas in Central America; the 1856 treaty required Britain to finalize a frontier treaty with Guatemala within two years. In 1859 the Anglo-Guatemalan treaty was signed, although it did not end the territorial dispute between the two countries. In 1854, meanwhile, Britain had, partly in response to this process and partly to satisfy the growing class of metropolitan owners of land and business in Belize, installed the first formal Constitution and a legislative assembly of eighteen members elected on a limited, property-based franchise.

The concentration of land and capital in metropolitan hands in the mid-nineteenth century—to the extent that one British company, the Belize Estate and Produce Company, Ltd., owned well over one million acres of land by 1881, which it maintained virtually intact into the 1970s—meant the collapse of the old settler elite as a major political and social force. Thenceforth, the capitalist class would be absentee, and political power would rest outside of the colony until well into the twentieth century.

The basic features of the economy endured up to the World War II. Several important developments, however, laid the foundations for later changes. In the first quarter of the twentieth century, the export of chicle to the United States grew and came to be dominated by U.S. firms acting through a new group of local foresters. Indeed, Belize Estate's dominance was so seriously challenged that the company claimed in 1931 that it would have to sell its interests to a U.S. firm from the British government—which it did. Another important development was the establishment in the 1930s of the citrus industry in Stann Creek. This created a small rural proletariat and, by attracting a number of businessmen from Belize City, served as the only challenge to the city's dominance of the colony's political economy. Finally, the commercial sector of importers and retailers grew, nurtured by the new industries and the growth of the population as well as by the contraband trade to the United States during the Prohibition years. Many of the new merchants were *mestizos*, who until the late 1930s were almost completely absent from the ranks of the civil service.

The majority of the colony's inhabitants continued to be dominated and exploited. Most of them worked in the mahogany industry or as workers/farmers collecting chicle and working in the citrus industry. The small peasantry, made up mostly of tenants of private and crown lands, lived a precarious existence. As a result of both private and government actions, many were evicted in the 1930s from lands they occupied.

What did develop during this period, however, was a small nonwhite elite that eventually would become more politically influential than the descendants of the white settler elite. In addition to the "creole" (of Afro-European stock) and *mestizo* businessmen in mahogany, chicle, and commerce, there emerged a new educated class—of lawyers, doctors, clergymen, civil servants, and teachers—that advocated constitutional change.

The changing economic and social structures also brought changes in the political institutions. In 1932, after a disastrous hurricane in 1931 had devastated the colony's finances, the British imposed "reserve powers," the power to pass a law despite the objection of the legislature, as the price for aid. This in turn revived local demands for elected representation in the legislature, to which the British reluctantly agreed. The elected members, however, remained a minority until the introduction of adult suffrage in 1954. Not only the minority status of elected members in the legislature, but also the narrow franchise (in the 1936 elections only 1.8 percent of the population were registered voters) meant that the people had no voice in the governance of the country. They were not, however, inactive.

The Rise of the People's United Party

World War II had brought a respite from the depressed economic conditions of the 1930s, as the mahogany and chicle industries revived and workers went to Britain to join the war effort. But the recovery was short-lived, and after the war economic conditions became increasingly desperate, culminating in 1949 with a disastrous drought. At the end of that year the British governor used his reserve powers to override the legislature and impose a devaluation of the currency that benefitted Belize Estate but brought further hardship on the masses. This became the immediate occasion for the formation of a group that soon established the country's first political party, the People's United Party (PUP), which later led Belize to independence.

Two developments in the previous decades made possible the formation and success of the PUP: the workers' movement and the rise of the "educated class." The rise in consciousness and the consequent capacity for workers' organization resulting from the Garveyite movement after World War I[1] and the workers' protests in the 1930s did not mature into the formation of trade unions until the repressive labor laws were repealed in 1943. Shortly thereafter the General Workers Union (GWU) was formed. It grew significantly in the next few years and extended its activities to the districts outside of Belize City. The educated elite, located almost exclusively in Belize City, were allied to the new creole business elements who had connections with the United States. Many of them were influenced by the U.S. Jesuits, who ran the most prestigious secondary school in the country. In the 1940s this educated elite was active in Belize City politics. Members of this "middle class" became the leaders of the PUP and took over the leadership of the GWU in 1950. The following year they consolidated their hold on the union; in the next four years they increased its membership four-fold. The union's branches in the districts became an indispensable organizational asset, and its members everywhere provided militants for the new party. By the time of the first universal suffrage elections in 1954, the union and the party were able to run a joint ticket.

The party leaders' objective was to achieve political independence, and in this they were supported by the vast majority of the population, particularly the workers and the peasants. By demanding the "Belizeanization" of leadership positions in all areas of society, they also attracted the support of sectors of the local business and educated elite. Still, in its first few years PUP was much too reliant on mass mobilization and support to win the confidence of the British. An intensive political struggle led to universal adult suffrage elections in 1954, which the PUP won overwhelmingly.

Following this victory a serious split occurred in the party, caused principally by differences of opinion as to how to deal with the British. The colonial policy of incremental decolonization, which allowed the locally elected leaders to have some say in the executive arm of the government, proved attractive to some leaders. But it was anathema to George Price, the party's most charismatic leader; in 1956 the party split, with Price retaining the leadership.[2]

Under Price the PUP maintained its strength, despite, or perhaps because of, the harsh opposition of the colonial regime, and in elections in 1957 it won all the seats. Rather than improving the party's chances for immediate constitutional advance, however, this victory proved to be an obstacle. In 1959 a British constitutional commissioner noted that the "essence of the British parliamentary system of government is the existence of two parties" that are credibly competitive, and he cited the dominance of the PUP in the two elections to recommend against self-government for Belize.

The 1961 elections brought a measure of self-government. The PUP won all eighteen seats; George Price became first minister and appointed a cabinet. The governor, however, still retained reserve powers. Two years later Britain agreed to introduce a "self-government" Constitution. Apart from the emergence of another credible political party, what convinced the British in 1961 to give up a measure of state power to the

PUP was the changed attitude of its leader. When the PUP won the elections in 1961 and was called on to form a government, Price realized that the party needed more than just mass support. It needed to deliver on its promises for social and economic improvements, which would require the cooperation of the British, the local business class, and the Creole middle class that also manned the state bureaucracy.

This meant, of course, that the masses' involvement in the anticolonial struggle would have to be reduced and the movement taken from the streets to the board rooms of government and business. Hitherto, Price had relied heavily on mass mobilization to win political concessions from the British; he would now have to shift his focus to obtain economic advances, the capital for which, he reasoned, could come only from the British themselves. This course was confirmed when, a few months after the PUP took office in 1961, a disastrous hurricane caused severe damage and negotiations had to be conducted with the British for reconstruction and the building of a new capitol.

Socioeconomic Conditions: Post–World War II

From the Second World War to 1964 two other important developments occurred: the expansion of the state and the diversification of the economy. The expansion of state activities had begun in the period just before the war in response to the popular disturbances throughout the West Indies in the 1930s and continued into the postwar period. In its attempt to lay the framework for a modern economy, the state developed institutions and laws; began to create infrastructure, particularly in transport and communications; and enlarged its social services. The legalization of trade unions was part of this process, as were incentives offered to businessmen and attempts to attract foreign investment. There were two important economic initiatives during this period. First, Mennonites were encouraged to settle in Belize in the 1950s; they purchased huge tracts of land and invested heavily in agricultural infrastructure, eventually becoming the major source of local agricultural activity. Second, and most significant for the country's political economy, was the British multinational Tate and Lyle's purchase of the struggling local sugar industry in the north in 1963. The company built a new sugar factory and greatly expanded the production of cane and the export of sugar, contributing decisively to the conversion of Belize from a forest economy to an agricultural, primarily sugar, economy. Within a few years sugar accounted for up to 60 percent of exports. In general, economic policy was based on the Puerto Rican model of development, with import substitution, industrialization by invitation, and export expansion. Despite attractive incentives, however, foreign investment was slow to materialize because Belize's small population (just over 100,000 in 1964) offered neither the markets nor the cheap labor force required by foreign investors.

After 1964 the state assumed a greater, more direct role in the economy. It invested in infrastructure that furthered the development of the economy and in productive enterprises such as banana and rice production. It also expanded state property and employment.

What social sectors benefitted from all this activity? Undoubtedly the workers and peasants made important gains in their standard of living, which was, after all, abysmal in the colonial era. But those who benefitted the most formed a small group that included the foreign operators and their local agents; the small local class of property owners; a new class of small industrialists, merchants, and the state and petty bourgeoisie. This latter group, what Clive Thomas called the "state petite bourgeoisie,"[3] controls the economic policy of the state and its property. It collaborates with foreign and local capitalists and encourages the creation and expansion of a local bourgeoisie. Of course these groups are not homogenous, and the state will sometimes first favor the claims of one sector and then those of another. Indeed this play of forces often forms the basis for the support different sectors of the elite give to the two political parties, support crucial to their existence.

In Belize the working class is particularly disorganized. At the time of the formation of trade unions, forestry was still the major occupational sector, yet it had only small gangs of scattered workers; few other industries have employed significant numbers of workers. Moreover, after the political party split in 1956 shattered the powerful GWU, the trade union movement never recovered. Party politics continued to divide the working class. In the late 1970s and early 1980s a strong trade union did develop, expanding from a firm base in the sugar industry to encompass the citrus, banana, rice, and timber industries. But it was quickly destroyed by the conservative wing of the government and by internal disunity. The existing labor laws do not require employers to recognize trade unions, so several industries simply refuse to allow unionization. The foreign-owned garment factory, which employs hundreds of women, is the prime example. In addition, workers frequently move from one region of the country to another; the rate of external migration, particularly to the United States, is also high.

The peasantry, for its part, has never, except in one instance, exhibited any ability to organize itself as a class to promote its own interests. Subject to uncertain tenure throughout its history, the peasantry finally received secure land tenure through the actions of the government in the 1960s and the 1970s, not through organized agitation.

Coming as it did as a gift from government, this important social process did little to raise the consciousness of the small farmer. Instead it fostered a dependence bred by colonialism. The class structure is more complicated and fluid because the economy exhibits different forms of production and types of economic relations. Thus, for example, many of the agro-proletariat are also small subsistence farmers who may produce a small surplus for an uncertain internal market, whereas in the towns the growth of an informal economy, including the activities associated with the drug trade and with tourism, further complicate the class structure. To the underdeveloped and fluid class structure must be added the importance of nonclass factors in the political economy. In Belize this refers primarily to the racial and ethnic divisions in the society, divisions that have a historical foundation but that have undoubtedly been exploited and aggravated by the elites over time. Space does not permit discussion of this most important factor, but it is one of the principal characteristics of the country's social structure and has important repercussions in both the economic and political spheres.

The Structure of Government

What was established in Belize in 1964 and carried through the Independence Constitution in 1981 is a variant of the British or "Westminster" model of parliamentary democracy. The House of Representatives elects from among its members the leader of the majority party as prime minister and the leader of the minority party as leader of the opposition. The Senate is little more than a rubber stamp of the House. Its members are nominated—five by the prime minister, two by the leader of the opposition, and one by the governor general, whose function is mostly ceremonial.

Except in a formal sense, the National Assembly does not "make laws for the peace, order and good government of Belize," as the Constitution requires. Under this system, the House is important only as the mechanism by which the cabinet is formed and through which the cabinet legislates. Certain features of cabinet government are stated in the Constitution, but much of cabinet practice is based on the British system, which developed by convention with the party system in the eighteenth century. Within the cabinet the prime minister is so powerful that it has been said that cabinet government has been replaced by prime ministerial government.

The prime minister names the Cabinet of Ministers from among members of his or her party in the National Assembly, which is composed of the House of Representatives and the Senate. This is the executive arm of government; no separation exists between it and the legislative branch. Municipal governments are elected but have no autonomy and no financial independence. The prime minister is the leader of the party and has sole authority to name the other ministers and their responsibilities. He or she presides over cabinet meetings, decides the agenda, controls the cabinet secretariat, and sees that cabinet decisions are carried out by various ministries, over which the prime minister maintains supervision and control. The convention is that cabinet decisions are not made by vote, only by consensus: it is the prime minister who declares the consensus. The prime minister also exercises a de facto authority over all public officers, or civil servants, whatever ministry they work in, and has the power to effectively appoint, discipline, and remove the senior public officers, including the heads of the police and the Belize Defense Force. Finally, the prime minister decides what measures the government shall put to the House of Representatives and when the parliament shall be dissolved. Of course, the members of the majority party in the House of Representatives can oust their leader, but this occurrence is unlikely.

Since 1981 the cabinet has had greater control over the civil service as well as over the security apparatus of the state, both of which were formerly held by the British. The judiciary is to a certain extent independent, but the inferior courts are manned partly by ordinary civil servants, who are subject to the executive's authority and transfer. Most of the judges of the Supreme Court are on short-term contracts, renewable by the executive. Despite the conventions of separation of powers and the preeminence of the rule of law, tremendous power is concentrated in the executive.

The Belizean people have not enjoyed a culture of freedom, nor have they had the opportunity to practice democracy. They have lived in a constitutional democracy whose structures did not develop out of the social and economic structure but were transplanted from a country with a different history. This transplanted model, as applied in Belize, has resulted in a fragile "democratic" system. Although regular elections are "free and fair and free from fear," the opportunities for authoritarian practice by the rulers are an integral part of the social, economic, and political structures.

The People's United Party

Origin and Structure

The PUP arose from groups outside of the parliamentary system. Although the early PUP opposed colonialism and appeared to oppose anything British, it still regarded the colonial institutions as legitimate and immutable. Even in demanding the right of self-government the nationalist leaders looked to England for a model to create the very institution that would fight British colonialism. Price has stated that the British Labour Party provided the model for the PUP.

The first PUP constitution divided the party into several districts. Yearly district conventions took place in which all the district party members could vote elected district party committees, candidates for local elections, and delegates to the General Party Convention, the party's supreme authority. The yearly general convention elected the national officers who, together with the chair of the district committees, formed the Central Party Council and also selected candidates for national office from among persons nominated by the various district party conventions.

After the major split in the party in 1956, George Price's personal influence became even greater within the party. He was able to build a party machine in the districts with individual leaders who were personally loyal to him. Following self-government in 1964, the locus of the party's power shifted from the party to the government, that is to say to the cabinet, where Price was the undisputed chief. This shift had major consequences for the PUP party structure. For all practical purposes the party constitution fell into disuse, and conventions became mere public shows held to ratify decisions of a small group of leaders and to rally support for the party.

On the party's twenty-fifth anniversary (1975) the party revised its constitution to give a greater and more organized voice to the rank and file. It maintains the basic structure of constituency branches, which at annual conventions elect delegates to a national convention, which in turn elects a central executive. It provides for a Central Party Council,[4] the governing body of the party. The central executive is comprised of the party leader, the deputy party leader, a chairperson, three deputy chairpersons, a treasurer, a youth organizer, and a national campaign manager and is charged with the organization and administration of the party. It also has the power to investigate disciplinary matters and to intervene in the affairs of any constituency branch and give binding directives to that branch. It is to meet at least once every month.

The constitution includes measures to guard against control of constituency conventions by local leaders, which sometimes resulted in undemocratic practices. In an attempt to wrest the control of party policy-making from the cabinet, the Central Party Council was empowered "to advise party members on public bodies in matters pertaining to the discharge of their public responsibilities and particularly to the effective implementation of Party policy and decision." It was also required "to prepare and enforce a code of conduct for the leadership of the Party with appropriate safeguards and penalties to ensure the effectiveness of such code." Finally, a provision was included that, in a stronger form, had been demanded by party militants in various constituency branches calling for the acceptance and institutionalization of self-criticism within the party.

Although the new constitution provided a model for the renewal of democracy within the party, it was never allowed to work. At the first convention under the new constitution, the leadership indicated that things were to remain the same. There was to be no democratic election of officers but, rather, automatic acceptance of a slate presented by the leadership itself, promoting itself. The constitution became a dead letter. Central Party Council meetings, to be called quarterly under the constitution, were summoned only rarely, in times of crises or elections. The central executive hardly ever met. None of the officers exercised their functions, and none could be challenged or changed. Under those circumstances, the party was and still is unable to create an organized youth wing.

In the constituency branches, the same pattern generally prevailed. Local leaders jealously guarded their positions. Organization and education were discouraged, conventions were fixed, participation and discussion suppressed. The personalism and paternalism stamped on the party at the national level were multiplied at the constituency level. Young people with new ideas for participation and action were barred from entry or, if they entered, discouraged away or even expelled.

The party still won elections, even the election of 1979, because it was the party of independence. Realizing this, a wide cross-section of people within the party perceived that, after independence had been achieved, reform would be essential. Various attempts at reform were made. In 1983, for example, several party militants in Belize City organized themselves as a pressure group within the party, calling themselves the Democratic Direction (DD). The group criticized the fact that the constitution was not being followed and accused the leadership of creating divisions by failing to adhere to the strategies, goals, policies, and programs of the party. The DD was frowned on by the leadership and attacked as "communist," in particular by the chairman, Louis Sylvestre, who was himself the main target of the group. It did, however, succeed in having a national convention called to elect the central executive of the party. For the first time in the party's history, delegates were accredited by the constitution, and they alone had a right to vote.

Yet because of the long autocratic history of the party, most of the delegates who represented constituencies outside of Belize City had been handpicked by the chairpersons of the branches, who were themselves indebted to and strongly influenced by the traditional leadership. Blatant irregularities at the convention allowed that leadership to secure the reelection of Sylvestre as chairman, and the rest of the slate was unopposed after it became clear that fair elections could not take place. The experience disillusioned many party militants and contributed to the party's subsequent electoral defeat later that year in the Belize City Council and the following year in the general elections.

After the electoral defeat in 1984, a national convention, delayed by continued internal disunity, finally took place in January 1986. The delegates passed a number of amendments to the party's constitution to allow for greater participation and to reduce the possibility of local leaders perpetuating their own status. At a national convention in 1988 the constitution was amended to allow for two deputy leaders. This resulted from a move to challenge the then sole deputy leader, Florencio Marin, who is unpopular with sectors of the party that consider him arrogant and authoritarian. Price managed to strike a compromise at the request of Marin who, as leader of the opposition in the House of Representatives, could not be alienated without creating serious problems for the party. A notable peculiarity of the PUP during most of its history is that it has never had a functioning bureaucracy. Even when it has had a secretary-general, that person has not carried out the functions specified in the constitution. Since 1982 the PUP has had no secretary-general.

With regard to a party organ or newspaper, the PUP in its first six years had the support of the *Belize Billboard,* which for most of that time was edited by PUP leaders Richardson and Goldson. After they split from the PUP, Price and Pollard, a union leader, created the *Belize Times* for the newly formed Christian Democratic Union. Later the *Belize Times* passed to the PUP and, in effect, became its official organ. Indeed, the buildings that since 1956 have housed both the *Belize Times* and the PUP headquarters are on land belonging to the George Price estate, over which Price himself has control. Since the convention of January 1986, the national executive has expressed the need to appoint an editorial board so that the party can more effectively control the political line of the newspaper, but this has still not been effected.

Membership and Leadership

For a brief crucial period in the PUP's history, from 1950 to 1956, it recruited its membership through advertisements in the *Belize Billboard,* appeals at public meetings and in house-to-house membership drives, and through its close, almost symbiotic, relationship with the GWU, whose members virtually automatically became members of the PUP. This latter phenomenon was especially crucial in the districts outside Belize City. In its first few years the party also relied heavily on working-class support as well as on that of the unemployed. Soon afterward, and more so after 1961, when it had some share in government and was able to commence a land distribution program, the party became strong in the rural areas, a strategic base no other party was able to seriously challenge until the 1980s. Since 1961 the PUP set the goal, which it succeeded in reaching, of becoming a party open to all classes and sectors of society.

At the same time membership has become more diffused; few persons are card-carrying members. The majority of those who vote for the party at elections consider themselves sympathizers or supporters rather than members. The party itself is unable to state how many members it has. Over the past several years, the practice developed of issuing membership cards only at the time of a constituency convention, when a vote would be taken to select the candidate for national elections, especially if it was known that the incumbent would be challenged. In such cases, the incumbent tried to control the issuance of party cards to known supporters and often paid the dues necessary to make the person being issued the card a financial member and thus eligible to vote. This, together with the absence of democracy, organization, and education in the party, had the effect of devaluing party membership. George Price succeeded in making his position as party leader unchallengeable. Even after the debacle of 1984 and despite his own humiliating electoral defeat, no one in the party dared suggest he step down. Price came to be regarded as something of a messiah, not only because he was seen as the "father of the nation," having single-mindedly fought for independence for so many years, but also because his lifestyle has been that of a social recluse, a man who has no life apart from his political activity, who lives simply and sparsely, and whose personal incorruptibility is unquestioned.

Apart from Price himself, the national leaders of the PUP have remained virtually the same for most of its history. In 1984, of the nine-man national executive, seven had been national political figures for twenty years or more and the other two had been locally active in the party for a like period. The 1986 convention produced some changes in this situation: only Price, Marin, and David McKoy from the previous executives remained in the new executive.

The leadership of the party has been dominated by Belize City people, but over a long period the trend favored openings for district candidates. Because of its historical development, the ethnic groups of

Belize have tended to be concentrated in particular districts, and, as Grant noted, the

> tendency, which had begun in the 1957 election, to recruit parliamentary candidates from their constituencies had its political advantages, but also limited the number of candidates who could have been selected from the intellectual repository of Belize City.[5]

As educational opportunities in the district expanded, however, district persons began to play a more pronounced role in the cabinet (the party's effective leadership body until 1984).

Affiliation and Ideology

In its first few years the PUP was closely linked with the GWU, and it was also able to call on the support of organizations such as cooperatives and credit unions and enjoyed a fairly close relationship with the Catholic church. But after 1961, when the party set out to embrace all sectors of society and began to take part in government, alliances quickly evaporated. As time went on, support from the various sectors was shared with the National Independence Party/United Democratic Party.

The party has not had any serious international affiliation. For a brief period in the 1970s, at the height of the internationalization campaign for independence, George Price flirted with the idea of joining the Socialist International, but that initiative was never pursued. A couple of years later the PUP did participate in a regional organization promoted by Mexico's *Partido Revolucionario Institucional* (PRI), the *Conferencia Permanente Partidos Politicos América Latina* (COPPAL), which, according to Marin (who attended its meetings on behalf of the PUP), was intended to represent a branch of the International Socialist Grouping in Latin America. COPPAL was inactive for several years, but in early 1987 it was revitalized. Said Musa attended a conference in Peru and returned with a commitment to strengthen the party's links with that organization. More recently, the party has also received cooperation from the *Friedrich-Ebert-Stiftung* of the Social Democratic Party in the Federal Republic of Germany.

Nigel Bolland recently described the PUP's ideology in a nutshell: "antisocialist as well as anticolonial and pre–free enterprise capitalism as well as pro-American."[6] From its early years, the party's pronouncements on social and economic policy were conflicting and confusing. Its only philosophical underpinning was nationalism, or the right of people to self-determination. As far as its economic policy is concerned, "the PUP has never wavered in its belief that heavy foreign capital investment is a prerequisite for economic growth. Furthermore, PUP policy continues to favor the exploitation of the country's natural resources by corporate American (U.S.) capital. "[7]

A statement of the party's aims and objectives was included for the first time in its 1975 revised constitution. The article in the constitution calls for "economic democracy," "development of the nation's resources for the benefit of all the people," for every Belizean to receive "a fair share of the national wealth," and for Belizean ownership and control of national resources. These principles were incorporated into the PUP's 1979 election "Manifesto for the New and Progressive Revolution," but they never served as guidelines for either the party or the government.

The party-government under Price had found that it had to govern in accordance with the wishes of the dominant class. This tendency was reinforced by the unremitting attacks from the United Democratic Party (UDP) accusing the PUP of communism and exploiting the differences between the so-called left and right wings of the party. U.S. influence on Price's policies, which began to grow at an alarming rate immediately after independence, cannot be overlooked either. This led Price, for example, to declare that although Belize was nonaligned, the United States was its "natural ally."

The United Democratic Party

Origin and Structure

The UDP was formed in September 1973 from a merger of the National Independence Party (NIP), the People's Democratic Movement (PDM), and the Liberal Party. Of these, the only substantial party was the NIP. For the origin of the UDP, therefore, one must go back to the NIP, which was itself formed in 1958 from a coalition of the HIP, a breakaway from the PUP, and the National Party, which had the greatest influence on the development of the NIP. The National Party was the creature of the colonial establishment's attempt to counter the nationalist movement and, according to Goldson, not a political party by modern political standards.

The first leader of the NIP was Herbert Fuller, who had been the leader of the National Party at the time of the coalition. Goldson, leader of the HIP, became the secretary of the NIP and was elected leader in 1961 when Fuller became too ill to function. For the next several years Goldson consolidated his position as undisputed leader and occupied a position in the NIP much like that of Price in the PUP, except that the NIP kept losing elections. Charging that "the NIP approach was too narrow to win an election," a group of young professionals supported

Dean Lindo as leader in the national convention of 1969. When they lost the bid, they broke away from the NIP and formed the PDM. Four years later, along with the Liberal Party, the PDM joined the NIP to create the UDP.

The UDP constitution declares that the party is a "union of self-governing constituency parties" but goes on to severely limit their autonomy. If the unit is recognized by the National Executive Committee (NEC) it is known as a "registered division" and can adopt its own rules and procedures providing they do not conflict with the Constitution. The unit can elect UDP candidates for national elections, subject to endorsement by the NEC.

The NEC consists of three officers of the party, the members of the parliamentary party, one representative of each registered division, five members elected at the biennial conference from among its delegates, the national presidents of auxiliary bodies, and representatives of affiliated bodies where this has been agreed to. The NEC, which should meet quarterly, is empowered to enforce the constitution of the party, to adjudicate intraparty disputes and give binding decisions, and to raise the funds for the party.

A central committee consisting of the officers of the party and of the parliamentary party is empowered to act as the Committee of the NEC, exercising its powers when the NEC is not in session. The "officers of the party" include the chairperson, three deputies, the secretary general and deputy, the financial secretary, treasurer and deputy, the director of organization, the national directors for women and for youth, and legal counsel. The parliamentary party includes party members in the House of Representatives and the Senate, as well as party candidates endorsed by the NEC who did not win a seat and were not appointed to the Senate.

The biennial conference, held every second year, is the supreme authority of the party and comprises the officers of the party, members of the NEC, members of the parliamentary party, five delegates from each registered division, one from each registered branch, delegates of affiliated bodies in accordance with the agreement of affiliation, two delegates from each auxiliary body, one from each overseas branch, and one delegate for every 25 members of a division over 100, up to fifteen delegates. The biennial conference elects 5 members for the NEC from among delegates generally, one representative for each registered division to the NEC on the nomination of the division, and the officers of the party (but not the leader and deputy leader) on the nomination of the NEC. There are special, complicated provisions for the election of the party leader and deputy leader, which no doubt reflect the tortured history of the party with respect to leadership.

Unlike the PUP constitution, which makes no reference to the governmental structure, the UDP constitution requires a candidate for the House of Representatives to be a person listed in the official candidates list. For a person not a member of the House to be eligible for election as party leader, the UDP must be in opposition, the person must be on the official candidates list, and the NEC must pass a resolution supported by a majority of UDP members in the House agreeing to this. This procedure was used in 1982 to elect Manuel Esquivel as leader when he was not a member of the House.

The UDP constitution also contains some draconian measures with regard to party candidates. For example, no person can be a UDP candidate for any national, municipal, or even village council election unless the NEC has endorsed his or her selection by a registered division or branch. Before even being considered by those lower levels, however, the candidate must appear on the "relevant official candidates list" approved by the Standing Committee on Candidates, comprised of the Central Committee of the party, which exercises supervision, direction, and control over all candidates. A person who wishes to be included in any of these lists must apply to the standing committee. Finally, the executive committee of a registered division or branch, with the approval of the NEC, may, prior to nomination day, remove any candidate, whether endorsed or not, and substitute another in his or her place, if the overriding interests of the party so demand.

Throughout its history the UDP has paid more attention to the party bureaucracy than did the PUP in the same period. The party constitution establishes a central office run by a secretary general, who is elected at the biennial conference and is the chief executive officer of the party. While the UDP was in opposition, the central office was the hub of its activity, but this has now shifted to the cabinet.

In 1987, long-simmering divisions within the UDP emerged at a biennial conference where Dean Lindo was replaced as chairman by Esquivel's hand-picked candidate. Several other leaders who were aggrieved by this refused to join the executive. The divisions continued and became more pronounced during 1988 for several reasons: the belief of some of the old party members from the NIP and PDM that the "Liberal Party" newcomers have usurped their position, the competition for power and economic reward, and the apparent privileges accorded by Esquivel to one particular business group that supports his faction over another that supports the Lindo faction. Some UDP leaders even complain that Esquivel is supported more by the *mestizo* and district leaders of the party, bringing the specter of ethnic divisions once more into the intraparty struggles.

In July 1988, the NEC, in partial response to dissatisfaction expressed by party members, established a select committee to receive representations from party members and agreed to develop rules to govern the procedure for upcoming conventions to elect party candidates for the 1989 general elections. Since then, despite the convention rules developed, there have been serious disputes with regard to the conduct of at least two constituency conventions, exacerbating and further publicizing the leadership divisions in the party.

Until 1987 the UDP had no official party newspaper, although the *Beacon* was so considered by all. The problem is that the *Beacon* is owned by Dean Lindo, who created it when he formed the PDM. After he was ousted from the chairmanship the party launched its *People's Pulse* as the official party organ. The *Beacon* continues to support the UDP, although it occasionally criticizes attitudes and actions of the Esquivel wing of the party.

With regard to financing, much the same considerations as stated in the section on the PUP apply here. The party does not collect much in the way of dues and relies heavily on support from business, especially for any election campaign. It has also found that being in government makes it easier to solicit funds from the business sector. According to Minister Curl Thompson, businessmen are nonpolitical; they are for money and go with the winning party. There is evidence the U.S. Republican Party assisted the UDP in raising funds in 1985, and since 1984 it has been widely assumed UDP also gets financial support from other U.S. sources.

Membership and Leadership

The UDP membership is basically that which was transferred to it through the NIP, which itself was gained by direct individual application. The UDP constitution makes provision for membership by individual application alone. Goldson has stated that the original National Party's support came mostly from the upper class. In this he included employers in the forestry and commercial sectors who had a vested interest in the colonial system of government and believed the PUP was a threat to their interest. He added that up to 1954 the civil service generally supported colonialism but has gradually come to accept change. UDP support has been mainly urban and middle class, but, according to Goldson, the party is reaching out to rural areas and seeks to embrace all ethnic groups and all classes. Like the PUP, the card-carrying membership of the UDP is not significant. What matters is the support they can muster from the various sectors of society at election time.

The UDP has gone through a period of collective leadership and three different leaders. It has built into its constitution provisions to make it difficult for a person to be the leader for more than ten years. Under the parliamentary system, however, it is unlikely the party leader will be changed if the party is winning elections. For example, Esquivel's ten-year limit ends in 1992, which, if the party wins the next election, will be two years into his term, with Esquivel as prime minister. He would almost certainly be confirmed as party leader again, and he is unlikely to be changed before the following election. If his party wins again, it is again unlikely he will be removed.

Esquivel moved quickly to assert his leadership. In early June 1986, just weeks after the UDP's biennial conference and after only eighteen months in office, Esquivel carried out a drastic cabinet reshuffle in which he appeared to discipline those ministers who were attracting the most public criticism and at the same time severely reduced the responsibility of Lindo, the only person who might still be thinking about making a bid for the leadership (because Goldson's age put him out of the race). The reshuffle enhanced Esquivel's stature, especially because many compare it with Price's prevarication when faced with much clearer evidence of abuse and incompetence. Since then, however, the deep divisions that have emerged at the leadership level have significantly eroded Esquivel's authority. As with the PUP, the leadership of the UDP has tended to be dominated by Belize City persons, but in his cabinet appointments Esquivel has struck the same balance reached by the PUP in his last cabinet—seven Belize City and four district persons.

Affiliation and Ideology

Although the UDP constitution provides for affiliated bodies, Esquivel has stated that there are no formal alliances, although the party has a good working relationship with various groups. According to the party's former secretary, there are presently four affiliated bodies: the youth wing (the party known as the Youth Popular Front) and three foreign UDP affiliates, which he refused to identify.

Internationally, the UDP is a member of the International Democratic Union (IDU), a grouping brought together in Washington in July 1985 under the aegis of the U.S. Republican Party and President Ronald Reagan. According to Esquivel, it consists of parties of the center or on the right and thus has a broad spectrum. In January 1986 the Caribbean Democratic Union (CDU) was formed in Kingston, Jamaica, with the collaboration of the U.S. Republican Party. Edward Seaga became chairperson of the CDU, and the UDP claimed one of the three deputy chairpersons. The Republican Party now has an opportunity to influence the region's political direction through the CDU and to channel funds for the various "like-minded parties" through that organization.

According to its former leader Dean Lindo, the UDP is right of center. He said the party is prepared to go along with the free enterprise system, within limits. It opposes central control. It has privatized the banana industry and would sell the statutory boards if it had a buyer. Esquivel, the present leader, asserts that the UDP is committed to as little government as is necessary to run the country and to preserve the rights and freedoms of all sectors of the community. He sees the party as centrist, to the right of the PUP, as supporting the free enterprise system as opposed to a more socialist concept.

The UDP has always been a cold warrior in the crudest tradition. Its 1979 manifesto declared communism "an evil which enslaves man and denies him of his religious, political, economic and intellectual freedom. As an economic system it strangulates development, and as a political system it crushes soul and mind." The policy statements of the UDP, in its manifesto and elsewhere, define it as a conservative, right-wing party committed to supporting free enterprise and to giving free reign to foreign investment.

The Elections of 1989

In the September 1989 general election the PUP won 51 percent of the total vote and fifteen seats in the twenty-eight-member House of Representatives. The UDP received 49 percent of the votes and won thirteen seats. As a result George Price again assumed the position of prime minister. Although then-prime minister Esquivel's UDP was strengthened by victories in local elections in 1985 and municipal elections in 1986, political infighting caused it to lose, by 1989, the landslide support that had earned it twenty-one House seats and the head of government in 1984. Esquivel's government was weakened by three controversies: alleged abuses connected with the Security and Intelligence Service (SIS), a body created in 1988 to suppress the illegal narcotics trade but used to scrutinize civil service appointees; accusations of suppression of the press by the PUP newspaper, the *Belize Times;* and allegations of foreign investment corruption, including improper sale of Belizian citizenship to foreign nationals.

Following its election, the Price government moved to disband the SIS and to end the issuance of citizenship bonds. It also committed itself to continuing negotiations with Guatemala regarding Belezian territorial integrity. These efforts were rewarded in September 1991 when the government of Guatemala recognized Belize's independence. As part of the agreement, both Belize and Guatemala endorsed the continuity of British troops and aircraft securing Belize's borders and attempting to limit drug trafficking.

Prospects for Democracy

Belize can only be understood in its historical context, a country that experienced a long period of colonial authoritarian rule and an independence achieved by the negotiation of rulers with the colonial power. The masses have been consciously excluded from that political process. Belize has seen changes in its dominant mode of production, from slavery to capitalism; in its economy, from forestry to agriculture; in its international status, from colony to independent state; and in its governments. Throughout all of these changes, the majority has remained poor and powerless, exploited and marginalized—and this is the basis of the authoritarian practices that have survived colonialism. The very constitutional and political structures that are supposed to guarantee democracy and freedom facilitate authoritarian practices.

Any analysis of Belize's political system today and its prospects must take into account its newly independent status and the circumstances surrounding the attainment of independence in 1981, which were inauspicious for the process of enhancing democratic practice. Months before independence the government was forced to declare a state of emergency to quell widespread riots ignited by opposition to its negotiating position with Guatemala. This meant bringing out British troops as well as the local security forces. There were ugly confrontations in the streets, arrests, and even—unprecedented for Belize—a death. Because the UDP, then in opposition, supported the rioters, and because it then maintained its opposition to independence and refused to participate in the constitutional conference, the nation was deeply divided when it became independent.

The Central American crisis, then at its height, in 1981 brought what for Belize's small population was a substantial flow of Salvadoran and Guatemalan refugees, which strained not only the economic resources, but also the cultural, social, and political fabric of the new state. This crisis caused the United States to take a special interest in Belize and the Belize government, which sought U.S. aid. This interest was accompanied by a cultural and political penetration that further tested the creation of a sovereign democratic state.

The long period of limited self-government, from 1964 to 1981, meant that the elected national government shared the country's rule with the colonial power. Given the social and economic policies of the national government, it was perhaps inevitable that the authoritarian practices of colonialism would rub off on the elected government. The independence Constitution, with its call for participatory democracy and its enshrinement of fundamental rights and freedoms, raised hopes for an enlargement of democratic practices, but it saved existing laws for five years, and the government was barely in power for three years before it was ejected from office by the general elections of 1984.

For the first time since universal adult suffrage in 1954 and after eight general elections, a change of government had been effected at the ballot box. This again raised hopes for a dismantling of authoritarianism and a new era of democratic, "open" government. The new government, however, took steps not only to maintain, but also to expand the suppression of freedom of expression, despite the fact that much of its electoral campaign was directed against the previous government's abuse of this right.

In 1988 the government passed a law banning the importation of any printed, audio, or visual media "which are, in the opinion of the Minister, contrary to the public interest." It is now proposing to amend the Constitution. According to the opposition party, this will enhance the government's ability to pressure or victimize civil servants and to control the electoral process. The Human Rights Commission of Belize denounced the increasing use of arbitrary violence against the public by the security forces, which it says is perpetrated under the pretext of the antidrug campaign and results from "an imported policy of national security that sees subversives in every shadow and around every corner."

In 1987 the UDP administration passed the Security and Intelligence Service Law, creating a political police charged with protecting the security of Belize from "sabotage" and "subversion." It required "security assessments" of the loyalty of any civil servant to the government. Apart from the regular employees, who are empowered to carry arms, a large number of unproductive part-time spies were employed throughout the country.

Why should a party that has so convincingly criticized the previous administration for its authoritarian rule not only maintain, but also extend and deepen such practices and increase the armory of repressive measures? One reason, of course, is simply revenge. Thus could a prominent minister write: "we want our pound of flesh...when we were the anvil, we bore. Now the roles are reversed; and the government has a duty to make it crystal clear...where the power lies." And the power lies, as the leaders of both parties see it, in the executive arm of the state. This attitude of seeking revenge means that successive changes of government are likely to bring successive, and larger, waves of selective repression; it also serves to reinforce the polarization of society along essentially irrelevant partisan lines. The most important consideration, however, is that both parties support the existing structure of class relations and oppression and are thus impelled to take whatever measures they consider necessary to maintain them. Thus, however many free elections are held, whether they result in changes of government or not, as long as the existing structures of production and social relations are supported within the context of the society's status as a dependent satellite in the world capitalist system, authoritarian practices will flourish, despite the supposed democratic nature of the political system.

Where then can one look for a democratic alternative to develop in Belize's political system? The political parties do not seem to offer much hope; their leaders are satisfied with the prevailing system and continue to have difficulty developing democratic practice even within their own parties. After the experience of the past four years, many Belizeans have become disillusioned with the party system, believing it offers them no choice.

In contrast to political parties in other Central American countries, those in Belize have not only played a dominant role in formulating national policy; they have also largely succeeded in monopolizing the political space, creating the impression that for any other body, active participation in political debate is illegitimate. And yet it is precisely in other entities in civil society that the best hope seems to lie for the development of democratic practice.

One unknown factor is the effect of those thousands of Central American refugees who, with their children, will probably account for a fifth to a quarter of the population by the year 2000. Indeed, the "central americanization" of Belize, seen by most observers as inevitable, will have an important impact on the prospects for democracy in Belize. Two further observations can be made with respect to Central America. The first is that we can dispense with the vicarious cultural arrogance that claims Belize is a model of democracy superior to that of its Central American neighbors because of its British tradition. To give two examples, the availability of alternative ideas in the press, radio, and television is far greater even in some of the more notoriously oppressive states than it is in Belize, and in Belize popular organizations are neither important nor strong, as they are in many Central American countries. Second, the current preoccupation with achieving the type of formal democracy that exists in Belize and in other Central American countries should not lull us into believing that, even if that is achieved, the expressions of authoritarian rule will cease. As the case of Belize so eloquently shows, these forms of democracy are inadequate to achieving democracy. Democracy can only be achieved by radically altering the production and class structures that gave rise to, and maintain, the oppression of the majorities.

Notes

1. A 1919 laborers' riot had to some extent been inspired by the Marcus Garvey movement's call to black consciousness. In 1920 a local branch of his United Negro Improvement Association (UNIA) was formed in Belize, with an executive comprised of the colony's few middle-class blacks. Although factionalism rendered the UNIA innocuous by 1926, it had ignited a spark that later led to the workers' protest of 1934–36. At that time the movement broke out of the traditional confines of the creole Belize City to embrace Mexican and Garifuna workers in the northern and southern districts and laid the groundwork for the trade union movement that emerged in the 1940s.

2. Because of its close ties with the party, the union movement was the most seriously affected; indeed, it was virtually destroyed. Membership of the GWU fell from 10,500 in 1954 to 700 in 1956.

3. Clive Y. Thomas, *The Rise of the Authoritarian State in Peripheral Societies* (New York: Monthly Review Press, 1984).

4. The Central Party Council comprises the central executive, the chairperson, and one other representative of each constituency branch; party members in the House of Representatives; one party member from each town board or city council; one representative from the youth, women, and men's groups; and six honorary members are appointed annually by the party leader. It must meet at least once every quarter.

5. C. H. Grant, *The Making of Modern Belize: Politics, Society and British Colonialism in Central America* (Cambridge: Cambridge University Press, 1976).

6. O. Nigel Bolland, *Belize: A New Nation in Central America* (Boulder, Colo.: Westview Press, 1986).

7. Grant, *Making of Modern Belize*, p. 229.

8

Parties, Programs, and Politics in El Salvador

Cristina Eguizábal

During the government of Gen. Maximiliano Hernández Martínez (1931–44), the military became the source of authority because the traditional agrarian elites abandoned that role. From that time on, the armed forces of El Salvador became the guarantor of the established order, and, little by little, in compensation, its members obtained access to wealth and social prestige.[1] Unfortunately, the military's efforts in public administration were not completely successful. Until the coup d'état of October 15, 1979, the governments that followed the *caudillista* dictatorship were incapable of creating a consensus over the legitimacy of the regime, largely because economic benefits, particularly access to land, continued to be unfairly distributed.

Two important efforts to establish relatively open regimes failed in the periods 1948–59 and 1961–72.[2] Both followed a similar pattern: political opening, which led to popular mobilization (perceived as subversion), followed by repression and closing. Indeed, as a governing elite the Salvadoran military was unable to resolve the contradictions inherent in the restricted democracy they wished for the country: How could they modernize the economy without the concomitant political and social mobilization becoming a destabilizing element? How could the dominant coalition be broadened and the hegemony of the landowning and financial oligarchy be maintained? How could the regime establish a base of legitimacy that would permit competitiveness without questioning the military's supremacy? As the principal political force in society, the Salvadoran military oscillated between greater and lesser degrees of repression.

135

Despite efforts at institutionalization and legitimation of the military's participation through the creation of political parties—the *Partido Revolucionario de Unificación Democrácia* (PRUD) and the *Partido de Reconciliación Nacional* (PCN)—the military was unable to consolidate a stable and legitimate regime. The traditional political parties, on the other hand, undertook fruitless efforts to construct a civilian alternative acceptable to the dominant class, in particular the more conservative sectors of this class, the great landowners.[3]

At the time of this writing in 1989,[4] a third effort was underway to establish a functional regime that would keep the country in the Western bloc and maintain the capitalist system internally. But, unlike previous efforts, this one, although guaranteed by an important group within the armed forces, was stimulated from abroad. It came at a time of economic stagnation marked by a climate unfavorable to poor countries internationally and by generalized violence internally.

Faced with grave doubts about the political system's effectiveness, the traditional economic elites have again taken on defense of their class interests, not only informally through their corporate associations, but also for the first time through their political party, the *Alianza Republicana Nacionalista* (ARENA). In many ways ARENA's program contradicts Washington's, which is supported by the armed forces and managed by the Christian Democratic Party (PDC).

Between Bullets and Ballots

Some months after the fall of Gen. Anastasio Somoza in Nicaragua, experts in the U.S. Department of State believed that El Salvador was on the brink of a similar popular insurrection. At the time Washington favored a reformist solution for Central America. Therefore, the United States regarded with some approval the coup d'état that took place in El Salvador on October 15, 1979, overthrowing the government of General Romero, considered by the majority of international observers one of the most repressive on the subcontinent.[5]

The military officers who succeeded to command positions in the government promised, one more time, to undertake the structural reforms necessary to transform Salvadoran society and build a dynamic economic democracy, grounded in periodic free elections.[6] But success did not depend only on good will. It also depended on successfully opposing the powerful agrarian interests. As it was, the October 1979 revolutionary junta was unable even to impose its authority over the elements of the security forces responsible for the repression. It was also unable to control political agitation by popular organizations. Thus, three months after taking power, the young military men and their civilian allies—many of them progressive Catholics who had been educated by Jesuits at the Central American University José Simeón Cañas—had been displaced by a more "moderate" sector of the armed forces. Backed by Washington, these "moderates" had allied with a majority faction of the PDC under the leadership of José Napoleón Duarte.[7]

The civilian-military Christian Democratic junta they formed maintained the reformist programs of its predecessor: agrarian reform, right of association for rural workers, nationalization of foreign commerce. To them the new junta added nationalization of the banks. It abandoned efforts to incorporate the political-revolutionary organizations in the reform process and adopted, thanks to massive aid by the United States, a more traditional counterinsurgency strategy to repress the civilian population mobilized by the guerrilla organizations.

The government of the United States became one of the key actors in domestic politics, and its political program became dominant. Washington's plan, an effort at political engineering, supported the creation of a political "center," which was lacking in Salvadoran society because of the opposition of the dominant class to reforms and the unwillingness of the military to surrender control of the state apparatus. The principal objective of U.S. strategy was annihilation of the insurgency by denying it its popular base through reform (and repression). The base would then change its loyalties and move toward the party of the reformist center. The training of the armed forces, the other dimension of the U.S. program, would make the military into an apolitical and professional body that would abandon its traditional governing function and develop the capability to protect the new "institutions."

Thanks to the participation of the PDC and the backing of the White House, the government of El Salvador could count on the support from the international Christian Democratic movement. In fact the Venezuelan governing party worked both inside and outside of the country to produce a better international image for the Salvadoran government. It was not an easy task. Spectacular political assassinations increased at a rate similar to that of more systematic crimes against the civilian population.[8]

Despite the limitations of the reformist measures, they dealt a harsh blow to the large native landowners and, consequently, to the country's big business. During 1980–81 the right regrouped, disconcerted over the traumatic reforms of October 1979. Behind the scenes, representatives of business interests conspired with the more conservative sectors of the army to displace the Christian Democrats. Others, in connivance with the "death squads," promoted violence and political assassinations.[9]

The left opposition, in response to the junta's strategy, began to regroup as well. The unification process led to the formation of two fronts, the *Farabundo Martí Para la Liberación Nacional* (FMLN), which had a political-military character, and the *Frente Democrática Revolucionario* (FDR), which incorporated the political forces that had supported the military option. Small groups participated in the FMLN—the *Partido Revolucionario de los Trabajadores Centroamericanos* (PRTC), in addition to revolutionary organizations such as the *Fuerzas Populares de Liberación Farabundo Martí* (FPL), the *Fuerzos Armadas de Resistencia Nacional* (FARN), and the *Ejército Revolucionario del Pueblo* (ERP). The Communist Party wholeheartedly embraced armed struggle after the failure of the first junta. Representatives of the revolutionary organizations, as well as important leaders of the leftist parties of the traditional civilian opposition, participated in the FDR. These included the *Movimiento Nacionalista Revolucionario* (MNR), the *Movimiento Popular Social Cristiano* (MPSC), the *Unión Democrática Nacionalista* (UDN), and a variety of popular organizations such as the *Movimiento de Profesionales y Técnicos de El Salvador* (MIPTES) and the important universities of the country.

The armed forces were divided. Some, along with the U.S. military advisers, publicly recognized that a counterinsurgency struggle should combine armed strategy with political work. Others called for a military offensive to eliminate once and for all the guerrillas and their support bases.

Despite growing internal and international pressure for a negotiated political solution to the civil conflict, the United States chose to maintain the military option while promoting elections. First constituent assembly, then presidential, and finally legislative elections were held, with the objective of giving the regime the international legitimacy it lacked. The electoral process had a decisive impact on Salvadoran political parties.

Initially the right did not support elections, but it decided to participate and add the vote to its already considerable resources. Eventually it hoped to displace the Christian Democrats in the government. In the meantime, it would attempt to neutralize the reforms.

In the election two divergent political programs confronted each other, symbolized by the two largest parties. The first was the program of the PDC, championed by Washington, whose strategy was to eliminate the guerrillas by undermining their support through the implementation of reforms. The second was the program of ARENA, which opposed the reformist strategy and sought to militarily defeat the insurgents.[10]

The first elections took place on March 28, 1982, under strict international observation. Observers concluded almost unanimously that honest elections took place. The results surprised many observers. First, the turnout was larger than expected, which some cited as proof of the lack of popular support for the guerrillas, who decided at the last minute to boycott the elections.[11] Moreover, the voters elected a rightist plurality, headed by ARENA, to the Legislative Assembly, even though ARENA leader Maj. Roberto D'Aubuisson had been linked to the 1980 murder of Monsignor Oscar Romero.

The PDC emerged as the major party, with 40 percent of the vote and twenty-four assembly seats. Nevertheless, the rightist parties organized a coalition, including ARENA, that obtained 29 percent of the vote and nineteen seats. The PDC was excluded from leadership of the Legislative Assembly. The United States, in alliance with the sector of the armed forces that supported its strategy, was able to force acceptance of the Christian Democrats' participation in government.

After a month of negotiations, an agreement was reached among all the parties—the Pact of Apaneca. The president of the republic would be Dr. Alvaro Magaña, who had the confidence of the armed forces. His government would be made up of representatives of all of the political parties participating in the elections, including the PDC, which maintained control of education, labor, and—important for image—foreign relations.

The right was able to counteract the reforms through its control of the Legislative Assembly, whose presidency fell to Major D'Aubuisson, and of the ministries of agriculture, economy, and foreign commerce. From these positions it also consolidated its share of power in the party system for the coming presidential and legislative elections in March 1984 and 1985.

The Pact of Apaneca was engineered by the U.S. government. Its objective was to diminish the struggle among competing parties and establish a minimum agreement among them. This was to be based, first, on representative democracy as the form of government and, second, on the need to maintain the reforms, at least for their cosmetic value.[12]

The Constitution of 1983 reflected, in great measure, the agreements reached at Apaneca. Agrarian reform was maintained, as was the limit of 245 hectares for landholdings, but the owners were given three years before expropriation so that they could parcel out or sell excess lands before losing them. Participation of the state in the economy was regulated, restricted to the already nationalized sectors. With respect to labor legislation, peasants retained the right of association, but seasonal workers were denied this right, even though they make up the majority of the rural labor force.

In a society as polarized as El Salvador's, military governments not only substituted for the lack of agreement between social forces, they also helped delay the development of a governing elite. This hampered the development of democratic procedures that could guarantee a stable and peaceful political system. At present, the absence of agreement on the rules of the game, the importance of the cosmetic aspect of electoral practices, the strong external influences, and the reduced citizen participation all signal the weakness of the institutions of representative democracy in El Salvador.

Apogee of the Christian Democrats, 1983–88

During the period of the Legislative Assembly, political struggle centered around the debates through which each of the political parties articulated its program. From the perspective of party politics, 1982–83 were years of growth for the PDC, thanks to the support of the United States, which made the PDC the base of the political center. After intense repression of radical labor organizations, Washington helped strengthen through economic and technical assistance a large number of moderate popular organizations that could buttress the Christian Democrats' program. The principal ones were in the *Unión Popular Democrática* (UPD), which brought together the cooperatives created under the protection of the agrarian reform law and various public sector unions. The former signed an electoral pact with the Christian Democrats in exchange for PDC promises to enact a number of measures favoring wage earners. In a parallel fashion, the revolutionary forces had noticeably deteriorated, less because of the success of U.S. military strategy than because of serious internal conflicts that fomented a severe leadership crisis.[13] This discord within the military was damaging to the government.[14]

The elections did help resolve conflicts that had arisen in the Government of National Unity and that were not overcome in the Legislative Assembly. Furthermore, moving up the election date in response to mounting international calls for a negotiated solution left little doubt about the elections' external legitimating functioning.

The presidential election campaign was marked once again by the rivalry between the PDC and ARENA, each representing a different political program and a different manner in which to conduct the war. The PDC's dominant theme was the "social pact," an expression of its desire to build alliances with labor. ARENA's theme was nationalism, conceived as the most important weapon against communist subversion and counterpoised to the "communitarianism" imported by Duarte.

Of the three major party candidates, in the first round Napoleón Duarte of the PDC obtained 43.41 percent of the votes, Roberto D'Aubuisson of ARENA, 29.76 percent, and Francisco José Guerrero of the PCN, 19.31 percent. In the second round, Duarte won 53.59 percent of the votes cast.[15]

Paradoxically, the 1985 campaign for the legislative elections was marked by its personalistic character. Thus, the elections became a plebiscite on the Duarte presidency. The Christian Democratic government had honored some of its electoral pledges to the UPD to consolidate its base of support and guarantee a positive outcome in the legislative and municipal elections. In addition, in a burst of boldness, President Duarte had, despite Washington's opposition, opened a dialogue with the insurgents in the fall of 1984.[16]

In 1985 the PDC won a majority of the mayoralties, as well as an absolute majority (thirty-three seats out of sixty) in the Legislative Assembly. ARENA had thirteen deputies, the *Partido de Conciliación Nacional* (PCN) twelve, *Partido Auténtico Institucional Salvadoreño* (PAISA) one, and *Acción Democrática* (AD) one. The electoral results showed the PDC to be a fundamentally urban party. Thanks to the support of the UPD and the themes articulated during the electoral campaign, it appeared as a party of the center-left with which popular sectors could identify. Its transition to an opposition party after 1982 had permitted it to gain some distance from the human rights abuses of the christian democratic–military junta (1980–82), while it benefitted from pushing a reformist agenda in the Legislative Assembly.

ARENA, for its part, had gained followers in the rural areas, mainly in those areas afflicted by the war, but also in those where productive activities continued in relative peace. ARENA had inherited a great part of the infrastructure of ORDEN, a paramilitary organization founded by the PCN in the 1960s and dissolved by the first junta in 1979. Nevertheless, ARENA's principal base of support did not come from the peasants, the small rural bourgeoisie, or the technocratic youth of the urban middle classes. Rather, it came from big business, through their trade associations—the National Association of Private Enterprise (ANEP) and the *Alianza Productiva* of El Salvador.

The PCN had lost its most important support, the armed forces. After the coup of 1979, it went through a severe identity crisis and was unable to rebuild an electoral clientele. Despite everything, the PCN still had the support of an important part of the electorate because it had developed the physical and economic infrastructure of the country and enacted important labor legislation.[17]

Although ARENA challenged the results of the legislative elections, the armed forces unequivocally backed the whole process. The officers' attitude clearly demonstrated that the relationship between the oligarchy and the armed forces had changed. It was obvious that the right had lost the battle to rebuild its traditional hegemony. To win the war, it would have to revise its strategy in light of the new rules of the game.

Following the elections, there was a political realignment. After Hugo Barrera left ARENA and formed the *Partido de Liberación,* which developed a more pragmatic platform, ARENA itself changed, favoring the less radical sectors led by Alfredo Cristiani and Armando Calderón Sol. In the PCN the leadership of the old guard, which had formed the alliance with ARENA, was replaced by new leaders who advocated a Social Democratic agenda. A majority of the AD decided to ally itself with the PDC, and thus many of AD's members were able to fill important positions in the government.[18]

In the electoral campaign of 1988, the parties of the right, particularly ARENA, applied the lessons of their past defeat. Aside from constantly accusing the government of corruption, they concentrated their campaign on economic issues. They emphasized the efficiency of private initiatives as opposed to state inefficiency but left their position on the reforms, which they had previously attacked so intensely, relatively obscure. Their message was favorably received. The PDC lost eleven deputies in the legislature and a majority of the mayoralties. ARENA obtained thirty-one deputies and 178 mayoralties, and the PCN received seven deputies and four municipalities.[19]

Paradoxically, as soon as the Christian Democratic Party won control of the state apparatus in 1985, it began to deteriorate as a political force. This deterioration led to the crushing electoral defeats inflicted by the right in 1988 and 1989. The reasons for the defeats had as much to do with the PDC itself and the way it took over administration of the state as with the balance of forces between the PDC and other parties.

The PDC's decision to ally itself with an important faction of the Salvadoran armed forces and to manage Washington's counterinsurgency program had serious repercussions for the party. Important leaders within the PDC refused to accept this alliance and had to leave the party. During 1980 and 1981 a significant number of Christian Democratic militants, most of them from the provinces, became the target of death squads, which led to the decline of the middle and lower ranks.

On the one hand, the party found itself without a leadership capable of maintaining enough structural autonomy from the government to permit the party to serve as a channel of communication between political authorities and civil society. On the other hand, the immediate responsibilities of conducting public affairs and the easy enrichment possible through this activity contributed to the PDC's forgetting the importance of training new men and women to assume government responsibilities. This situation led to the formation of two factions: the *argolla* (ring) personalist faction, led by Julio Adolfo Rey Prendes, and the reformist and modernizing sector, led by Fidel Chávez Mena and Antonio Morales Ehrlich. This conflict culminated with a new schism led by ex-minister Rey Prendes after he lost the party's presidential nomination in 1989.[20]

The war, the earthquake, the drought, the fall in the price of coffee in the international market, and the absence of productive investment all hurt the economy. Monetary devaluations and increases in the cost of living, in addition to chronic unemployment, resulted in a marked deterioration in living conditions. Faced with this situation, the labor organizations that once had served as a vehicle for the PDC in its efforts to rebuild a base of popular support redoubled their actions on behalf of labor and gradually distanced themselves from the PDC. An important faction of the UPD, in alliance with militant labor groups, formed the *Unión de Trabajadores Salvadoreños* (UNTS). To counteract the power of the new organization, the government reorganized its sympathizers into the *Unión Nacional Obrero-Campesino* (UNOC), which subsequently also became critical of the government's efforts.

For ideological and economic reasons, the government of President Duarte and his party were unable to obtain the support of the Salvadoran private sector for their development program. Private enterprise continued to consider him their chief enemy, even though Washington defended the interests of the Salvadoran dominant classes in their conflict with the revolutionary movement.[21]

Militarily the forces were at a standoff. Neither side appeared to be capable of winning the war, although both parties could inflict serious losses on the enemy. Within the armed forces conflicts continued to exist, and, although a majority of the officers accepted the strategy known as "low intensity warfare," the implementation of the U.S. program did not mean they accepted the Christian Democrats' policies.

Relations between Duarte's government and Washington also deteriorated over the course of his presidency. After the first years of his government, when progress was made on human rights, the U.S. Congress became more preoccupied with corruption. Congressional investigations impugned the Christian Democratic administration.

The adherence of the Salvadoran government to the Esquipulas II agreements also did not help relations with the White House. It did, however, have positive repercussions in the domestic sphere. There it awakened hopes of reestablishing a dialogue with the guerrillas and broadening the political arena. The most concrete consequences were the return of the leaders of the MNR and the MPSC (members of the *Frente*

Democrático Revolucionario [FDR]) and the formation of the Democratic Convergence, a new electoral option to the left of the existing parties.

The Elections of March 1989

The nature of the electoral processes has changed in the last few years. Although the military has certainly continued to condition the political game and the United States has continued to be a key actor in national politics, the elections are no longer a mere facade, as they were during most of the first three-quarters of this century, and they have gradually become a mechanism of governmental change. With the participation of the ARENA party at one extreme and the MPSC and the MNR at the other, the party system covers for the first time in many years practically the entire Salvadoran political spectrum.[22]

ARENA's Political Program

The political power of ARENA was consolidated after its success in the legislative and municipal elections of 1988. It controlled the Legislative Assembly, with a majority of thirty-two deputies, and almost all of the country's municipalities, including the mayoralties of all of the departmental capitals. Besides exerting a strong influence on the Supreme Court of Justice, it had the support of the press and maintained close ties with an important sector of the armed forces.

Continuing in the direction outlined after the electoral defeat of 1985, ARENA appeared in the eyes of many to have left behind its initial association with indiscriminate violence. The theme of its campaign was that the Salvadoran crisis was fundamentally economic, the product of an inefficient, corrupt administration. The activists of the extreme right, headed by Major D'Aubuisson, have gradually been abandoning leading roles in ARENA. They have been replaced by successful entrepreneurs of the upper middle class, educated at the best universities in the United States and closely tied to the members of the traditional oligarchy.

Ideologically, ARENA has been adjusting its proposals along neoliberal lines. Following ideas popular throughout the region, it has declared itself in favor of a market economy in which the state "is at the service of man" and against a program in which "interventionism and regulatory excess have atrophied the functioning of the economy."[23]

The party's political platform had few references to the need to promote political development and negotiation. The vagueness of the proposals showed the right remained deeply suspicious of politics. For many years the dominant classes in El Salvador refused the responsibilities of government and refused to organize a political party to represent their class interests. They preferred to work through their powerful corporate organizations. In its political program, ARENA called for peace with dignity through a "National Peace Proposal"—negotiations on a cease-fire and on ways to incorporate the FMLN into the political system.[24]

Chávez Mena and the Renewal of the Christian Democrats

Disorder reigned in the Christian Democratic ranks. After months of veiled confrontations between the dominant factions, the party split. Rey Prendes and his new party, the *Movimiento Auténtico Cristiano* (MAC), kept the support of two-thirds (16 out of 22) of the PDC deputies elected in the 1988 elections. However, Fidel Chávez Mena, the candidate preferred by Washington, was able to maintain control of the party structure.

On economic policy, Chávez Mena tried to distance himself from the Duarte administration. To get closer to the private sector he proposed a "social pact" that would depolarize relations between the business community and his future government. He offered to correct errors in the structural reforms, which did not come from "Christian Democracy [but] from the armed forces and were presented in the Proclamation of the armed forces."[25]

For many Christian Democrats, the war, not the economy, was the main problem. The way to end the conflict, they believed, was first to strengthen the party system and domestic political processes and second to negotiate with the FMLN.[26] Unlike ARENA, whose strength resided in its support from the dominant sectors and whose capacity for popular mobilization appeared unimportant, the Christian Democrats believed their most important political resource was their party's ability to mobilize the people. Despite the fact that the party depended on political and financial support from Washington and the international Christian Democratic movement and that the Duarte government was maintained through the benevolence of the armed forces, the PDC generated enough of its own resources to give it a degree of autonomy, even though the party hesitated to use it.

The mistakes in state management—the waste and corruption among high functionaries—contributed to the deterioration of the image of the Duarte government, not only within El Salvador, but also among its international allies. Candidate Chávez Mena, however, was able to retain an image of integrity and efficiency amid the accusations that multiplied against his party.

The Strategy of the Democratic Convergence

Notwithstanding the limitations of the process begun by the Esquipulas Peace Accord, it undoubtedly opened political space in El Salvador and permitted the participation of the left in politics—though not without danger to its leaders. President Duarte's illness, disputes within the Christian Democratic Party, and the resulting power vacuum created the opportunities for the left to build its popular support at a time when the worker and peasant masses appeared to be demobilized and apathetic in the face of a recrudescence of violence.[27]

There was much speculation about how the participation of the parties of the FDR in the Democratic Convergence—the coalition of the MPSC, MNR, and the *Partido Socialista Demócrata* (PSD)—and in the elections of 1989 would affect the alliance between the democratic left and the extreme left.[28] During the campaign, both the politicians of the FDR and the militants of the FMLN denied that important differences existed between them. According to the official declarations of the Convergence, the idea was to take advantage of the political space provided by the electoral process to encourage a negotiated political solution.[29] According to the leadership of the FMLN, the participation of the left in the elections allowed it to use the elections as a "political battlefield."[30] Nonetheless, the transportation boycott decreed by the FMLN during election week demonstrated strong differences over how the two coalitions defined the significance of the electoral process.

In its electoral platform, the Convergence presented itself as inheritor of the *Unión Nacional Opositora* (UNO), unanimously considered the winner of the 1972 elections and member of the *Foro Popular*, whose revindications were at the base of the coup d'état of October 1979 and the Proclamation of the Armed Forces that followed it. Based on these antecedents, the Convergence appealed not only to the popular classes, but also to the middle classes who, apart from the intellectuals, had refused to identify with the revolutionary program but supported the reforms proposed by the civilian opposition parties.

The Democratic Convergence's economic proposals were vague. The leaders declared themselves in favor of a reformist strategy. They rejected the reforms undertaken by the Christian Democrats as incomplete and invalidated by the counterinsurgency program through which the reforms had been defined and implemented. In their electoral speeches, the Democratic Convergence candidates insisted on redistribution, leaving changes related to production to be debated "among all of those national sectors involved in the productive effort."[31]

In addition to reiterating their commitment to the search for a negotiated political solution, the Democratic Convergence candidates emphasized the need to regain national sovereignty. They stressed as a necessary condition for the development of democratic process respect for human rights, the "total elimination of the death squads, the cessation of indiscriminate captures and disappearances of citizens calling for justice, the abolition of all forms of torture and the repeal of laws restrictive of civil liberties," freedom of association for all workers, and the return of all refugees and displaced individuals.[32]

The feverish activity of the leaders of the left and their many public appearances to debate their proposals with leaders of ARENA cloud the fact that frequent threats were directed against them.[33] To many observers Dr. Guillermo Ungo was selected as the coalition's candidate for the presidency because of the high profile he had maintained in the Socialist International. International opinion became a protective shield for the most important figures of the coalition, if not for the militants who daily risked their lives in anonymity.

The Proposal of the FMLN

On January 24, in the midst of the physical and rhetorical violence that characterized the presidential campaign, the FMLN publicly announced a "political proposal, with the aim of giving the elections a greater objective, [to] contribute [to] a lasting peace." The rebels proposed the elections be postponed until September 15. If the proposal were accepted, the FMLN would agree to call on all of its supporters to participate in the elections, back the candidates of the Democratic Convergence, and accept the election results. Regarding the armed forces, the FMLN only asked that those military officers suspected of human rights violations be tried.

First reactions to the FMLN proposal from the right, the Christian Democratic government, and the armed forces were negative. When the U.S. Department of State expressed cautious interest, the Salvadorans quickly reconsidered their initial rejection.[34]

The FMLN's offer was followed by explanatory statements from them and counterproposals by the government and the political parties. The political parties of the Legislative Assembly played a central role during this time, presenting original proposals parallel to, yet different from, those of the executive branch. Despite a meeting between the legal parties and the commanders of the rebels in the Mexican resort of Oaxtepec on February 20 and 21, no substantive agreement was reached, and the electoral calendar remained unchanged. The FMLN returned to its position of rejecting the electoral process, despite the exhortations of the candidate of the Democratic Convergence to suspend the boycott of transportation on election day.

Electoral Results

Of the over 2 million potential voters, of whom 1,834,000 were registered to vote, only 1,003,153 went to the polls. Despite the violent conditions at the time, the elections took place in a relatively normal climate.

A crushing victory by ARENA was foreseeable early on. According to the figures of the Central Electoral Council (CCE), Alfredo Cristiani won 505,370 votes; Fidel Chávez Mena, Christian Democratic candidate, 338,369; Rafael Morán Castañeda of the PCN, 38,218; Guillermo Ungo of the Democratic Convergence, 35,642; and Adolfo Rey Prendes of the *Movimiento Auténtico Cristiano,* 9,300 votes.[35]

ARENA's victory did not surprise anyone, but the magnitude of the PDC's defeat was unexpected. With no second round of elections, the hopes of the Democratic Convergence, the PCN, and the MAC to act as balancing forces were dashed. The PDC had lost more than 150,000 votes in four years, more than all of the votes obtained by the other losing parties. ARENA, however, had been progressively winning votes. From 1985 its electorate increased by more than 200,000. For these elections it was able to bring together a disparate and incoherent coalition: technocrats and young professionals confident that the entrepreneurial capacity of the new leaders of the party could end the country's economic difficulties, old oligarchs dreaming of repealing the reforms, conservative peasants who missed the stability of the past, and members of military who wanted to rid themselves of the limitations of human rights practices imposed by the United States.

The PCN went from representing almost 20 percent of the electorate (19 percent of the valid votes) to representing .04 percent of it, whereas the MAC had no impact on the PDC. The Democratic Convergence received such scant support because of the FMLN's rejection of the elections, the violence the FMLN encouraged, and the ambiguity of the rebels' support for the left's candidates. In addition, the Democratic Convergence encountered serious difficulties in its campaign efforts, and its message did not mobilize the voters.

Perspectives of the New Government of Alfredo Cristiani

As expected, the period of presidential transition was characterized by violence and uncertainty. Guerrilla activity increased and new extremist right-wing commandos appeared, created by the more recalcitrant sectors of ARENA unhappy with the pragmatism and openness adopted by the new leaders. In the midst of all of this, proposals for negotiation proliferated.[36]

The Negotiating Process

Cristiani's inaugural speech marked a change in his party's traditional positions, and even his own during the electoral campaign. Although he maintained a neoliberal economic position, Cristiani emphasized the problem of the war rather than the economic crisis or the failures of his predecessor, as he had previously done. He accepted the existence of internal structural problems beyond the intervention of foreign actors. He also characterized the conflict as a "fratricidal war," accepting the FMLN as an actor in Salvadoran politics, even though it was operating "illegally."[37] President Cristiani proposed the initiation of dialogue as soon as possible. His minister of the presidency, Dr. Rodriguez Porth, was to be responsible for forming the governmental commission to undertake conversations with the FMLN.

One week after taking on his new position, Porth was assassinated. In response to the attack, the president presented the Legislative Assembly with proposed reforms of the Penal and Procedural Codes. These reforms were antiterrorist and reminiscent of the Law of Public Order under which the old military governments had committed their worst human rights abuses.[38]

Two rounds of negotiation took place, during September and October 1989, between a governmental negotiating team composed of intellectuals, cabinet members, and top members of the FMLN. Little progress was made. The main achievement was that both parties expressed willingness to continue the meetings. Radicals on both sides held a significant share of power and viewed any concessions as unacceptable. Their intransigence was especially evident whenever more substantive dialogue was attempted. Violence erupted each time the conversations closed, initiated either by guerrillas' urban commandos or by death squads close to the armed forces. Moreover, the causes that had once justified the armed struggle had not disappeared, and ten years of war had left rancor and hate in all sectors of society.

There had, however, been changes for the better. The political system had opened up, and, in spite of right-wing calls for reestablishing the state of emergency, President Cristiani maintained constitutional guarantees. Unfortunately, abuses against the civilian population continued to abound, further evidence of the power of the extremists.

The objective of negotiation was peace, but not everyone involved in the talks seemed to have the same conception of it. The government team negotiated exclusively on the cessation of hostilities and on the mechanisms that would allow the rebels to abandon the armed struggle and reenter civilian life within the framework of the current regime. The government negotiators seemed to consider reduction of the armed forces their main concession.

On the other hand, the insurgents were negotiating for a "social pact," the only outcome that, in their view, would justify ending the armed struggle and entering the legal political arena. Thus, in both negotiating sessions they demanded important changes in the constitution as well as the adoption of economic and social welfare policies aimed at a wider distribution of wealth.

With both parties negotiating different things, a climate of mutual trust had little chance to emerge. After the bombing of the FENESTRAS offices, the FMLN withdrew from the negotiations.[39]

The Battle of San Salvador

On the night of November 11, the FMLN launched a surprise attack against the presidential palace and the private homes of the president, the vice president, and the president of the Legislative Assembly. These assaults marked the beginning of an FMLN offensive in San Salvador that lasted two weeks.

To the international media the FMLN explained that the offensive had been prepared since January but had been postponed because the new government appeared willing to negotiate. Confronted with the "bad faith" of the Cristiani negotiating team, the FMLN believed it had no alternative except to force the government to negotiate seriously.[40]

San Salvador's population gave the rebels an indifferent reception at best. In the wealthy neighborhoods they were feared and, once the fighting was over, hated as never before. International public opinion condemned the air raids launched by the government against the civilian areas, which the FMLN was using as shields. The slaying of six Jesuit priests, their housekeeper, and her daughter by government soldiers confirmed the worst fears of human rights advocates, and the FMLN skillfully used the slayings as a public relations coup. But this incident was soon neutralized by the crash of an airplane coming from Nicaragua loaded with anti-aircraft missiles. Cristiani pointed to this as evidence of Nicaraguan involvement in Salvadoran internal affairs and of the rebels' dependence on foreign intervention.[41] Following the plane crash he announced the suspension of relations with the *Sandinista* government and his decision not to attend the presidential meeting scheduled to be held in Managua on December 3.[42]

The summit did take place, a few days later than originally scheduled, in San José, Costa Rica. President Cristiani proposed resuming the negotiation process on the condition the rebels lay down their weapons. The FMLN perceived this as asking them to surrender. Cristiani emerged from the presidential summit as the clear winner on the diplomatic front, after receiving from the other presidents, including Daniel Ortega, a declaration of support in his struggle against the FMLN.[43] On the military front, the situation continued to be a stalemate. For the 1989 Christmas and New Year holidays, the FMLN high command declared a unilateral cease-fire that was respected, but the guerrillas resumed attacks on economic targets as soon as the new year began. It did not appear that the rebels had lost their capacity to mount an offensive, despite official claims after the battle of San Salvador.

President Cristiani had to prove, particularly to the U.S. Congress that he had control over the military. The proof would be identification and prosecution of those responsible for the Jesuit priests' assassination. In his first public declaration of the new year, President Cristiani named suspected military officers and confined them to their barracks, but the investigation proceeded slowly.

For his government to continue receiving U.S. economic and military aid, President Cristiani had to do better than that, and he knew it. His handling of the matter proved the seriousness of his intentions, but the outcome was uncertain.[44]

Post–Cold War Prospects for Democracy

Since President Cristiani's inauguration, the world scene has changed dramatically. The East-West conflict is now dead. Communism is no longer a threat to Western free market societies.

U.S. policy toward El Salvador has already shown signs of change: military aid for the next fiscal year was reduced 50 percent because of the lack of progress in the investigation of the killings of the Jesuit priests. The U.S. government is likely to maintain its pressure, however contradictory, on Salvadoran authorities to secure at least a few democratic gains. In the economic realm, Violeta Chamorro's and Guillermo Endara's problems acquiring U.S. aid for reconstruction in Nicaragua and Panama are not encouraging precedents and raise doubts about the capacity of the Salvadoran government to generate enough aid to meet the needs of the post–civil war period.

Today one question remains unanswered: Will the changing world order have an impact on the Salvadoran conflict any time soon? After eleven years of fighting, most accept that the causes of the violence have not been imported, that they have grown from inequalities deeply rooted in Salvadoran society. The communist threat having vanished, the ruling civil and military elites will not be able to explain continuation of the civil war without acknowledging that the main reason for the fighting has been the defense of enormous privileges for the few.

Yet from the insurgent coalition's point of view, the breaking up of the socialist bloc, Cuba's increasing economic difficulties, the Soviet withdrawal from costly political commitments, and the *Sandinista* defeat in neighboring Nicaragua have dramatically reduced their outside political, economic, and ideological supports. This is forcing them to make their political program Social Democratic in orientation.

Paradoxically, in spite of the internationalization of the conflict throughout the decade, most of the Salvadoran political forces, from the right as well as from the left, have retained a high degree of autonomy. Now that the superpowers are disentangling from Third World conflicts (the Persian Gulf notwithstanding), the conflict in El Salvador will assume its true proportions after a time.

The main result of American political engineering has been the strengthening of the armed forces in correlation with the power of the traditional economic elites. Even if the military seems unable to defeat the FMLN, it remains the single most powerful institution in the country. Political parties have been unable to go much beyond the role of electoral machines. Furthermore, after the Christian Democrats' defeat in the last presidential elections and the subsequent paralysis of the PDC, the political party system lost a good deal of its ability to channel demands and extract support from the civil society. ARENA's incipient modernization as a political institution is in jeopardy. If no significant party contest appears, we will be facing a disintegration of democratic processes and the settlement of political conflict through direct confrontation between contenders for power. The state of war and the use of noninstitutionalized violence would spread instead of retreat.

Will the political parties have a significant role to play as vehicles of civilian participation? The maintenance of a strong civilian presence in Salvadoran politics is impossible without demilitarization. This goal still seems far off, but from what has filtered down from the negotiations, we know that demilitarization is at least under discussion.

Conclusion

In the wake of the guerrillas' November 1989 offensive in San Salvador, both the FMLN and the government returned to the nego-tiating table with new seriousness. The strength of the guerrilla assault demonstrated to the government, and to Washington, that a military victory by the armed forces was impossible in the foreseeable future. At the same time, the refusal of the citizenry in San Salvador's poor neighborhoods to rally to the FMLN's calls for a general insurrection demonstrated that the guerrillas could not expect a military victory either. With the conflict clearly stalemated, the only alternative to a protracted and inconclusive war of attrition was a negotiated settlement. With the population increasingly eager for peace, both sides came to believe that they had more to gain by stopping the fighting.

International circumstances reinforced that calculus. The end of the cold war and the collapse of communism, first in Eastern Europe and then in the Soviet Union, removed the Salvadoran conflict from the East-West struggle. Throughout the 1980s, Washington backed the Salvadoran government's counterinsurgency war and tolerated its poor human rights record because a guerrilla victory was regarded as unacceptable; it would give the Soviet Union another ideological ally in Washington's "own backyard." Once that fear evaporated, both Congress and the executive branch were less willing to accept the Salvadoran army's human rights abuses or finance an interminable war.

In 1990, Congress cut military aid to El Salvador by 50 percent (from $85 million to $42.5 million) and threatened to cut it even further unless the government conducted good faith negotiations with the guerrillas and an honest investigation of the murders of the six Jesuit priests, their housekeeper, and her daughter. President Bush restored full military aid after the FMLN launched a new offensive at the end of 1990, during which an FMLN unit captured and executed two U.S. advisers after shooting down their helicopter. But Bush did not disburse the aid for another six months, instead using it as leverage to further both the peace talks and the Jesuit investigation.

While the new international context led Washington to press its Salvadoran allies to end the war, it had a parallel effect on the guerrillas. The Soviet Union, in consultation with Washington, urged the FMLN to show flexibility at the bargaining table as well. Moreover, the demise of communism weakened the ideological underpinnings of the guerrillas' revolutionary socialism, making them more willing to participate in a political system based on pluralist democracy and a modified market economy. Finally, the electoral defeat of the *Sandinistas* in Nicaragua robbed the Salvadoran guerrillas of their main regional ally and complicated their logistical situation considerably. In the light of such circumstances, a military victory appeared permanently out of reach.

Unlike prior talks between the government and the guerrillas, the negotiations begun in 1990 were actively mediated by United Nations Secretary General Javier Pérez de Cuellar and his personal representative Alvaro de Soto. In July, the two sides signed a preliminary agreement pledging to end human rights abuses against civilians and prisoners and to have U.N. observers monitor compliance once a cease-fire was achieved. But then the talks deadlocked on the issue of reforming the Salvadoran military. Hopes that the war might end soon enough for the FMLN to participate in the March 1991 legislative elections were disappointed.

The March election, however, gave new impetus to the peace process. The Democratic Convergence, led by politicians who had been close allies of the guerrillas, did surprisingly well, winning 12 percent of the vote (about three times its vote in the 1989 presidential election) and eight seats in the new assembly. The success of the Convergence showed the guerrillas that the electoral system offered real possibilities for the left, and it showed President Cristiani that, if he could not end the war soon and begin to revive the economy, ARENA could suffer electoral collapse as had its predecessor in power, the Christian Democratic Party.

Within a month, the negotiations produced a major agreement on constitutional changes that strengthened the independence of the judiciary, reorganized the police as a civilian agency rather than a branch of the armed forces, and created the Truth Commission to investigate the human rights abuses of the 1980s. Although the changes would not take effect until a cease-fire was reached, agreement on these political issues left military reform as the main stumbling block to the settlement of the war.

At first the guerrillas insisted on elimination of both the armed forces and the rebel army, leaving El Salvador, like Costa Rica, with only a police force. That, needless to say, was unacceptable to the armed forces. The FMLN's fall-back position was more practical; it called for a reduction in the size of the military to prewar levels and a "purification" of it—that is, the removal of officers guilty of serious human rights abuses. In addition, however, the guerrillas still wanted some form of merger between its combatants and those of the regular army.

The deadlock over military reform was finally broken in September 1991, during a marathon negotiating session in New York attended by all five of the FMLN's principal commanders. The government agreed to reduce the size of the military and create an independent civilian commission to review the human rights records of individual officers, essentially giving in to the FMLN's demands. In exchange, the guerrillas agreed to accept participation in the new civilian police force rather than in the military. With the signing of that agreement, all the fundamental political and military issues dividing the two sides had been resolved. Only the technical details of a cease-fire and separation of forces remained unsettled.

Just one day after the agreement was signed, the Jesuits case went to trial, and for the first time in modern Salvadoran history, two officers were convicted for the politically motivated murder of civilians. Most significantly, Col. Guillermo Benavides, the highest ranking officer charged, was found guilty of ordering the killing of the Jesuits. Yet Salvadoran justice remained imperfect. Seven other soldiers were acquitted despite their own confessions and overwhelming evidence against them. It seemed clear that the price for getting the army to accept Benavides's conviction was that the rest of the participants be exonerated and that the investigation proceed no further.

As 1991 drew to a close, almost at the stroke of midnight, El Salvador seemed on the verge of ending its decade-long agony of civil war, a conflict that claimed some seventy-five thousand lives and devastated the country. The transition to peace and democracy was by no means completed, let alone consolidated, but on both sides of the barricades Salvadorans voiced an unprecedented optimism and hope for the future.

Final differences between the government and the FMLN were agreed on as the new year brought all parties back to New York to hammer out a final accord. The peace accord, signed January 16, 1992, in Mexico City, set up the framework for the next nine months. In that document, "The parties commit themselves to maintaining the atmosphere necessary to continuing and broadening the unilateral decisions they have taken to avoid any military action." On February 1, 1992, a cease-fire will come into effect, and demobilization of the army will begin as will the creation of the new police force, the Policía Nacional Civil (PNC).

Notes

1. For a detailed account of the history of the previous period, see Rafael Guidos Vejar, *El Ascenso del Militarismo en El Salvador* (San Salvador: UCA Editores, 1980), pp. 69–132; and Rafael Menjívar, *Formación y Lucha del Proletariado Industrial Salvadoreño* (San José: EDUCA, 1979), pp. 51–94.

2. For an analysis of these efforts at political opening and the reasons for their failure, see Cristina Eguizábal, "Los Partidos Políticos, las Elecciones y el Desarrollo de la Democracia Representativa en El Salvador (1948–1988)," in *Guía de los Partidos Políticos en Centroamérica*, ed. P. Albarracín et al. (San José: CAPEL-IIDH, forthcoming).

3. Cristina Eguizábal, "Poder Militar y Luchas Civiles en El Salvador (1961–1982)," *Polémica* 4–5 (San José):267–77; and "El Salvador: Elecciones sin Democracia," *Polémica* 14–15 (San José):16–33.

4. This article was revised again in 1991.

5. For a view of the foreign policy of the Carter administration, see Viron Vaky, "La América Central and la Encrucijada: Testimony Before the House Committee on Foreign Relations, 11 September 1979," in *El Juego de los Reformismos en Centroamérica*, ed. H. Assman (San José: DEI, 1981), pp. 153–70; and William Bowdler, "Testimony Before the Sub-Committee of Inter-American Affairs," in *El Juego de los Reformismos*, pp. 171–81.

6. For an original analysis of the coup d'état of 1979, see F. Flores Pinel, "El Golpe de Estado en El Salvador: ¿Un Camino Hacia la Democratización?" *ECA* 34, 372–373 (San Salvador):885–904.

7. The formal division of the PDC followed the formation of the Christian Democratic junta. During the first weeks, many of those who had taken part in the movement that culminated with the overthrow of President Romero participated in the highest levels of government. They would later make up the MPSC.

8. In 1980 at least forty Christian Democratic mayors and aldermen had been assassinated by the "death squads." Monsignor Romero was killed while officiating mass. In November the principal leaders of the FDR were murdered, including its president, Enrique Alvarez Córdoba. In December, four U.S. religious workers were brutally raped and executed. Finally, in January 1981, two American Institute for Free Labor Development (AIFLD) workers were gunned down in a luxury hotel in San Salvador.

9. High-ranking military officers and the political and trade associations of the most conservative Salvadorans participated in the coup attempts. These included the *Frente Amplio Opositor*, the forerunner of ARENA; the *Partido de Orientación Popular*; and the *Alianza Productiva de El Salvador*, which at the time replaced ANEP in its function of corporate leadership. See Sara Gordon, "Las Vías de Reconstrucción del Régimen Político Salvadoreño," paper presented at the Seventh Central American Sociology Congress, Tegucigalpa, November 2–7, 1986. Mimeographed.

10. The other parties that participated in the elections were *Acción Democrática*, made up of intellectuals of the moderate right; the former official party, the PCN, reorganized with bureaucratic and professional members of the middle class and part of its traditional clientele in the countryside; the *Partido Popular Salvadoreño* (PPS), an old party with liberal members; and the *Partido de Orientación Popular* (POP), organized around Colonel Medrano, previously director of the *Guardia Nacional* and founder of ORDEN, subsequently a convert to the populism of the right.

11. A study of the Universidad José Simeón Cañas (UCA) establishes that the number of voters was inflated by the CCE, with the acquiescence of the participating political parties, as a result of the proportions of the number of votes obtained by each one of the parties. See *ECA* 37, 402 (San José):243; and ibid., 37, 403/404:573–96.

12. The Pact of Apaneca had been inspired by the Pact of Punto Fijo, signed by representatives of the large Venezuelan parties, *Acción Democrática*, COPEI, the Social Christian Party, and the *Unidad Republicana Democrática*, party of the non-Marxist left. Thanks to this pact, the rules of the game were established for the transition toward representative democracy after the fall of General Pérez

Jiménez. See D. H. Levine, "Venezuela Since 1958: The Consolidation of Democratic Politics," *The Breakdown of Democratic Regimes: Latin America,* ed. Juan Linz and Alfred Stepan (Baltimore: The Johns Hopkins University Press, 1978), pp. 93–94; and Terry Lynn Karl, "After La Palma: The Prospects for Democratization in El Salvador," *World Policy Journal* (Spring 1985):310. In El Salvador the Pact of National Unity proposed a broad amnesty for the armed opposition and guarantees for their participation in the next elections. See Gordon, "Las Vías de Reconstrucción," p. 11.

13. The sectors in favor of negotiation strongly opposed those that favored a strategy of prolonged struggle. The confrontations led to the assassination of Commander "Anamaría," Mélida Anaya Montes, number two in the FPL, and the subsequent suicide of Cayetano Carpio, the commander-in-chief of that organization.

14. The military strategy to be followed was not evident; even the Salvadoran officers sympathizing with the Pentagon clashed among themselves. Some favored a strategy of the massive use of the battalions in a regular fashion and others were inclined to pursue activities associated with counterinsurgency. These disagreements accentuated the main schism in the armed forces, between officers disposed to support the reformist project and officers loyal to the project of the traditional oligarchy. The absence of a clear strategic line had unfavorable repercussions in the battlefield, where the FMLN was able to maintain the strategic initiative and insist on its negotiation proposals from a position of relative strength. See Francisco A. Moreno, "El Reformismo en El Salvador," *Cuadernos Americanos* (January–March 1985):75 ff.

15. PAISA and the PPS, which had again presented Dr. Rodriguez Porth as its candidate, supported ARENA. MERECEN and POP pronounced themselves in favor of the PDC. The PCN on various occasions stated that it was neutral, even though it was possible to detect arguments critical of ARENA. This was not the case for the PDC. Nevertheless, the base tended to support the candidate from the right. See Eguizábal, "Los Partidos Políticos."

16. In his speech before the General Assembly of the United Nations, President Duarte announced an offer of dialogue to the FDR-FMLN. From that offer arose the meetings at La Palma on October 15 and Ayagualo on November 30, 1984, during which the discrepancies and lack of conviction about a negotiated solution became evident. For a detailed account of the proposals and counterproposals of dialogue, negotiation, and mediation in the Salvadoran conflict, see "Cronología del Proceso de Diálogo Entre el Gobierno Salvadoreño y el FDR-FMLN," *ECA* 51, 454–55 (August–September 1986):769–88.

17. The *Partido Auténtico Institucional Salvadoreño* (PAISA) and the *Movimiento Estable Republicano Centrista* (MERECEN), both products of schisms of the PCN, had participated for the first time in the presidential elections of 1985. Roberto Escobar Garcia, candidate of PAISA, was unable to obtain the votes traditionally obtained by the PCN and won only 1.22 percent of votes. Juan Ramón Rosales y Rosales of MERECEN received 0.52 percent of votes. See Eguizábal, "Los Partidos Políticos."

18. In December 1987, AD broke its alliance in light of the deterioration suffered by the governing party.

19. The Liberation Party obtained control in one municipality. Of the seven deputies of the PCN, one deserted and allied himself with ARENA, which raised the number of deputies of that party to thirty-two. Statistics of *ECA* 43, 473–474 (March–April 1988): passim.

20. After the electoral authorities annulled his selection as presidential candidate of the PDC for the elections of 1989, Adolfo Rey Prendes formed the *Movimiento Auténtico Demócrata Cristiano*, which later allied itself with MERECEN to form the *Movimiento Auténtico Cristiano*, whose first decision was the nomination of the ex-Christian Democratic leader as its presidential candidate. At a second national convention, whose validity was recognized by the CCE, Fidel Chávez Mena was elected as candidate of the PDC. The followers of Chávez Mena had undertaken an effort without precedent in the recruitment of new militants before the presidential election. One of the reasons its partisans did not accept the results of the first Extraordinary National Convention was that many new militants were unable to vote. During the convention the followers of Rey Prendes forced a decision in which the participation of about four thousand members of the party was considerably reduced, leaving about two thousand voting members. See *Centroamerica Hoy* (San José), no. 3, April 28, 1988; and ibid., no. 6, June 30, 1988.

21. Open confrontations took place over the fiscal measures that the Christian Democratic government, pushed by its creditors, attempted to impose through the *paquetazos* (packages) of January 1986 and January 1987. The coffee growing and export groups have also maintained constant pressure in favor of the reprivatization of international trade.

22. The FMLN accepts the participation of the MPSC and the MNR in the electoral game, without totally accepting the legality of the regime. The UDN party, member of the FDR, also participates in the electoral process, but without, to this date, taking part in the Democratic Convergence.

23. "ARENA Hacia el Rescate Nacional," *El Diario de Hoy* (San Salvador), October 18, 1988.

24. Ibid.

25. *La Prensa Gráfica* (San Salvador), October 19, 1988. Among the corrective measures, Chávez Mena proposed to establish margins of privatization in foreign trade.

26. In this sense they considered the participation of the FDR's political parties in the electoral process to be a success for the party system, according to the declarations of an important leader of the Christian Democrats. *La Prensa Gráfica*, October 17, 1988.

27. Beginning with September 1988, the FMLN multiplied its actions in the capital, making San Salvador into a real "war front." The main attacks were directed against military objectives (urban garrisons); however, the detonation of car bombs in different parts of the city harshly hit the civilian population. The recrudescence of violence was felt throughout the country, principally with the campaign of threats against the ARENA mayors and the execution of those who refused to abandon their posts. See *Centroamerica Hoy*, no. 16, January 17, 1989, p. 11.

28. Apparently the FMLN was unable to rebuild and broaden its base beyond the traditional circles of support. Indeed, the actions of the guerrillas, transportation strikes, sabotage, and terrorist attempts all could have contributed to the political apathy reigning in the country. By August 1987, 58.8 percent of urban Salvadorans believed that no political group could resolve the problems of the country. Only 3 percent believed the PDC, 6.3 percent ARENA, and 0.6 percent the FDR/FMLN could resolve the problems. See Ignacio Martín-Baró, *Así Piensan los Salvadoreños Urbanos (1986–1987)* (San Salvador: UCA Editores, 1987), p. 116. In any event, the candidates of the Democratic Convergence criticized on numerous occasions the guerrilla campaign against the local governments, as well as the use of car bombs.

29. See "Comunicado de la Convergencia Democrática," *Proceso* 9, 349, August 24, 1988. In fact at the end of November 1988, in a poll on the voter preferences of urban Salvadorans undertaken by the University Institute of Public Opinion of the Central American University, only 5.9 percent of those polled indicated they would vote for a candidate of the Convergence (as contrasted with 26.2 percent for the candidate of ARENA and 21.3 for the candidate of the CD), *Centroamerica Hoy*, no. 14, November 27, 1988.

30. See the declarations of Comdr. Leonel González in *Le Monde* (international edition), no. 2087, October 27–November 2, 1988, and the more critical ones by Comdr. Joaquín Villalobos in Mexico: "We cannot tie our strategy to an electoral component, but we are not afraid of elections," *El País* (international edition), 6(287), November 21, 1988. In the FMLN, the ERP favored a military solution and developing terrorist tactics, whereas the FPL was more pragmatic and tried to increase their political presence.

31. "Pronunciamento de la Convergencia Democrática," *Proceso*, 8 (313), November 25, 1987; and *Proceso*, 8 (314), December 2, 1987.

32. "Pronunciamento de la Convergencia Democrática."

33. This explains in great measure the MPSC's difficulties in obtaining the 3,000 signatures necessary for its legal registration as a political party. People feared to openly identify with a leftist option. Despite ARENA's declarations affirming its intention to respect individual rights, the violations of human rights have increased. The activity of the death squads multiplied and the violence of the military against the civilian population, especially in the rural areas, escalated. *Centroamérica Hoy*, no. 12, October 31, 1988, summarizes the reports confirming the escalation of violence from America's Watch, Interamerican Human Rights Commission, Amnesty International, and "Tutela Legal."

34. The arguments justifying the rejection revolved around the question of the constitutionality of the proposal. The church and the labor movement, including the UNOC (progovernment), considered the proposal a step in the direction of peace. See *Proceso* 9 (370), February 1, 1989; *Proceso* 9 (371), February 3, 1989; and ibid. (372), February 22, 1989, passim.

35. *ECA* 44, 485 (March 1985): "Document" section.

36. The violent urban actions affected the vice president-elect, Francisco Merino, whose residence was attacked with explosives. A few days after the assault against Merino, the climate of violence intensified with the assassination of the attorney general of the republic, Roberto García. On May 16 the

residence of the president of the Legislative Assembly was attacked; this was the only action claimed by the urban commandos of the FMLN. Both the government and ARENA accused the FMLN of being responsible for the three terrorist actions, notwithstanding the reports of well-informed parties that the authors of the former two actions had identified themselves as the "Gerardo Barrios Civic Forces," a right-wing group that separated from ARENA unhappy over its loss of leadership within the party with the election of Armando Calderón Sol to the presidency of the party. See *Centroamerica Hoy*, no. 21, April 24, 1989, p. 5; and *Proceso* 9 (384), May 17, 1989.

37. Taken from the speech by the president of the republic, Alfredo Cristiani, reproduced in *La Prensa Gráfica*, June 2, 1989.

38. The law was condemned by the opposition deputies, the church, labor leaders, and important legal practitioners. At the time this chapter was being written the law had not yet been approved. See *Centroamérica Hoy*, no. 24, June 30, 1989, pp. 15–17.

39. *New York Times*, November 11, 1989.

40. *Le Monde*, November 15, 1989.

41. Contrary to their usual behavior, the *Sandinista* authorities did not deny their participation and support of the rebels. Furthermore, the plane crash appeared as a diplomatic defeat for Managua because it diverted attention from the vital issue of the demobilization of the *Contras*. See *New York Times*, December 3, 1989.

42. *New York Times*, November 26, 1989; and *La Prensa Gráfica*, November 30, 1989.

43. See *New York Times*, December 13, 1989. Commenting on the outcome of the San José meeting, Humberto Ortega, Nicaragua's Minister of Defense, confirmed his government's refusal to "act as a guerrilla force supporting another guerrilla force" and its recognition of the Cristiani government's electoral legitimacy. See *El Nuevo Herald*, December 20, 1989.

44. Not until the fall of 1991 did a trial take place against the accused officers. A guilty verdict resulted, with officers receiving prison terms, a first in El Salvador's history.

9

The Origin and Development of Political Parties in Honduras

Ernesto Paz Aguilar

The historical development of political parties in Honduras can be divided into three clearly defined stages. The first, dominated by liberals and conservatives, lasted from independence in 1821 until 1891. These "factions were the direct ancestors of the main contemporary political parties and originated in the groups of notables that defined the political life of Honduras. There were liberals and there was a Liberal Party. However, although there were conservatives, there was no Conservative Party. This period corresponds to what historians of Central America call "the anarchy"—a time of unsuccessful attempts to build a unified national state in the region.[1] At the time, electoral struggles were a marginal mechanism for attaining power. The favored means to obtain and maintain power was armed struggle. Political power was legitimated through armed struggle and fraudulent elections. The "factions" appeared as bands of armed men under the leadership of *caudillos* organized at the national level. They represented fragile and precarious alliances of *caudillos*, whose stability rested on a complex web of family ties and *compadrazgos*.[2]

The political structures of the time reflected the economic and social structure of the country. They corresponded to a closed, self-sufficient economy in which no economic surplus was generated and the fundamental economic unit was the cattle ranch. Thus, the rancher, the large landed estate owner, and the political leader were one and the same person. In this way, economic and political power were concentrated in a small elite, which made the organization and functioning of political parties impossible. Only during the Liberal Reform were the material and intellectual conditions ripe for the organization of political parties.

The Traditional Parties, 1891–1948

The traditional parties began to organize at the beginning of the Liberal Reform. It is well known that a party system's chances for survival are a function of a society's degree of economic and social development. In addition, those who make up the political class must observe a minimum respect for the rules of the political game. These are the necessary preconditions for a party system. During the Liberal Reform these conditions were met. A process of economic and social development was initiated that incorporated Honduras into the world economy.

The liberal governments of Marco Aurelio Soto and Luis Bográn developed a policy of conciliation that permitted a more equitable distribution of resources among the political groups. The motto "better to spend money than bullets" is attributed to Soto. His view contrasted with the embarrassing policy of "money, bullets, and cudgels" that prevailed during the "anarchy"[3]—that is, money for friends, bullets for enemies, and cudgels for the indifferent ones. Marco Aurelio Soto was, as noted by a Honduran historian, "able to build a provisional throne for culture."[4]

Under these circumstances, the Liberal Party was organized out of the liberal faction directed, until his death, by Celeo Arias López. On February 5, 1891, the party's first convention was held under the leadership of Policarpo Bonilla Vásquez. Another traditional party, the National Party, appeared on March 28, 1902. Its founder was Manuel Bonilla Chirinos. The National Party emerged out of personal differences within the Liberal Party and was essentially a splinter group of it. In this way, a two-party system appeared in Honduras, and political life between 1902 and 1948 was marked by a social and legal bipartisanship: social because the two great traditional parties represented the economic and social structure of the country and legal because these parties were the only two officially recognized.

Two events primarily shaped the bipartisan period: the growing political power of the banana companies and the dictatorship of Carías Andino. Other historical events influenced the first efforts to organize new parties, but to a lesser extent. The Mexican Revolution inspired youth to attempt once more to reconstruct the *"Patria Grande"* through the Central American Unionist Party. The Bolshevik Revolution contributed to the organization of the Honduran section of the Communist International in 1922.

The Liberal Reform envisioned an open door for foreign capital. This contributed to the denationalization of the nascent agricultural bourgeoisie. Thus, gradually, Honduras became the prototype "banana republic." A "banana enclave" formed that eventually became a state within a state. One consequence of the enclave was the interpenetration of the banana companies and partisan politics. The United Fruit Company established close ties with the National Party, and the Cuyamel Fruit Company allied with the Liberal Party. These alliances help explain many of the civil wars, *montoneras* (guerrilla wars), and armed insurrections between 1902 and 1932. Some arose from disputes between the banana companies; others from quarrels among the *caudillos*.

The influence of the banana companies also undermined the political morality of the country. The dictatorship of Carías Andino can be attributed in part to the withdrawal in 1929 of the Cuyamel Fruit Company, which had previously helped finance electoral campaigns, *montoneras*, and civil wars for the Liberal Party. Revolutions are made by human beings but require money and weapons as well. When the Liberal Party's financing from the Cuyamel Fruit Company disappeared, the dictatorship of Carías Andino became more likely. At the time, Honduras did not have a professional military. Carías Andino encouraged the professionalization of the air force (the most expensive and sophisticated service branch) and thus strengthened his control over it. The modern combat aircraft were piloted by North Americans and guarded by indigenous soldiers loyal to Andina. Thus, until 1947, all the commanders and a majority of the pilots in the Honduran air force were foreigners. In contrast, Carías Andino opposed the professionalization of the army because he feared a coup d'état would result, just as a number of his counterparts elsewhere in the region had experienced.

Another factor that contributed to the long dictatorship of Carías Andino was the Depression. During the 1930s, Central America suffered a plague of dictatorships—Ubico in Guatemala, Hernández Martínez in El Salvador, Carías Andino in Honduras, and Somoza in Nicaragua. (The honorable exception was Costa Rica.) This club of tyrants signed a nonaggression, mutual defense pact: that is, to say, they agreed to protect each other.

Finally, one must consider the role of the U.S. government, which approved of Andino's reign. Moreover, this attitude was reinforced by the desire of the United States during the World War II to keep countries in the Western hemisphere in the Allied camp at a time when some Latin American countries displayed sympathy to the Axis powers.

The Modern Parties, 1948–87

The decline of the Carías Andino dictatorship began with the Allied victory in World War II, which created a climate favorable to democratic regimes. A renewed fight against dictatorship began, headed by the Liberal Party. Opposition elements at the margins of the traditional parties began to gain strength as well.

The awakening of the Liberal Party and the appearance of the modern parties were consequences of several phenomena, both national and international. Nationally these included (1) the diversification of the activities of the banana enclave, (2) the capitalist development of agriculture, and (3) the modernization of the state. At the beginning of the 1950s the banana enclave began to diversify and extend its operations into industry, banking, and commerce.

Capitalist development in agriculture produced an agricultural export economy based on coffee, cotton, sugar, meat, and lumber. The appearance of the agro-industrial bourgeoisie and the development of the agricultural proletariat were intimately tied to this phenomenon.

The traditional parties did not escape the effects of modernization; the struggle between conservatives and reformers gave rise to new parties. In 1954 the National Reformist Movement (MNR) was founded, the product of a division within the National Party. The Liberal Party also suffered from divisions, leading to the founding of the Orthodox Republican Party (PRO) in 1958. The National Reformist Movement, as well as the Orthodox Republican Party, was unable to survive for long.

International events—the Guatemalan Revolution (1944–54), the Cuban Revolution (1959), the Second Vatican Council (1961), the Sino-Soviet conflict (1967–69), the Honduras–El Salvador War (1969), and the Nicaraguan Revolution (1979)—contributed to the development of modern parties.

The Guatemalan process contributed significantly to the creation of the Honduran Democratic Revolutionary Party (PDRH) in 1948. This political group brought together artisans, intellectuals, and important sectors of the working class. The political project of the PDRH had two main objectives: to restore a democratic regime and encourage autonomous capitalist development. The successful growth of the party led the government to resort to repression. The PDRH was declared illegal, and its newspaper, *Vanguardia Revolucionaria*, was closed. The ban led to a crisis within the party, which then split. In 1952 a sector of it entered the left wing of the Liberal Party, and two years later the other sector founded the Communist Party of Honduras (PCH).

The Cuban Revolution produced a demonstration effect in Latin America. In almost all of the countries of the continent, guerrilla groups appeared that proposed to build socialism through armed struggle. In Honduras two organizations of Castroite inspiration arose: the Francisco Morazán Movement (MFM) and the Revolutionary Party (PR). Both organizations began as dissident groups of the left wing of the PCH.

After the military coup d'état of October 1963, the Liberal Youth, the Communist Party, and the Castroite organizations attempted to develop guerrilla *focos* (cells) in different parts of the country. The *focos* were destroyed, some of their members killed, and others were imprisoned or expelled from the country. In the end, the MFM and the PR proved ephemeral.

The Second Vatican Council was a landmark for the Catholic church, which had been the traditional ally of conservatives. Beginning with Vatican II, the church "changed trenches" and began to promote reform and democracy. In Latin America, this process became more intense with the Bishops' Conference of Medellín (Colombia) in 1968, after which pastoral action was increasingly directed toward the most needy. With the Conference of Puebla (Mexico) in 1978, the idea of "a preferential option for the poor" was further refined.

In Honduras, beginning in the 1960s, the Catholic church stimulated the development of unions, peasant leagues, and student fronts of Social Christian inclination. In 1968, a group of lay persons linked to the social work of the church founded in 1968 the Christian Democratic Movement of Honduras (MCDH). In 1975 this movement became the present Christian Democratic Party of Honduras.

The rivalries and disputes between the two giants of the socialist world, the USSR and the People's Republic of China, provoked tensions and divisions in the world's Communist parties. In Honduras, the clandestine Communist Party, hit by repression after the coup of 1963 and weakened by the Castroite organizations, suffered a new split. In 1967 some members of the Central Committee and the Political Commission clashed, leading to a series of expulsions. The internal conflict was prolonged until 1971, when one of the groups took the name of Communist Party (Marxist-Leninist) of Honduras. The first group was recognized by the Communist Party of the USSR; the second aligned with the Communist Party of China.

The armed conflict between Honduras and El Salvador was a hard test for the Honduran nation. The causes of the war resided in the structure of landownership in El Salvador. Historically, Salvadoran governments have been reluctant to undertake land reform. The unfair structure of landownership in El Salvador pushes thousands of peasants into neighboring countries, especially Honduras. War appeared inevitable when the government of Honduras decided to exclude Salvadoran peasants from the benefits of the agrarian reform. By the late

1960s, rural instability in Honduras had reached alarming dimensions; during 1967, two land recoveries or invasions by peasants occurred every day, with both Honduran and Salvadoran peasants participating.

The war opened wounds that have not yet healed. The governing National Party lost credibility and prestige because of its incompetence in handling the war. When the hostilities ceased, a climate supportive of national unity developed in the country, as did consensus for the need to renovate political institutions.

A group of citizens led by Dr. Miguel Andonie Fernández decided to create a new political party—the Party of Innovation and Unity (PINU). Andonie Fernández, a wealthy businessman, was the president of the National Defense Committee and many of the members of the local committees of national defense were present at the foundation of the PINU.

The Nicaraguan Revolution in 1979 provoked in Honduras a process of differentiation among political parties, of the left as well as the right. Honduran political forces simultaneously experienced both radicalization and polarization. The radicalized right formed death squads and the radicalized left organized guerrilla movements.

On the left were the Morazanist Front for the Liberation of Honduras (FMLH) (1979), the Popular Revolutionary Forces "Lorenzo Zelaya" (FPR) (1980), the National Liberation Movement (MPL) (1980), "Cinchoneros," and the Revolutionary Party of the Central American Workers (PRTC) (1983). On the extreme right were the Association for the Progress of Honduras (APROH) (1982) and the Alliance for Anti-Communist Action (AAA) (1987).

Features of the Honduran Political System

The Honduran political system has the following characteristics: (1) it is a limited and restricted democracy, (2) it is a presidential regime, (3) the armed forces have a tutelary political role, (4) interest groups have a growing influence, and (5) the U.S. embassy plays a proconsular role.

Theoretically Honduras is a liberal democracy. Liberal democracies are characterized by elections and pluralism. In Honduras armed struggle has been the favored way to take power and fraudulent elections the most efficient means to legitimate it. In 164 years of independence, more than one hundred changes of government have occurred, and for years no civilian president transferred power to another civilian president.

Although Honduras is a country with an authoritarian past, in the 1980s there were three free and honest elections. These elections have not, however, taken place in a pluralistic framework, that is, in a climate that guarantees the free play of all political parties, with all ideologies having equal opportunities. The electoral game has been circumscribed by a truncated political spectrum that extends from the right to the center. Even when legal impediments for the registration and free functioning of the political parties of the left were absent, the conservative sectors successfully thwarted their operation. They have still not learned the first lesson of democracy—tolerance.

According to the Honduran Constitution the form of government is republican, democratic, and representative. It is exercised by three branches—legislative, executive, and judicial—which are complementary, independent, and not subordinate to each other. In practice, the executive branch dominates the others.

The president of the republic is also the head of the party, and presidential elections coincide with legislative and municipal elections. For this reason, the winning party almost always obtains a majority in Congress and in municipalities. Furthermore, the president has at his disposal important economic resources through a budgetary mechanism commonly known as the "confidential account." The confidential account is a sum of money, often not included in the national budget, available to the president for use at his discretion. It can be used to provide drinking water to a community, help a party member in need, or finance a political campaign.

Even though the president makes power concrete and personalizes its exercise, he is also forced to share it with an institution: the armed forces. The Honduran Constitution indicates that the armed forces are a permanent national institution—professional, apolitical, obedient, and nondeliberating. The last three characteristics are simply fictitious. The armed forces of Honduras form the principal political force of the country and thus exercise a tutelary role over the other institutions of government. The armed forces constitute a de facto power, not subordinated to civilian political power.

In the first place, the armed forces are charged with fulfilling eminently political functions: maintaining the rule of the Constitution, the principles of free suffrage, and the alternation of the office of the presidency of the republic. In any liberal democracy these are the tasks of the judicial branch. Because of the armed forces' role in judging the conduct of civilian government, Honduran democracy finds itself under the permanent threat of a coup d'état. The armed forces determine, in fact, whether the civilian government is maintaining the Constitution.

The political tutelary function of the armed forces rests with the National Security Council. Theoretically, the council is a consulting body to the presidency of the republic; here civilians are an evident minority. For some time the National Security Council has been a suprapower where matters most important to the country were discussed and decided, from the national budget to the position of Honduras in the Central American peace process to the government's response to a union strike. The armed forces, through the National Security Council, have institutionalized their intervention in political life. In this sense, Honduras' experience follows to the letter authoritarian presidential systems colored by a national security doctrine, as were found in Chile, Haiti, and Paraguay.

The functioning of the power structure in Honduras is not as simple as it appears. To the political parties–armed forces scheme must be added the growing role of interest groups. Curiously, Honduras, the most economically backward country of the region, is equipped with a dynamic and flexible superstructure. Beginning in the postwar period, two new actors appeared in the Honduran political system: the armed forces and the worker-peasant movement, which erupted onto the political scene after the banana workers' strike of 1954. From this moment on, the state recognized union organizations, and later the Labor Code and the Agrarian Reform Law were promulgated.

The rise of the unions stimulated the corporate development of the economic elite, which organized the Private Business Council (COHEP). In the past, communication between the economic elite and the state apparatus had taken place through informal mechanisms.

The political parties, especially the traditional ones, were unable to adequately represent the interests of the emerging social groups. They also proved inept at resolving intraparty conflicts, which resulted in the diminution of party influence and the rise of interest group influence. Two instances in recent Honduran history make this evident: the signing of the National Unity Pact in 1971 and the Act of Settlement in 1986.

Finally, the U.S. embassy exercises enormous influence on domestic policy by playing a proconsular role. Within the present political system, the president of the republic, the commander-in-chief of the armed forces, and the U.S. ambassador are the most important people in Honduras. The days of the "banana republic," when the executives of the banana companies had a decisive influence, have been left behind. But the influence of the diplomatic representatives of the United States is enormous.

Because the United States constitutes the greatest source of external financing, many ministries have units that execute projects and programs financed by the Agency for International Development (AID). In this way, AID has created a "parallel government" directed from the U.S. embassy. The embassy participates in almost all important decisions. This has led a Honduran analyst to conclude that the influence of the United States has come to be "a very sui generis internal factor."[5] Howard Wiarda has stated that "the United States is not only the most important external power operating in Central America...the North American embassy functioning in its proconsular capacity, is also a very important, or even, the most important force."[6] The proconsular role of the U.S. embassy is concomitant with the presence of foreign troops on Honduran national soil.

Honduras endured the presence of the U.S. armed forces and the army of the Nicaraguan counterrevolution. The government recognized the presence of U.S. troops and justified it by a disputable interpretation of the Treaty of 1954. In truth, the military presence of the United States in Honduras has acquired a permanent character owing to military maneuvers. Yet the government officially denied the presence of the *Contras* in Honduras until after the 1990 Nicaraguan election because it was contrary to international law.

There are different perceptions of the military presence. I share the opinion of Leticia Salomón, who indicates that the military presence of the United States,

> was not merely a matter of U.S. imperial design, but rather a response to real or fictional security threats in which Honduras was a player...besides, U.S presence was not due to internal objectives, the eradication of an opposition force, but rather U.S. troops pursued external objectives of dissuasion.[7]

Yet regardless of the objective of the U.S. military presence, it has produced growing opposition from the population, especially in the regions where the troops are quartered. In the end the presence of North American troops is creating unprecedented anti-American feeling among a majority of Hondurans.

The Electoral System

Because Honduras is organized as a republic, elections have theoretically been the mechanism that permit citizens to choose their government. The Honduran electoral system follows the general lines of electoral systems in contemporary liberal democracies. The Electoral and Political Organizations Laws of 1977 and 1981 represent a significant advance in this direction.

The Honduran electoral system is based on the principle of universal suffrage. The Constitution of 1982 stipulates that the electorate is made up of all Honduran citizens nineteen years of age or older, of both sexes, who have civil and political rights. Thus, suffrage is conceived as a right and as a public function of the citizen.

Yet the Constitution also defines certain restrictions on suffrage. Mental incapacity or criminal conviction may result in a loss of the right to vote. To prevent the politicization of the armed forces, active members of the armed forces and the state security corps cannot exercise the right to vote (Article 37 of the Constitution and Article 10 of the Electoral and Political Organizations Law). This restriction, however, has not produced the expected results, for the armed forces intervene in politics through other means.

Registration in the National Electoral Census is the second condition of the right to vote (Article 135 of the Electoral Law) and the duty of every citizen (Article 40 of the Constitution). Finally, Hondurans who reside outside of the national territory are prevented from voting, owing to the manifest negligence of the government authorities. Their number is significant. For example, the fourth largest Honduran city (in number of Honduran residents) is New Orleans, Louisiana, in the United States.

The constitutional regulation of political parties is relatively recent. Only in the Constitution of 1957 were political parties recognized as "institutions of public law." The independent candidacies are also a novelty, created by the Electoral Law of 1977. According to the Honduran Constitution, political parties must have the following characteristics and observe the following rules:

1. They must be organized to "promote the national welfare and the strengthening of representative democracy."
2. Their objectives must be achieved "through democratic and representative means" and must "avoid violence and respect the will...of the majorities."
3. They must observe the principle of the nonsubordination "to national or foreign entities that make attempts against the sovereignty and independence of Honduras, its form of government, and the legally constituted authorities."

Honduran political parties guarantee their members direct and representative participation in the election of their officers and their candidates for public office. Internal elections take place according to the statutes of each party, respecting the principle of proportional representation, and are supervised by the National Tribunal of Elections. The different movements, currents, or internal tendencies that participate in such elections must register lists in more than half of the departments and municipalities of the country. These internal elections tend to give a preponderant weight to the competing currents, which weakens party structure. In addition, the internal elections are "open primaries"—all eligible voters can participate. To be more representative of the parties, these elections should be limited to party members.

A political party must have twenty thousand members, organized in more than half of the departments and municipalities of the country. The registration of parties takes place at the National Electoral Tribunal, at any time except in the six months preceding general elections. The registration of a political party may be canceled if the party obtains less than ten thousand votes in elections for higher offices.

The electoral process includes three stages: the preparation of elections, the official vote count, and, eventually, the results themselves. In a country with an "authoritarian past," the electoral process presents complex problems. On the one hand, political forces tend not to respect the rules of the electoral game. On the other hand, the frequent coups d'état have undercut party activity.

The electoral or campaign period is defined as the time between the call for elections and the elections themselves—six months under current electoral law. General elections (presidential, legislative, and municipal) take place every four years. The electoral campaign begins on the day after the call for elections and is carried out until five days preceding the elections. In practice, however, Hondurans are first subjected to almost permanent proselytizing campaigns between and within parties.

There are, however, certain restrictions. Meetings and political marches must be first authorized by the government. Furthermore, five days before the elections, the parties cannot organize meetings or marches, and debates on television, radio, newspapers, and by other means of communication are suspended. The distribution and sale of alcoholic beverages are prohibited during the meetings and marches and also on election day.

The state contributes to the financing of political parties. Each legally registered party that participates in the general elections receives five *lempiras* for each valid vote cast in the last elections. With this measure the state seeks to secure the independence of the party organizations from economic interest groups and provide equal opportunity in the electoral struggle.

Although the state's financial contribution to political parties is an advance, the cost of campaigns is much higher. Millions more are invested in the electoral campaigns, and those parties with greater resources have a better chance of persuading voters to support them. All means of mass communication are privately owned, and the majority are managed as profit-making businesses. Publicity is expensive: one minute on the television channel with the largest audience costs 900 *lempiras*. The gross national product per inhabitant is 500 *lempiras*. Local political analysts have calculated that the 1985 political campaign of Rafael Leonardo Callejas cost more than 5,000,000 *lempiras*,[8] and the campaign of the 1985 winner, José Azcona, cost more than 3,000,000.[9]

Elections can be challenged for legal or procedural violations. To regulate elections, two systems have been used: political regulation through the National Congress and jurisdictional regulation through special bodies. The system of political regulation was in effect from 1894 to 1957. The National Congress was responsible for acting on requests for the annulment of elections for president of the republic and deputies (Article 55 of the Electoral Law of 1895). This system made the legislature the judge of its own membership. The Constitution of 1957 established the system of jurisdictional regulation by creating the National Council of Elections. Today the National Tribunal of Elections is made up of a representative of the Supreme Court of Justice and a representative of each recognized political party. The National Tribunal of Elections serves as a court of first instance; appeals can be made to the Supreme Court of Justice.

The Current Political Climate

Possibilities exist for incorporating the parties of the left into the democratic-electoral game. This will depend in part on the political parties themselves as well as on the degree of tolerance and openness among the political elite and the armed forces. To this day guerrilla organizations have marginal political importance. Their growth and influence are directly proportional to the capacity of the system to resolve the fundamental problems of the Hondurans. As the regime emerges from over a decade of internal wars, Honduras's political growth and the increased ability for civilian leadership appears more promising.

In November 1989 Honduras held its fourth national election since the country's return to civilian rule in 1981. Four political parties—the *Partido Nacional* (PN), the *Partido Liberal* (PL), the PINU, and the *Partido Democrata Cristiano* (PDC)—ran candidates for the presidency. Also to be decided were 3 vice presidential slots, 132 representatives to Congress, 284 municipal offices, and 20 representatives to the Central American Parliament.

Rafael Leonardo Callejas, the opposition candidate of the PN, won the election with 51 percent of the votes, with the PL candidate, Carlos Flores Facusse, receiving 43 percent. The PN also captured 71 out of 128 seats in the legislature, 212 municipalities out of 289, and won in 16 out of 18 departments. Callejas's election reflected public dissatisfaction with the Liberal administration of José Azcona del Hoyo in the midst of the continuing deterioration and mismanagement of the Honduran economy. The PL had governed Honduras since its return to civilian rule in 1981.

The backdrop of the campaign was a sea-change in the region's military activity. By 1989 Honduras's position as a strategic ally of the United States in Central America had ended. In the 1980s Honduras served as a sanctuary for the Nicaraguan rebels, or *Contras,* inside Honduras's border. The winding down of the regional civil wars evoked new nationalist sentiments against a large-scale foreign presence. The Tela Agreement, which Honduras signed in 1989, provided for voluntary demobilization and repatriation of the *Contras* back to Nicaragua and reinforced the position of nationalist political forces. The Honduran military was wary of Washington's unreliable support for the *Contras.*

The most pressing issue of the campaign, however, was the economy. In spite of the infusion of foreign assistance during the 1980s, Honduras remained the region's second poorest nation after Haiti. Both candidates were forced to address the issue of reactivating the nation's economy. During the campaign, the PN emphasized that the Liberal's rule had produced a further downturn in economic conditions. PL candidate Flores stressed the need for an efficient public sector, the removal of tariff barriers, and increased export levels. Yet the austerity measures requested of PL President Azcona in early 1989 by the International Monetary Fund had never been implemented. Fearing that such measures would lead to further deterioration of social and economic conditions during an election year, Azcona chose to halt interest payments on Honduras's external debt, causing a freeze on additional inter-national loans. This move, by itself, may have proven the more disastrous political course for the Liberals.

Conclusions

Callejas's victory marked a growing trend in Central America of electing more conservative, free market–oriented leaders. As the region emerges from a decade of civil war to one in which economic revitalization will hold the key to future success, political parties in Honduras will be challenged to develop platforms that provide vision and hope for one of the region's poorest countries. Parties may also provide the only effective organizing institution to counter the continued behind-the-scenes power of the Honduran military in the political arena.

Honduras is a precarious and limited democracy where the armed forces have a function of political tutelage and the embassy of the United States has a proconsular role. The trend of "corporatizing" power will likely be accentuated because of the growing importance of interest groups and the inability of the political parties to produce a representative leadership.

Notes

1. Edelberto Torres Rivas, *Interpretación del Desarrollo Centroamericano* (San José: EDUCA, 1971), pp. 37–57.

2. Relation of a godfather to the parents of a child.

3. Romulo E. Duron, *Biografía del Doctor Marco Aurelio Soto* (Tegucigalpa, D.C.: Tipografia Nacional, 1946), p. 50.

4. Phrase attributed to Honduran historian Rafaél Heliodoro Valle (1891–1959).

5. Victor Meza et al., *Honduras: Pieza Clave de la Política de los Estados Unidos en Centroamérica* (Tegucigalpa, D.C.: CEDOH, 1986), p. 8.

6. Quoted by Mark Rosenberg, "Democracia en Centroamérica?" *Cuadernos de CAPEL* 5 (1985):17.

7. Leticia Salomón, "Honduras: Sistema Político, Fuerzas Armadas y Crisis Centroamericana," *Honduras, Panorama y Perspectivas* (Tegucigalpa, D.C.: CEDOH, 1989), pp. 26–27.

8. Anibal Delgado Fiallos, *Honduras: Elecciones 85* (Tegucigalpa, D.C.: Editorial Guaymuras, 1986), pp. 68–69.

9. Information provided by President José Azcona to the author.

10

Nicaragua, 1944–84: Political Parties and Electoral Processes

Virgilio Godoy Reyes

History

The Colonial Period

In Nicaragua, as in other Central American countries, the genealogy of the political parties can be traced to the middle of the sixteenth century, when the conquest of America concluded and the colonial period began. The colonial period generated an insoluble contradiction between two sectors of Spaniards who lived together in the colonial domains without accepting each other. On the one hand were the creoles *(criollos)*, descendants of the conquistadors or the first colonizers. They maintained that their historical roots gave them certain prerogatives, which they believed the crown was constantly diminishing. On the other hand were the peninsulars *(peninsulares)*, who as direct representatives of the crown held power and privileges that aggrieved the creoles.[1]

The clash between creoles and peninsulars for reasons of ancestry and economic interests was transformed over the years. In the eighteenth century, it became ideological and produced embryos of the political parties, which became clearly defined at the culmination of the Civil War of 1854–57.

The old rivalry between creoles and peninsulars climaxed as a result of another European development: the Napoleonic invasion of Spain. The hostility between social groups, forged during almost three centuries of colonial rule, came to a head when royal power crumbled in Spain. The vacuum left by Spain created an opportunity for the creoles to achieve their old emancipatory aspirations, now reinforced by the participation of the *mestizo* sectors of society. This settling of accounts between the Spaniards of Spain and the Spaniards of America was fought above the "great productive mass of the population, which [was] only a passive observer."[2]

Following the example of the Spanish insurgents against Napoleon, the creoles organized governing juntas to redefine power in their favor. What happened in Nicaragua in December 1811 illustrates this trend. Peninsular authorities were deposed and replaced by creoles. The Nicaraguan rebels of 1811, besides rejecting peninsulars and royalists, revealed well-defined political and economic views. In León, "the rebels passed through the streets of the city asking for the appointment of new judges, the establishment of a new government, the abolition of the alcohol monopoly, the reduction of the price of tobacco by two *reales*, the cheaper sale of stamped paper, the suppression of sales, wagon, and cattle slaughter taxes, and the release of prisoners."[3] In Rivas the claims of the people were even broader. In addition they demanded the reduction of tribute paid by Indians and the return of excessive levies assessed against the Indians, the control of prices and speculation, a moratorium of up to five years on the payment of taxes by poor debtors, the complete abolition of slavery, and the prohibition of Europeans from engaging in retail commerce and holding public office.[4]

Emancipation and Political Parties

The expulsion of the French from Spain and the restoration of the absolute monarchy of Ferdinand VII did not dissolve the emancipatory aspirations of the colonial domains. On the contrary, this struggle accelerated throughout the 1820s. In the city of Guatemala, seat of the royal government in Central America, the creole ideological discourse acquired greater clarity and strength. In 1820, two publications, *El Editor Constitucional* (The Constitutional Editor), directed by Pedro Molina, and *El Amigo del la Patria* (The Friend of the Fatherland), guided by José Cecilio del Valle, framed the great political-ideological debate that marked the last days of the colonial regime, and "around these newspapers were formed the first groups that would originate the political parties of the future."[5]

In the gestation period of political parties, a new social sector—"the middle sectors of society *(mestizos,* mulattos, and *zambos),*" already a third of the population of the kingdom of Guatemala[6]—appeared alongside the Indian masses. In this environment the political parties of Central America and Nicaragua were formed: the Liberal Party and the Conservative Party.

> The Liberals formulated a program based on the secularization of political life oriented toward progress, having as its pillars the unrestricted defense of civil liberty as a dike against despotism and social equality as a barrier against corporate privileges. The Conservatives...with the maintenance of national Hispanic traditions...proposed, without euphemisms, a dictatorship of the army, land owners, and the clergy.[7]

The parties clashed and then redefined and realigned themselves immediately after the eclipse of colonial power. The *cacos* or *fiebres* (liberals) became the Federalists, while the *gazistas* or *serviles* (conservatives) became Centralists. Civil war became the mechanism of exchange between the heirs of the old regime and the new social actors *(mestizos* and Indians). In the difficult period following independence, the process of political redefinition between social elites and popular sectors led to high degrees of polarization and crudity. In the heat of battle, the political parties recently created in Nicaragua forgot the classifications "liberal" and "conservative" and instead referred to *calandracas* (hungry ones) and *timbucos* (tired ones) or *desnudos* (ragged ones) and *mechudos* (dandy ones).[8] These labels underlined the different social origins of the members of the political parties, as well as the reasons for the parties' confrontation.

During the period of anarchy (1821–56), armed assaults and irregular elections characterized access to power in Nicaragua. This time was also rife with devastating civil wars. Many authors have attributed the rivalry between León ("liberal," agricultural, and the seat of local government) and Granada ("conservative" and commercial) to the redefinitions and mimicry that occurred before and after independence and to the immaturity of the political parties, whose lack of organization made them vulnerable to the influence of *caudillos* and the military. This strife between cities and groups is, however, better explained as a remnant of colonial disputes.

Political parties developed differently than those in Europe and North America, which began with the first parliament and then were furthered by external factors, but always after the consolidation of the state.[9] In Nicaragua, the embryos of the parties that emerged before independence and the proto-parties active immediately after independence were defined simultaneously with the formation of the national state in the crucible of civil war.

The 1850s

In the 1850s, one can see almost all of the elements influential in Nicaraguan politics in the nineteenth and twentieth centuries. The decade began with the Clayton-Bulwer Treaty of April 19, 1850, which buried English pretensions to control interoceanic communication through Nicaragua and the adjacent territories and implicitly recognized U.S. might. In 1854, civil war exploded again, and in June 1855, William Walker's filibusters disembarked in the Realejo, invited by one of the contenders in the civil war. In April 1856, proclamations by the centrist (conservative) *caudillo* Gen. Fruto Chamorro, and the federalist (liberal) *caudillo* Gen. Máximo Jeréz established the Legitimist Party and the Democratic Party. Walker supplanted his allies and forced his election to the presidency of the republic in September. The Nicaraguan Civil War then became the Central American National War Against the Filibuster. On September 12, legitimists and democrats made their peace and united to fight the usurper, thus giving birth to the Binary Government. Two days later Walker's troops were defeated at San Jacinto. In 1858, a new Constitution liquidated the parliamentary regime and introduced a strong executive. The next thirty-five years, the most peaceful ones of that century, witnessed the consolidation of the conservative regime of the "Thirty Years," which was overthrown in 1893 by the last Liberal revolution in America. This Liberal revolution brought with it two developments that transformed the state: first, the creation of a professional army and, second, the growth of a strong nationalist spirit. These developments led to the recovery of Mosquitia and conflicts with the United States that would lead to the Liberals' fall in 1909. The Liberals did, however, leave a substantial legacy of support for individual rights and universal suffrage, codified in the Constitution of 1893. Intervention by the United States in 1909 disrupted the relative autonomy of Nicaraguan politics. From then on the parties' struggles for power would be resolved in terms of U.S. interests.

From Postwar to Revolution

During the nineteenth century and the first half of the twentieth, the Liberal and Conservative parties dominated the national scene. Even the external factors that affected the history of the republic did not alter the bipartite political system born with it. The parties alternated power for relatively long periods (Conservatives, 1858–93; Liberals, 1893–1909; Conservatives, 1909–28; and Liberals, 1928–79).

Nonetheless a change, at first imperceptible, began to take place during the 1920s. The presence of new political figures and different forms of social and political organization warned of the system's progressive exhaustion. Labor groups began forming in 1912 and became belligerent by the 1920s. The class-based party of 1922 (Labor Party) and the one that followed it in 1931 (National Nicaraguan Worker's Party) provided another expression of change.

Loss of faith in the system resulted from a series of factors: the impetus given to social and economic development by the seigniorial regime of the conservative "Thirty Years" and the Liberal regime of Zelaya; the decay of the historical parties and their leadership during the U.S. intervention; the consolidation of external dependence; the acceleration of demographic growth; the example of social strife in other countries and advances in communication; the rivalries and conflict between the great powers and the internationalization of politics to promote social consciousness; and the disposition of the people for struggle.

The global economic crisis of the thirties and its after-effects only accelerated the crisis of the bipartite system. A wave of strikes rocked the country between 1941 and 1945 at the same time Allied propaganda against the Axis powers emphasized the promise of a world "free of misery and fear."

Diversification of Parties

In the tense and uncertain atmosphere of the Second World War, the political parties that would certify the end of the bipartite system emerged in 1944. These parties were the Socialist Nicaraguan Party (PSD) and the Liberal Independent Party (PLI). Some years later other parties appeared.

The Socialist Party of Nicaragua (PSN) was created by a small group of labor leaders who had been a part of the left wing of the Nicaraguan Workers Party (PTN). When the latter party was dissolved in 1939, this group went to Costa Rica and joined the Communist Party for two years, after which it returned to Nicaragua better equipped ideologically and politically to organize a class party clearly framed by the canons of Marxism-Leninism. This party was illegal. Conditioned by its ideological framework, by the social composition of its membership, and by legal prohibition, the PSN abandoned its social and political negotiating capacity by involving itself in the labor movement, trying to take over the organization of the incipient labor class.

The PLI originated with the fissure of the old Liberal Party caused by the elections of 1936. The Liberal and Conservative parties boycotted these elections, although factions of them did participate to validate the election of Gen. Anastasio Somoza García, head of the *Guardia Nacional*, as president. The fissure in the Liberal Party became a complete rupture seven years later when, in 1944, General Somoza García announced his intent to seek reelection for a third time. The independent Liberals, who already acted under this name within the Liberal Nationalist Party (PLN), rose in revolt against the reelection pretensions of the first Somoza. The PLI then emerged to defend political democracy in terms of the alternation of power. It was an extralegal birth because the Constitution of 1939 and the Electoral Law of 1923 only recognized the permanent existence of the "principal" parties. Nevertheless, the PLI did not question the bases of the system but, rather, sought to rescue its principles and norms, which the PLI considered threatened by the group in power.

These two parties, the PSN and the PLI, were born restricted, the former by law and the latter by the de facto power. In spite of these limitations, they did obtain legitimacy when they were recognized and admitted by political society. The country's instability and the fragility of the governing party forced Somoza Garcia to seek a broader base of support. In a typical populist game, he attracted the PSN with the promise of passing a Code of Labor to protect wage earners, a promise he fulfilled in 1945. The PLI, prevented from participating in the elections because of lack of legal recognition, allied itself with a "principal" party (the Conservatives). This alliance resoundingly defeated the government in the elections of 1947. Despite this victory, the official candidate was declared elected through the most scandalous electoral fraud in national history.

The attempts since the end of World War II to form new political parties have corresponded to the crises of bipartite rule. But the war, the reactivation of the economy in the fifties (particularly with the cotton boom), and later the expectations created in the process of Central American economic integration in the sixties also had an impact on the creation of parties. This period witnessed the birth and death of nearly two dozen political organizations, almost always founded by individuals of the middle class. These persons—reformist in most cases, but sometimes radical—often carried ideological baggage acquired in trips or studies abroad.

Aside from the historical parties, before July 19, 1979, only the Conservative Nicaraguan Party obtained legal recognition by the government in 1956, as an ad hoc alternating party, because of the abstention of the other "principal" party. The other parties had de facto recognition, at times illegal (e.g., PSN, *Sandinista* National Liberation Front [FSLN], Communist Party of Nicaragua [PCdeN], Popular Action Movement [MAP]), sometimes extralegal (e.g., PLI, Social Christian Party [PSC], Authentic Liberal Party [PLA], Authentic Conservative Party [PCA], Democratic Nicaraguan Movement [MDN], Popular Social Christian Party [PPSC], Democratic Conservative Party [PCD]). When one of these parties was able to acquire parliamentary participation (e.g.,

PLI, PSC, PLA), it was because of alliances with the Conservative Nicaraguan Party, one of the two legally recognized parties.

Pacts and Alliances

A review of recent history indicates that from 1924 to 1984 eleven general elections took place, one every five and a half years. Despite this regularity, Nicaraguan elections remained far from democratic, which prevented Nicaraguan democracy from gaining credibility among the citizens of the country and the international community.

To reduce the noticeable disadvantage of competing against a party installed in the state, decidedly monopolizing its power, the opposition developed a valuable instrument to increase its electoral capacity and negotiating power: the political alliance. The party in power, harassed by a strengthened opposition, would try to weaken it through the use of two instruments: (1) the recognition, or threat of recognition, of another political party as a political alternative, and (2) the celebration of political pacts with the "principal" party of the opposition, thus dividing the alliance through the granting of certain favors and privileges to the "principal" party. If the alliances were always, or almost always, organized with an electoral perspective, the pacts came as a response to acute crises of the government in power.

Between 1944 and 1984 two pacts were made between the government party (Nationalist Liberal) and the other "principal" party (Conservative) of Nicaragua. The first, arranged in 1950, was the Pact of the Generals. It established a ceiling and a floor for the composition of the National Congress (two-thirds for the majority and one-third for the minority). The second pact, made in 1972, is known as "Kupia Kumi" (one heart). It established new representative parliamentary limits (60 percent for the majority and 40 percent for the minority). These pacts expressed the will to accommodate political adversaries who were unable to either eliminate each other or modify each other's positions.

In the same period thirteen political alliances were formed, the majority of which (twelve) had an electoral objective and only one (National Opposition Union [UNO], 1959) of which was constituted to support an armed movement. Of the thirteen, only two participated in elections and none displaced the party in power.

Rupture and Postrevolution

The Somoza family regime, which dominated public power for more than forty years, disintegrated in Nicaragua on July 17, 1979. It was undermined and ultimately overthrown by internal and international factors activated in the critical years of 1978 and 1979. which produced the political unity of the opposition and internal insurrection, in addition to external intervention—political, diplomatic, and military. The circumstances under which the dynastic dictatorship collapsed implied not merely the replacement of a few people but the dismantling of an entire power structure.

On June 18, 1979, one month before the breakdown of the Somoza regime, a provisional government was organized in Costa Rica. The government in exile announced in its first proclamation that one of its principal objectives was the organization of a democratic system in Nicaragua. This promise was ratified soon afterward, on July 9, with the release of the Program of Government, in which the government committed itself to promulgate

> the necessary legislation for the organization of an effective democratic regime, of social justice and progress, which fully guaranteed the right of all Nicaraguans to political participation and universal suffrage, as well as the organization and functioning of political parties, without any ideological discrimination, with the exception of the parties and organizations promoting the return of Somocismo.[10]

The Program of Government proposed to create a legislative body of corporate character, which expressly included political parties. Eleven days later, on triumphantly entering the Nicaraguan capital on July 20, 1979, the provisional government dictated the Fundamental Statute of the Republic of Nicaragua. This became the legal base on which the new state was organized. Its first article established that the immediate purpose and task of the government was to implement the Program of Government, published on July 9. This implied the juridical recognition of a plurality of political parties heretofore unknown and, simultaneously, the legal liquidation of the bipartite system. Article 16 of the statute confirmed these developments and indicated that the FSLN, PLI, PPSC, PCD, MDN, MLC, PSN, and United People's Movement (MPU) were organizations with the right to participate in the (co-legislative) Council of State. A new statute of the Rights and Guarantees of Nicaraguans, approved a month later, established in Article 25 that "All citizens will have the unrestricted right to organize political parties or groups or to be a part of them."

The dismantling of the *Somocista* power structure and the definitive rupture of the bipartite political system appeared to inaugurate a pluralism indispensable to a democratic regime. The enthusiasm, however, did not last long. In a relatively short time the new regime moved to a limited pluralism. It justified this retreat by establishing the priority of reconstruction and defense of the revolution. This move signified a policy of restricting the activities of the political parties, except the government party, the FSLN.

The FSLN approved the first Law of Political Parties in the history of Nicaragua (August 17, 1983) in which political parties were forced to "promote and support the patriotic unity of the nation."[11] The law could have resulted in the cancellation of the legality of a party considered to transgress it. The restrictions included in the Law of Political Parties suggested a change in orientation in the *Sandinista* leadership with respect to both political parties and elections in the national political process. Public statements by high officials of the FSLN indicated that elections were not needed because "the people have already voted with guns" or because "we will not lose with votes what we gained with bullets." In addition, pressure was applied to political parties by the official party through its own agencies or through the state's apparatus.

Seen from this perspective, there was no important difference between the bipartite system of the old regime and the limited pluralism of the *Sandinista* regime because both systems operated as mechanisms of containment or dissuasion over the power aspirations of the parties. Bipartite government induced control through the political alternator (the other "principal" party), which became the catalyst of support. Limited pluralism controlled through the dispersion of equal political organizations but limited their rights so they could not compete effectively with the ruling party.

The first elections that took place in Nicaragua after July 19, 1979, were those of November 4, 1984, five years after the new regime was installed and almost ten years after the last elections of the old regime (1975). The electoral project faced a difficult road, both because the country required so much attention to bring it back to normality after the destruction of the dictatorial regime and because of repeated statements against elections by FSLN leaders who were also high government officials.

The requests of political parties, as well as a growing international concern, forced the government to elaborate basic laws. The Political Parties Law was ready in July 1983 and the Electoral Law was prepared in December. The Electoral Law was widely publicized during its preparation and provided a few new measures, such as the right to vote without restrictions at the age of sixteen. The electoral apparatus itself was almost identical to the one established previously. The introduction of a national identity document, with an electoral function, was rejected by the government, along with other measures geared to guaranteeing the purity of the vote.

In January 1984 the government surprised the political parties with a new decree that speeded up the electoral process. The electoral campaign was to be conducted from August to October and the vote held on November 4. These changes had been suggested by some foreign governments and international organizations (e.g., the Socialist International) to prevent the U.S. government from justifying more aid to the armed irregulars opposed to the FSLN since 1982. This armed opposition justified its existence because of the antidemocratic nature of the FSLN.

The electoral process was plagued by irregularities of all kinds. A state of emergency was maintained until July 31, thus restricting the parties' preparatory activities for the elections. Advance funding for electoral campaigns was distributed when the campaigns had already begun. The territorial demarcations necessary for registration and voting were not released to the political parties so they could prepare their representatives in a timely fashion. The registration process was verified under the exclusive control of the FSLN and the *Sandinista* Defense Committees, a partisan organization charged with notifying the citizens where they had to register. The use of electronic media discriminated against nongovernmental parties and favored the official party. The Supreme Electoral Council fixed a thirty-minute limit of television time and forty-five-minute limit of radio time per week for each party. In reality the FSLN was never subject to these limits because, as the party in government, it had continued access to the state radio station.

Two additional elements served to disadvantage the nongovernmental parties: the first was the selective use of compulsory military service to demobilize the opposition's youth; the second was the attacks of official shock groups *(turbas)* on opposing politicians. For these and other reasons, three of the original ten parties initially participating in the elections withdrew, leaving seven: the FSLN, PLI, PCD, PPSC, PSN, PCdeN, and the Marxist-Leninist Popular Action Group [MAP-ML]. Under these circumstances, along with the conditions of war, the first electoral process of the post-1979 years took place on November 4, 1984.

The results of the 1984 elections gave a victory to the government party, the FSLN. According to the Supreme Electoral Council, the FSLN obtained 67 percent of the valid votes, thus winning the presidency, and 63.5 percent of the seats in the National Assembly, against 36.5 percent of the seats assigned to the other six participating parties.

The comfortable majority obtained by the FSLN in the 1984 elections permitted it to model the country's institutions according to its ideological interpretation of social reality. Limited, however, by the surrounding geopolitical environment, the FSLN was forced to proceed with ambiguity in developing the juridical framework of the state. The civil war, governmental incapacity, and corruption radically diminished the following of the official party, whose capacity to influence came to reside with the military and security apparatus.

The Nicaraguan political process in 1984 did not yet offer acceptable levels of confidence for participating political parties. Sometimes the failures could be attributed to the party system, which had not yet matured, but external stimuli also caused instability and rigidity. The most notable result of this process was the exclusion practiced from the seat of power and boycott or abstention frequently used by the opposition. Nor did the 1984 elections do anything to resolve Nicaragua's basic internal conflicts. The boycott by the major opposition parties exacerbated the animosity between them and the *Sandinistas*, making national dialogue and reconciliation harder to achieve.[12]

Notes

1. Severo Martínez Peláez, *La Patria del Criollo* (San José: Educa), pp. 37, 107.

2. Filander Díaz Chávez, *Sociología de la Desintegración Regional* (Tegucigalpa, D.C.: Universidad Autónoma de Honduras, 1972), p. 116.

3. Tomás Ayón, *Historia de Nicaragua* (Managua: Ediciones del Banco de América, 1977), 3:444.

4. Ibid., pp. 453–56.

5. José Mata Gavidia, *Anotaciones de Historia Patria Centroamericano*, (Guatemala City: Editorial Universitaria), p. 273.

6. Martínez Peláez, *La Patria*, p. 259.

7. Edmundo Vásquez Martínez and Jorge Mario García Laguardia, *Constitución y Orden Democrático* (Guatemala: Universidad de San Carlos, 1984), pp. 40–41.

8. José Dolores Gámez, *Historia de Nicaragua* (Managua: Ediciones Banco de América, 1975), pp. 473, 540–41.

9. Maurice Duverger, *Los Partidos Políticos*, 9th ed. (Mexico City: Fondo de Cultura Económica, 1984), p. 16.

10. "Programa de Gobierno (Original), Area Política, 1.1," in *Leyes de la República* (Managua: Ministerio de Justicia, 1979), p. 10. Emphasis added.

11. Article 7, "Law of Political Parties" (Managua: Publications of the Supreme Electoral Council, n.d.).

12. In 1990, Virgilio Godoy Reyes, author of this article, ran as a vice presidential candidate under the UNO coalition. This chapter was written two years earlier, when Godoy was still working as an opposition leader within his country. The chapter that follows, by William M. LeoGrande, brings the Nicaraguan story up-to-date.

11

Political Parties
and Postrevolutionary Politics
in Nicaragua

William M. LeoGrande

Although political parties proliferated in Nicaragua during the decades after World War II, the ruling Somoza family never allowed them to play a central role in politics. Constrained by legal limitations and repression, most parties remained small, weak, and divided. Rarely did they develop any significant grass-roots organization; their realm of operation was normally restricted to the middle and upper classes. The legitimacy of these parties was undercut by their willingness to cooperate with the regime. Time after time, Somoza lured them into unequal "alliances" with the government. Among the populace, such coopted politicians were scorned as *zancudos*—blood-sucking mosquitos.

When Anastasio Somoza Debayle was overthrown on July 19, 1979, Nicaragua's political landscape was dominated by a single non-traditional party: the *Sandinista* National Liberation Front *(Frente Sandinista de Liberación Nacional,* FSLN). Although the *Sandinistas* allowed other parties to exist (and many new ones formed as the traditional parties went through multiple fissions), the *Sandinistas'* vision of the new Nicaraguan polity was less than pluralistic. They conceived of the FSLN as a political vanguard that would monopolize political power while directing a revolutionary transformation of society.[1]

Fragmented in a welter of civic and business groups, the opposition to the FSLN was badly disorganized and had no access to the government. To exert influence, it had to rely on the same weapons it used to good effect against Somoza: control over much of the economy and enough foreign contacts to make or break the international reputation of the regime. The private sector tried to use its economic muscle to extract political concessions from the *Sandinistas,* warning that the "rules of the game" both economically and politically had to be codified in law before business confidence would improve enough to spur production. Despite their tenuous political position, most businessmen were determined to stay in Nicaragua and struggle with the *Sandinistas* for the right to define Nicaragua's future. "We are not like the Cuban upper class," vowed one Nicaraguan businessman. "We are not going to Miami."[2] In the United States, both the Carter and Reagan administrations sought to bolster the "civic opposition," as it was called, by providing various groups (business associations, trade unions, political parties, and the media) with both overt and covert financial support through the U.S. Agency for International Development and the Central Intelligence Agency (CIA).[3]

From the beginning, the issue of elections was one of the main points of conflict between the *Sandinistas* and the conservative wing of the anti-Somoza coalition. The civic opposition pressed for immediate elections after Somoza was ousted in 1979, whereas the *Sandinistas* argued that the nation's energies should first be devoted to economic reconstruction; elections could wait. The *Sandinistas'* refusal to schedule elections contributed to Alfonso Robelo's and Violeta Chamorro's resignations from the governing junta in April 1980. As part of the negotiated settlement resolving this first crisis between the *Sandinistas* and the civic opposition, the *Sandinistas* pledged to announce a date for elections by July 19, 1980. The deadline came and went, however, with no announcement. The opposition was not much happier when the *Sandinistas* finally announced that elections would not be held until 1985. In early 1984, the *Sandinistas* accelerated the timetable by scheduling elections for president, vice-president, and a ninety-member national assembly on November 4, 1984.

During the early 1980s, the increase in armed attacks on Nicaragua by exile forces (known as the "*Contras*") based in Honduras and Costa Rica polarized Nicaragua's domestic politics and poisoned relations between the *Sandinistas* and the civic opposition. Escalating *Contra* attacks strengthened the hand of hard-liners on both sides. Many opponents of the *Sandinistas* had been willing to seek accommodation because the only alternative was exile. But as Washington's commitment to the *Contra* War escalated, hard-liners in the civic opposition could credibly argue that, one way or another, the United States would eventually remove the *Sandinistas.* A strategy of accommodation was unnecessary.

Among the *Sandinistas,* the civic opposition's intransigence in dealing with the government and its willingness to collaborate with the *Contras* seemed to prove the hard-line *Sandinistas* right when they argued that civic opponents were nothing but *vendepatrias*—a fifth column willing to sell out their country to the United States. The *Sandinistas'* tolerance for internal opposition declined as the war intensified. Emergency laws were imposed restricting the opposition's ability to organize and criticize the regime. "We're in war.... We won't accept neutrals," explained junta member Sergio Ramirez, who was by reputation one of the *least* hard-line *Sandinistas*. "Either you're against the [counterrevolution] or you're for it. We can't accept disguised support for the counterrevolutionaries, be it religious, political, or whatever."[4]

Small to begin with, the opposition political parties were hamstrung by censorship, harassment, and the emergency laws banning outside rallies or demonstrations. The laws didn't prevent *Sandinista* supporters *(turbas)* from demonstrating outside the homes and offices of opposition leaders, sometimes breaking up their meetings. Police frequently detained opposition politicians for questioning, warning them to mend their counterrevolutionary ways. Some who were businessmen had their property confiscated. Only the Catholic church enjoyed a limited immunity from such constraints, and its archbishop, Miguel Obando y Bravo, soon emerged as the leading critic of the *Sandinista* regime.

The 1984 Elections: For External Consumption

The civic opposition was divided over whether to participate in the 1984 election. Several parties that had been coalition partners with the *Sandinistas* decided to run against them from the right: the Democratic Conservative Party (PCD), the Independent Liberal Party (PLI), and the Popular Social Christian Party (PPSC). Three small leftist parties ran against the *Sandinistas* as well. But the parties that had been the most vocal critics of the *Sandinistas* since 1979 were united in a loose coalition called the Democratic Coordinating Committee, known popularly as *La Coordinadora Democratica*. Many of its members were unwilling to legitimize the *Sandinistas* by participating in an election that they did not believe they could win.[5]

Few people thought the *Sandinistas* could be defeated even in a fair election, let alone one in which they could take full advantage of their incumbency. Even the U.S. embassy expected the *Sandinistas* to win at least a plurality of the vote.[6] And if they won, they were unlikely to change their domestic policies significantly. For both the *Sandinistas* and their opponents, the 1984 election was more important for influencing international audiences than for allocating political power inside Nicaragua.[7]

The *Sandinistas* urgently needed to improve their international image. The limitations on political liberty imposed by the state of emergency at the beginning of the *Contra* War in 1982 had tarnished the *Sandinistas'* reputation among Latin American and Western European democrats. Countries like Mexico and Venezuela, which had helped the *Sandinistas* both financially and politically, were becoming impatient with Nicaragua's growing authoritarianism.[8] With the country running an annual balance of payments deficit of $500 million, economic aid from Latin America and Europe was indispensable. A reasonably fair election might reopen their coffers.

The 1984 elections were also aimed at Washington. The absence of democracy in Nicaragua was one of the "pretexts" the Reagan administratration used to justify its hostility toward the *Sandinistas,* explained Bayardo Arce, National Directorate member in charge of the campaign. A key reason for holding elections was to "take away from American policy one of its justifications for aggression against Nicaragua."[9]

Arce represented the radical tendency within the *Sandinista* leadership, which regarded the elections not as an exercise in democracy but as a "nuisance" forced on the FSLN by international circumstances. "If we did not have the war situation imposed on us by the United States," Arce confided in a speech to the Marxist Nicaraguan Socialist Party, "the electoral problem would be totally out of place in terms of its usefulness." Elections were a "bourgeois formality" that interfered with the construction of socialism. But, like the continued existence of the private sector, they were necessary.[10]

Like the *Sandinistas,* the civic opposition also saw the elections more as a battle for international legitimacy than for domestic power. Badly fragmented into ten different parties, none of which had much organization or grass-roots support, the opposition was no match for the highly organized and disciplined FSLN. "They have no leaders, no program, and so few members that they would have a hard time coming up with poll watchers in an election," said one western ambassador in Managua.[11]

Some members of the civic opposition argued that even if they stood little chance of winning, the campaign would give them an unprecedented opportunity to organize, present their message to the Nicaraguan people, and establish an important democratic precedent—that political power is subject to periodic elections. A rejectionist group argued that participation played into the hands of the *Sandinistas* by ratifying their legitimacy. The precedent of elections would be worth little if the *Sandinistas* were able to consolidate their rule. The election should be boycotted. "They are doing this just to put up a front and fool the world," said Superior Council of Private Enterprise (COSEP) president Enrique Bolanos in calling for an election boycott.[12]

Both in Nicaragua and abroad, attention focused on whether the *Sandinistas* could entice the reluctant *Coordinadora* parties into the election. In Washington, especially, the participation of this major opposition coalition was regarded as the litmus test of whether the election was fair. The *Coordinadora* nominated Arturo Cruz as a candidate, but despite marathon negotiations between the *Sandinistas* and the *Coordinadora* facilitated by Colombia, Venezuela, and the Socialist International, agreement could not be reached on campaign conditions. Cruz refused to file as a candidate and the *Coordinadora* urged its supporters to boycott the election.

Once Cruz was irrevocably out of the race, the United States worked diligently behind the scenes to pressure all the conservative opposition parties to join the boycott. "In an election that the opposition could not win, it was better to have them out," explained a State Department official.[13] Virgilio Godoy's Independent Liberal Party withdrew from the race; however, the withdrawal occurred so late that Godoy's name remained on the ballot. "Under the conditions they are giving us, we have as much chance as a cat who is tied into a sack and thrown into a river," Godoy said by way of explanation.[14] The Democratic Conservative Party split over whether to withdraw.

On November 4, 1984, 75 percent of registered voters participated in the first Nicaraguan election since the ouster of Somoza, but with most of the major opposition parties boycotting the process the result could not be taken as a real test of the *Sandinistas'* support. Though the *Sandinistas* won handily, they did not do as well as many observers expected. Daniel Ortega received 67 percent of the presidential vote, Clemente Guido (Democratic Conservative Party) came in second with 14 percent, Virgilio Godoy (Independent Liberal Party) finished third with 9.6 percent, and Mauricio Diaz (Popular Social Christian Party) was fourth with 5.6 percent. Three leftist opposition parties together polled only 3.8 percent of the vote.[15] In the assembly elections, the *Sandinistas* won 63 percent of the vote and 61 of the 96 seats. The Democratic Conservatives won 14 seats, the Independent Liberals 9, the Popular Social Christians 6, and the leftist parties 2 each.[16]

In taking a third of the vote, the conservative opposition showed surprising strength, given the fact that the *Coordinadora* boycotted the race and the parties that participated did so half-heartedly. A high-ranking U.S. diplomat in Managua lamented that if the opposition had participated fully, it might have done even better and initiated a real process of democratization. The election, he said, was "a terrible missed opportunity," and it was not all the fault of the FSLN. "I give 60 percent of the blame to the *Sandinistas* and the rest to COSEP."[17] Arturo Cruz agreed and later said he regretted not staying in the race.[18]

The Crisis Deepens

Nicaragua's 1984 elections did nothing to resolve the country's conflicts. The boycott by the major opposition parties exacerbated the animosity between them and the *Sandinistas*, making national dialogue and reconciliation harder to achieve. The United States refused to accept the elections as legitimate and continued its policy of covert funding for the *Contras*.

When, in the summer of 1985, the U.S. Congress voted to resume aid to the *Contras* after a one-year ban on such assistance, the *Sandinistas* responded by closing the limited political space that had been opened for the 1984 election campaign. In October 1985, President Daniel Ortega announced a new state of emergency, which effectively suspended all civil liberties for a year. Although Nicaragua had been under a formal state of emergency since the beginning of the *Contra* War in March 1982, most limitations on the political rights of the opposition had been relaxed during the 1984 campaign. The new emergency decree reimposed tough restrictions, suspending the right to assembly, freedom of speech, freedom of the press, the right to travel, the right to strike, and most guarantees of due process. Ortega justified the decree as a necessary response to Washington's resumption of *Contra* aid and its enlistment of "allies and agents of imperialism" in "political parties...communications media or religious institutions" to engage in "political destabilization."[19]

Another catalyst for the crackdown appeared to be an escalating confrontation between the *Sandinista* regime and the Catholic church. The government's first act under the new decree was to confiscate the entire print run of a new Catholic periodical, *Iglesia,* which criticized the unpopular military draft. Several opposition party leaders were summoned to the Ministry of Interior and warned not to violate the new decree; some were briefly arrested. But except for intensified censorship of *La Prensa,* opposition leaders carried on much as before.[20]

A year later, in 1985, when the U.S. Congress approved Ronald Reagan's request for $100 million in *Contra* aid to escalate the Nicaraguan War, the *Sandinistas* again responded by punishing the internal opposition. The government closed the newspaper *La Prensa,* expelled from the country outspoken critics in the Catholic church hierarchy, and warned opposition parties that the limits on political expression under the state of emergency would be strictly enforced. "The United States takes actions, and we pay the price," lamented opposition leader Virgilio Godoy.[21]

In the years after the 1984 election, the *Contra* War became the central fact of Nicaraguan life. The war dragged on, costing Nicaragua billions of dollars in destroyed infrastructure and lost production and some 50,000 casualties. War damage, U.S. economic sanctions, and ill-conceived *Sandinista* economic policies combined to send the economy into a tailspin.

The most significant effect of the war was the diversion of resources from economic development to military defense. By 1986, 55 percent of the government's budget was devoted to fighting the war, a figure that held constant through 1988. With production declining, tax revenues could not begin to cover the costs of the conflict, so the government closed the fiscal gap by simply printing money. That, of course, unleashed inflation. In 1987, the inflation rate was 1,800 percent. The government took its supplies of old 20 and 50 cordoba bank notes and simply printed three more zeroes on them to make 20,000 and 50,000 cordoba notes.[22] In 1988 the government's austerity measures, intended to control inflation by reducing public spending, triggered a severe recession. The economy contracted 9 percent, and the fiscal deficit widened. Inflation raged completely out of control, reaching 36,000 percent—hyperinflation of the sort experienced by only a few nations in history. As money became worthless, the economy was reduced to primitive barter, further dislocating production and exchange. By the end of the year, unemployment stood at 33 percent and real income had fallen 90 percent from its 1979 level.[23]

From Esquipulas to the 1990 Elections

For the *Sandinistas*, peace became imperative. In August 1987, Daniel Ortega, along with the other four Central American presidents, signed the Central American (Esquipulas II) peace accord. Each government pledged itself to democratic pluralism, free elections, and a concerted effort to end internal fighting by seeking a cease-fire with its armed opponents and initiating a process of political reconciliation. Each country promised to refrain from providing support or refuge for armed insurgents in the region, and together they called on other governments to do the same.

To comply with the agreement, the *Sandinistas* created the National Reconciliation Commission, which included an opposition party leader, a neutral Protestant clergyman, and, as chair, Cardinal Miguel Obando y Bravo, their harshest critic. Over the next few weeks, the government allowed the Catholic radio station to resume broadcasts and *La Prensa* to resume publishing, allowed exiled members of the Catholic church hierarchy to return to the country, and lifted restrictions on the internal opposition's right to hold demonstrations.

When the Central American presidents met in Costa Rica on January 15, 1988, to review progress on the Esquipulas accord, Daniel Ortega stole the headlines by finally agreeing to open direct talks with the *Contras*. He also announced that the *Sandinistas* would lift the state of emergency limiting the civic opposition's political liberties, hold free elections, and give up political power if they lost.[24]

In March the *Sandinistas* and *Contras* meeting in the small Nicaraguan town of Sapoa signed a cease-fire agreement. The agreement embodied most of the *Contras* demands. The *Sandinistas* agreed to a general amnesty for both the *Contras* and the remaining members of Somoza's National Guard still imprisoned for war crimes. Exiles would be allowed to return to the country without fear of prosecution and could participate fully in national political life. The *Contras* would be allowed to send delegates to the "national dialogue" between the *Sandinistas* and the civic opposition over how to carry out the Esquipulas agreement. Although sporadic fighting continued throughout the next two years, full-scale combat operations did not resume.

Once the *Sandinistas* relaxed legal constraints on free expression, as mandated by the Esquipulas agreement, the civic opposition roared to life. A new, broad coalition of opposition parties, the Group of Fourteen, was formed in 1987, and included most of the parties from the Democratic Coordinating Committee that boycotted the 1984 election and the parties (even some of the leftist ones) that participated in that election. With the Nicaraguan economy disintegrating, the civic opposition saw a tremendous opportunity to rally public opinion to its side. The *Sandinistas* saw that possibility, too. Fearful that Washington's financial support would transform the opposition into a formidable foe, the *Sandinistas* sought to constrain its activities. But the guarantees of democracy in the Esquipulas accord limited what the government could do. Its main strategy was harassment and intimidation. In January 1988, for example, shortly after the state of emergency was lifted, the *Sandinista* police arrested twelve opposition leaders to question them about their ties to the *Contras*. All were released within a day or two, but the *Sandinista* newspaper, *Barricada*, warned that the opposition should not treat the restoration of civil liberties as "a blank check for irresponsibility and subversion."[25]

In February 1989, the five Central American presidents met again at Tesoro Beach, El Salvador, and signed another accord specifically designed to resolve the Nicaraguan conflict. The *Sandinistas* agreed to move up their national elections from November to February 1990 to guarantee full freedom for the opposition to organize and campaign and to allow extensive international observation to assure the fairness of the electoral process. In return, the other presidents called, yet again, for the demobilization of the *Contras*.

Over the next year, election preparations were made under close international supervision by the Organization of American States, the United Nations, and a delegation headed by former U.S. President Jimmy Carter. In June 1989, the Group of Fourteen formed the *Unión Nacional Opositora* (UNO) as an electoral coalition to run against the *Sandinistas*.[26] Over the years, however, fragmentation of the opposition had become so severe that eight opposition parties (four on the left and four on the right) remained outside the UNO coalition, determined to run on their own.[27]

In August 1989, on the eve of another Central American presidents' summit, the *Sandinistas* signed a sweeping accord with all of the opposition parties, settling almost all of the outstanding disputes over the conduct of the upcoming election. "Ninety-five percent of our demands have been met," said an opposition leader emerging from the final negotiating session. In exchange for these *Sandinista* concessions, the opposition echoed the government's call for demobilization of the *Contras* and repudiated any covert (i.e., CIA) interference in the election campaign.[28]

Popular discontent with the *Sandinista* government, mainly resulting from the economic collapse, was undoubtedly high. If UNO could unify behind a single candidate and put forward a credible political program, it would stand an excellent chance of winning the February 1990 election. But centripetal forces were intense within the diverse coalition, which included both rightists and communists. The UNO nearly fell apart when it deadlocked over who to select to head its ticket. The rightist parties wanted to nominate COSEP president Enrique Bolanos; the moderates wanted PLI leader Virgilio Godoy. As a compromise, they settled on Violeta Chamorro, the publisher of *La Prensa* and widow of editor Pedro Joaquin Chamorro, whose murder in January 1978 sparked the insurrection against Somoza. The UNO barely held together through the campaign; without encouragement and occasional mediation by the U.S. embassy, the coalition might well have collapsed.

Political advice was not all Washington offered. The Bush administration also provided material assistance to the opposition. Fearing that the United States would try to affect the election's outcome by pouring resources into the opposition's campaign, the *Sandinista* majority in the Nicaraguan National Assembly had passed a law in October 1988 making it a crime for Nicaraguan parties to accept foreign funds for political purposes. Under intense international pressure, however, the *Sandinistas* relented in early 1989 and legalized foreign campaign contributions, providing that 50 percent of the funds went to the Supreme Electoral Council to defray the administrative costs of the election.

Washington then channeled most of its aid to UNO through the quasi-public, quasi-private National Endowment for Democracy (NED). The NED had been providing aid to Nicaraguan opposition trade unions and press outlets since 1985. No one pretended it was nonpartisan. As one of NED's directors, Sally Shelton-Colby, described its operations in Nicaragua, "The whole thrust of this program is to help the opposition coalesce and overcome their historical differences, and develop a national political structure with a view to getting their message into all corners of Nicaragua."[29]

Still, NED's charter explicitly prohibited it from giving money to "finance the campaigns of candidates for public office." Recipients of NED funds were not supposed to use the money for campaigning in support of Chamorro, but they were allowed use it for voter registration and education, poll-watching, and "party-building" activities. These were distinctions without much difference; no one had the slightest doubt that the aid was intended to strengthen UNO's ability to challenge the *Sandinistas* at the polls. In all, NED provided $11.6 million to the opposition ($3.9 million appropriated for fiscal year 1989 and $7.7 million for 1990)—a program that NED President Carl Gershman admitted "dwarfed" previous NED election support programs in Chile and the Philippines. An additional $1.2 million was approved to finance international observation of the election process.[30]

Although the opposition parties complained at first that the Supreme Electoral Council would be biased in favor of the *Sandinistas,* its exemplary administration of the electoral process was applauded by all concerned.[31] The campaign was conducted throughout the fall of 1989 under close international observation and with a minimum of violence. When incidents of fighting and rock throwing escalated in November and December, climaxing in a riot at an UNO rally in the town of Masatepe in which one person was killed, the internal observer missions (especially the one headed by President Carter) and the Electoral Council mediated an agreement between the *Sandinistas* and UNO to head off further violence. Incidents between the two campaigns subsided, although a number of *Sandinista* campaigners were killed by *Contras* in conflicted areas.[32]

In the months before the election, several major independent public opinion polls showed Ortega running far ahead of Chamorro. Some reporters had doubts about the polling results because they seemed to contradict the population's widespread discontent with the economy, but in most cases, the doubts were submerged by the extraordinary *Sandinista* campaign, which was far more extensive and sophisticated than UNO's.

FSLN organizers, banners, and assorted paraphernalia were everywhere, while UNO was virtually invisible until just before the election. The *Sandinistas* out-spent the opposition by a wide margin, using every accoutrement of the modern political campaign—direct mail, automatic telephone dialing, rock concerts, and television advertising. Even with help from Washington, UNO had nothing comparable. *Sandinista* rallies were routinely much larger than the opposition's, culminating in the final FSLN rally of 300,000 people—almost five times the size of UNO's closing rally on February 21.[33] In most elections, such stark differences in the quality of two campaigns would be enough to settle the outcome.

In the end, the campaign itself probably meant little. The election was a referendum on ten years of *Sandinista* rule, and no campaign could overcome the government's record of economic calamity. The *Sandinistas* tried to diffuse the economic issue by appealing to nationalism, linking UNO with the *Contras* and the United States. Polls indicated that the issue of the war seemed to benefit the *Sandinistas*, whereas the issue of the economy favored UNO. By focusing on the war, the *Sandinistas* hoped to escape, Houdini-like, from the political consequences of the country's economic collapse. It didn't work. Eight years of the *Contra* War had destroyed all of the material gains of the revolution's first few years, leaving little in its wake but death and privation.

On February 25, 1990, the election was held without incident and UNO won in a landslide victory. Chamorro won 54.7 percent of the popular vote to Ortega's 40.8 percent, and UNO won fifty-one seats in the ninety-three-member National Assembly compared to the *Sandinistas'* thirty-nine. The decisive issues were the terrible state of the economy, the *Sandinistas'* refusal to end the highly unpopular military draft, and the public's doubt that the *Sandinistas* would be able to make peace with Washington and bring the *Contra* War to a definitive conclusion.

The transfer of power from Ortega to Chamorro proceeded with surprising smoothness. The stunned *Sandinistas* accepted their unexpected defeat and prepared to transform themselves from governing party into loyal opposition. Transition teams from the outgoing and incoming administrations negotiated agreements on key issues, such as control over the armed forces and maintenance of the agrarian reform program. But the main obstacle to a peaceful transition was the continued existence of the *Contra* army, which, despite several agreements among the Central American presidents, had still not been demobilized. The *Sandinistas* warned repeatedly that the *Contras* would have to be disbanded before Chamorro's inauguration or else civil war might erupt.

Both the UNO transition team and the United States urged the *Contras* to disarm and repatriate to Nicaragua, but the *Contras* themselves were reluctant to lay down their weapons as long as the *Sandinistas* retained control of the armed forces. On March 23, 1990, *Contra* commanders signed an agreement with the Chamorro transition team in which they promised to demobilize their Honduran-based troops by April 20, five days before Chamorro's inauguration. But simultaneously they began infiltrating most of their fighters back into Nicaragua, where they agreed in principle to disarm but procrastinated in accepting any specific deadline. On April 19, the *Sandinista* government, the Chamorro transition team, and the *Contra* commanders signed agreements for a cease-fire and the demobilization of the *Contras* inside Nicaragua beginning on inauguration day and concluding three weeks later, by June 10.[34] Nicaragua's long and bloody conflict had finally come to an end.

On April 25, 1990, Violeta Chamorro was inaugurated president in the national stadium, where *Sandinista* supporters and UNO supporters sat on opposite sides, jeering at one another, but avoiding any incidents of violence.

The *Sandinistas* in Opposition

The *Sandinistas* settled into the new and unfamiliar role of electoral opposition, but they retained important bases of power. They were still the largest single political party and by far the best organized. With supporters all across the country in trade unions, peasant associations, and student groups, the *Sandinistas* had the capacity to "rule from below," as Daniel Ortega put it. They could mount mass demonstrations and strikes to force their demands on the UNO government and, in the event of confrontation, make Nicaragua virtually ungovernable, as happened when *Sandinista* unions called general strikes in May and July 1990.

The *Sandinistas* retained considerable influence within the government bureaucracy, especially the military, much of which had been staffed by *Sandinista* loyalists after the fall of Somoza. Despite opposition from hard-liners within her own UNO coalition and from the United States, Chamorro decided to retain *Sandinista* leader Humberto Ortega as commander of the armed forces as a gesture of reconciliation. In exchange, the *Sandinistas* agreed to allow the dismantling of the internal security forces attached to the Ministry of the Interior and to accept substantial reductions in the size of the regular armed forces.

Chamorro's appointment of Ortega opened the first rift between Chamorro and a more conservative element of the UNO coalition led by her vice president, Virgilio Godoy. Over the next two years, Nicaraguan politics evolved into a three-way struggle among Chamorro and her supporters, Godoy and his, and the *Sandinistas*. Chamorro advocated a policy of national reconciliation to heal the deep wounds in the body politic. In pursuit of that objective, she was willing to cooperate with the *Sandinistas*. Godoy criticized the president for being too conciliatory toward her former adversaries. The *Sandinistas*, for their part, sought to strike a balance between cooperating with Chamorro to stabilize the economy and defending the interests of their poor constituents who were hard hit by the government's stabilization plan. They also underwent an agonizing internal debate over their failures while in power and the future of socialism in the aftermath of events in Eastern Europe and the Soviet Union. At times Chamorro loyalists and *Sandinista* delegates in the assembly joined forces to defeat Godoy's conservatives. On other occasions, the original UNO coalition came back together to defeat the *Sandinistas*.

By far the worst problem facing the country in 1991 and 1992 was still the economy, which deteriorated even further during Chamorro's first two years in power. Political violence reappeared as some former *Contras* took up arms against the Chamorro government for failing to provide the economic benefits promised when the *Contras* demobilized. Some *Sandinista* supporters in remote areas took up arms as well to defend themselves against raids by these "re-*Contras*." Whether Nicaragua would develop a stable electoral democracy depended in large measure on the ability of its principal parties to set aside their differences long enough to reverse the country's economic decay. Failing that, the danger of a new civil war lurked ominously in the background.

Notes

1. Dennis Gilbert, *Sandinistas: The Party and the Revolution* (Cambridge, Mass.: Basil Blackwell, 1988), pp. 19–34.

2. Interview with COSEP official William Baez, Managua, Nicaragua, November 1980.

3. Don Oberdorfer and Patrick E. Tyler, "U.S. Backed Nicaraguan Rebel Army Swells to 7000 Men," *Washington Post*, May 8, 1983; Leslie H. Gelb, "Argentina Linked to Rise in Covert U.S. Actions Against Sandinistas," *New York Times*, April 8, 1983.

4. Alan Riding, "Sandinistas Say U.S. Seeks to Overthrow Them," *New York Times*, March 27, 1983.

5. The *Coordinadora* included the Superior Council of Private Enterprise (COSEP), the opposition newspaper *La Prensa*, two conservative trade union federations (the Confederation for Labor Unification, CUS, which received aid from the AFL-CIO's American Institute for Free Labor Development; and the Nicaraguan Workers Central, CTN, which was linked to the Social Christians), and four political parties—*Partido Social Cristiano* (PSC), *Partido Liberal Constitucionalista* (PLC), *Partido Social Democrata* (PSD), and *Partido Conservador Nicaraguense* (PCN).

6. Robert G. Kaiser, "Yankees Are a Sandinista's Best Enemy," *Washington Post*, January 16, 1983.

7. Dennis Gilbert, "Nicaragua," in *Confronting Revolution: Security Through Diplomacy in Central America*, ed. Morris J. Blachman, William M. LeoGrande, and Kenneth Sharpe (New York: Pantheon, 1986), pp. 88–124.

8. Stephen Kinzer, "Nicaragua Offer of Conciliation Aimed at Critics," *New York Times*, November 25, 1983.

9. "Las elecciones son parte integral de la defensa," *Barricada* (Managua, Nicaragua), 21 July 1984, as quoted in William I. Robinson and Kent Norsworthy, "Elections and U.S. Intervention in Nicaragua," *Latin American Perspectives* 12, no. 2 (Spring 1985):83–110.

10. U.S. Department of State, *Comandante Bayardo Arce's Secret Speech Before the Nicaraguan Socialist Party* (PSN).

11. Interview with a senior western diplomat, Managua, Nicaragua, August 1983. This was no exaggeration. None of the opposition parties was able to put poll watchers at more than 10 percent of the polling stations on election day. *The Electoral Process in Nicaragua: Domestic and International Influences*, Report of the Latin American Studies Association (LASA) Delegation to Observe the Nicaraguan General Election of November 4, 1984 (Austin, Tex.: LASA, 1984), p. 13.

12. Edward Cody, "Sandinista Foes Doubt Pledges on Elections," *Washington Post*, January 17, 1984.

13. Roy Gutman, *Banana Diplomacy: The Making of American Policy in Nicaragua, 1981–1987* (New York: Simon and Schuster, 1988), p. 253.

14. UPI, "Ortega Hits Vote Pullout by Party," *Washington Post*, October 23, 1984.

15. *Electoral Process in Nicaragua*, p. 17. The three leftist parties were the *Partido Comunista de Nicaragua* (PCdeN), *Partido Socialist Nicaraguense* (PSN), and *Movimiento de Acción Popular Marxista Leninista* (MAP-ML).

16. Stephen Kinzer, "Sandinistas Win 63 Percent of Vote in Final Tally," *New York Times*, November 15, 1984.

17. Robert J. McCartney, "Vote Boycott Lamented," *Washington Post*, November 3, 1984.

18. Robert A. Pastor, *Condemned to Repetition: The United States and Nicaragua* (Princeton: Princeton University Press, 1987), p. 250.

19. Edward Cody, "Nicaraguan Crackdown Seen Aimed at Church," *Washington Post*, October 17, 1985.

20. Stephen Kinzer, "Nicaraguans Split on Curbs Effect," *New York Times*, October 17, 1985; Stephen Kinzer, "In Nicaragua, Rights Curbs Bring Uncertainty and More Censorship," *New York Times*, October 24, 1985.

21. Stephen Kinzer, "Sandinistas Indefinitely Shut Down Opposition Paper," *New York Times*, June 28, 1986.

22. Julia Preston, "Inflation Runs Away in Managua," *Washington Post*, January 22, 1985.

23. Guy Gugliotta, "Nicaraguans Suffer in Sick Economy," *Miami Herald*, January 26, 1989; Mark A. Uhlig, "Managua Acts to Revive Business," *New York Times*, February 2, 1989; Tim Coone, "Nicaragua Economic Policy Attacked After Fares Rise," *Financial Times of London*, January 6, 1989.

24. James LeMoyne, "Nicaragua Agrees to Talk Directly with Contras," *New York Times*, January 17, 1988.

25. Quoted in Stephen Kinzer, "Managua Detains Five More Leaders of the Opposition," *New York Times*, January 20, 1988.

26. UNO included *Partido Liberal Constitucionalista* (PLC); *Movimiento Democratico Nicaraguense* (MDN); *Partido Accion Nacional* (PAN); *Partido Popular Social Cristiano* (PPSC); *Partido Socialist Nicaraguense* (PSN); *Partido Nacional Conservador* (PNC); *Accion Nacional Conservador* (ANC); *Partido Democratica de Confianza Nacional* (PDCN); *Partido Comunista de Nicaragua* (PCdeN); *Partido Neo-Liberal* (PALI); *Partido Social Democratica* (PSD); *Partido Alianza Popular Conservador* (PAPC); *Partido Liberal Independiente* (PLI); and *Partido Integracionista de Centro America* (PICA).

27. They were *Partido Social Conservatismo* (PSOC); *Partido Liberal de Unidad Nacional* (PLIUN); *Partido Social Cristiano* (PSC); and *Partido Conservador Democrata de Nicaragua* (PCDN) on the right and *Partido Revolucionario de los Trabajadores* (PRT); *Partido Marxista Leninista* (MAP-ML); *Partido Unionista Centro Americano* (PUCA); and *Movimiento de Unidad Revolucionaria* (MUR) on the left.

28. Mary Speck, "Sandinistas, Opposition Reach Sweeping Election Agreement," *Washington Post*, August 5, 1989.

29. Robert Pear, "U.S. to Help Anti-Sandinista Parties," *New York Times*, April 25, 1989.

30. Robert Pear, "U.S. to Pare Aid in Nicaragua Vote," *New York Times*, September 29, 1989; Martin McReynolds, "U.S. to Send Funds for Nicaragua Vote," *Miami Herald*, December 9, 1989.

31. *Electoral Democracy Under International Pressure*, Report of the Latin American Studies Association Commission to Observe the 1990 Nicaraguan Election, March 15, 1990 (Pittsburgh, Pa.: LASA, 1990), p. 28.

32. *Electoral Democracy Under International Pressure*, pp. 29–30.

33. Mark A. Uhlig, "Ortega Says He Won't Arm Rebels in El Salvador if He Is Re-elected," *New York Times*, February 24, 1990.

34. Mark A. Uhlig, "Cease-Fire Begins in Nicaragua as the Contras Agree to Disarm," *New York Times*, April 20, 1990.

12

Political Parties, Party Systems, and Democracy in Costa Rica

José Luis Vega Carballo

Participatory regimes that are tolerant of legitimate ideological opposition are clearly products of historical development and are not merely constructed. They are established only through a long and complex process of negotiations between the state and the civil society. Central to this process are political parties. Of special interest here are political systems with a predominant party, particularly as in the case of Costa Rica.

The central argument of this chapter is that Costa Rica's democratic regime was possible only because the social forces that formed the state opted for the political party as the instrument by which to organize their participation. Thereby they created strong, dominant parties that would have an impact across generations. Only in this way was it possible to consolidate a strong political center that was moderate, pluralistic, open, and capable of discouraging informal, often explosive, intervention from outside the political system. The management of disputes within the "power bloc" under such conditions permitted periodic renewal (although not always through peaceful means) and the execution of long-term compromises among the principal actors inside this bloc.[1] Costa Rican democracy thus evolved without adopting any prior organizational model. Particularly important has been the ability of Costa Rican elites, despite their different interests, to compromise instead of becoming polarized.[2]

It is possible to distinguish two phases in the evolution of the Costa Rican party organizations. The first phase, or First Republic, extended from 1889, when the first parties appeared on the political scene, until the Civil War of 1948, when a critical realignment of political and institutional forces occurred. The second phase began with the civil war and continues through the so-called Social Democratic Second Republic up to the present.

Origins of Party Democracy: The First Republic

During the first phase of their development, the political parties of Costa Rica were appendages of the modernizing agro-exporting oligarchy. The oligarchy accepted and promoted parties as an alternative to the old, expensive method of carrying out the presidential successions through coup d'états *(cuartelazos)*. At the time the country was benefitting from profitable coffee exports to European markets. The compulsory, free primary education paid for by the state contributed to forming a citizenry ever more politically aware and desirous of participating in elections. Elites wished to put their university knowledge and experience to work resolving the problems of rapid modernization and urbanization.[3] At the end of the 1880s the first steps were taken by political elites—heirs of the power of Gen. Tomás Guardia (1870–82) and his efforts as a liberal to promote "order with progress"—to organize political parties "from above."

Besides the civil oligarchy, no organized social forces existed in Costa Rica. Thus, these parties behaved like parties of notables, with their cadre, in the classic sense defined by Maurice Duverger.[4] Costa Rica's political parties did have a parliamentary origin because they grew out of the factions developing in the Congress at the time. Their activity also guaranteed the retirement of the military from political activities.

The predominant role of the agro-exporting oligarchy as well as the popular acceptance of the centralized state guaranteed sufficient resources and power for the parties to function.[5] Because of the growing autonomy of the political-institutional power of the state and the political parties, the entrepreneurs were unable to completely control the economy or manage the political structure. This left an opening for the middle and lower classes to channel their demands through the system while they were being integrated into national life. Thus, the political regime developed in this manner at the end of the last century because civil society was able to maintain the necessary distance and autonomy to introduce political changes. For that reason, Costa Rica developed a much more integrated social structure than that of other Central American societies.

Even before the electoral processes had matured and the political parties were institutionalized, Costa Rican society had also been democ-

TABLE 12.1 Voter Participation in National Elections, 1897–1940

Year	Population	No. of Voters	Percentage
1897	275,000	24,065	8.75
1901	310,000	35,722	11.52
1905	314,000	51,789	15.18
1909	341,000	51,623	13.62
1913	378,780	51,623	13.62
1913	410,000	64,147	15.64
1919	421,000	47,497	11.28
1923	460,000	71,545	15.55
1928	471,564	50,447	13.05
1936	591,862	88,324	14.92
1940	660,000	108,145	15.70

Source: Samuel Z. Stone, *La Dinastía de los Conquistadores* (San José: Editorial Educa, 1975), p. 236.

ratizing. The election in 1889 of opposition candidate José Joaquín Rodriguez as president has been taken as the birth date of competitive democracy and a party system in Costa Rica. Since then, the political, constitutional, and electoral processes have been interrupted only twice. The first instance was during the dictatorship of the Tinoco brothers, Federico and Joaquín, between 1914 and 1917, which ended with their violent fall under oligarchic and popular pressure. The second was the brief lapse during which the Founding Junta of the Second Republic governed, between 1948 and 1949.

In Costa Rica in the middle of the nineteenth century barely 2 percent of the population registered and voted in the secondary elections, which were carried out in ritualistic manner between military uprisings and other disturbances. By the end of the century participation increased to only 10 percent (see Table 12.1).

Beginning in 1901, participation stabilized at around 15 percent. Not until the middle 1950s would it increase again, when, along with other factors, voting by women was introduced and the minimum voting age reduced. The voting rate remained constant during the period of the oligarchic republic preceding World War II. Yet the figures do not illustrate an even more important characteristic of a democratic system—the existence of an active opposition, which was not excluded by force, persecuted, or terrorized. In addition to the legitimate opposition, which gave a democratic character to the elections, during this period the formal political game of the political parties was established. Parties were irreversibly institutionalized, if not as permanent structures with defined ideological orientations then at least as *caudillist* patronage machines important to the liberal political system restored under the leadership of experienced personalist leaders like Ricardo Jimenez and Cleto González. Among these clientelist machines, the Republican or National Republican Party (PR) excelled because it appeared in the 1890s and was able to overcome the Civilist Party and a myriad of other small, short-lived parties. The PR maintained its status during the period of personalist parties in different forms and under different names.[6]

The versatile machinery of the PR found ways to continue to dominate the political scene. It produced leaders or contributed to establishing other organizations, which it then assimilated or weakened through alliance or cooptation. The PR successfully employed these tactics for a half a century, until the 1940s, when organizations appeared that stubbornly refused to play the electoral game or be absorbed.[7]

The PR successfully alternated in power with an opposition so similar to it that its competitors did not dare present viable alternatives. Moreover, the PR kept up with the times and quickly embraced the causes of some pressure groups within civil society. The PR furthered these causes but always endeavored to do so moderately. Many times the PR even came to approve reforms after calculated postponements, struggles, negotiations, even street brawls. In this way the initiative would remain under the control of the PR.

The crash of 1929–30 hit Costa Rican society hard. Tensions had previously existed because the rapid economic growth had unleashed new social forces coming from social differentiation and the diversification of the agro-exporting productive structure. But in the following decade acute poverty and urban expansion resulted in growth of social protest movements with nationalist, unionist, or socialist orientations. The Communist Party of Costa Rica (PCCR), founded in 1931, began to unionize workers of the banana plantations owned by the United Fruit Company. This resulted in the famous strike of 1934, which was resolved through negotiations, thereby establishing an important precedent. The union and Communists' electoral activity created fear among the upper classes and among some middle-class conservatives. The Communists had founded the Bloc of Workers and Peasants and obtained nearly 10 percent of the total of votes cast. Despite some cases of fraud and limitations imposed by the PR, the PCCR's representation in the Congress and in some municipalities increased. When the PR obtained 90 percent of the votes cast in the elections of 1940 and brought Dr. Rafael Angel Calderón Guardia to the presidency, calm and confidence seemed to return, especially in view of the anticipated support of the Catholic church for the innovative social reforms promised by the young president in his inaugural speech.[8]

The Social Democrats, however, who had begun to organize politically in the early 1940s, and the Communists began to attack the new government and soon established an alliance to gain the approval in Congress of a Labor and Social Guarantees Code that would establish social security and welfare as objectives of the state. The Communists opposed the capitalist circles that saw their wealth and political security threatened by a far-reaching reform. The Social Democrats, who represented the interests of the rising professional and entrepreneurial middle classes, considered the reforms demagogic and lacking any economic content. Meanwhile the PR saw its electoral margin decrease because the PCCR-Social Democratic alliance was attracting fractions of the capitalist, centrist, and conservative anticommunist and conservative sectors. As a result, the PR's strength in civil society weakened and its traditional political center began to fracture. The center was unstable after the elections of 1944, 1946 (parliamentary), and February 1948. The PR consequently lost its balancing role in the political system, could not get the state to manage social tensions, and had to resort to electoral fraud and police coercion to maintain the social reforms of 1942. In this way, the PR distanced itself from its long-standing role as a political integrator. When the opposition, called the "National Compact," claimed victory in the elections of February 1948 the government annulled the electoral results. In response a group of young Social Democrats led by José Figueres, who had founded the Social Democratic Party (SDP), militarily toppled the government of President Teodor Picado and, at the end of April 1948, constituted the Founding Junta of the Second Republic.[9]

The New Dominant Party System:
The Second Republic

Nearly two thousand deaths were the price the country paid for the political opening through which new national leaders emerged. They reappeared in 1951 as the National Liberation Party (PLN), founded by Figueres and others. They offered a new program of national development that sought to deepen the far-reaching reforms that Figueres and the governing junta had initiated three years before. These reforms included state control of private banking, the constitutional abolition of the army as a permanent institution, and the creation of Uruguayan-style autonomous institutions geared to resolving technical, economic, and social problems.

The oligarchic circles that negotiated the new political Constitution with Figueres (more progressive in many cases than the Constitution of 1871) did not imagine that he and his group of Social Democratic reformers would return to power.[10] But the PLN won with 64.7 percent of the votes cast in the elections of 1953—elections in which it faced an amalgam of forces belonging to the old regime, which adopted the name Democratic Party (DP). At the time the Communists could not directly participate because Figueres had made them illegal in 1949 in response to the pressure of the cold war climate and to consolidate his power. For their part, the principal leaders of the old Republican Party were still in exile. The losing parties in the Civil War of 1948 would gradually integrate into political life by the 1960s. In 1974 the communists returned under the protection of a constitutional reform that Figueres and the PLN backed to demonstrate the strength and maturity that (according to them) had been achieved by the Costa Rican democratic regime.

The PLN dominated from the elections of 1953 to those of 1986, which brought Dr. Oscar Arias Sanchez to power. Notwithstanding the realignment in favor of the PLN, the party system did not change. It continued to be a multiparty system with a dominant party. The PLN appears to continue to control and effectively manage the middle of the ideological spectrum. It even accommodates the opposition of the right and the left and holds enormous influence over the state apparatus and its substantial resources.[11] This kind of domination is similar to that held by the old Republican Party within the oligarchic-liberal power structure.[12] The structure has been partially transformed and now includes the techno-bureaucratic middle classes—also called the "new small bourgeoisie"—and other sectors of the working and peasant classes, almost the same ones with which the leaders of that oligarchy established negotiations that preserved the democratic regime.

Although there have been obvious changes in the political system, interesting lines of continuity exist. Therein may lie the secret of the system's success in transforming periodic crises into integrating rather than disintegrating events, contrary to the experiences of other Central American states.[13]

Thus, the PLN emerged from a quasi-rupture of the traditional scheme of parties that had existed since the last decade of the nineteenth century. Founded in 1945 as the Social Democratic Party (SDP), it was able to impose its partial hegemony over the nascent regime of the Second Republic, immediately placing itself at the front of a vast capitalist modernization project based on the moderating intervention of the welfare state. After a long Liberal period, it preserved its role as a guarantor of the civil and electoral rights of the citizens. (It was precisely the lack of respect for civil rights which ended the domination of the old Republican Party in the 1940s.) This transformation simultaneously permitted the party to contribute to the growth of the middle social and entrepreneurial classes. It thus gave power to a techno-bureaucratic elite that could win elections and direct both the public sector and private enterprise.

Within this context, the opposition the PLN has faced since 1963 has in great measure been adjusted to the needs, conditions, and limitations indicated by the dominant party. Recent evidence of this is the fact that in 1983, when the antiliberationist center-right forces finally constituted a political party, the United Social Christian Party (PUSC), its formation as a party could only take place via an accord with the then-PLN president Luis Alberto Monge. Monge had determined that it was time this opposition coalition stopped being a disparate group of factions unified solely for elections and finally become a modern political party. Through this pact with the PLN an effective consolidation of a more powerful political center, made up of both groupings, became possible. This center includes almost 95 percent of the electorate. The PUSC may eventually adopt a defined program and ideology and reappear with different colors in front of the national electorate. Even more, President Monge indicated that this effort at political engineering is, in the first place, a challenge and a stimulus for the renewal of the PLN and of the entire party system that will bring the country closer to a classic two-party system. Second, it is a way to invigorate democracy via the construction of strong parties and the lessening of factionalism.

The results of this strategy, which is supported in the PLN ranks, remains to be seen. What is clear is the powerful influence the PLN continues to have over the political scene. This influence, however, may not always be available to the dominant party wherever and whenever it chooses to act, as the results of the 1990 elections have demonstrated.

On February 4, 1990, Rafael Angel Calderón Fournier, the candidate of the Costa Rica's PUSC, was elected president with 51.4 percent of the vote. The PUSC also gained control of Costa Rica's Legislative Assembly, winning 29 of 57 seats. Calderón out-polled Carlos Manuel Castillo, the candidate of the PLN, who garnered 47.3 percent of the vote. The PLN had won five of Costa Rica's previous six presidential elections, and Calderón was seen to have benefitted from a national desire to avoid concentration of political power.

During the campaign Calderón claimed that his predecessor, President Oscar Arias Sanchez, had neglected domestic issues in pursuit of a Central American peace plan. Calderón promised to stress Costa Rica's role in global disarmament and human rights while also working for internal growth. Outgoing President Arias, constitutionally banned from reelection, kept a high profile during the election campaign, promoting peace in Central America. At this writing Calderón's presidency has strengthened the consolidation of the PUSC, which, together with the PLN, continues to command the loyalties of more than 90 percent of the Costa Rican electorate.

As noted above, through 1989 and 1990 the PLN has had to face the consequences of negotiation with its principal opponent: it won the elections of 1986 but lost in 1990. At the same time, its leadership has promoted a process of rotation and generational change within the party, renewing the party statutes and promoting competition among rising leaders through the so-called struggles of tendencies. These measures seem to have been encouraged to confront diverse problems, including the loss of the founding father of the party, José Figueres, in May 1990; the necessity of renewing the ideological and programmatic platform in view of competition from the PUSC; the possibility the left may also unite for the elections of 1994 as it did in 1978; and the likelihood new currents that emerge from civil society demand from the PLN new answers.

The great question for the future is whether the political regime as such will have sufficient resources to efficiently, legitimately, and quickly effect a peaceful and negotiated transition to a different stage of national development. This stage will likely require revising the old formulas of the interventionist benefactor-state. Following orthodox liberalism will undoubtedly have high social and political costs that could bring defeat not only to the PLN, as occurred in February 1990, but also to the PUSC. Similarly, the political system is challenged with institutionalizing the transition to a new two-party system, considered by many beneficial for the development of Costa Rica's democratic regime.

Yet for Costa Ricans to sustain democracy they must not take it as only ideological discourse or mistakenly believe that democracy is ready-made. Democracy is a long-term policy commitment. It requires the creative reconstruction of relations between the state and civil society, which eliminates the mechanisms that prevent sustained, shared economic growth. It also requires a persistent and never-ending search for social equality combined with the promotion of individual opportunities. Both major political parties' experimentation in the last decade with neo-liberal economic policies cannot guarantee such readjustments without higher social costs. Thus this experimentation threatens the political and democratic stability and reformist capacity of the Costa Rican political system.

Notes

1. Even though these lasting accords or "social domination pacts" have not been closely studied and information on the Costa Rican case has barely begun to receive attention in the comparative studies of stable democracies or breakdowns, these pacts are critical to guaranteeing the alliance politics of forces associated with the power bloc of a society, as well as the use of the state apparatuses to put them into practice for the long term. For Alain Rouquié's contribution, see Alain Rouquié and Jorge Schvarzer, eds., *Cómo Renacen las Democracias?* (Buenos Aires: Emecé, 1985).

2. The interested reader can find an in-depth study of the circumstances that favor both the establishment of moderate and lasting compromises between social forces in conflict and the progressive stabilization of the centralized structures of the national state in my *Poder Político y Democracia en Costa Rica* (San José: Editorial Porvenir, 1982).

3. In this respect, the differences between Costa Rica and the rest of Central America are explored in various studies on the "Liberal Epoch" or the "Liberal Reform." See Mario Rodriguez, *Centroamérica* (New York: Prentice-Hall, 1965), especially chap. 3; and Edelberto Torres-Rivas, *Interpretación del Desarrollo Social Centroamericano* (San José: EDUCA, 1971).

4. Maurice Duverger, *Los Partidos Políticos*, 9th ed. (Mexico City: Fondo de Cultura Económica, 1984), pp. 93–101.

5. Cf. Vega Carballo, *Poder Político*. Also, the author has studied in detail the vicissitudes of this process of structural differentiation and the forces that moved and accentuated it in the social and economic spheres and the formation of the centralized state beginning in 1821, when Costa Rica became independent from the Spanish colonial empire in *Orden y Progreso: La Formación del Estado Nacional en Costa Rica* (San José: Editorial del Instituto Centroamericano de Administración Pública, 1982). Some interesting references to the same problems in more recent times can be found in Rolando Franco and Arturo Leon, "Estilos de Desarrollo y Estructura Social en Costa Rica," *Pensamiento Iberoamericano* 6 (July–September 1984):65–92, published by the Instituto de Cooperación Iberoamericana in Madrid, Spain.

6. These trends and a global analysis of this period can be found in Vega Carballo, *Poder Político*.

7. Abundant observations and facts about the evolution of the PR and other personalist-*caudillist* parties of the classic liberal period can be found in Oscar Aguilar Bulgarelli, *Democracia y Partidos Políticos en Costa Rica* (San José: Editorial de Costa Rica, 1968).

8. With regard to this time, see John Patrick Bell, *Guerra Civil en Costa Rica* (San José: Editorial Costa Rica, 1978); and Jorge Mario Salazar, *Política y Reforma en Costa Rica* (San José: Editorial El Porvenir, 1981).

9. The events that led to the arrangements and negotiations that made possible not only the termination of the conflict, but also the approval of a new Constitution, can be found in the work by Oscar Aguilar Bulgarelli, *La Constitución de 1949* (San José: Editorial Costa Rica, 1949).

10. Much of the information on the origins and a great part of the trajectory of the PLN used in this section can be found in Araya Pochet, *Historia de los Partidos: Liberación Nacional* (San José: Editorial Costa Rica, 1968).

11. For a valuable account of the electoral activities of the left in Costa Rica, see Manuel Rojas and Elisa Donato, *Sindicatos: Política y Economia* (San José: Publicaciones de CEPAS, 1985).

12. This great control has not completely ended. It can easily be established through the references and analysis that appear in the work of Jorge Rovira, *Costa Rica en los Años 80* (San José: Editorial El Porvenir); and Mylena Vega, *El Estado Costarricense de 1974 a 1978: CODESA y la Fracción Industrial* (San José: Editorial Hoy, 1982).

13. Some aspects of this dynamic are correctly pointed out by Edelberto Torres-Rivas, "Centroamérica: La Transición Autoritaria Hacia la Democracia," *Polémica* no. 4 (second series) (January–April, 1988):2–13.

13

Panama:
Political Parties, Social Crisis,
and Democracy in the 1980s

David A. Smith

To understand Panama's political process and party system, one must understand its peculiar political heritage. Carved from a rebellious province of Colombia and shaped by U.S. diplomats and business interests, Panama's political heritage is split. It lies both in Latin American institutions and in U.S. aspirations to promote constitutional democracy. Knowledge of this political heritage is essential for evaluating the current political crisis, the role of political parties, and the characteristics of political confrontation in pursuit of democratic development.

Panama's prolonged confrontation with the United States over sovereignty, administration, and control of the Panama Canal Zone and enjoyment of the zone's economic benefits have influenced political events. Likewise, U.S. economic, political, military, and diplomatic presence in Panama has inhibited the nation's autonomy and independence. The overwhelming U.S. influence has affected cultural and sociopolitical life in Panama.

Panama's political heritage is characterized by

- *The fragility of the political party system.* Until 1934 one party dominated; after that fragmented multiple parties existed, until 1968.
- *The predominance of elections decided by alliances.* Eleven out of sixteen alliances were formed from 1904 to 1968; alliances were again made in 1984 and 1989. From 1968 to 1980, during

the Torrijos regime, political institutionalization occured without political parties.[1]

- *The predominance of Latin American* **caudillismo.** During most of its history, Panama has been ruled by *caudillos:* Dr. Belisario Porras, 1903–30; Dr. Arnulfo Arias Madrid, 1931–68; and Gen. Omar Torrijos Herrera, 1969–81. Since 1981, Panama has had neither *caudillo* nor any political leader of national and international stature to resolve the political conflict.

- *The growing tendency of political and social forces to channel their demands and actions through nonpartisan organizations that frequently have become politically belligerent.* These organizations include the Inquilinary Front (1920s);[2] the Communal Action Association (CAA), which directed the first political coup in January 1931 and also produced Dr. Arnulfo Arias; Panama's Student Federation (1940s to date); Panama's Teachers Union (periodically during the past forty years); labor unions (throughout the past fifty years); chambers of economic and free enterprise (such as the Construction Chamber and the Commercial and Industrial Chamber); and civic clubs and associations (such as the Rotary, Lions, and Kiwanis clubs), the National Opposition Front, the National Civilian or Civic Coordinator, and most recently, the National Civic Crusade.

- *The growing presence of the military in the political scene.* The military first served as an instrument of oligarchy during the 1940s and 1950s. During the 1960s, 1970s, and 1980s it became a more independent and autonomous political institution. The military's growth as a political institution without explicit moral responsibilities or obligations to a social base or electorate has become significant during the past two decades. It has at times been autocratic and repressive, at other times, consultative.

Political Parties in Panama

The Initial Bipartisanship

The development of political parties began in 1903, out of the liberal versus conservative confrontation that characterized Latin America during the post-Independence period (1821–1900). The evolution of Panama's national state included open and explicit foreign intervention, especially during its first thirty-two years.

The Panama Canal Treaty and the National Constitution authorized administrative, political, and military intervention by the United States. The intervention was solicited by national leaders during periods of social strife and political struggle (from 1906 through 1928). Liberals and conservatives alike responded promptly to this mechanism and used it to control elections.

The Liberal and Conservative parties guided political life and conflicts from the end of the nineteenth century to the 1912 general elections, which were won by the Liberals. Their victory began a period of Liberal predominance that was to last until 1934.

Bipartisanship with Liberal Predominance

With the exception of the 1914 elections, all other elections during the period were dominated by the Liberals. The 1920s marked the beginning of more defined nationalist feelings, organization, and actions. Popular and middle-class groups became increasingly anti-oligarchic and also expressed antiliberal sentiments. The popular perception was that Liberal continuity in government was tantamount to an antinational regime, a government controlled by the United States.

This situation gave rise to the first significant nonpartisan organization in Panama, the Communal Action Organization (CAA). Founded in 1923, it served to channel political needs and demands. The association was conspiratorial and created the conditions for the January 1931 coup. Although CAA was anti-oligarchic and antiliberal, the lack of a political program and CAA's own recognition of its political immaturity prevented it from controlling the government after the coup. Instead, the government was retaken by the Liberal vice president. The most significant long-term result of this coup was the breakup of the Liberal Party in 1934.

Fragmented Multipartisanship

The Liberal Party's predominance was weakened after the coup. The ensuing liberal factions adopted different names. The Doctrinaire Liberal Party brought together those that favored the 1931 coup or political change (both members of the CAA and the Liberals). The 1931 CAA group took the name Renewed Liberal Party. Other factions included the United Liberal Party, grouped around the *caudillo* of this first thirty-year period, Dr. Belisario Porras. The Democratic Liberal Party also emerged, although the traditional leaders remained with the old Liberal Party.[3]

The most immediate and significant result of this political disruption and dismemberment was the elimination of the treaty clauses of Panama's Constitution, which had allowed U.S. political and military intervention. In addition, the business classes negotiated the extension of their interests in the economic activities derived from operating and administering the Panama Canal. From this perspective, the anti-oligarchic and antiliberal movement ironically permitted the consolidation of national oligarchic control and economic expansion. It also created a political vacuum as evidenced by the growing nationalist and anti-oligarchic attitudes.

The expansion of the Canal Zone market during World War II brought to Panama certain economic activities and the appearance of industrial growth. With the influx of U.S. and allied troops stationed in and passing through the Canal Zone came an increase in demands for consumer products and services. But, with the end of the war, this situation changed. The increased wartime demand had no relation to Panama's national market. Thus, the postwar era initiated economic and political polarization, with the traditional economic groups on one side and the new industrial and professional groups on the other.

The traditional groups, which had economic interests in commercial and administrative activities and services in the Canal Zone, had no reason to pursue modifications of United States-Panama relations or of the treaty. In one area the interests of these traditional groups and the new social and economic sectors converged: both sought to overcome oligarchic economic and political control and modernize the national economic infrastructure and relations as a way of expanding economic facilities and possibilities. Meeting this objective required political and institutional modernization and an important modification of international relations, primarily a new Panama Canal treaty.

The period from 1934 to 1968 gave birth to a national-populist political leader and *caudillo,* Dr. Arnulfo Arias Madrid, from the CAA. His political discourse appealed to the lower classes—urban workers, peasants, and housewives, who had little or no political education but longed for a national identity. The Arias phenomenon turned out to be the most egregious expression of the political system's immaturity during this entire period. Arias ran for office four times, won four times, and was deposed three times, thus creating an aura of martyrdom.[4]

The rise of Arias as a political figure had its roots in the Liberal breakup of 1934. Arias helped create the National Revolutionary Party, which backed Juan Demostenes Arosemena in the 1936 elections, in alliance with the traditional Liberal Party faction that opposed the United Liberal Party. The United Liberal Party, in turn, had established alliances with the Democratic, Renovated, and Doctrinaire Liberal factions; the Popular Front; and the Socialist Party. In the 1940 elections, the National Revolutionary Party won the elections in alliance with the Traditional Liberals, the United Liberals, the Democratic Liberals, and a reborn Conservative Party.

Thus, party politics from 1904 to 1968, and more explicitly from 1934 to 1968, consisted of the preelectoral multiplication of parties, the creation of ephemeral alliances, and the growing absence of political leadership, both by individuals and organizations. Only six of the seventeen presidential elections from 1904 to 1968 were won by a single party. These six cases occurred during 1910–34, the predominantly Liberal phase. In the other eleven elections, in 1904, 1908, 1916, and in all eight elections from 1936 to 1968, political campaigns were based on pre-electoral alliances that varied from one election to another. In one case, this consisted of "reconstituted liberalism"; in another, as joint opposition; and in yet another as "officialism" in alliance with earlier opposition parties and factions. In six out of eight elections, from 1936 to 1968, the defeated candidate was also backed by an alliance.

This changing of factions illustrates how fragile party programs, principles, doctrines, and leaders were characterized largely by opportunism, internal conflicts, and fragmentation. According to H. Conte Porras, social, economic, and family relations played a small role in deciding allegiance to one party or another. Political party allegiance was more the result of accident or convenience. Without changes in the political structures of government, the rise and fall of either political group was considered of little or no importance. On four occasions, 1940, 1948, 1952, and 1968, the elected president was overthrown and replaced by his vice president. This kind of legal coup, second only to legal succession, demonstrates the predominance of the personal over the programmatic. Furthermore, in no way were the preexisting cordial relations of the leaders of the different parties affected by electoral outcome. These relations were established through the back door, behind the political facade presented every four years.[5]

After the first Arias populist experience ended with his downfall in 1941, the 1945 constituent elections were dominated by Liberals, who won 70.8 percent of deputies elected and 71.8 percent of votes collected.[6] The 1948 election demonstrated even more dramatically these easy reversals. Arnulfo Arias ran for president in 1948 backed by his recently created Authentic Revolutionary Party and opposed by the National Revolutionary Party, the party he once led.

Table 13.1 shows the political dispersion in the 1960, 1964, and 1968 elections. As we can see from Table 13.1, in 1964 there were nineteen political parties, vying for 317,171 votes, with the *Panameñista* Party (the new name for Arias's party) winning a majority of the votes (37.6 percent). Nonetheless, it lost the elections to a large alliance of opposing political parties.

TABLE 13.1 Panama's Political Parties and Presidential Elections

Party	1960(%)	1964(%)	1968(%)
Liberal National	17.6	15.3	20.7
Republican	10.8	10.2	11.1
Third Nationalist	6.7	3.6	3.3
National Liberation Movement	6.4	4.1	6.5
National Patriotic	35.6	7.5	5.9
Liberal Civil	12.0	1.3	-
Renovated	4.0	1.3	-
Progressive	3.6	3.1	4.7
DIPAL	3.3	1.0	-
Panameñista	-	37.6	30.9
Agrarian Labor	-	3.6	9.7
Democratic Action	-	3.5	3.4
Christian Democrat	-	3.1	3.6
Six Other Parties	-	4.9	-

Notes: Figures are rounded.

Sources: Raúl Leis. Radiografía de los Partidos. Panama City: Ediciones Centro de Capacitación Social, 1984; J. Conte Porras. Arnulfo Arias Madrid. Panama City: Litho Impresora Panamá S.A., 1980.

TABLE 13.2 Panama: Elections and Abstention, 1948–68

Election Year	Total Votes	% of Electorate	
		Voting	Abstaining
1948	216,214	70.9	29.1
1952	231,848	67.5	32.5
1956	306,770	79.3	20.7
1960	258,039	59.24	40.8
1964	326,401	67.1	32.9
1968	327,048	60.1	39.9

Source: Electoral Statistics, 1972 Elections. Panamanian Statistics, Year XXXI—Statistics and Census Supplemental Directory.

In 1968 nine small parties disappeared. Despite the growth of the National Liberal Party and the relative loss of influence of the *Panameñista* Party, Arias still won the elections, because of the alliance he had masterminded. On the other hand, nonvoting rose from 29.1 to 39.9 percent during the twenty-year period, with a high of 48.8 percent during the 1960 elections. The 1960 figure resulted from a boycott by the populist masses because of the exclusion of Arias as a presidential candidate (see Table 13.2).

The 1941 and 1949 coups were carried out on behalf of oligarchic interests channeled through the military. The 1952 presidential campaign and triumph of Gen. José A. Remon Cantera, founder of the Patriotic National Coalition, showed an increased political presence within the *Guardia Nacional*. The final stage witnessed the *Guardia Nacional* return to office deposed president Marco A. Robles. This action, in part, resulted in his alleged open support of the official candidate prior to the 1968 elections.

A 1968 October coup overthrew Arias for the third time. Economic, social, and political conditions were creating a backdrop for political deterioration. The lack of political leadership and institutionalization of the executive was accompanied by a slow but progressive professionalization of the *Guardia Nacional* as a military organization.

In addition, growing popular disenchantment with political parties, the obvious distance between the parties and the voting masses, and the strengthened nationalism that resulted from the January 1963 confrontation between the United States Southern Command Armed Forces stationed in the Panama Canal Zone and Panamanian students and citizens only reenforces this view of a debilitated political system and an almost illegitimate party structure.

The Torrijos Era and Beyond: The Political Project

After a repressive two-year interim (1968–70),[7] which included an internal military purge, the *Guardia Nacional* put forth a new form of political intervention in Panama. As in 1931, this period marked a new stage in the evolution of the political system.

Under Torrijos the call for national unity increased social participation; its aim was to consolidate a more explicit national identity. Thus began a period in which political reforms, state intervention, and economic development became main issues. Economic diversification and growth were pursued and accompanied by institutional and political modernization.

New was the Torrijos regime's call for political and professional intellectuals to assist in establishing a program for national unity. For the first time in Panama's political history a team was brought together and a program set forth that could serve as a guideline for organizations, institutions, and individuals to follow or to oppose.

Three stages can be identified in the development of Panama's political system:

1. *Oligarchic stage.* This stage is best characterized by a governing style of social exclusiveness. The government moved rapidly toward illegitimacy because of the economic interests it established, particularly its close ties to the denationalized and unproductive sector of the economy.

2. *Nationalist and popular stage.* This phase was led by middle-class professionals and popular leaders whose historical awareness allowed them to become a leading force in Panama's political life. Relying on anticolonial and anti-oligarchic principles, new leaders and social sectors aligned themselves during this stage of political development. This sector sought national sovereignty; national control of the Panama Canal; and economic, social, and political modernization.

3. *Democratic bourgeois stage.* This phase, based principally on a capitalist modernization strategy, was rooted in the nationalist movement, the expression of the need to establish autonomous modes of economic expansion, such as economic diversification; control and expansion of a national market; and the growth of technology and economic competitiveness. To pursue economic development, the goal during this stage was political and social stability. Bourgeois leaders initially established an alliance with General Torrijos in response to his call for national unity. Torrijos and the bourgeois leaders shared objectives, such as the defeat of the oligarchic system, economic growth, and the attainment of political modernization and stability. Although led by the new *caudillo* Torrijos, the alliance that resulted from the 1969–72 cooperation helped establish a new political system in response to the deterioration and limitations of the old one.

The "1970–1980 Strategy for National Development Program" (*Dirección General de Planificación,* 1970), the political reform (a new Constitution and the establishment of the 505-member National Popular Assembly in place of the traditional Deputy Parliament of about fifty members), a new labor code, and educational and agrarian reforms paved the way for ample social support during the early 1970s. The results were a remodeling of the political system, exclusion of political parties, and engagement in a corporate form of politics.[8]

Party politics during the Torrijos and post-Torrijos era can be subdivided into two subperiods. The first refers to a corporative[9] consolidation of the political scheme, with the absence of political parties, 1969–78. A second, 1978–89, is characterized by the reopening of party politics, either multipartisan or bipartisan, and by a recognized political role for the military. Political analysts either point out the abnormality of military intervention in politics or claim that the political crisis, which resulted from twenty years of military intervention, will lead to a solution of Panama's political system with or against, but not without, the military.

Without a party framework, the consolidation of the new political system was accompanied by the institutionalization and professionalization of the military. Because political parties played no role in framing political debate, different institutions had to serve as vehicles for political expression and confrontation. State institutions took on the role of official standard-bearers. Nongovernmental organizations such as the associations, chambers, trade unions, and clubs began adopting similar roles, establishing an opposition to official alignments.

Two national elections took place during the first subperiod. In each case the votes of the electorate determined the members of the new National Popular Assembly, entrusting them with indirect election of the president. In these two elections abstentionism fell to 10.8 percent in 1972 and to 16.5 percent in 1978, making the new political experiment relatively credible.

Certain political analysts consider 1969–78 as one of the most democratic periods in Panama's political life in terms of voter response, mass participation, and electoral climate. These were years of establishing national unity and explicit development plans and seeking the building of an economic infrastructure, economic diversity, social reforms, and identifiable political leadership on an individual, institutional, and organizational level.

This period also contrasted with the political ambiguity that preceded it. Certain political positions were clarified, but such stands were not ideological. Torrijos stressed that his regime was with neither the left nor the right, but with Panama. According to Ricaurte Soler, Torrijos was supported by both the left and the right.[10] The political romance ended in 1976, 1977, and 1978.

Economic restraints, precipitated by increased public debt, the failure of state enterprise, and the failure of agrarian reform; unfulfilled expectations raised by the Torrijos-Carter Canal Treaty (signed in 1977); and the 1978 elections brought to the surface the personalism, corruption, and political incapacity of the National Assembly. Popular frustration with the unfulfilled economic bonanza anticipated as a result of the new canal treaty marked the end of this subperiod. The Torrijos regime and the political system were discredited. The indirect presidential election was now considered subject to political manipulation. Many supported a return to the party system. There was discussion of limiting the military's presence in politics and government; labor unions sought revitalization, having lost influence as a result of the December 1976 counterreform.

The second subperiod, which began in 1978 with a general mobilization against the regime, ended with the May 1989 general elections.[11] It was characterized by economic and political crisis. In 1978 the military decided to reopen the political scene by reviving the party system. The arrival and regrouping of deposed political leaders increased political instability. Yet the most significant occurrence was General Torrijos's sudden death in 1981. This eliminated the *caudillo*, the political leader, the real head of state.

Another political vacuum appeared in the midst of a reemerging political life; the whole system awoke to sudden crisis. Several realignments occurred: inside the armed forces, in the precarious development of civilian autonomy, and in the relations between the military and the civilian political structures and government.

As the 1984 general election drew closer, party politics and instability in the ranks of the military and government prevailed. There were three different commanders-in-chief of the *Guardia Nacional*—Flores, Paredes, and Manuel Antonio Noriega. There were also three presidents—Royo (overthrown by Paredes), De La Espriella (Royo's first vice president, overthrown by Noriega), and Illueca (Royo's second vice president and first in line to De La Espriella), who finally turned the office over to Nicolas Ardito Barletta, proclaimed winner of the 1984 elections by less than 2,000 votes.

Since the 1984 elections, Panama's regime, its leaders, and its military have increasingly lost legitimacy. Denunciations of electoral fraud, growing military power, and corruption at all levels of public life have increased. The subperiod 1978–89 shows the absence of military and political successors to Torrijos. It also demonstrates the inconsistencies of the so-called generational relay, which Torrijos claimed so many times.

Social Crisis and Democracy in the 1980s

The intended reorganization of the political system, the search for an alternative leader, and the military's stubbornness in wanting to play a principal role in political developments contributed to a sense of crisis. Yet the absence of an alternative political plan with enough credibility to successfully replace the efforts of the 1969–72 project also hastened the deterioration of conditions.

The most dramatic outcome of the crisis resulted from retired Col. Roberto Diaz Herrera's declarations in June 1987 accusing General Noriega of fraud in the 1984 elections and responsibility for the death of an important opposition leader, Dr. Hugo Spadafora. This opened a bitter feud inside and outside the military. It corralled General Noriega and his military allies and political counterparts. It also dramatized the need for modifying the role of the military in civilian politics.

During the 1978–89 subperiod, alongside the reestablished party system, nonpartisan organizations became the channels for registering political demands. The first of these was the National Civic Coordinator. It was followed by the National Civic Crusade. There also was the Popular Unitary Front, which supported the National Liberation Coalition for the 1989 general elections.

The recurrence of political party alliances is still characteristic of national elections in Panama. Examples include the National Democratic Union (UNADE) versus the Opposition Alliance (ADO) in the 1984 elections; this emerged in 1989 as the Civic Opposition Alliance versus the National Liberation Coalition. These modern alliances have shown the traditional inconsistencies and have dispersed after election. The Christian Democratic Party (PDC), however, claims that the ADO, its precursor, is the longest lasting political alliance in Panama.[12]

Political Parties in Recent Years

From 1984 the following political parties have played important roles: the Democratic Revolutionary Party, the Authentic *Panameñista* Party, the Christian Democratic Party, the Agrarian Laborist Party, the Liberal Party, the Republican Party, and the National Renovated Liberal Movement. The Democratic Revolutionary Party and the Authentic *Panameñista* Party were the highest vote-getters; the remaining parties lagged further behind in popular support—a difference of at least 10 percent of the votes for president and deputies to parliament (see Table 13.1).

Only the following parties had sufficient stability and party organization to gain grass-roots support: the Democratic Revolutionary Party, the PDC, the Agrarian Laborist Party, the Liberal Party, the People's Party (communist), and the two minor left-wing parties, the Workers Revolutionary Party and the Socialist Worker's Party. The Authentic

Panameñista Party is not on this list for two reasons: the death of its populist leader and the recent party split in 1988. Also excluded is the Republican Party because of a similar 1988 split, which resulted in a loss of party leadership.

The most important parties are the Democratic Revolutionary Party (the official governing party until 1989), the PDC (the main opposition party), and the Liberal Party, the only party that has endured factions and realignments.

Although Panama superficially has a multipartisan system, it tends toward bipartisanship with the Democratic Revolutionary Party and the PDC at the forefront.[13] The three major political parties, discussed in more detail below, represent the left/center and right/center.

The Christian Democratic Party (PDC)

The PDC has belligerently opposed the government. An ideologically organized party, it has international links with European and Latin American Christian Democrats. Its leaders take part in the directorate of the Latin American Christian Democrat Organization. Besides engaging in political training and grass-roots organization, their leaders and publications give the impression that the party's strength results from being the victim of political repression.[14]

A PDC document entitled "Ideological Foundations" points to the party's antiliberal, antitotalitarian, antimilitary, and anticommunist stand. It calls for political responsibility and simplistically characterizes the PDC as good and its opponents as bad. This document stresses the need for political formation of the populist masses according to the four elements of the party's opposition stand: ideological formation, organization, political leadership, and solidarity with Christian Democrats worldwide.

The party's reach is nationwide; it has established grass-roots organizations in many communities. The *Instituto Panameño de Estudios Comunitarios,* the party's training center, has held seminars during recent years, offering a balance of internal unity, new, valuable leaders, and the image of an organized and ideological party. The PDC claimed, in its May 1988 convocation, to be a popular party, and it has identified itself with the aspirations of the working majorities. Yet the party is criticized for being right wing and conservative. Its leaders are well-to-do intellectuals and professionals who can dedicate themselves full time to the party while their personal enterprises and economic activities support them. It is also said that they have been absent during crucial nationalist and popular reform movements.[15] The PDC has been a significant member of the Civic Opposition Alliance, which has prompted accusations by the official National Workers Council of PDC support for U.S. intervention in Panama and economic blockade. The council also believes the PDC does not support the canal treaties.

The PDC's November 1988 Ordinary Congress accused the Noriega regime of being a dictatorship that systematically violated human rights, militarized the state, and established friendly relations with the Communists, thus jeopardizing the future of the canal. They placed responsibility for economic disintegration on the regime, which they also accused of being responsible for worsened living conditions. Christian Democrats call for development with social justice, without the military, and through pacific dialogue as a way of guaranteeing democracy.

The Authentic Panameñista Party (PPA)

A charismatic and populist-oriented party, the PPA has appealed to the electorate through personality as well as programs. For this reason, with the recent death of its *caudillo,* Arnulfo Arias, its future role is in question.

During the 1987 mobilization against the regime, the PPA did not present a political program. In a March 1988 document entitled "The PPA Program for Democratization," party leaders stated that the solution to the crisis required giving government control to Arias, the legitimate winner of the elections. They also spoke of the need to change the composition of the High Command of the Public Defense Forces (the new name for the military). The party denounced a "twenty-year dictatorship," identifying it as the main cause of Panama's crises. Yet this argument, shared by the PDC, ignores the political developments of 1970–78.

National Civic Crusade

The *Cruzada,* as it is called, brought together a heterogeneous grouping of social, economic, and political perspectives. United by rejection of the regime, it was unable to join together in a common ideological position. The June–December 1987 incidents that took place in the suburban, middle-class areas of Panama City and in the administrative and banking district were called by some the "Reebok–Gloria Vanderbilt mobilization," a reference to the upper middle-class nature of the *Cruzada* membership.

Both the PDC and the PPA were part of the National Civic Crusade. The parties and the *Cruzada* were openly confronted by the popular sectors and working classes, who denounced the programs of these organizations as lacking specific reference to the effect of the *Cruzada's* opposition to the regime on the masses. For example, the National Organized Workers Council judged the crusade a right-wing, "old-time" oligarchy. On the other hand, April 6, 1988, marked the birth of the Popular Civilist Movement, which identified itself with a similar antimilitary viewpoint. This new group revitalized nationalism and populism. The Popular Civilists drew up a platform that went beyond the social and economic considerations of the *Cruzada*.

Another reason for the popular rejection of the *Cruzada* was that the National Private Enterprise Council was an important part of the *Cruzada* opposition. Its October 1988 document on the reasons for the crisis and solutions to it had always been considered elitist and bourgeois.

The Democratic Revolutionary Party (PRD)

The opposition and political analysts consider the PRD to be the creation of the government, a party developed from the top down. It is also considered a bureaucratic party, unable to meet the needs of Panamanians or address the issues facing society. Yet it has become an alternative party organization. Nationalism, anticolonialism, Latin American solidarity, cultural identity, and antiimperialism are the essence of PRD ideology. The Torrijos ideals, the role of the military in the political scheme, the Panama Canal Treaty, Panama's future administrative control, and Panamanians' right to solve their own problems without foreign intervention provide the basis for the PRD's political organization, its grass-roots appeal, and its campaign program.

Principal member of the *Union Nacional Democrática* alliance during the 1984 elections, the PRD was the main member of the National Liberation Coalition in the 1989 elections. The party reaches Panamanians from all provinces and social classes. The National Secretariat includes subsecretariats covering peasant and gender issues, the indigenous sector, health, the enterprise sector, and child and family issues. The party is frequently in confrontation with the U.S. political and diplomatic delegation stationed in Panama. The PRD's political platform of March 1988 viewed the U.S. economic blockade as aggression toward a long-standing historical ally.

The party also stresses international relations. Its leaders consider it as having social democratic tendencies. The PRD identifies itself as revolutionary, democratic, nationalist, populist, and supportive of ideological pluralism. In the international field it defends self-determination, neutrality, nonalignment, anticolonialism, and the peaceful solution of conflicts.[16]

The National Executive Committee of the PRD presented its platform to the party in a document dated October 11, 1987, entitled "Popular

Liberation or Slavery." In it the PRD recognized political errors that had accumulated over the years; it referred to its inability to gain a consensus on main issues, its lack of political direction, and its inability to face changing conditions and new realities in Panama.

The general crisis in Panama has forced the PRD to develop planning, negotiation, and confrontation skills. This led to party reorganization and redefinitions, which party leaders believe will prepare it to fight for the country's survival with the changing social and economic conditions.

Political Parties Since 1984

Since the elections of 1984, which returned Panama to civilian rule, and the May 1989 elections, which were annulled, three political parties have dominated the political arena. The PDC, the PRD, and three factions of the followers of Dr. Arnulfo Arias Madrid, allied in the *Partido Panameñista Democratico* (PPD), the PPA, and the *Partido Panameñista Revolucionario* (PPR).

The events that led to this national crisis are partially explained by the relationship between the United States and Panama, in particular between the United States and Gen. Manuel Antonio Noriega. In June 1987 Col. Roberto Diaz Herrera, the retiring deputy commander of the Panamanian Defense Force, publicly accused Noriega of drug trafficking, rigging the 1984 elections, and ordering the murder of Dr. Hugo Spadafora, a former health minister under the Torrijos government. These charges launched an important opposition election, the *Cruzada Civilista,* or National Civic Crusade, a coalition of two hundred business, professional, student, and labor groups, who organized a series of demonstrations against the Noriega government. This prodemocratic alliance played a crucial role in civic education and kept up the pressure for new elections, which ultimately took place in May 1989.

On February 4, 1988, a grand jury in Miami, Florida, indicted Noriega for drug trafficking and racketeering. Three weeks later, on February 25, President Eric Arturo Delvalle attempted to fire Noriega as commander-in-chief, in a televised announcement. Immediately after the announcement, the legislature convened without opposition leaders present and ousted the president and his vice president, Roderick Esquivel, and appointed Minister of Education Manuel Solis Palma to the position of minister-in-charge of the presidency. The United States continued to recognize Delvalle, and relations between the United States and Panama continued on a downslide. By May 1988 negotiations to end the crisis ended in a stalemate. Under increasing international pressure, Noriega decided to hold elections, hoping this move would provide his regime with some legitimacy in the world community. The absence of public support for the de facto rule of General Noriega was made clear by pressure to hold elections in May 1989. By late 1988 the political parties in Panama began a process of realignment and coalition building in preparation for presidential and National Assembly elections in May 1989. Two coalitions emerged: the progovernment *Coalition de Liberacion Nacional* (COLINA), which included the parties and groups loyal to Noriega and the opposition forces, representing a broad ideological spectrum, which united their parties under the ADO.

With the death of Dr. Arnulfo Arias Madrid, Panama's political system was left without an heir-apparent. Arias's PPA, the leading opposition party, divided in December 1988, shortly after his death. The Noriega-appointed Electoral Tribunal recognized the faction of the PPA led by Hildebrando Nicosia and his colleagues, who were granted official use of the party symbols. This faction joined COLINA in its progovernment coalition. In what many believe was a move engineered by Noriega, the other PPA faction, led by the party secretary general Guillermo Endara, joined the opposition coalition, ADO, rather than support Noriega.

To understand the background of the events that led to the elections of May 7, 1989, one must go back to the May 1984 elections and the coalitions that emerged at that time. The progovernment coalition, COLINA, included five parties that belonged to the ruling coalition elected in 1984 and two parties from the left, one of which was formerly aligned with the opposition. The remnant of the 1984 coalition included the PRD, the *Partido Laborista* (PALA), the PPR, the *Partido Liberal* (PL), and the *Partido Republicano* (PR). The *Partido del Pueblo* (PPP) and the *Partido Democratico de los Trabajadores* (PDT) represent the Communist and left Labor parties, which were part of the COLINA alliance.

The PRD was COLINA's leading party. Its president, Carlos Duque, a business associate of Noriega, was the coalition's presidential candidate in 1989. Ramon Sieiro, the coalition's candidate for first vice president, came from the PALA party; Sieiro is Noriega's brother-in-law. Aquilino Boyd, former foreign minister and former ambassador to the United States, the United Nations, and the Organization of American States (OAS), ran as the coalition's second vice president.

In December 1988 the ADOC included the PDC, the *Movimiento Liberal Republicano Nacionalista* (MOLIRENA), the Arnulfista faction of the PPA, the PLA, the unregistered *Partido de Acción Popular* (PAPO), and the *Partido Nacion Popular* (PNP). Arnulfista loyalist Guillermo Endara became the coalition's candidate for president, with Ricardo Arias Calderon of the PDC and Guillermo (Billy) Ford of MOLIRENA, first and second vice presidential candidates, respectively. This unified ADOC ticket came about only after intense negotiations among coalition members.

On May 7, 1989, Panama held presidential elections witnessed by international observers. Two former U.S. presidents, Jimmy Carter and Gerald Ford, and several high-ranking Latin American and European Community leaders also participated. The elections marked a turning point in the regime of Gen. Manuel Antonio Noriega. That elections were being held at all was part of Noriega's strategy to convey some legitimacy to the status quo. In the government's view the problems Panama faced were the direct result of U.S. intervention; thus, holding an election with international observers would elevate Panama's intentions to promote democratic governance in the eyes of the international community.

On May 8, just one day after the balloting, former U.S. president Jimmy Carter, head of the National Democratic Institute's delegation, denounced the election process as defective. On the same day, the Episcopal conference of the Catholic church announced that the opposition, ADOC, had won the election by a three to one margin over the progovernment coalition, COLINA, based on a parallel vote count reported by party officials collecting data from election sites around the country.

In spite of the evidence of opposition victory, on May 10, 1989, the Electoral Tribunal, whose members had been appointed by Noriega, nullified the elections, alleging foreign interference in the process and the absence of sufficient documentation to declare a winner. On the same day, ADOC leaders Guillermo Endara, Billy Ford, and Ricardo Arias Calderon were brutally beaten by thugs sent by progovernment forces, Noriega's famous "dignity battalions." The bloody encounter, memorialized on videotape by international television coverage, dramatized the brutality of the Noriega government. Rather than elevating Panama to an improved standing in the international community, the election backfired on Noriega. World reaction to the election and its subsequent nullification marked the countdown to Noriega's ultimate ouster from the Republic of Panama. On May 17, 1989, the OAS met in emergency session to condemn Panama's actions.

The election was a prelude to the final chapter of Noriega's control of Panama. Although the United States continued to insist Noriega relinquish power to the legitimate winners of the May election, there was no effort to move toward a peaceful resolution of the dispute between Noriega and the United States and the world community. An abortive coup in October 1989 against the Noriega regime only strengthened the U.S. government's resolve that Noriega had to be removed. On

December 20, 1989, after months of efforts to negotiate an exit for Noriega, the United States invaded Panama in an operation known as "Just Cause." Within days the Panamanian Defense Force had surrendered to U.S. troops, and Panamanians danced in the street as Noriega fled the city. Taking refuge in the residence of the papal nuncio in Panama City, Noriega ultimately surrendered in early January to U.S. authorities and was removed to Miami, Florida, to stand trial on federal drug and money laundering charges. A trial is currently in progress in the fall of 1991; as yet no decision has been made as to Noriega's guilt or innocence, only further unraveling of the long and tragic episode of Noriega's relationship with the United States.

The three victors in the May 7, 1989, elections, Guillermo Endara, Ricardo Arias Calderon, and Billy Ford, were restored to office with the U.S. invasion of Panama on December 26, 1989, by Decree 127. As of the fall of 1991 all three are still engaged in a bitter competition for power in the struggle to move Panama and its political parties toward a more democratic system of government.

Panama's first elections since the events of December 1989 were for the legislative assembly. These elections, held on January 27, 1991, were to fill nine National Assembly seats that had remained vacant since the May 1989 elections. Although twelve political parties participated in this election, turn-out was low, with an abstention rate of 54 percent for the Legislative Assembly seats and 73 percent for election of local neighborhood *corregidores*.

The low voter turn-out in the January election is not surprising, given the electoral history of the nation. Public opinion had continued to demonstrate low public esteem for the government of Guillermo Endara. The perception is that the regime represents a return to the period of oligarchical families rather than a step forward for citizen participation in the wake of Noriega's years as de facto ruler.

Of the twelve parties that participated in the January 1991 elections only the PDC, PRD, MOLIRENA, PALA, and PLA received significant voter support. The PDC remained the largest single force in the assembly with twenty-eight of fifty-eight seats.

In late May 1991, dissonance among the multiparty coalition that rules Panama came to a head when the PDC announced that it was going to serve as an opposition party to the government, of which it had previously been the strongest component. First Vice President Ricardo Arias Calderon, though still one of the three officers of the executive branch, lost the five cabinet posts his party held in the government, as well as other important positions. Although he considers himself the leader of the new democratic opposition, he is an executive without a portfolio.

The events of May 1991 also strengthened and elevated the importance of the PRD in the National Assembly. This political organization, created by Omar Torrijos and manipulated by Noriega, can now use its ten assembly seats to leverage either the PDC or MOLIRENA pluralities, thus becoming a key player in legislative initiatives.

Polls taken in June 1991 reflected the popular perception that Panama's political chaos had halted the initially favorable climate for economic recovery. Although the same poll showed 45 percent of the public saw a need for new political parties, the public mood reflected a sense of despair over the continued deterioration of the political system and the low credibility of the government, a sense that Panama was headed down a dead-end street. Only one legislative act, passed by the National Assembly on June 14, 1991, as a constitutional amendment, made clear one change from preinvasion times: The Republic of Panama would not have an army. This amendment reaffirmed legislative support for the *Fuerza Publica*, or public force, that was formed after the army was dissolved during the U.S. invasion.

Presidential elections are not scheduled until 1994, but the campaign has already begun, with second vice president Billy Ford showing the highest popularity and recognition ratings as of June 1991, with 39.5 percent of the vote, followed by Ricardo Arias Calderon and Guillermo Endara as second and third choices. The issues in the campaign are already clear: Who will defend the Panama Canal in the wake of the army's dissolution? Who will provide the best plan for economic recovery? Will a new political force that is more populist replace the parties whose leaders still represent the vestiges of the oligarchical past? One thing is clear. The United States may be unwilling at this juncture to fill the political vacuum that had in the past guided the decisions among Panama's political class.

Conclusion

The most delicate aspect of Panama's political situation has been the polarization of the two main political forces. Each side called for the exclusion of the other, defining the 1989 elections more in terms of supporting or opposing the regime, the military, and U.S. intervention, than in terms of offering economic, social, and political solutions to the crisis.

Panamanians have faced unconventional political development for the past two decades, characterized by military control. In the 1970s there was unprecedented improvement of economic, social, and political conditions. This period has ended and is unlikely be repeated. Yet society still lacks political maturity. In the face of elections and political reorganization, the political system is now seriously at risk. There are no specific alternative political programs; ideological discourse has replaced action.

With or without conflict, democracy needs a chance. It needs planning and programs, actors and actions. It must extend beyond elections, but must occur through elections. The heightened economic, social, institutional, moral, and political crisis in Panama during the past two years has dealt a great blow to the combined military and civilian regime inherited from Torrijos.

The underprivileged classes are most affected by the crisis of political confidence. In response, the crisis has increasingly spawned important grass-roots organizations and renewed alliances through social organizations and programs. Despite the general polarization, there is evidence of a capacity to negotiate in the midst of an openly conspiratorial political system. These factors must all be considered from a democratic perspective, without ignoring the precarious viability of national democratic development under transnational geoeconomic and East-West geopolitical influences that limit efforts at effective self-determination. Panama's fragile democratic opening may be no more than a brief episode in yet another effort by external actors to jump-start political development.

Notes

1. See page 219, which refers to the Torrijos Regime, and page 220, which mentions the corporate scheme implemented as an alternative to political parties, which were deemed unrepresentative of the interests of the masses.

2. *Inquilinos* (Spanish for *tenants*) of Panama City went on strike in October 1925, refusing to pay the high rents charged by their landlords. This mobilization of the lower classes against the property-owning elites was finally suppressed by President Rodolfo Chiari's government, who called on U.S. troops to help disperse the masses.

3. Victor R. Goytia, "Los Partidos en el Istmo," in *Revista la Antigua* (Panama City, 1975); H. Conte Porras, *Arnulfo Arias Madrid* (Panama City: Litho Impresora Panama S.A., 1980).

4. H. Conte Porras, *Arnulfo Arias Madrid* (Panama City: Litho Impresora Panama, 1980).

5. Jilma Noriega de Jurado, *Verdad y Miseria de Nuestros Partidos Políticos* (Panama City: Talleres de Editoria Renovación, 1978).

6. Victor F. Goytia, "Los Partidos Políticos en el Istmo," in *Revista la Antigua* (Panama City, 1975).

7. MNL–29–11, *Declaración de Panamá* (Mexico City: Editorial Diógenes, 1971).

8. An accurate summary of the political atmosphere is evident in a poster placed at different ministries:

I am the little red ball, I go to the left.
I am the little blue ball, I go to the right.
I am the little white ball, I go to....

Red symbolized the Liberal Party, and blue identified conservative, right-wing political tendencies. White implied that now without parties, no one knew where to turn.

9. Refers to representation of the people through guilds instead of through political parties, a concept promoted by "Nationalist" governments as a means of assuring participation of the various sectors of society.

10. Ricaurte Soler, *El Pensamiento Político en los Siglos XIX y XX* (Panama City: Universidad de Panamá, 1988).

11. This subperiod can be subdivided as follows: (1) 1978–81, from the beginning of the mobilization to the sudden death of General Torrijos in a plane accident; (2) 1981–84, from Torrijos's death to the general elections; and (3) 1984 to the present, or up to the May 1989 general elections. See Editors' Note.

12. Partido Demócrata Cristiano, *Declaración de 9no Congreso Ordinario* (Panama City: November 1988). In 1984 it was claimed that the UNADE obtained 47 percent of the presidential votes, winning the election by 0.4 percent. Yet official statistics show the UNADE winning the elections for deputies, mayors, and National Popular Assembly members by obtaining over 65 percent of each of the respective votes. If fraud took place at the presidential level, then we might have to accept that UNADE turned out to be the main political force in the general elections but could not oppose the last *caudillo*, Dr. Arnulfo Arias, presidential candidate for the ADO.

13. In late 1988 the National Congress was dominated by two parties, the PRD and PDC, with the election of presidents, vice presidents, secretary-generals, members of the respective political committees, and the different secretariats.

14. Partido Demócrata Cristiano, Secretaria de Comunicación y Propaganda, *Informe Sobre una Verdadera Agresión* (Panama City: November 1988).

15. Raúl Leis, *Radiografía de los Partidos* (Panama City: Ediciones Centro de Capacitación Social, 1984).

16. Soler, *El Pensamiento Politico*.

Political Parties and
Their International Connections

14

Projecting Democracy in Central America: Old Wine, New Bottles?

Cynthia J. Arnson and
Johanna Mendelson Forman

If constitutional democracy has been America's religion, the propagation of this faith has been a constant feature of our history.[1] Whether the United States attempted to promote democratic institutions abroad through heavy-handed interventions or tried to foster democracy through economic aid or "political development" programs, U.S. efforts all represent a long-standing conviction that our brand of government promotes individual rights and economic well-being better than other systems of governance.[2] Latin America has been a particular object of U.S. missionary zeal. Whether the United States was sending gunboats to Caribbean and Central American ports under the banner of democracy at the turn of the century or sending economic aid dollars in the firm conviction that capitalist development would foster pluralistic political systems, the idea that U.S. actions were beneficial to democracy has pervaded this century.[3] In the postwar era, the politics of the cold war made its mark by making military assistance and the concomitant search for "stability" and "security" part of a larger economic assistance package. President Harry S. Truman expanded military aid to the hemisphere to protect it from external (i.e., Soviet) attack. In the wake

Special thanks to Elizabeth Cohn and Maria Davila for their invaluable research assistance.

of the Cuban Revolution of 1959, President John F. Kennedy launched the Alliance for Progress, an aggressive plan to promote economic development on the assumption that growth would result in political democracy.[4] Little understood by policymakers was the extent to which the cold war objectives of the Alliance for Progress conflicted with democratic goals: counterinsurgency doctrines promulgated in the name of fighting pro-Castro guerrilla movements encouraged the most anti-democratic sectors of the Latin American military. Nevertheless, the Kennedy approach brought several novel elements to U.S. assistance programs. The newly founded U.S. Agency for International Development (USAID, or AID) focused on grass-roots projects, encouraging civic participation through a "bottom-up" approach to the creation of a new civic culture in Latin America.[5]

Despite its promises, the Alliance for Progress failed to bring significant political or economic improvement. The linkage in theory between economic growth and democracy gave way to the strengthening in practice of the wrong political institutions. Military rather than civilian institutions flourished.[6] In the late 1960s and early to mid-1970s, the armed forces in Chile, Brazil, Argentina, and Uruguay created unprecedented security states, most of them welcomed, if not directly fostered, by the administrations of Lyndon B. Johnson and Richard M. Nixon.

The late 1960s and early 1970s marked a shift in U.S. foreign assistance policy, largely promulgated by the Congress. Political repression in so many parts of the globe and rising dissent over the Vietnam War sharpened the view of congressional liberals that assistance should concern itself not only with economic development, but also with civil liberties, human rights, and economic redistribution. A major revamping of economic aid legislation in 1966 and the linking of U.S. aid to political as well as economic factors were enshrined in various foreign assistance laws during the 1970s. The new consciousness of political liberties as a criterion for U.S. foreign assistance peaked under President Jimmy Carter, elected in 1976. Carter's human rights doctrine linked the protection of individual rights to economic and military aid, even if the standard was unevenly applied and often discarded when "national security" concerns competed.

In the Reagan years, 1981–88, U.S. foreign assistance departed from the traditional combination of military and economic assistance, marshaling U.S. dollars to promote what was called democracy in ways that differed dramatically from earlier programs.[7] The larger policy debate centered on whether the United States should provide military assistance to resistance forces in Third World countries deemed communist by the administration, campaigns that were justified in the name of democracy. In addition, quasi-governmental agencies were created for the stated purpose of exporting democracy, while AID itself adopted a "democratic initiatives" program that detached attempts to foster democratic political systems from levels of economic development.[8]

This chapter focuses on Reagan administration policies aimed at promoting democracy, as well as on the political rationales for those programs. While U.S. government aid attempted to reform judicial systems and promote human rights, the most important aspect of democracy promotion was seen as the holding of free and fair elections. This chapter reviews the modern roots of the programs of the 1980s, the congressional mandates of various foreign assistance acts, and the implementation of legislative directives by AID and the National Endowment for Democracy (NED). It shows how the fierce anticommunism of the cold war was marshaled for a new ideological offensive against the Soviet Union and how the State Department policy used the notion of democracy to promote a variety of political ends. Finally, the chapter shows how the Reagan administration was forced to abandon its early ideological preference for authoritarians over totalitarians and ultimately demonstrate a preference for centrist political parties and nonmilitary governments.[9]

Central America has received the bulk of electoral assistance funding in the 1980s from both federal and quasi-governmental forces (see Table 14.1). Of the eight Latin American nations that have received electoral assistance from the U.S. government or private organizations since 1980, five are Central American states: El Salvador, Guatemala, Honduras, Nicaragua, and Panama.[10] In fact, Central America became the laboratory for controversial foreign policy experiments carried out in the name of democracy. The emphasis given to these electoral assistance programs in the 1980s must be examined within the context of U.S. development policy and the political environment that produced such efforts.

USAID and Congressional Directives

The key federal agency charged with providing technical assistance for electoral processes is the United States Agency for International Development. AID's recent activities in electoral promotion form yet another phase of that agency's long-standing involvement in political development aid programs.[11] Recent efforts share with their predecessors an emphasis on the technical aspects of carrying out an election, under the foreign policy guidance of the State Department. Although such an arrangement suggests a harmonious division of labor, AID and the State Department have fought bitterly over policy priorities. "To AID people

TABLE 14.1 National Endowment for Democracy Latin America Funding, FY 84 to FY 89 (in U.S.$)

Country	FY 84	FY 85	FY 86	FY 87	FY 88	FY 89	Total
Argentina	135,000	273,640	353,289	336,824	443,310	496,030	2,038,093
Bolivia	—	60,000	108,000	108,000	142,500	88,000	506,500
Brazil	—	395,000	87,309	205,620	140,375	157,800	986,104
Chile	210,000	500,000	682,447	629,822	1,623,909	682,257	4,328,435
Colombia	—	155,988	141,000	86,811	219,550	100,000	703,349
Ecuador	—	80,000	21,711	—	—	33,000	134,711
Guyana	—	—	127,429	30,000	—	—	157,429
Paraguay	—	50,000	163,954	121,880	209,304	743,400	1,288,538
Peru	—	370,000	377,368	218,780	328,000	382,000	1,676,148
Surinam	—	112,500	—	—	—	—	112,500
Uruguay	—	231,100	167,500	15,000	30,000	95,140	538,740
Venezuela	—	—	60,250	—	—	—	60,250
Subtotal S.A.	345,000	2,228,228	2,290,257	1,752,737	3,136,948	2,777,627	12,530,797
Costa Rica	—	75,000	103,500	176,432	164,900	88,000	607,832
El Salvador	—	—	—	10,647	—	—	10,647
Guatemala	127,500	292,730	270,228	16,000	120,000	168,000	994,458
Honduras	—	—	—	—	—	36,000	36,000
Nicaragua	—	360,000	240,000	454,757	807,242	3,600,000	5,461,999
Panama	41,500	—	66,000	98,800	112,430	198,665	517,395
Regional C.A.	—	166,100	58,560	303,856	322,540	446,000	1,297,056
Subtotal C.A.	169,000	893,830	738,288	1,060,492	1,527,112	4,536,665	8,925,387
Mexico	—	100,000	273,000	94,418	188,700	138,000	794,118
Cuba	60,000	—	110,000	110,000	170,000	130,000	580,000
Dominica	—	74,200	56,535	170,500	90,000	54,500	445,735
D.R.	—	178,510	278,281	153,000	115,000	76,000	800,791
Grenada	—	—	75,000	—	50,000	—	125,000
Haiti	—	—	400,881	271,912	180,000	209,229	—
Car. General	—	276,940	495,547	171,500	240,000	252,705	—
Subtotal Car.	60,000	529,650	1,416,244	876,912	845,000	722,434	1,951,526
Reg. L.A. & Car.	—	1,092,000	1,275,025	935,009	1,917,740	555,440	5,775,214
Total L.A.	574,000	4,843,708	5,992,814	4,719,568	7,615,500	8,732,166	32,475,756

Note: FY 84 did not specify amounts allocated to each country. These sums do not include funds for multiregional projects. Reg. = Regional; Car. = Caribbean; D.R. = Dominican Republic.

State is a treacherous betrayor of development," explained a senior U.S. policymaker, "because State's emphasis is political and short term." The State Department, meanwhile, "sees AID as technocrats who don't see the need for a political content to programs."[12]

Three key legislative mandates form the statutory authority for AID's role in what has come to be known as "democratic initiatives" (see Table 14.2).[13] The first emerged from the original Foreign Assistance Act (FAA) of 1961, which offered a broad definition of development that included "economic, political, and social institutions" to improve the quality of life.

In 1966 Representative Donald Fraser (D-MN) authored Title IX of the Foreign Assistance Act of 1967 (amending the FAA of 1961). He was concerned that the assumption behind the Alliance for Progress, that economic development led directly to political development, did not always hold. Title IX held that U.S. aid programs should emphasize "assuring maximum participation in the task of economic development on the part of the people...through the encouragement of democratic private and local government insitutions." In its report on the legislation, the House Foreign Affairs Committee directed AID to foster "cooperatives, labor unions, trade and related associations, community action groups, and other organizations which provide the training ground for leadership and democratic processes."[14] In contrast to the emphasis of the Reagan years, in Title IX grass-roots organizations were seen as key to the development of democracy.

Title IX was an important precursor to AID electoral assistance programs in the 1980s, even though the two initiatives differ. In the late 1960s Title IX encouraged the creation of a special office, the Civic Participation Division of the Bureau of Program and Policy Coordination. That division funded university-sponsored research on "how best to incorporate considerations of social, political and economic development into AID projects."[15] Universities developed projects on effective participatory methods, which resulted in training in social and political development. The office also published materials on participation as a feature of U.S. development strategy.[16] The Civic Participation Division was abolished at the beginning of the Reagan administration and later absorbed into ongoing programs in the Policy Planning Coordination Bureau of the agency.

The mid to late 1960s saw other efforts to engage the U.S. government in assisting political groups abroad. One such effort had its origins in a Johnson administration review of covert U.S. support for nongovernmental organizations in the late 1960s. Some administration officials believed covert U.S. support for private groups compromised them if the

TABLE 14.2 Strengthening Democratic Institutions

Year	Legislation/Initiatives	Key Concepts
1961	Title VI of the Foreign Assistance Act of 1961 (the Alliance for Progress)	Social and economic development with democratic institution-building as one of its goals
1961	Amendment on Cooperatives of 1961 (Humphrey Amendment)	Development and use of cooperatives, credit unions, and savings and loan institutions to increase popular participation
1962	Amendment on Community Development (Zablocki Amendment)	Development of popular participation at the local government level in countries with agrarian economies
1967	Title IX of the Foreign Assistance Act of 1961	Maximum participation from the masses of people in private government institutions; political and economic approaches development; consideration of needs and desires of individual countries; training of country's people to develop leaders, strengthen democratic institutions, and encourage participation in democratic processes
1973	Foreign Assistance Act of 1978 ("New Directions" mandate)	New direction to help the poor majority, primarily the rural poor, by supporting equal distribution of wealth and more active participation in their countries' development
1974	Amendment of the Foreign Assistance Act of 1961 502B (added by the Foreign Assistance Act of 1974)	Security assistance based on country's adherence to human rights
1975	Section 116(e) of the Foreign Assistance Act of 1961	Economic assistance conditioned on adherence to human rights and fundamental freedoms in all countries and adherence to civil and political rights

funding was exposed[17] and proposed creating a "quasi-autonomous non-governmental organization," a so-called QUANGO, to substitute for governmental support. In 1967, Florida Democrat Dante Fascell introduced legislation to create an "Institute for International Affairs" to carry out such public activities, but his proposal was overshadowed by attempts in Congress to cut off or limit covert activities over the next several years.[18]

A third thrust toward greater involvement in explicit efforts to promote democratization came as a congressional mandate in the early 1970s. This effort, represented by a series of amendments to the FAA, was Congress's response to the failure of the Johnson and Nixon administrations to pursue policies that fostered democracy in the developing world. Prompted by disaffection with the Vietnam War and by revelations of a covert U.S. role in the overthrow of the elected Allende government in Chile, a Democratic Congress in 1974 passed Section 502B of the FAA. This law expressed the "sense of Congress that U.S. military aid should be tied to a recipient country's adherence to human rights standards. Such linkage was extended in stronger fashion to economic aid with the Harkin Amendment, Section 116(e) in 1975, which denied economic aid to human rights violators."[19] AID's policy determination on human rights directed the agency to "carry out programs and activities which will enhance adherence to civil and political rights."[20]

Section 116(e) greatly expanded AID's political mandate. It provided the legislative support to pursue projects on such themes as research and discussion of civil and political rights in developing countries, adherence to the rule of law through a legal framework conducive to civil and political rights, free and democratic electoral systems, and increased access of women and ethnic groups to the judicial system.[21] AID's ability to implement such political programs, however, was often circumscribed by foreign policy concerns that had little to do with promoting democracy. The effectiveness of fulfilling the intent of 116(e) was also a function of other such assistance programs managed by the Department of Defense.

If Title IX represented a grass-roots approach to democratic development, the Democratic Initiatives program of the 1980s was the trickle-down version, focusing on political party assistance, national institutional development, and leadership training. Most of AID's experience in electoral assistance has been drawn from its work in Latin America and the Caribbean. In 1984 AID established the Office of Democratic Initiatives, largely based on and funded by the recommendations of the National Bipartisan Commission on Central America (the Kissinger Commission).

Betraying the long-standing conviction that a stable Latin America is in the best interest of U.S. security,[22] the Democratic Initiatives set as its goal "support[ing] the evolution of stable, democratic societies." Such support would entail strengthening competent civilian-run government institutions and encouraging pluralism.[23] Reflecting the belief that elections remained the key to democratic government, AID's Latin America and Caribbean Bureau listed the need to "improve the effectiveness and strengthen the institutional capacity of the country to administer free, fair and open elections" as second in a list of nine strategic objectives.[24]

From 1984 to 1987 AID spent $25 million in electoral support in Latin America.[25] Most AID money for elections has come from the general Economic Support Fund, which goes for overall budget support in a host country rather than for particular projects. The U.S. Department of State controls this source of funds.[26] Funding for elections included cash transfers to governments to generate local currency; electoral commodities such as indelible ink, ballot boxes, and ballot paper; and technical assistance such as training of election workers and support of international observer teams.

Training of election workers and observers has been performed by the Inter-American Center for Electoral Assistance and Promotion (CAPEL), a Costa Rican institution affiliated with the Inter-American Commission on Human Rights.[27] Although AID critics state that CAPEL is just a Latin American arm of AID's wider program in electoral assistance, CAPEL is a Latin American creation.[28] It grew out of a meeting of Latin American foreign ministers in October 1982.[29] Although it receives support from AID, it also receives support from international organizations such as the Organization of American States (OAS), the United Nations, and from other private voluntary organizations.

Background to the Reagan Years

If President Jimmy Carter's human rights doctrine served domestically to repair the wounds of America's cold war debacle in Vietnam and reconstruct a sense of the U.S. global mission, then President Ronald Reagan's zeal for democracy helped transform the final years of the cold war into a moral drive to crush communism through democratic institutions. David Shipler has aptly characterized the efforts at democratic institution-building abroad in the 1980s as a new era of missionary zeal.[30]

For President Reagan and other prominent officials within his administration, the promotion of democracy was an extension of the ideological struggle with the Soviet Union that posited the moral superiority of the institutions of the West over the totalitarianism of the East. In the president's view, the global struggle between East and West would ultimately be determined, not by "bombs and rockets," but by a "test of wills and ideas, a trial of spritual resolve."[31] Marxism-Leninism was headed for the "ash heap of history," in Reagan's words,[32] and U.S. support to noncommunist groups behind the Iron Curtain and in the developing world could further the process of decay. An interagency working group meeting as early as 1981 drew up a proposal for a "Project Democracy" to support both overt and covert programs to spread the ideas of democracy abroad.[33] Although formally part of the U.S. Information Agency (USIA), the project was to be coordinated by the National Security Council, a way ostensibly of keeping the project distinct from CIA programs.[34]

President Reagan unveiled the proposal in a June 1982 speech before the British Parliament. He urged that the United States "assist the campaign for democracy" overseas, by "foster[ing] the infrastructure of democracy—the system of a free press, unions, political parties, universities—which allows a people to choose their own way, to develop their own culture, to reconcile their own differences through peaceful means."[35] Reflecting the ideological thrust of the program, National Security Decision Directive No. 77, which President Reagan signed in January 1983, authorized "political action strategies" to counter moves by the "Soviet Union or Soviet surrogates."[36]

To carry out this effort, the Reagan administration in early 1983 asked Congress for $150 million for Project Democracy over a three-year period to support five areas of democratic development: training of leadership, education, support for nongovernmental organizations such as parties and unions, dissemination of ideas through conferences and publications, and development of personal ties between U.S. organizations and individuals and their foreign counterparts.[37] Congress refused to fund the plan, and critics viewed the program as a front for covert action. Congress embraced instead a plan for such programs to be carried out by a semiprivate organization, the National Endowment for Democracy.

There is strong evidence that almost a year and a half before the June 1982 speech, State Department and AID officials had begun their own examination of ways to promote the "infrastructure" of democracy.[38] These officials, mostly career foreign service officers, began to cloak earlier projects defended in the name of human rights in the new garb of "democracy." Although new political appointees at the State Department considered Carter's policies on human rights destabilizing and sought to undermine or discard them, some in State and AID sought to preserve a focus on civil and political liberties.[39]

Asked to determine how existing programs could be refocused as part of the new democratic gospel, State and AID officials suggested exchange programs for political leaders interested in supporting democratic institutions, civic education, and electoral assistance.[40] These officials within State and AID found the anticommunist rhetoric of the White House useful in marshaling domestic support for foreign assistance programs. Never popular, foreign aid was increasingly difficult for U.S. politicians to justify to their constituents during the Reagan years of rising budget deficits and slashed domestic spending. Only in 1984, following the election in El Salvador of José Napoleón Duarte, did Congress approve expanded economic and military assistance to the entire Central American region, as was recommended by the Kissinger Commission. Congress also increased the amount of money available to AID for its Office of Democratic Initiatives (ODI).[41] These funds were to be used for electoral support, judicial reform, and human rights programs. In practice, electoral assistance absorbed the majority of ODI funding.[42] The State Department articulated its rationale this way:

> The consolidation of democratic governments in Latin America... depends in large measure on increased public confidence in the electoral process and the institutional capacity to administer it. U.S. assistance, training, and material resources to help establish sound laws and procedures, administer elections, carry out measures to prevent fraud, and educate citizens about the voting process.[43]

Other Organizations Promoting the New Democratic Initiative

If Congress had been wary of the Reagan administration's ideological offensive in the name of democracy, it proved willing to support private or semiprivate organizations to carry out a similar agenda. The origins of the quasi-governmental National Endowment for Democracy are distinct from the Reagan administration's Project Democracy, but political forces behind NED were able to take advantage of the Reagan administration's foreign policy orientation to get federal funding for their proposed organization. Juxtaposed to the Reagan administration's proposal to spend tens of millions of dollars on political groups abroad, NED's semiindependent status appeared a more attractive alternative to skeptical members of Congress.

NED's beginnings were in the Democracy Project of the American Political Foundation, a bipartisan group founded by Freedom House consultant George Agree. Project director Allen Weinstein and a board of notable political leaders of both the Democratic and Republican parties advanced the idea that it was in the interest of U.S. political parties as well as labor and the private sector to foster democratic institution-building and political exchange abroad.[44] If the Democracy Project's approach was to emulate the political party foundations of Europe (particularly those of West Germany), this bipartisan effort also had an underlying ideological bias that equated promoting democracy with undermining communism. That it attracted supporters from all ideological viewpoints, however, is attributable to the political skills of the project's directorate, which assembled a leadership base from both parties and thus avoided the careful scrutiny Congress would normally accord such a highly political project.[45]

The American Political Foundation's efforts dovetailed with those of the Reagan administration in mid-1982. Immediately prior to President Reagan's speech to the British Parliament in June, the foundation's chairman, co-chairman, and another Republican official wrote the president to propose a study of the "ways and means" the United States could help in the growth of democracy.[46]

AID provided $300,000 for the study; the Democracy Project headed by Weinstein was created to carry it out. The executive board was comprised of such leading government and private figures as Sen. Christopher Dodd (D-CT); Rep. Dante Fascell (D-FL); Michael Samuels, international vice president of the U.S. Chamber of Commerce; and Lane Kirkland, president of the AFL-CIO.[47] In April 1983 the group proposed the founding of the semiprivate National Endowment for Democracy as well as foreign policy foundations of the two major political parties. Congress created NED in November 1983 in legislation signed into law shortly thereafter.

NED is what the British call a QUANGO—a quasi-autonomous nongovernmental organ. Funded by the government but directed by private citizens, NED's charter states that its role is to promote democratic values in developing countries and, where possible, in communist ones. Among its promoters were liberals who wanted to see covert aid to political parties transformed into open assistance subject to public scrutiny. When NED was created, then-CIA Director William Casey issued a public statement promising that NED would "not be used to conduct intelligence activities" or employ intelligence agency personnel, except as agreed to by Congress.[48]

In spite of direct financial support from Congress, NED receives its annual money from a grant appropriated through funds for the USIA. An independent board of directors oversees NED's grant-making abroad. NED has four principal grantees: the two political party institutions (the National Democratic Institute for International Affairs and the National

Republican Institute for International Affairs [NRI]), the Free Trade Union Institute of the AFL-CIO, and the Center for International Development of the U.S. Chamber of Commerce. The two party institutes receive most of the indirect funding for electoral assistance.

NED also receives special "pass-through" money from AID for programs deemed important to U.S. foreign policy. These additional funds come from AID's Economic Support Fund (ESF) and have been especially important in the electoral assistance furnished by NED to groups in Nicaragua, Chile, and Poland. Together, NED and AID have funneled tens of millions of dollars overseas over the last decade for political opposition groups, election observer missions, and technical assistance.

Despite the apparent bipartisan consensus over the desirability of promoting democracy abroad, U.S. experience in that domain has not been without controversy. The notion that the United States could fund genuinely nonpartisan activities abroad—seminars on how to set up a voter registry, for example—has clashed with the reality that both U.S. and NED-funded programs are frequently aimed at securing a particular political outcome in a field of many choices. That the choice in Latin America is frequently between different democratic forces across the ideological spectrum rather than between dictatorship and democracy only compounds the problem. NED in particular has been a lightning rod for criticism.

Under the best circumstances, providing taxpayer-funded grants to organizations involved in the internal politics of foreign countries would raise questions about the motives of the grant-makers. But the prominence of foreign policy conservatives in the NED leadership, including Director Carl Gershman, a former aide to Reagan's UN ambassador, Jeanne Kirkpatrick, has opened NED to charges that it is less interested in democratic development than in the promotion of a narrow, conservative foreign policy agenda.[49] In the early years of its existence, for example, NED provided over half a million dollars to a far-right French student group with ties to an extremist paramilitary organization opposed to the French government. When disclosed by French journalists, the grant provoked such a furor that its remaining portions were suspended by the NED board.[50]

NED is prohibited by charter from funding overseas campaigns for public office, but the line between funding candidates and funding activities that support the candidates' campaigns is thinly drawn. Moreover, as the following examples illustrate, NED grantees have often been involved in highly partisan activities that compromise the organization's stated purpose of strengthening "democratic institutions throughout the world through private, nongovernmental efforts."[51]

- In Panama in 1984, a trade union funded by the Free Trade Union Institute campaigned for Nicolas Ardito Barletta, the candidate backed by Gen. Manuel Antonio Noriega and the military. On learning of the contribution, the U.S. House of Representatives voted to cut off funding for NED.[52] The State Department was also backing Ardito Barletta over the opposition candidate, Arnulfo Arias, in 1984, and AID provided funds for the election. By 1989 the State Department shifted its support to the opposition coalition in an effort to oust General Noriega.[53]

- In Costa Rica, the NRI provided $434,000 to groups opposed to then-President Oscar Arias, including the Association for the Defense of Liberty and Democracy, a group with close ties to the center-right Social Christian Unity Party. A NED-funded magazine attacked Arias's peace plan for Central America, which ran counter to Reagan administration support for the *Contras* in Nicaragua, charging that the plan was "impugning the national virility" of Costa Rica. Congressional Democrats questioned the project, which was "reoriented," according to NRI president Keith Schuette.[54]

- In Nicaragua, NED made grants of over $350,000 between 1984 and 1986 to a U.S. group, PRODEMCA, to support the opposition newspaper *La Prensa*, to translate and distribute outside of Nicaragua the reports of Nicaragua's Permanent Commission on Human Rights, and to support a "private, nonpartisan center" for the vague purpose of studying democratic ideas.[55] In 1986, PRODEMCA became deeply involved in efforts to rally moderate and liberal U.S. support for the Nicaraguan *Contras* and took out full-page ads in the *Washington Post* and the *New York Times* supporting military aid to the rebels. The PRODEMCA-funded "nonpartisan center" was to be formed for the purposes of the NED grant and included on its proposed board of directors opposition leaders of the *Coordinadora*, an anti-*Sandinista* group representing the traditional parties and private sector.[56]

Yet not all NED grants or those made by its four core grantees have bordered on the directly partisan. NED has funded YMCA youth programs in Panama, supported the Guatemalan reconciliation commission in seeking a peace settlement between the Guatemalan guerrillas and the government, and funded bipartisan election observer missions that have played key roles in preventing or documenting electoral fraud.

In attempting to judge the appropriateness of NED's foreign policy activities, analysts have offered differing perspectives. One view of NED is that it will fund diverse, and controversial, projects because its competing constituencies—the two U.S. political parties, business, and labor—themselves have different conceptions of how to promote democracy.[57] A more critical view is that NED is less interested in supporting democracy abroad than in promoting a narrow foreign policy agenda that serves U.S. security objectives and that NED programs differ little from previous covert efforts to manipulate foreign political systems.[58] The controversy over NED thus extends beyond a simple calculus of whether one supports or opposes those whom NED has made beneficiaries to a question of the ultimate objectives for which that aid is provided.

A review of NED's programs from 1984 to 1990 shows that the bulk of NED-assisted programs are on the moderate to conservative end of the political spectrum—no doubt because three of NED's four core grantees represent private sector, anticommunist union, and conservative political interests. In addition, Latin America has figured disproportionately in NED's overall portfolio of grants, a trend mirrored in historic U.S. efforts to carry out foreign policy in the name of democracy. Further, NED funding of foreign groups is involvement of the sort that the United States does not permit in its own political system.[59] NED has thus served as an instrument for foreign policy elites to use the banner of democracy to promote a wide range of political objectives. This NED shares with U.S. policy, which has attempted to reconcile self-interested intentions in the Third World with loftier professed principles.[60]

State Department Initiatives

The aim of promoting democracy proved politically useful in justifying Central American policy during the Reagan administration, even if that goal was inconsistently pursued throughout the region and typically served as a means to other ends. The Reagan administration failed to support opposition forces in Panama in 1984, for example, partly because the existing government was viewed as a more predictable guarantor of U.S. interests in the Panama Canal and partly because Panamanian Defense Forces leader Gen. Manuel Antonio Noriega provided certain advantages to U.S. intelligence services.[61]

In Honduras in 1985, moreover, the State Department sought credible elections, in part to convince Congress to appropriate large sums of aid for the Honduran military, a key pillar of the anti-*Sandinista Contra* effort. AID provided $5–$10 million for materials and equipment in the 1985 elections; by one account, embassy officials assembled ballot boxes in their offices and made sure they were distributed to the polls.[62] The 1985 elections marked the first time in Honduras that one popularly elected civilian government succeeded another.

The centerpieces of Reagan administration policy in Central America were El Salvador and Nicaragua. In both cases, U.S. rhetorical support for democracy masked a narrower effort to defeat the left, an objective the Reagan administration described as vital to U.S. security. In El Salvador, building democracy was equated almost exclusively with holding elections, seen as the necessary political component of a military effort to defeat left-wing guerrillas vying for power. In Nicaragua, particularly after 1983, democracy was equated with the replacement of the *Sandinista* regime. It served as the banner of war for a *Contra* military effort to overthrow the *Sandinistas*. When that failed, the Bush administration hoisted democracy as the banner of defeat, shifting the focus of U.S. policy to elections and supporting the opposition as a means of getting the *Sandinistas* out of power through the ballot box.

El Salvador

Initial Reagan administration policy in El Salvador had little to do with democracy. Key policymakers viewed the guerrilla war and external support from Cuba and the Soviet Union as a threat to U.S. security and expanded a program of military aid and advisers to wage a counterinsurgency war. Elections entered the policy framework belatedly, as part of a two-pronged effort in support of security goals. This was for two reasons. First, Congress opposed the Reagan administration's emphasis on communist subversion in El Salvador, rather than on such issues as socioeconomic reform and human rights, and called for reductions in aid and for a political settlement through dialogue. Second, senior administration policymakers who clashed with administration ideologues realized that political reform in El Salvador, whose history was replete with fraudulent elections, would have to complement military efforts to defeat the rebels if the Salvadoran government was to gain legitimacy. In the spirit of both considerations, Assistant Secretary of State for Inter-American Affairs Thomas Enders in July 1981 called on "all parties that renounce violence...to participate in the design of new political institutions and the process of choosing representatives."[63]

In March 1982, El Salvador held elections for a national assembly to draft a new constitution. To help secure the credibility of those elections, AID spent $200,000 on a bipartisan U.S. observer mission. In addition, the CIA provided funds for commodities, including invisible ink, that would prevent voters from casting more than one ballot.[64]

U.S. support for the elections extended beyond the technical aspects addressed by AID to political issues relevant to U.S. policy. As a result of the balloting, a coalition of right-wing parties gained control of the assembly and threatened to appoint a reputed death squad leader, Roberto D'Aubuisson, as provisional president. The State Department and the U.S. embassy exerted pressure on the Salvadoran armed forces and the political parties to prevent that outcome, arguing that Congress would cut U.S. aid if D'Aubuisson were named president. U.S. officials helped organize a prominent congressional delegation to deliver the same message. As a result, the Salvadoran Assembly appointed a more neutral figure, Alvaro Magaña, as provisional president.

The March 1982 Salvadoran elections were a public relations coup for the Reagan administration and may have been a factor in the administration's public launching of Project Democracy later that year. Huge numbers of people in El Salvador waited hours in the hot sun to vote, an apparent repudiation of the guerrillas' call to boycott the election and continue armed struggle. President Reagan devoted several paragraphs of his speech to the British Parliament in June 1982 to the Salvadoran vote. Subsequently, the administration invoked El Salvador's elections by way of comparison to Nicaragua, whose leaders had seized power through violent means and had postponed elections until 1985.

When El Salvador held presidential elections in 1984, the United States was again less interested in the exercise of democratic rights than in a political outcome favorable to the United States. Under a $3.4 million elections project launched in 1983, AID officials again supported technical aspects of the elections.[65] But the State Department feared a victory by D'Aubuisson's extreme right-wing ARENA party over the Christian Democratic candidate, José Napoleón Duarte. Over the objection of some AID officials, and in pursuit of a Duarte victory, the CIA channeled funds to the Christian Democrats, particularly to those rural areas where the party was weak. Policymakers in the United States feared not only the congressional reaction to a D'Aubuisson victory, but also the polarizing effect it would have inside El Salvador.[66]

Even revelations of the CIA's role by D'Aubuisson supporters did not detract from the acclaim bestowed on Duarte following his May 1984 victory.[67] And U.S. support for a particular outcome in the Salvadoran elections paid off politically for the Reagan administration. Following Duarte's election, Congress voted record amounts of economic and military aid. The bipartisan consensus that supported U.S. policy in El Salvador endured for the remainder of Reagan's two terms, only to fray under President George Bush following the murder of six Jesuit priests, their housekeeper, and her daughter during a November 1989 guerrilla offensive.[68]

Nicaragua

For most of the decade Reagan administration policy toward Nicaragua centered on efforts to sustain a covert, then overt, war waged by *Contra* rebels to oust the *Sandinista* government. Because the *Sandinistas* maintained extensive military ties to the Soviet Union and Eastern bloc and had expressed solidarity with other Central American revolutionaries, key conservatives within the Reagan administration viewed replacement of the regime as vital to U.S. security.[69] The notion of democracy was only peripheral to this military effort, rhetorically embraced by the Reagan administration as a major theme of U.S. policy after Congress refused to continue supplying the *Contras* with military aid in October 1984.[70]

During the second half of the decade, during which time Congress renewed and then again cut off *Contra* aid, a democratic Nicaragua became the stated goal of policymakers with widely divergent political views. For the Reagan administration and its supporters, democracy was synonymous with the ouster of the *Sandinistas*, who were totalitarian and repressive. A second group, comprised mostly of centrist Democrats in the Congress, sought vaguely defined internal reform in Nicaragua and saw the *Contras* as useful in pressuring the *Sandinista* government to make concessions to its internal opposition and open up its political system.[71] A third group opposed *Contra* funding altogether. It viewed the war and its hardships as responsible for the absence of political freedoms under *Sandinista* rule and held that only when the war stopped could the *Sandinista's* stated commitments to democracy be tested.

During the Reagan administration, support for non-*Sandinista* political groups as a way of bringing about democracy took back seat to the *Contra* War, even though there were reports of covert funding of opposition politicians, particularly at the time of Nicaragua's 1984 presidential elections. From 1985 to 1988,[72] a small amount of overt U.S. assistance went to opposition groups, primarily through NED. Between 1984 and 1988, non-*Sandinista* parties, business, labor, and media groups received approximately $1.9 million through NED.[73] In 1987, *Contra*-aid supporter Sen. Lloyd Bentsen (D-TX) sponsored legislation to send $250,000 to Nicaraguan opposition groups through NED, arguing that the United States was doing too little to support the *Sandinistas'* nonarmed opposition. Ironically, Bentsen had vigorously opposed foreign funding of U.S. elections in the early 1970s. The process of congressional "earmarking" set the stage for an expanded program of assistance in Nicaragua prior to the 1990 elections.

The principal event that shifted U.S. attention from the *Contras* to overt funding for the Nicaraguan political opposition was the peace plan offered by President Oscar Arias of Costa Rica in August 1987. Through a series of accords spanning the next two years, Central American leaders committed themselves to democratizing their own political systems, to ending military interference in the conflicts of neighbors, and to negotiating solutions to their own guerrilla wars. The peace plan offered the

Sandinistas the prospect of ending the *Contra* War in exchange for a commitment to hold broadly contested elections.

The Arias peace plan, together with the Iran-*Contra* scandal, which erupted in late 1986 and festered throughout the following year, eroded congressional support for military aid to the *Contras*. In February and March 1988, Congress cut off military aid. Congress continued a small amount of nonlethal aid, both to allow members to avoid charges that they had abandoned the opposition and, ostensibly, to sustain the *Contras* in the field as a form of pressure prior to the holding of fair elections. As the military effort wound down, Congress directed NED to expand its support for the Nicaraguan internal opposition. In October 1988, Congress designated $2 million for NED activities in Nicaragua as part of the Fiscal Year 1989 foreign aid appropriations bill. A supplemental spending bill that passed in mid-June 1989 included an additional $1.5 million for the "promotion of democracy" in Nicaragua.[74] But the Reagan administration, its *Contra* policy discredited, largely stood on the sidelines of efforts to refocus U.S. policy.

The incoming Bush administration made support for the non-*Sandinista* opposition the centerpiece of its Nicaraguan policy. If opponents of the *Contras* had supported the Arias plan's emphasis on elections as a way of stopping the *Contra* War, *Contra* supporters now saw elections as the way to rid Nicaragua of the *Sandinistas*. Neither the administration nor Congress wanted to prolong bitter partisan struggles over Nicaraguan policy. President Bush and House and Senate leaders signed a bipartisan agreement in March 1989 that, among other things, released the $2 million appropriated in October 1988 for opposition political activity. The purpose of the aid, according to Sally Shelton-Colby, a member of NED's board, was "to help the opposition coalesce and overcome their historical differences and develop a national political structure with a view to getting their message into all corners of Nicaragua."[75]

With U.S. urging, Nicaraguan opposition parties did come together to nominate Violeta Chamorro as their presidential candidate in early September 1989. Within weeks, the administration asked Congress for an additional $9 million to support the opposition through NED. In return for overt funding from the Congress, the administration promised not to provide covert assistance for the Nicaraguan elections, a pledge long sought by opponents of covert activities.[76]

The administration initially considered asking Congress for a change in NED's charter to support Chamorro's candidacy directly.[77] But bowing to criticism that such aid would taint Chamorro's campaign, the administration instead asked for funds vaguely targeted at opposition political activities. Pointing to the *Sandinistas'* control of the state apparatus and their domination of the media, Secretary of State James

Baker III stressed "how important it is that we do everything possible to level the playing field during the Nicaraguan electoral campaign."[78] Congress approved the aid by wide majorities in October 1989; even liberals supported the funding to avoid being blamed if the opposition lost the election.[79]

In practice, the line between "leveling the playing field" and directly supporting the opposition campaign was a thin one, at times vanishing as U.S. leaders made it eminently clear that they preferred a Chamorro victory. According to President Bush, "Violeta Chamorro has told us that the opposition needs our assistance desperately, and that only by receiving help can it make a real contest of this election."[80] Chamorro herself told Congress "how important this help is to us in our struggle to bring democracy to Nicaragua."[81]

The national Democratic and Republican institutes, which administered the bulk of the grants in Nicaragua, drew up elaborate guidelines for their activities in Nicaragua. Under the category "party-building," for example, the two party institutes could provide such physical items as office space, vehicles, office equipment, supplies, and support for office staff. They could also support civic and voter education, including generic presentations, literature, and communications (T-shirts, flags, and banners) to promote democracy and pluralism and to encourage voting. None of the vehicles provided to the National Opposition Union (UNO), however, could be used as sound platforms, and the party institutes could not fund public meetings that endorsed or featured a candidate for public office.[82]

But these detailed distinctions did not prevent UNO from being the principal, if unintended, beneficiary of U.S. funds. UNO itself was slated to receive $1.8 million in U.S. goods, and the Institute for Electoral Training and Promotion (IPCE), which it dominated, $1.3 million.[83] Judging the impact of these funds on the outcome of the election, however, is difficult. First, *Sandinista* obstructionism and bureaucratic delays in the United States held up all but several hundred thousand dollars until just weeks before the election. The tangible benefits of U.S. assistance must thus be seen as marginal.[84] Second, isolating the impact of U.S. support from other factors behind an opposition victory—most notably, widespread disaffection with the *Sandinistas*, resentment of military conscription, and the disastrous state of the economy—is next to impossible.

To the extent that the training of pollwatchers, which did take place, led to faith in the confidentiality of the vote, U.S. funds may have contributed to a more fair electoral process. (This, no doubt, was also the function of observers from the OAS and the United Nations, as well as, to a lesser extent, a prominent bipartisan U.S. observer delegation.) The most important impact of U.S. funding, however, may have been the intangible psychological advantage it conferred on the opposition. In this respect, the assistance helped achieve what its sponsors in the administration and Congress had hoped for: the defeat of the *Sandinistas* through the ballot box.

Conclusions

Electoral assistance emerged in the 1980s as an ostensibly new foreign policy initiative in Central America, but the roots of that policy were at least several decades old. Political development programs in Latin America dated as far back as 1961 during the Alliance for Progress, when the Kennedy administration sought to promote democratic governments by expanding popular participation, even as the administration subverted democratic aspirations by exporting anticommunist doctrines to Latin American military establishments. Congressional efforts to focus economic aid on programs that would enhance pluralism culminated in the passage of Title IX to the Foreign Assistance Act, which formally launched AID's Civic Participation Division. As government after government in Latin America was overthrown by the military, Congress again moved to tie U.S. assistance to political rights. Long before President Carter embarked on the politics of human rights, Congress passed amendments linking foreign economic and military aid to a recipient nation's ability to guarantee individual liberties.

During the early 1980s, the congressional directive that foreign assistance be linked with respect for individual rights took on a new ideological dimension. For the Reagan administration, fighting communism became the equivalent of supporting democracy, which by definition rested on free enterprise. Congress had had enough experience with anticommunist crusades, however cloaked, to enthusiastically embrace the administration's approach, but both liberals and conservatives supported efforts to reinforce noncommunist groups abroad through the creation of a quasi-governmental organization, NED, in late 1983.

During the Reagan administration, policy planners at the Department of State and the Agency for International Development were divided as to what democracy meant at an operational level. On the one hand, some saw the support of free and fair elections as the essential component of democracy in Central America: a nation's ability to hold a clean election, this was an end unto itself. On the other hand, a different group of policymakers saw electoral assistance as only one part of a broader ideological war that operationally became a more martial affair, manifested in support for the *Contra* rebels or in increased military assistance programs in El Salvador and Honduras. By militarily supporting opponents of Soviet-backed governments or insurgencies, proponents of the military victory approach believed democracy could emerge out of the barrel of a gun.

Some observers have said that the tension between AID and the Department of State over electoral assistance was rooted in AID's technical as opposed to the State Department's political approach.[85] This chapter suggests, however, that the bureaucratic tension was much deeper. It stemmed from divergent views of how to achieve victory over the communist enemy in the name of democracy. Achievement of that victory militarily or through peaceful participatory means more accurately characterizes what divided the two agencies. Less obvious, albeit significant, is that, as the decade progressed, AID no longer considered democracy a means to developmental goals and did not tie it to economic development at all. This was a major departure from the 1960s, however flawed the original assumptions about the relationship between development and democracy might have been.

In further contrast to earlier decades, the 1980s saw a plethora of new actors participating in electoral activities in Central America. Not only was the U.S. government involved both directly and indirectly, other groups such as the National Endowment for Democracy, the National Democratic Institute, the National Republican Institute, and the Center for Democracy (the outgrowth of the Democracy Project funded by AID) also played roles in electoral programs. In Central America, the creation of CAPEL in 1983 embodied the desire of Central American presidents to promote a peaceful resolution to the ongoing civil wars through development of a training center dedicated to teaching electoral process and providing hemispherewide assistance. In the ensuing years, CAPEL became closely identified with U.S. assistance programs.[86]

Ultimately one of the principal products of U.S. policy in Central America during the 1980s was a domestic one—the creation of an uneasy liberal-conservative consensus that, in Latin America, U.S. interests are better served by democratic governments that support free elections than by authoritarian regimes that carry out repressive policies in the name of stability. If conservatives, including leading ideologues in the Reagan administration, were forced to abandon their preference for stable authoritarians, liberals had to swallow the expansion of U.S. programs that promised the consolidation of democracy, even if it meant interference in Latin American political systems. Needless to say, neither side can claim total vindication of its beliefs.

Yet is this new U.S. political consensus relevant to the problems of Central America in an era of post-cold war politics? Certainly the ability of Central American societies to rebuild after a bloody decade of civil wars will depend on inclusionary political processes, of which elections are only a part. Support for elections to guarantee democracy must be part of a larger program that assists in maintaining the opening of political space that elections can bring, if only temporarily, to civic culture. This means that democracy also depends on the behavior of institutions that traditionally have seen the opening of political space as threatening and that definitions of democracy must expand to encompass new levels of participation (e.g., an independent judiciary is essential to maintaining an open political space for the electoral process).

The linkage between political democracy and economic development, however, remains problematic. Although the Latin American experience in the 1980s shows a weak correlation between economic crisis and the slowing of the transition toward civilian government, the depth of the economic crisis in Central America and the relatively less developed political systems there offer scant hope for democratic advancement. Ironically the promotion of free enterprise that the Reagan administration viewed as central to democracy and a key to economic recovery became derailed by the overwhelming efforts to crush what the administration viewed as communist-inspired movements.

Ultimately, although the United States has proven relatively successful in raising the technical standards of election-holding, it has proven deficient in addressing those structural problems in Central American societies that impede democratic development. The ongoing power of Latin American militaries to circumscribe civilian authority and to repress their populations and the socioeconomic structures that historically have gone hand-in-hand with the curtailment of political liberties remains intact in most Central American countries.

In Central America initiatives to create or expand political openings or to reinforce civilian leadership over other powerful elements of society must be sui generis. The United States, through official and private efforts, can contribute to a process of democratization, but it cannot substitute for a local consensus that affirms the necessity and desirability of reform. Above all, the United States must refrain from using democracy as a catchword for a variety of self-interested policies whose end results may contradict the goals of democracy. Rather, democracy as it develops in the Central America must chart its own course and implement broad goals that promote civic participation, freedom of speech and assembly, and, above all, justice to those who need it most.

Notes

1. As the United States embarked on its famous foreign policy effort in the 1960s, the Alliance for Progress, historian Robert Quirk commented that "There is still today the insistence upon the universal beneficence of the American brand of equality and individualism and on the superiority of American enterprise and technology. There also persists the urge to force upon 'backward peoples' whether they want them or not. And there is still present what Latin Americans have resented most about the United States—an insufferable air of superiority in our relations with others, even when we are trying to help them." *An Affair of Honor* (New York: Norton, 1962), Preface, w/n.

2. See, for example, Louis Hartz, *The Liberal Tradition in America: An Interpretation of American Political Thought Since the Revolution* (New York: Harcourt, Brace and World, 1955).

3. See, for example, Walter LaFeber, *Inevitable Revolutions* (New York: W. W. Norton, 1984); Michael Hunt, *The Ideology of U.S. Foreign Policy* (New Haven: Yale University Press, 1987); Albert K. Weinberg, *Manifest Destiny* (Baltimore: The Johns Hopkins University Press, 1935); Bryce Wood, *The Making of the Good Neighbor Policy* (New York: Norton, 1961).

4. For an overview of the evolution of U.S. assistance policies and their underlying ideologies, see Robert A. Packenham, *Liberal America and the Third World* (Princeton, N.J.: Princeton University Press, 1973).

5. The extent to which AID programming in the "political development" area achieved intended effects is unclear. But AID stressed the ways in which aid could be used to strengthen cooperatives, unions, and other aspects of a pluralistic political system. See Packenham, *Liberal America*, pp. 67–68.

6. Jerome Levinson and Juan de Onis, *The Alliance That Lost Its Way* (Chicago: Quadrangle Books, 1970); Dennis Rondinelli, *Development Administration and U.S. Foreign Aid Policy: Studies in Development Management* (Boulder, Colo.: Lynne Rienner Publishers, 1987).

7. See, for example, Carl Gershman, "The U.S. and the World Democratic Revolution" *The Washington Quarterly* (Winter 1989):125.

8. From USAID, LAC Bureau, internal policy statement, dated July 24, 1990.

9. See Jeanne Kirkpatrick, "Dictatorships and Double Standards," *Commentary* (November 1979):34–45. Kirkpatrick argued that totalitarian regimes were impervious to change from within, whereas authoritarian regimes could evolve in a more democratic direction. The thesis suggested that the United States should tolerate the excesses of pro-U.S. dictators rather than destabilize them through pressures to reform.

10. United States Department of State, Bureau of Public Affairs, *Democracy in Latin America and the Caribbean: The Promise and the Challenge*, Special Report 158, Washington, D.C., March 1987, pp. 20–21. Bolivia, Chile, Paraguay, and Haiti are the other Latin American states; Washington Office on Latin America (WOLA), Discussion Paper, "U.S. Electoral Assistance and Democratic Development in Latin America: Chile, Nicaragua and Panama," Washington, D.C., January 19, 1990, p. 15. Hereinafter WOLA Discussion Paper.

11. A review of AID programs and projects based on computer print outs using the word *democracy* revealed over 700 projects since the 1960s. In reviewing the project descriptions, it is clear that foreign development assistance administrators have always viewed a pluralism component as part of any economic development program. Therefore, democracy was more a subconscious component of many a program than an overt attempt to achieve a political end.

12. Interview, Ambassador Luigi Einaudi, October 9, 1990. It also has been suggested, even in internal agency reviews, that AID has not always been receptive to carrying out congressional mandates to build democratic institutions. To deal with congressional mandates AID has established special offices or the work has been contracted out to private voluntary organization, "thus presumably removing AID from the onus of everyday involvement in promoting these initiatives. See John P. Mason, "AID's Experience with Democratic Initiatives: A Review of Regional Programs in Legal Institution Building." AID Program Evaluation Discussion Paper No. 29, February 1990 (USAID).

13. Funding for electoral assistance programs is channeled through USAID's Latin America and Caribbean Bureau (LAC) and its Office of Democratic Initiatives (ODI). LAC/DI was created out of the increased funding for the region that followed the release of the Report of the National Bipartisan Commission on Central America (Kissinger Commission). Not only does this part of AID provide electoral assistance, but it also supports municipal governments, aid to judiciaries, labor unions, and the press. LAC/DI's largest program has been the Administration of Justice, which receives approximately $20 million a year. Creative Associates, *A Retrospective of A.I.D.'s Experience in Strengthening Democratic Institutions in Latin America, 1961-81*, Washington, D.C., September 1987, and Washington Office on Latin America, ibid.

14. Quoted in Packenham, *Liberal America*, p. 100.

15. Mason, "AID's Experience," Appendix B.

16. Agency for International Development, "Popular Participation in Development: Title IX, A Selected List of References," *AID Bibliography Series*, Washington, D.C., August 15, 1978.

17. This had been the case, for example, with the National Student Association and the Asia Foundation, two private groups that received CIA money.

18. The Democracy Program, "The Commitment to Democracy: A Bipartisan Approach," Interim Report, April 18, 1983, p. 2.

19. For a discussion of congressional legislation leading up to the provisions tying military and economic aid to human rights, see Lars Schoultz, *Human Rights and United States Policy Toward Latin America* (Princeton, N.J: Princeton University Press, 1981), chaps. 4 and 6.

20. "A Retrospective of AID's Experience in Strengthening Democratic Institutions in Latin America, 1961–81," September 1987, prepared under contract with Creative Associates for AID, LAC Bureau, Office of Administration of Justice and Democratic Development.

21. See Mason, "AID's Experience," p. 6.

22. Viron P. Vaky, "Democratization as a Foreign Policy Goal," paper presented at World Peace Foundation program, "How the United States Can Promote Democracy in Latin America: Some Lessons from the Past," Washington, D.C., May 23, 1989.

23. "Democratic Initiatives Program Structure," USAID, July 24, 1990, w/n.

24. Ibid., w/n.

25. WOLA Discussion Paper, p. 17. For example, Honduras alone received $15 million in electoral assistance during this period.

26. AID's bilateral electoral assistance is now a small component of the democracy programs in Central America. Of the FY89 budget of $12.9 million, bilateral electoral programs comprised only $1.07 million with low cash transfers. WOLA, Discussion Paper, ibid., p. 17.

27. Thomas Carothers, "U.S. Electoral Aid to Latin America: The Question of Political Neutrality" (Paper presented at WOLA Conference on "U.S. Electoral Assistance in Latin America: Chile, Panama, and Nicaragua," Washington, D.C., January 19, 1990), pp. 8–9.

28. Ibid., p. 9.

29. See State Department Special Report No. 158, p. 20.

30. David K. Shipler, "The Role of the United States in an Age of Democratic Revolution" (Paper presented at the WOLA Conference on "U.S. Electoral Assistance and Democratic Development in Latin America: Chile, Panama, and Nicaragua," Washington, D.C., January 19, 1990).

31. Address by President Reagan before the British Parliament, "Promoting Democracy and Peace," June 8, 1982, reprinted by the Department of State, *Current Policy*, No. 399, p. 4.

32. Ibid., p. 4.

33. Thomas Carothers, "The Resurgence of United States Political Development Assistance to Latin America," unpublished manuscript, p. 3; and John Felton, "Committees Revamp 'Project Democracy,'" *Congressional Quarterly Weekly Report*, June 4, 1983, p. 1112.

34. Joel Brinkley, "Iran Sales Linked to Wide Program of Covert Policies," *New York Times*, February 15, 1987.

35. Address by President Reagan before the British Parliament, p. 4.

36. Brinkley, "Iran Sales." The article erroneously reported that the National Endowment for Democracy was the overt side of Project Democracy, a term later adopted by Lt. Col. Oliver North to describe his program of covert assistance to the Nicaraguan contras.

37. Felton, "Committees Revamp 'Project Democracy,'" pp. 1112–14; Secretary of State George Shultz, "Project Democracy," February 23, 1983, testimony before a House Foreign Affairs Subcommittee, reprinted in Department of State, *Current Policy*, No. 456, February 23, 1983, pp. 2–3.

38. Marilyn Zak, "Assisting Elections in the Third World," *Washington Quarterly* 10, 4 (1987):175.

39. Interviews with AID official, February 28, 1990; and with Ambassador Einaudi, October 9, 1990.

40. Funding for these efforts was already available under the broad mandate of Section 116(e) of the Foreign Assistance Act.

41. Zak, "Assisting Elections," p. 175.

42. Washington Office on Latin America (WOLA), "U.S. Electoral Assistance and Democratic Development: Chile, Nicaragua and Panama," *Proceedings of a Conference*, January 19, 1990, February 1990, pp. 1–2.

43. U.S. Department of State, Bureau of Public Affairs, "Democracy in Latin America and the Caribbean: The Promise and the Challenge," p. 20.

44. See the Democracy Program, "The Commitment to Democracy," p. 2.

45. The Resource Center, "The Democracy Offensive," Bulletin No. 18, Fall 1989, p. 3. See also Ralph M. Goldman, "The Democratic Mission: A Brief History," in *Promoting Democracy*, ed. Ralph M. Goldman and William A. Douglas (New York: Praeger, 1988), p. 18. For example, American Political Foundation Director Agree recruited former Republican National Committee Chairman William E. Brock III and Democratic National Finance Council Chairman Charles T. Manatt as chairman and vice-chairman, respectively. The foundation sponsored a series of bipartisan political exchanges, principally with Europe. Later, Brock and others convened a series of meetings to explore creating a nongovernmental agency to support political entities abroad.

46. See the Democracy Program, pp. 3–6 and Appendix A (text, letter from William Brock III, Charles T. Manatt, and [Republican official] Richard Richards to President Reagan, June 4, 1982, p. 2); Goldman, "Democratic Mission," pp. 18–20.

47. The AFL-CIO's American Insitute for Free Labor Development was reportedly looking for an alternative to CIA funding lost in the late 1960s. See Carothers, "Resurgence," p. 4.

48. The agreement was struck with Sen. William Proxmire (D-WI), as an alternative to his proposed legislation to prohibit the NED from hiring any individual with a prior intelligence association. See *Congressional Record*, November 17, 1983, p. S 16430.

49. For the political background of key officials connected with the NED, see Michael Massing, "Trotsky's Orphans," *New Republic*, June 22, 1987, pp. 18–22.

50. See David Shipler, "Missionaries for Democracy: U.S. Aid for Global Pluralism," *New York Times*, June 1, 1986.

51. National Endowment for Democracy, "Statement of Principles and Objectives," p. 1.

52. Shipler, "Role of the United States," p. 6. U.S. ambassador to Panama James E. Briggs cabled Washington that "it would be embarrassing to the United States if the labor institute's use of endowment funds to support one side in Panama's elections became public knowledge. The Ambassador requests that this project be discontinued before the U.S. Government is further compromised." Quoted in Ben A. Franklin, "Project Democracy Takes Wing," *New York Times*, May 29, 1984.

53. Remarks by John Dinges, in Washington Office on Latin America, "U.S. Electoral Assistance..." *Proceedings*, p. 27.

54. Robert S. Greenberger, "U.S. Group Aided Arias's Costa Rica Foes," *Wall Street Journal*, October 13, 1989; and National Endowment for Democracy, *Annual Report*, 1986, p. 35.

55. National Endowment for Democracy, *Annual Report*, 1985, pp. 11 and 46; and *Annual Report*, 1986, p. 42.

56. Julia Preston, "U.S. Finances Rights Group in Nicaragua," *Washington Post*, July 11, 1986. NED director Carl Gershman complained to the *Post* that the PRODEMCA relieved itself of the *La Prensa* grant prior to the appearance of the PRODEMCA ad supporting *Contra* military aid. (The grant was taken over by Delphi Research Associates.) But PRODEMCA did not relieve itself of the grant to the human rights commission.

57. David Shipler in Washington Office on Latin America, "U.S. Electoral Assistance..." *Proceedings*, p. 12.

58. See, for example, David Corn, "Foreign Aid for the Right," *The Nation*, December 18, 1989, pp. 744–46; and The Resource Center, "The Democracy Offensive," Bulletin No. 18, Fall 1989, Albuquerque, New Mexico, pp. 1–6. In supporting its claims, the Resource Center notes the preponderance of right-wing Social Democrats on NED's board, including NED director Carl Gershman.

59. Congress tightened restrictions on foreign funding of U.S. elections after the Watergate scandal. In the words of Sen. Lloyd Bentsen (D-TX), "I do not think foreign nationals have any business in our political campaigns. They cannot vote in our elections, so why should we allow them to finance our elections? Their loyalties lie elsewhere." Quoted in John Spicer Nichols, "Get the N.E.D. Out of Nicaragua," *The Nation*, February 26, 1990.

60. For further elaboration of the U.S. image of its role and purpose in the world, see Vaky, "Democratization," pp. 1–2.

61. See John Dinges, *Our Man in Panama* (New York: Random House, 1990).

62. Carothers, "Resurgence," p. 8.

63. Cynthia Arnson, *Crossroads: Congress, the Reagan Administration, and Central America* (New York: Pantheon, 1989), pp. 69–70.

64. The CIA also provided the Salvadoran government with "information and capabilities" to reduce the supply of weapons to the Salvadoran guerrillas and to "break up guerrilla formations intended to destroy the election." See William J. Casey, "How the C.I.A. Helped in Salvador's Election," *New York Times* (letter to the editor), July 30, 1982.

65. The Salvadoran government contributed an additional $8.75 million in local currency for the 1984 and 1985 elections, money generated from U.S. Economic Support Funds. Telephone interview, Lorraine Simard, El Salvador desk officer, Office of Central American Affairs, U.S. Agency for International Development, October 18, 1990; USAID, Abstract, "Salvadoran Elections Program, FY 83–85," Project Paper PD-KAA-750, August 16, 1983; and USAID, "El Salvador: Assistance to Elections," undated factsheet.

66. Some U.S. officials warned against the covert aid, arguing that it would detract from the credibility of the elections and of Duarte's mandate. An official of AID did receive death threats after news of the covert funding seeped out and subsequently had to flee El Salvador. Following the elections, the right also reportedly plotted to assassinate U.S. Ambassador Thomas Pickering. See Arnson, *Crossroads*, pp. 149–50. A different account is that the CIA provided $1.4 million to the Christian Democrats and the National Conciliation Party

(PCN) out of $2.1 million spent on the election. See Jeff Gerth, "C.I.A. Has Long Sought to Sway Foreign Voters," *New York Times*, May 13, 1984.

67. A notable exception was Sen. Jesse Helms (R-NC), who railed against the CIA's involvement in the May 8, 1984, *Congressional Record*. Helms was reportedly rebuked by the Senate Intelligence Committee for revealing classified information.

68. AID provided additional assistance for El Salvador's 1988 municipal elections ($300,000 for an election observer mission) and for the 1989 presidential elections ($2 million in local currency for voter registration, distribution of voter cards, observer missions). WOLA Discussion Paper.

69. These officials included CIA Director William Casey, National Security Adviser William Clark, U.N. Representative Jeanne Kirkpatrick, and Under Secretary of Defense Fred Ikle.

70. From mid-1982 through mid-1983, some State Department officials, including Assistant Secretary of State Thomas Enders, viewed the *Contra* War as a means to force the *Sandinistas* to make political concessions, including concessions over democratization. By July 1983 Enders had been forced out of office; dominant hardliners, informed by Jeanne Kirkpatrick's thesis that totalitarian regimes are impervious to reformist pressures, sought instead a *Sandinista* overthrow.

71. Text, Sen. Sam Nunn (D-GA), Speech to the Coalition for a Democratic Majority, April 17, 1985, in *Congressional Record*, April 23, 1985, p. S 4595; and Bernard Aronson, "Another Choice in Nicaragua," *New Republic*, May 27, 1985, pp. 698–99.

72. In a three-year period, Congress moved from a position of opposition to *Contra* aid, to a position of nonlethal, then lethal aid to the rebels, and finally to a position of no military aid at all. For an explanation of the shifts, see Aronson, *Crossroads*, 169–206.

73. National Endowment for Democracy, *Annual Reports*, 1984, 1985, 1986, 1987, 1988.

74. John Felton, "Rare Aid Funding Bill Comes Down to the Wire," *Congressional Quarterly Weekly Report*, October 1, 1988, pp. 2735–36; David Rapp, "Conferees Finish Supplemental, Remain Split on Drug Funds," *Congressional Quarterly Weekly Report*, June 17, 1989, p. 1454.

75. Robert Pear, "U.S. Allots $2 Million to Aid Anti-Sandinistas," *New York Times*, April 25, 1989. In April, the Nicaraguan Assembly lifted a provision in Nicaraguan law that prohibited foreign political donations and mandated prison terms for those who accepted them; instead, the Assembly required that 50 percent of the donation go to the Supreme Electoral Council to defray the costs of the election.

76. The Intelligence Authorization bill for FY90 contained no funds for covert assistance to the elections in Nicaragua.

77. This idea originated with several members of the civic opposition (including Alfredo Cesar, Guillermo Potoy, and Adan Fletes) who traveled to Washington in September 1989. The $9 million figure also originated with them. Interview, Program Officer, National Democratic Institute, July 25, 1990. Section 505(a)(1) of NED's enabling legislation states that "funds may not be expended,

either by the Endowment or by any of its grantees, to finance the campaigns of candidates for public office." Cited in *Congressional Record*, October 4, 1989, p. H 6629.

78. Text, letter from James A. Baker III to Thomas S. Foley, September 20, 1989, p. 1. An attached fact sheet "Funding for the Nicaraguan Internal Opposition," broke down the $9 million as follows: $5 million for NED activities, including "election monitoring, voter registration, get-out-the-vote efforts, communications support and building party infrastructure" and $4 million for "additional non-partisan, technical support for the election process," including the "minimum contribution to satisfy the Nicaraguan Supreme Electoral Council's 50% 'tax.'"

79. The funds provided assistance to "political organizations, alliances, independent elements of the media, independent labor unions, and business, civic, and professional groups." Text, P.L. 101–119. The funds went to AID, which granted $7.735 million to NED. Of that, $4.12 million went to the National Democratic Institute and the National Republican Institute, $493,013 went to the Free Trade Union Institute, and $220,000 to the Internal Foundation for Electoral Systems. NED used close to $3 million to meet the Nicaraguan requirement for a 50 percent donation to the Supreme Electoral Council and to supplement other projects. See George Vickers, "U.S. Funding of the Nicaraguan Opposition: A Preliminary Assessment," unpublished manuscript, p. 2ff.

80. Text of letter to Senate Minority Leader Robert Dole, *Congressional Record*, October 17, 1989, p. S 13532.

81. *Congressional Record*, October 17, 1989, p. S 13523.

82. Allowable Program Activities and Related Costs," and "Examples of Allowable and Unallowable Activities and Related Costs," Grant Agreement Between National Republican Institute for International Affairs and National Democratic Institute for International Affairs and *La Unión Nacional Opositora*, Grant No. 90/10.89-5.90/NIC.U.1, December 1989. The same provision appeared in the grant agreement with the *Instituto Para la Promocion y La Capacitacion Electoral* (IPEC), Appendix C.

83. PCE was to carry out voter and civic education, registration verification, and poll-watching. One IPCE board member, Alfredo Cesar, was Violeta Chamorro's principal campaign adviser. Another, Luis Sanchez, was UNO's official spokesperson. IPCE was incorporated on October 17, 1989, the same day Congress approved funding for the Nicaraguan election. See Vickers, "U.S. Funding," pp. 8–9. For details on the overlap between UNO and IPCE, see also Jacqueline Sharkey, "Nicaragua: Anatomy of an Election," *Common Cause Magazine* (May/June 1990): 20–29.

84. See, for example, Robert Pear, "U.S. Aid Just Dribbles in to Nicaragua Opposition, but Sandinistas Profit," *New York Times*, February 4, 1990; and AFP, "Government Releases Campaign Funds to IPCE," *Foreign Broadcast Information Service*, February 2, 1990, p. 38.

85. Carothers, "U.S. Electoral Aid," pp. 8–9.

86. Ibid., p. 9, states: "As a non-governmental organization, CAPEL operates independently of larger national policies and focuses exclusively on non-partisan, technical electoral assistance. Nonetheless, in some cases, [such as Haiti in 1987] the U.S. government has in effect used CAPEL as an instrument of U.S. policy by urging CAPEL to carry out election assistance projects in situations where a U.S. government project might offend local political sensitivities."

15

Esquipulas: Politicians in Command

William Goodfellow and James Morrell

Esquipulas is the story of militarists and ideologues being supplanted by politicians, with their penchant for messy compromises, their suppleness in dealing with questions of hallowed principle, and their genius for finding solutions that satisfy nobody yet somehow stop the shooting. From the moment the five presidents of Central America—some with enthusiasm, some with reluctance—strode up the aisle of the Guatemalan National Palace on the afternoon of August 7, 1987, to sign the Arias plan, notice was served to the ideologues in Washington and to the army officers of Central America that politicians' ways would now be applied to Central America's disputes.

These politicians knew well that they were working in a highly circumscribed area, but they were used to that. Central American politicians had spent their lives working in the narrow space left for them by the region's militaries and the United States. For decades they had supplied their nations with a shadow political life—the full regalia of multiple political parties, candidates, platforms, and elections but with truncated power once in "office." How natural now that they should engage in shadow diplomacy—ostensibly diplomacy among the five Central American countries, but, because these countries were not fighting each other, in reality in negotiations between Nicaragua and any interlocutors they could find in Washington.

And just as an enduring dynamic of party politics in Central America was always to expand the power of civilian politicians vis-à-vis their military overlords, so the dynamic of Esquipulas was to make the surrogate negotiations real. The Reagan administration refused to negotiate, but Congress eventually would, and it increasingly embraced the deal offered by the Central Americans: effacement of *Sandinista* radicalism in return for calling off the *Contras*.

The *Sandinista* diplomats had proven incapable of pulling off such a deal by themselves. Since 1979 *Sandinista* diplomacy had progressed from a series of failures in bilateral relations with the United States to concertation with Latin America's political class. Contadora was the first forum in which this concertation took place. After four years of frustration, from 1983 to 1987, the Contadora plan became the Arias plan—a plan that seemed capable of deflecting further U.S. attacks. The ideologically driven hostility of the U.S. right wing and much of the Washington political establishment would not cease. But once it became clear the *Contras* could not win, a series of politically adroit concessions by Managua in regional negotiations demonstrated a pragmatism that undermined the Reagan administration's case in Congress for more aid to the *Contras*. Forced by dire necessity, *Sandinista* diplomats learned the patience, flexibility, and political wile that enabled them to extract benefits from a diplomatic forum in which they were frequently outnumbered four to one by Washington's allies in Central America. However disadvantageous the forum, it offered safety in numbers and gave the *Sandinistas* a mechanism for making concessions on internal matters—above all, elections—on which, for reasons of pride, they could never negotiate with the United States.

U.S. hostility was the backdrop to all diplomatic efforts. Although the hostility moderated during the first years of the revolution (1979–81), it returned with full force during the Reagan years. To be sure, within the State Department some career officers worked hard for an agreement and sincerely believed a bilateral or regional treaty that contained the *Sandinistas* would best serve U.S. national interests. But Ronald Reagan, William Casey, Caspar Weinberger, William Clark, Oliver North, Elliott Abrams, and others at the top simply wanted to get rid of the *Sandinistas*. For them negotiations, either bilateral or regional, under the sponsorship of the Contadora countries got in the way of stronger measures that could be used to oust the government in Managua.

Given the Washington ideologues' stranglehold on policy, the failure of bilateral negotiations with Nicaragua was inevitable. As former U.S. ambassador to Nicaragua Lawrence Pezzullo put it, "No matter what you do, you are always going to get a new approach by the right that will shoot you down. Because all the people in this administration are people who shoot down negotiations rather than people who negotiate."[1]

The collapse of U.S.-Nicaraguan negotiations and the launching of the *Contras* motivated Mexico to convene a meeting of its foreign minister and those of Colombia, Panama, and Venezuela on Contadora

Island in January 1983. The goal of the Contadora group was to guide the five Central American countries toward reaching a peace agreement among themselves that would limit superpower (mainly U.S.) intervention in the region. Contadora filled the diplomatic vacuum left by the United States. Because the Reagan administration refused to negotiate seriously, Contadora would arrange a regional settlement and confront the United States with the result.

Contadora was a major step forward, if only because it put in the lead politicians who wanted to negotiate instead of Washington ideologues who wanted to "shoot down" negotiations. Moreover, Contadora cobbled together a negotiating group—the five Central American countries—and a forum that in this context had not previously existed.

For a year and a half Contadora marked time as the Central Americans argued about details. Nicaragua was wary of the provisions about internal democratization that smacked of foreign interference, and Secretary of State George Shultz seized on this as an example of the *Sandinistas'* inflexibility. Nicaragua, he charged, "has rejected key elements of the draft, including those dealing with binding obligations to internal democratization and to reductions in arms and troop levels."[2]

Shultz was wrong: the rigid nationalists of 1979, the *Sandinistas*, were becoming politicians. On September 21 Nicaraguan president Daniel Ortega shocked Washington with this reply to Contadora: "We inform you of the Nicaraguan government's decision to accept in its totality, immediately and without modifications, the revised proposal submitted on September 7 by the Contadora group."

All a flabbergasted State Department official could say was, "It's not at all clear to me that in the long run Nicaragua won't come to regret its precipitous action." Nicaragua's offer to sign he dismissed as a "good negotiations ploy" but one that would "come back and haunt them....So it remains to be seen who will get the last laugh on this one."[3]

Nicaragua's response was significant because for the first time one of the major parties to the dispute had said yes. It would take until October 30 before the National Security Council staff could report,

> We have trampled the latest Nicaraguan/Mexican efforts to rush signature of an unsatisfactory Contadora agreement....We have effectively blocked Contadora group efforts to impose the second draft of the Revised Contadora Act. Following intensive U.S. consultations with El Salvador, Honduras, and Costa Rica, the Central Americans submitted a counter-draft to the Contadora states on October 20, 1984. It reflects many of our concerns and shifts the focus within Contadora to a document broadly

consistent with U.S. interests....Contadora spokesmen have become notably subdued recently on prospects for an early signing.[4]

One problem, however, perplexed the administration in its continued efforts to weld the other four Central American countries into an anti-*Sandinista* bloc (the "Core Four"):

> The uncertain support of Guatemala for the Core Four is a continuing problem. Continuing personality problems...continue to hamper efforts to keep the Core Four together. We will continue to exert strong pressure on Guatemala to support the basic Core Four position.[5]

The United States never did prod Guatemala back into the fold, and U.S. diplomatic strategy would completely collapse when, far from recruiting Guatemala, it would lose Costa Rica as well.

This loss was still in the future. The failure of Costa Rica, El Salvador, and Honduras to sign the revised Contadora draft in 1984 sent negotiations into a tailspin. These three countries met in Tegucigalpa on October 19, 1984, to produce a counterdraft, which no longer prohibited U.S. military bases, exercises, and advisers in the region.

In the bubbling cauldron that was the Reagan administration, Secretary of State Shultz bobbed temporarily to the top in the spring of 1984. He conceived of a new negotiation with Managua that President Reagan let go forward because Congress was balking at aid to the *Contras*. For the president this was the decisive point: "How do we get that support in the Congress?"[6]

Shultz met Ortega at the Managua airport to propose bilateral talks, which began in Manzanillo, Mexico, in June. By August the U.S. negotiator finally had clearance to present a proposal, left incomplete by action of the right in Washington. In return for Nicaragua expelling all Soviet and Cuban military advisers, the United States promised only to take Nicaraguan actions into consideration. The *Sandinistas* came back in October with a counteroffer based on the Contadora agreement. Once Reagan was safely reelected, the U.S. side broke off the talks in January 1985.

The Manzanillo failure again left the field to the four Contadora countries, who were soon joined by a "support group" of Argentina, Brazil, Peru, and Uruguay. Foreign ministers of the eight countries met in Caraballeda, Venezuela, and issued on January 12, 1986, the rousing "Caraballeda Message," insisting on simultaneous, parallel work in both signing Contadora and preparing the groundwork (i.e., stopping aid to the *Contras*). Three days later, the Central American presidents found themselves together in Guatemala City for the inauguration of President

Vinicio Cerezo—that country's first elected civilian politician in many years. An energetic politician, Cerezo corralled the other presidents into endorsing the Caraballeda Message.

The Esquipulas Process

Cerezo also persuaded the presidents to reconvene at Esquipulas, Guatemala, intending at this meeting to clear the last obstacles to Contadora's signing. It soon became evident, however, that they had come to argue. The newly elected president of Costa Rica, Oscar Arias, who had left Ortega off the invitation list for his inauguration, now argued with him about democracy. The presidents went away empty-handed. Their foreign ministers followed suit a month later by failing to sign Contadora. Nicaragua and Guatemala apparently would have signed, but the traditional trio of Costa Rica, El Salvador, and Honduras demurred. Reagan promptly persuaded the House of Representatives to pass $100 million in military aid for the *Contras*.

Genesis of the Arias Plan

Arias began his role as an international negotiator inauspiciously. Yet over the course of his presidency his skills in this area became evident. One of the key moments in the Central American peace process had already occurred at the beginning of 1986, late at night over bottles of wine as he met with his advisers to hammer out the strategy for his presidential campaign.

Arias was trailing in the polls, and some advisers blamed the *Contra* issue. People were saying that the candidate who took the hardest line against Nicaragua would win. *La Nacion,* the leading newspaper in Costa Rica, said that 90 percent of the Costa Ricans supported the *Contras*. "I would rather lose the election than run a prowar campaign," Arias declared. And with this he decided to run on a peace platform. Then, when he won the election, he not only would take office but would also be secure in public support for his policies.

He already had in mind a peace plan. But coming to office he found Costa Rica clandestinely involved in the *Contra* War: it was authorizing use of a CIA airstrip at Santa Elena to supply the *Contras*, allowing aid to the *Contras* to flow through its territory and serving as a base for hundreds of CIA agents.[7] It took Arias a year to close down the airstrip and begin clearing out the CIA agents.

In February 1987, Arias called a meeting of Central American presidents, again excluding Ortega, to discuss the plan he had quietly composed. The meeting appeared to inaugurate Nicaragua's isolation. Instead, however, it produced a plan for Nicaragua's reentry into the Central American community.

This was the Arias plan, essentially the same as was finally signed by all five presidents in August 1987. The plan carefully balanced requirements for internal democratization and an end to external support for rebels. It was a politician's plan. It dispensed with Contadora's elaborate military provisions against bases and foreign military involvement in the region and other evocations of Third World neutralism and concentrated on ending the *Contra* War in return for internal changes in Nicaragua.

The other presidents arrived in San José expecting a one-sided plan against Nicaragua. They were shocked by the clauses against the *Contras*. El Salvador's President José Napoleón Duarte said, "If I sign this plan, you might as well shoot me here, because I will be shot when I return."

Meanwhile, in Managua, President Ortega was fuming, furious at President Arias for excluding him. Costa Rica was a "neocolony" and a "traitor," he snapped. But he quickly forgot his harsh words. President Cerezo stopped off in Managua on his way back from San José and briefed Ortega on the summit. By February 18, Ortega reversed himself, finding much in the Arias plan worthy of study and pledging to go to the next Esquipulas meeting. The same game of musical chairs had gone on so long within the Contadora, that it is not surprising negotiations now began again. As Nicaragua began to favor a peace plan, the U.S. allies turned against it.

Such was the confused, tumultuous birth of the Arias plan. A Costa Rican diplomat noted the irony: "At first we did not reveal the plan. So the people who should not be in agreement with the plan did agree with it, and those who should agree with it did not."[8] Apart from its intrinsic logic, the plan was a device by which Costa Rica could leave the Tegucigalpa bloc and join the peacemakers. By May the plan was threatening a diplomatic disaster to the Reagan policy. Both Nicaragua and Guatemala were lining up to support it. That made it a majority of three for the plan, putting Washington's remaining two clients in the minority.

The U.S. Position

On June 17, Arias, who was on a private trip to the United States, was invited to the White House. President Reagan lambasted the plan as too lenient toward Nicaragua. "The greatest concern is the need for the *Sandinistas* to act on genuine democratization before pressure on the regime is removed in any way," Reagan told Arias. The Costa Rican stood his ground, vainly trying to convince the president to give his peace plan a chance.[9]

In the region, Honduras kept voicing new problems with the plan. Twice the summit meeting of the five presidents was postponed, as Salvadoran president Napoleón Duarte kept remembering last-minute appointments in Europe. At last the five foreign ministers agreed to meet in Tegucigalpa at a session mediated by the Contadora ministers to set the agenda for the summit meeting in Guatemala a few days later.

The Talks

The change was visible as the foreign ministers arrived in the Honduran capital. The Hondurans started by issuing an entirely new peace plan text—in effect another counterdraft requiring many more months of negotiations. But in introducing the plan under the icy gaze of the Mexican foreign minister Bernardo Sepúlveda, Honduran foreign minister Carlos Lopez Contreras insisted that it was merely a series of suggestions that the participants could consider as they chose. The suggestions were promptly disregarded, and the participants went on to discuss the Arias plan.

The changes they made were minor, but they tightened up the plan in two crucial respects. First, the original Arias plan mentioned only declaring a cease-fire. The Hondurans argued successfully that there was no sense in the governments declaring a cease-fire because they were not fighting each other. The cease-fire needed to be worked out between the government and the guerrillas of each afflicted country, even though this meant the *Sandinistas* would have to talk to the *Contras*. This was agreed to and was the genesis of the many rounds of later cease-fire talks. Second, Contadora also tightened up the original Arias language against aiding the region's rebels. From *suspension* of aid it went to *cessation* and from *military* aid it went to *all* aid, except that for repatriation or resettlement, prefiguring the U.S. congressional formulas of 1988 and 1989.

The five presidents arrived in Guatemala City. The momentum for an agreement was palpable. When, on August 5, just as the summit meeting began, the White House released its own peace plan for the region, which it had just worked out with then-House Speaker Jim Wright, the Central Americans took it in stride. With a broad grin, President Cerezo told reporters, "We welcome plans from any quarter, from the United States, from Europe, from the Soviet Union, or even the Middle East. But we are here to sign the Central American peace plan, and that is what we are going to do."[10]

The effect of the Reagan-Wright plan was to legitimize what the Central Americans were doing. Arias held them to the task. When Honduran president José Azcona de Hoyo showed signs of getting cold feet, Arias's aides called Speaker Wright in Washington to announce that agreement was imminent. Just as Salvadoran president Duarte had finally tired of canceling summit meetings, now Azcona, the president of Honduras, did not want to be singled out as the spoiler. The politician in him won out.

The Signing

Miraculously, then, all five presidents walked up the aisle of the Guatemalan National Palace to sign the plan. Heralded by a drum roll and fanfare from a brass band, the five presidents strode into the ornate reception hall, listened to their national anthems, watched President Arias read his peace text, and then signed the Procedure for a Firm and Lasting Peace in Central America.

The sublime moment, four and a half years after the first meeting of the Contadora group, was not only a key victory for patient *Sandinista* diplomacy, it was also an important marker in Central America's political modernization. The five presidents agreed, above all, that they—not the military, not the guerrillas, not the Americans—were in charge of their respective countries. They were the constitutional authorities and would not tolerate endemic guerrilla warfare, the "Lebanonization" of the region.[11]

The historic agreement pledged the five countries to take the following actions in ninety days: (1) decree amnesty for irregular forces (which would also be obligated to release their prisoners); (2) call for a cease-fire in countries where armed conflicts were underway; (3) promote a pluralistic, participatory democracy, with no outside interference, guaranteeing complete freedom of the press and assuring all political parties access to the press, radio, and television; (4) call on the governments within and without the region to cease all aid, whether military, logistical, financial, or propagandistic, to all irregular forces or insurrectional movements, with the exception of aid for repatriation or relocation; and (5) prevent irregular forces from using the territory of any Central American state to attack other Central American states or to establish supply bases.

After the signing of the accord, the Nicaraguan government moved the most quickly to implement it. Nicaragua was the first country to set up a national reconciliation commission, required by the accord. President Ortega appointed Cardinal Miguel Obando y Bravo, an outspoken critic of the regime, as the commission's chairman. *La Prensa* and *Radio Católica* reopened. Political opposition rallies took place, even though one opposition leader was arrested. The government and opposition met in the National Dialogue.

The more difficult provisions of the plan were implemented later. President Ortega waited the full ninety days but on November 5, 1987, announced to the gasps of his audience the beginning of indirect talks with the *Contras* on a cease-fire. The *Sandinistas* had been vowing for five years never to talk to them.

The Alajuela Summit

The presidents had agreed to meet in a new summit, which was held in Alajuela, near San José, on January 16, 1988. The issue before them was whether they could agree on a common statement when the plan so far had failed to stop the region's wars. Much hung on the outcome, as the administration had asked Congress for $270 million to fund the *Contras*.

Alajuela would clarify the dynamics of the Arias plan, which the evenhandedness of the bare text only masked. Nicaragua benefitted chiefly by being included at all. It got a pale, reflected legitimacy, in biased U.S. eyes, by being associated with its four conservative neighbors in a process that included a call for an end of aid to the *Contras*, even though one of those neighbors continued to harbor the same *Contras*. On the debit side was the fact, now starkly revealed, that all the rigors of the Arias plan were being applied to Nicaragua alone. Apart from Costa Rica, where democratic procedure was already in place, only Nicaragua was doing anything to comply.

Thus, Ortega arrived at this summit already outnumbered four to one. He could argue and defy, as he had at Esquipulas I; then the summit would break up in discord and Reagan would get his money. Or he could accept the double standard. He chose to deal rather than defy and announced a series of concessions.

Whatever its weaknesses, the joint declaration also reiterated the call for an end to *Contra* aid. This issue was now finally coming onto the U.S. congressional agenda for decision. Elliott Abrams had begun 1987 by confidently predicting Congress would vote the aid because it had no alternative. Now it had an alternative in the Arias plan.

Among the sixty undecided "moderates" in the House who held the balance, the progress of the Arias plan was decisive. In a situation so evenly balanced, President Ortega's concessions on January 21 and impetus toward a cease-fire nudged the debate in the direction of the Arias plan. The House leadership also promised wavering members, if military aid were defeated, the chance to vote for nonlethal sustenance aid, misnamed "humanitarian." This way they could both uphold Arias and avoid "abandoning" the *Contras*.

During the last week of January, Congress was subjected to a public barrage it had rarely experienced on any issue in the 1980s. Calls came in overwhelmingly against *Contra* aid from around the country, and even in the conservative, rural border-state districts of the undecideds, calls usually ran at least two to one against aid. The administration so feared this onslaught that it reduced its request from $270 million to $36 million.

Nevertheless, the progress of the Arias plan, the leadership's adroit strategy, and the indignation of millions of Americans combined at the same moment. The administration had jockeyed itself into a position of opposing a diplomatic solution. On February 3, the House voted to deny the administration's request for military aid to the *Contras;* the margin of victory was eight votes. Twelve Republicans voted against aid; nearly sixty southern Democrats went with the administration.

The Alajuela summit and the House vote set the stage. Acting on his commitment at Alajuela and sensing the *Contras* were ready to move, Ortega instituted direct talks between them and the *Sandinistas*. At the February 1988 talks in Guatemala, the positions narrowed markedly; both sides accepted the proposal of Cardinal Obando, the mediator, "in principle." Then the appointment of higher ranking delegations and the proposal to hold the talks on Nicaraguan soil directly, without a mediator, brought the top players together in mid-March 1988. The *Contras,* beaten in both Congress and the field, embraced the logic of the Arias plan. The government, by reopening *La Prensa,* lifting the state of emergency, and releasing prisoners, had already done so.

Sapoa Cease-Fire Agreement

After the February House vote, the agreement signed between the government and *Contras* at Sapoa, Nicaragua, on March 21 was the Arias plan's greatest triumph: the first true agreement between warring factions. Yet it only suspended the war. The *Contras* were to retain their weapons during the sixty-day negotiating period that began on April 1. During this period a permanent cease-fire was to be sought. The *Contras* were to relocate in zones. More prisoners were to be granted amnesty. Sustenance aid recently passed by Congress was allowed the *Contras.* They were invited to join the National Dialogue and rejoin political parties.

The Alajuela summit, the House vote, and the Sapoa cease-fire were the most concrete achievements of the Arias plan and vindicated President Ortega's strategy of concessions designed to keep negotiations going. The momentum toward massive aid to the *Contras,* regional war, and U.S. intervention had been turned back. Ortega pocketed the lesson for future application and turned to the talks with the *Contras* to make the cease-fire permanent.

On April 17 the government presented a comprehensive proposal for a permanent cease-fire, building on the Sapoa agreement. It was immediately rejected by the *Contras,* but meanwhile *Contra* leader Alfredo Cesar had initiated back-channel talks with government negotiators Paul Reichler and Gen. Humberto Ortega. Cesar gave Reichler a list of political concessions that, if accepted, Cesar said would enable him and other members of the directorate to sign an accord.

At the penultimate, May 26–28, round in Managua the government formally accepted all these points, abandoning its previous position that political questions were to be negotiated with the internal opposition, not illegal rebels. Nevertheless Cesar and the others did not sign but insisted on the extreme demands of the faction headed by former National Guard colonel Enrique Bermudez.

June 9 Round in Managua

The *Contras* returned to Managua in June 1988 with their extreme demands and then at noon on June 9, the last day, piled on a new series of demands, including the right of draftees to leave the army any time they chose, forced resignation of the Supreme Court, restoration of confiscated property that had been distributed to smallholders or cooperatives, and opening of *Contra* offices in Managua. The government would have to carry out these actions while the *Contra* army remained armed and in its enclaves; it would take until January 31, 1989, to disarm. The *Contras* gave the government two hours to accept these demands; if it did not, they would walk out.

Cesar denied that these were new demands; he was merely "putting into effect and implementing the points" made in their previous proposal, he said at the press conference. "But whenever the Resistance tries to move to a discussion of written accords the government avoids making this type of commitment," Cesar charged.[12] This sort of exaggeration outraged government negotiator Paul Reichler on June 9 and prompted him to go public with the back-channel negotiations, where he had met Cesar's demands for written accords on democratic reforms.

The *Contras* had persistently escalated their demands each time agreement seemed near. Their walkout from the June 1988 Managua negotiations was intended to force a crisis that would trigger new U.S. military aid, one of their leaders later admitted.[13] The walkout effectively ended talks between the government and the *Contras* for the year, although the two sides would meet in September 1988 in Guatemala for an afternoon of talks that failed to yield agreement even on the site of the next negotiating round.

Resumption of Esquipulas Process

Nevertheless, the peace process was not dead. In February 1989 the Latin American statesman Carlos Andres Perez was inaugurated president of Venezuela. Four Central American presidents—all except the ailing Duarte—converged on Caracas, as did Fidel Castro, Alan Garcia of Peru, and Felipe González of Spain. Perez got all of them together in a hotel room on February 2 and hammered out with them a full peace agenda for 1989.

It was here that President Ortega made the fateful decision to apply fully the strategy of concessions that had worked so well to date—to stake his entire rule on an election wholly designed to fulfill the letter and spirit of the Arias plan, end all questions of the legitimacy of the government, and deprive the United States of grounds for attack. With Castro nodding his assent, Ortega agreed to forego advantages of incumbency the election law gave him while braving the protest vote that was the natural disadvantage of incumbency. Only elections with international observers and credibility would reopen international aid flows and ease U.S. hostility, the assembled Social Democrats told Ortega. When Ortega said he doubted the opposition would even run, they promised to apply their full powers of persuasion. In return for this extraordinary concession by Ortega, the other presidents promised to move diplomatically against the *Contras*.

El Salvador Summit

The Washington debate over Nicaragua had hinged on how best to encourage Nicaragua to democratize. On the one hand, the Reagan administration and its allies in Congress, Republicans and hard-line southern Democrats, insisted that the Nicaraguan government would respond only to force. On the other hand, the Democratic leadership in both the House and Senate, President Arias, and most of the United States' Latin American and European allies argued that a combination of diplomatic pressure and economic enticements would best draw the Nicaraguans into the democratic camp. The summit would be the first test of the carrot approach.

For Washington, the summit's most startling development was the news that the five presidents had asked their foreign ministers to come up with a plan within ninety days to disarm and resettle the *Contras*. Nicaragua had been hoping for a bilateral agreement with Honduras but considered it a long shot. Now Honduras decided it was safest to multilateralize the plan.

The *Contras* were the big losers at the summit. Although they held a nonstop press conference across the street from the presidents' meeting, they were ignored by the presidents and most of the press. The presidents' clearly stated opposition to any aid that did not disarm and relocate the *Contras* made it much harder for the Bush administration to keep the *Contras* encamped indefinitely in Honduras.

The new Bush administration had not drawn up its own wish list in time for the conference. This inactivity would not last forever. Yet by moving decisively to demobilize the *Contras*, the presidents limited the Bush administration's options. Moreover, by rescheduling their elections, releasing the ex-guardsmen, and opening further the political system, the Nicaraguan government hoped to remove any reason the new administration in Washington might give for resuming the Reagan administration's war against it.

Nevertheless, a measure of how deeply the U.S. onslaught had impaired Nicaraguan sovereignty was Ortega's agreement to negotiate with foreigners wholesale changes to a national electoral law and invite virtual U.N. supervision of his election. The decision to use the most intimate exercise of national sovereignty for international legitimation was to have unforeseen consequences.

Adjusting to the Bush Administration

After the encouraging start at Caracas and the El Salvador summit, the peace process went into a holding pattern during March–August 1989 as the various actors oriented themselves to the new administration. Honduras reverted to a familiar pattern of backsliding, Congress approved new logistical aid to the *Contras*, and Arias struggled to find a point of balance.

Moving to get the Hondurans back in line, the Bush administration sent an official to Tegucigalpa in March with a request to leave the *Contras* alone until February 1990—the month of the Nicaraguan election. When the Central American foreign ministers met in San José at the end of March, Honduras's Lopez Contreras stalled on the demobilization plan and attached a crippling reservation to the U.N. peacekeepers' force as well.

Turning to Congress in April for the *Contras'* money, Secretary of State James Baker tried to move beyond the usual rancorous debate by yielding on questions of principle. Given the makeup of Congress, he had no doubt he could push through nonmilitary aid, but he wanted an agreement with the Democratic leadership as well—a "bipartisan accord." The administration pledged to support the peace process, refuse money to *Contras* who launched offensive operations, make the money available for *Contra* demobilization, and submit to a midterm review at which Congress could block further money if the administration were found in noncompliance. The Democratic leadership agreed, and Congress voted some fifty-five million dollars in sustenance aid to the *Contras*. The legacy of Reagan's trade embargo and anti-Nicaraguan rhetoric was continued.

Thus, when in late April Nicaragua made its first electoral changes, giving those who boycotted the 1984 elections equal standing with those who had run, the State Department immediately belittled the concessions as did various self-appointed commissions set up by U.S. right-wing foundations. Yet the Nicaraguan electoral law they criticized was modeled on that of other Latin American countries, as a series of studies by the United Nations, the Organization of American States (OAS), the U.S. Library of Congress, and the Venezuelan electoral commission all confirmed. Nevertheless, the media and Congress faithfully echoed the administration's complaints. With *Contra* demobilization and U.N. peacekeeping already stalled by Honduras, the cacophony against the electoral reforms also mired the third plank of the presidents' El Salvador program in controversy.

The poisoned atmosphere made Arias worry about whether the opposition would indeed boycott the election, as it had in 1984. At the El Salvador summit in February he had foreseen that a mere perfunctory reform by Nicaragua, combined with an adamant opposition stance, could lead to such a boycott. He had then requested the Nicaraguans give him powers to impose binding arbitration, but they refused. He began in May to pressure President Ortega for more concessions. In June, Ortega appointed a balanced Supreme Electoral Council—a key issue he had discussed with Arias and Perez in Caracas. Although by the results of the 1984 elections the *Sandinistas* were entitled to put three *Sandinistas* on the five-person board, they now gave up their majority. The opposition, which had wanted to name four of the five members, predictably complained, but Arias and his advisers found the change acceptable.

Arias was still not finished. In a seven-hour face-to-face session in San José on July 14, 1989, he extracted Ortega's agreement to further enticements of the opposition. Ortega agreed to try again to open a national dialogue with the opposition parties together, instead of meeting with them individually as he had been doing.

National Political Dialogue

This last decision immediately yielded a two-fold result. On August 3–4, Ortega held a marathon twenty-two-hour televised public dialogue with twenty opposition parties. It produced the first-ever agreement between the *Sandinista* government and the opposition parties. It also helped weld the squabbling oppositionists together into a formidable bloc they appeared incapable of achieving on their own.

In the dialogue the opposition finally agreed to participate in the February 1990 elections, and the government agreed to further concessions, such as abolishing a mild public order law and advancing the date for turnover of power to the winner of the elections. It also agreed to suspend the military draft until after the elections.

The opposition took another stride toward a common Nicaraguan position: it joined in a declaration calling on the Central American presidents in their upcoming summit in Honduras to demobilize the *Contras* and asked foreign countries not to channel covert aid to the electoral campaign. With this political accord one of the last essential pieces of the Arias plan fell into place.

Tela Accord

The political accord within Nicaragua cleared the way for the five presidents to end the stagnation and impel the process forward. Abandoning all previous reservations, they now formally put into action all three planks agreed on in their previous El Salvador meeting: endorsement of Nicaragua's electoral preparations, deployment of the United Nations Observer Group Central America (ONUCA) peacekeepers, and dismantlement of the *Contras*. This last was to be carried out by the newly created International Commission of Support and Verification (CIAV), made up of the U.N. and OAS secretaries-general.

Undermining the Tela Accord

For the *Contras*, the Tela accord was the signal to reinfiltrate Nicaragua, both to avoid demobilization and to attack an election they feared could render them irrelevant. From August to October 1989 they sent some twenty-three hundred fighters back in, stepping up attacks on remote roads and farms. Most victims were civilians, but on October 21 they scored a lucky hit and killed eighteen reservists on a road that was supposed to have been covered by the army.

Furious, President Ortega resolved to draw attention to the unfolding violence through the only means open to him: he canceled the unilateral cease-fire with the *Contras*, the remaining achievement of the Sapoa accord. U.S. newspapers, which had scarcely reported the escalation in *Contra* attacks, gave front-page coverage to the cancellation. Even though the *Contras* were engaging in offensive operations, Congress did not activate the provision in the law to cut off their aid but instead passed more resolutions against Ortega.

At the root of the Democrats' inaction was not only a change in personnel—Speaker Jim Wright had resigned, to be succeeded by Tom Foley—but a calculation based on domestic politics. Once the administration had ceased confronting Congress with incessant *Contra*-aid requests, Congress simply disengaged, not wanting confrontation with the administration over such a volatile, unpredictable issue as Nicaragua.

Reviving the Diplomatic Process

Called together by CIAV, the Nicaraguan government and the *Contras* met in New York and Washington on November 9–21 to attempt to renew the cease-fire, but, sustained by the continued flow of aid, the *Contras* refused to either demobilize or withdraw from Nicaragua. Deputy Foreign Minister Victor Hugo Tinoco entered the talks with a position based on the Tela accords and with carefully prepared fallback positions to demonstrate flexibility. The strategy almost worked when the *Contras* threatened to walk out entirely, but they did not, and Tinoco then retreated to his last fallback position by accepting CIAV's compromise proposal to evacuate only those *Contras* who had reinfiltrated since Tela. But the *Contras* refused to move a single man. By the end Tinoco and his follow-negotiator Reichler joked that "[we had been] negotiating against ourselves." The remark well summarizes Nicaragua's entire diplomatic experience with the United States and the *Contras*.

San Isidro Emergency Summit

What the *Contra* negotiations did produce, however, was an exhaustive record of *Sandinista* attempts to resolve the problem peacefully. Nicaragua urgently called for a new meeting of Central American presidents to consider the situation the *Contras* had created.

Not only had the cease-fire broken down and the deadline for demobilization passed, but in November 1989 an offensive launched by the rebels in the Farabundo Martí National Liberation Front (FMLN) made sure that the issue of El Salvador would be high on the summit agenda. Ortega apparently let the FMLN use Nicaragua as a base for arms shipments and flights—whether inadvertently or in a deliberate effort to gain greater leverage for removal of the *Contras* was unclear. But El Salvador's recently elected President Alfredo Cristiani refused to go to the summit unless the presidents endorsed him and called for demobilization of the FMLN. As he said, until now Nicaragua had extracted all the benefits of the peace process and he wanted them for El Salvador as well. The army's murder of six prominent Jesuit clergymen in November revealed how dreadfully far El Salvador had to go to comply even minimally with the plan, whose benefits Cristiani now demanded cost-free. Until now, the Central American peace process had scarcely dealt with El Salvador, although formally the provisions of the agreement applied to all five countries equally. In fact, President Arias believed the plan had to work in Nicaragua before it could be applied to El Salvador.

The emergency meeting the five presidents held in San Isidro de Coronado, outside of San José, on December 10–12, 1989, was their most difficult since Alajuela. One the one hand, they could scarcely fail to meet after offensives in two of their countries. On the other hand, the disputes among them were severe. Cristiani's price for attendance was high, and Ortega paid it with utmost reluctance to eke out progress on the *Contras*. The presidents agreed to demand that all remaining aid to the *Contras* be immediately transferred to CIAV, the commission they had set up in August. They also agreed to expand ONUCA's mandate.

The results of the San José emergency meeting were consistent with the entire record of *Sandinista* diplomacy since their unexpected acceptance of Contadora in 1984: make extensive concessions to extract progress. A completely unbalanced pronouncement on El Salvador hurt Ortega and damaged the peace process, but this was the price of progress for Nicaragua.

Enigma of the Arias Plan

By the beginning of 1990, the election in Nicaragua had become the centerpiece of the peace process—the supreme regional effort to transfer its disputes from the military to the political arena. By conducting a credible election under the auspices of a regional diplomacy that mobilized all five countries and the United Nations and OAS as guarantors, Nicaragua rendered the *Contras* irrelevant, despite the continued funding the *Contras* received from Washington.

Nevertheless, to hold elections under conditions of gravely impaired national sovereignty and to use the elections for international purposes created unpredictable dynamics. Left to themselves, the Nicaraguan miniparties would have boycotted and squabbled. Only the combined efforts of the *Sandinistas* and foreigners persuaded them to run and come together into a formidable bloc. The *Sandinistas,* who had previously refused even to discuss electoral matters with the United States, now allowed open U.S. government aid to the opposition. So fundamental had the economic issue become that this aid, which few countries in the world would have tolerated, had less the effect of tarring the opposition as collaborators than of advertising them as the ones who could deliver U.S. largesse. Invited to participate in an election held to please foreigners, the majority voted exactly the way indicated.

The unexpected outcome of the election removed from power the most dedicated proponents of the regional peace plan and cast a shadow over the revolution's social achievements in a region that desperately needed successful examples of closing the social chasm. But the same pragmatism and moderation that the opposition first showed at the Managua political dialogue just before Tela it now displayed in victory. Indeed Violeta Chamorro best captured the spirit of the times with her statement that reconciliation was more beautiful than victory. Her team negotiated demobilization accords with the *Contras* and left redistributed land in the hands of the peasantry.

What began as an ideological confrontation between Washington and Managua now ended in a politicians' deal within Central America. Beginning as a revolutionary vanguard, the *Sandinistas* transformed themselves into a political party playing the role of loyal opposition. The Reagan administration had sought to eliminate them entirely, even at the cost of convulsing the region in war. Arias, Ortega, and the region's other politicians found another way: they moved the Nicaraguan drama from the battlefield to the congresses and rallies of the country's political parties.

Notes

1. For a comprehensive account of Reagan-era diplomacy in Nicaragua, see Roy Gutman, *Banana Diplomacy: The Making of American Foreign Policy in Nicaragua, 1982–1987* (New York: Simon and Schuster, 1988), from which this quote is drawn (p. 78).

2. Unpublished cable from U.S. Secretary of State George Shultz to the European Economic Community, September 7, 1984.

3. State Department official L. Craig Johnstone, unpublished press briefing, October 1, 1984.

4. U.S. National Security Council internal memorandum, October 20, 1984, first revealed in *Washington Post*, November 6, 1984.

5. Ibid.

6. National Security Planning Group Meeting, June 25, 1984, unpublished document made available by the National Security Archive, Washington, D.C. The authors are grateful to Peter Kornbluh for drawing this passage to our attention.

7. Interview with Arias adviser John Biehl in *APSI* (a Chilean weekly) no. 253, May 23–29, 1988, p. 59.

8. Interview of Melvin Saenz, an adviser to Costa Rican foreign minister Rodrigo Madrigal Nieto, by Lidwien Michiels, of the *Oficina por la Paz en Centroamérica* in Managua on May 14, 1987.

9. *New York Times*, June 8, 1987.

10. Authors' notes, President Cerezo's press conference, Camino Real Hotel, Guatemala City, August 6, 1987.

11. The presidents had frequently talked about Central America becoming another Beirut.

12. Statement by Alfredo Cesar at press conference in Managua, June 9, 1988.

13. Roy Gutman, "Contra Peace-Talks Ploy Disclosed," *Newsday*, July 5, 1988.

16

The Soviet Union and Cuba in Central America: Guardians Against Democracy?

Wayne S. Smith

A thesis frequently put forward during the early years of the Reagan administration and still accepted in some quarters is that the turmoil in Central America was largely of Soviet and Cuban making—that Soviet-Cuban objectives in Central America were to communize the region and were therefore antithetical to efforts at democratization. This chapter will examine this thesis in light of Soviet and Cuban policies, actions, and objectives. Do Moscow and Havana oppose democratization in the Central American countries? Are their policies likely to pose serious obstacles to the democratization process? Or, conversely, might they be induced to play a constructive role in the quest for peace and democracy in the region?

Historical Background

For the most part, Soviet tactics and policies in Latin America between 1918 and 1959 were cautious and decidedly less than aggressive. During most of those years, local Communist parties were ordered to form alliances with other progressive groups, participate in elections, and even cooperate with those governments that showed some tolerance toward the parties. Only during the period 1928–35 were these popular front tactics abandoned in favor of militant communism. During those years, the parties were ordered to eschew relationships with progressive but noncommunist groups and to confront bourgeois governments wherever feasible. Communist-led or inspired uprisings followed in Mexico (1929), El Salvador (1932), Cuba (1933), and Brazil (1935). The results of that period were disastrous for the Communist parties and for the Soviet position in the hemisphere. By 1935 all the uprisings had been crushed, Communist parties had been declared illegal in most countries, and Mexico and Uruguay, the only two countries maintaining diplomatic relations with the Soviet Union, had severed them.

In a sense, the Latin American Communist parties never recovered from the traumas of the 1928–35 period. Few ever again had any confidence in the efficacy of armed struggle. A few did return to such tactics after 1959, but only with obvious reluctance and with no real hope of success. For almost a quarter of a century, from 1935 until 1959, no Communist party in Latin America even advocated violent revolution; rather, they returned to the popular front tactics employed prior to 1928. They participated in elections, formed alliances with noncommunist groups where possible, and concentrated on recruitment and ideological proselytizing so as to prepare for the historical moment (perhaps well into the next century) when the so-called objective conditions for socialist revolution might obtain. For the most part, Communist parties had little influence and played unimportant roles in the political lives of their respective countries. The most notable exception was Guatemala. There, between 1945 and 1954, the Communists came to have a limited role within the government (mostly in the agrarian reform agency) and some influence with President Jacobo Arbenz (1950–54). This is by no means to say that Arbenz was controlled by the Communists or that they had taken over the Guatemalan Revolution. Far from it. Much less was the revolution orchestrated from Moscow. Indeed, the Guatemalan Revolution sprang entirely from conditions and circumstances within the country. Perhaps the Communists pushed their programs too loudly, but they were not on the verge of taking control. True, the Communist Party was legalized—but then the Communist Party in the United States has always been legal. True, there were a few Communists in mid-level governmental positions and four in the National Assembly, but there were none in the cabinet and few in the armed forces or security forces. True, President Arbenz did in 1954 purchase arms from the Eastern bloc, but only after he had tried unsuccessfully to purchase them in the West.

The U.S.-backed overthrow of Arbenz in 1954 seems to have been triggered more by his decision to nationalize land belonging to the United Fruit Company than by evidence Guatemala was becoming a tool of Moscow. His ouster took place shortly after the nationalizations began. Secretary of State John Foster Dulles's law firm represented United Fruit. CIA Director Allen Dulles had been a member of its board. After Col. Carlos Castillo Armas had ousted Arbenz and made himself president, Castillo Armas returned United Fruit its land. None of this seems to have been coincidence.

In any event, whether because of some exaggerated cold war concern over Communist conspiracies or, as seems more likely, in an effort to make Guatemala safe for United Fruit, the United States helped crush one of the few genuine social revolutions to emerge on the Latin American scene in decades. What followed was one bloody dictator after another, occasionally separated by a year or so of civilian government at the sufferance of the military. It would be difficult indeed to argue that democracy was furthered by the U.S.-engineered coup of 1954.

Elsewhere in Latin America Communist parties prior to 1959 seemed more intent on collecting membership dues than on preparing for revolution. That changed, of course, with the triumph of the Cuban Revolution. Suddenly, inspired by Castro's example, revolutionaries began taking to the field all over the hemisphere. Guerrilla fronts appeared in Venezuela, Colombia, Peru, Argentina, Nicaragua, and eventually Bolivia. New groups began operations in Guatemala.

Following the line accepted by all Communist parties in Latin America, the Cuban Communists had eschewed armed struggle and had not supported Castro's revolt against Batista until the eleventh hour, when it was already clear Castro would win. Nor did Castro receive help from Moscow. Neither Castro nor his movement were communist, but by late 1959, despite the earlier failure of the Soviets and their local protégés to support his cause, Castro, with a view to advancing his own objectives (specifically to acquire a shield against U.S. power behind which he might continue to pursue those objectives), moved to associate himself with the Soviet Union and the Cuban Communists. This eventually led to his own conversion to Marxism-Leninism and to the restructuring of the Cuban state along Marxist-Leninist lines.

Castro's alliance with Moscow did not mean he accepted the latter's recommendations for policies and strategies in Latin America. Quite the contrary, he scornfully rejected Moscow's popular front tactics in favor of the encouragement of guerrilla fronts and armed struggle. This was not at all to Moscow's liking. It believed such tactics would eventually produce the same results as in 1928–35. Yet Castro's own victory made it difficult to argue the point convincingly. Accordingly, in 1964 Moscow and Havana reached a compromise. In some countries—Venezuela, Colombia, Guatemala, Honduras, Paraguay, and Haiti—armed struggle was endorsed as the appropriate tactic, and in these countries the Communist parties were to support, or even organize, guerrilla fronts. Elsewhere popular front tactics were indicated, and in these countries Cuba was supposed to work through the orthodox Communist parties rather than through *Fidelista* guerrilla groups.

The compromise was ignored by both sides more often than it was honored. Castro, for example, continued to support guerrilla groups in both Peru and Nicaragua. Neither Moscow nor the local Communist parties pushed for armed struggle in Haiti, Paraguay, or Honduras.

In any event, the compromise was of short duration. By the end of the sixties it was clear Castro's tactics had failed. Rural guerrilla fronts had everywhere been defeated, and the urban guerrillas who took their place in Brazil, Uruguay, and Argentina would meet the same fate by the mid-seventies. Ernesto "Che" Guevara's defeat and death in Bolivia in 1967 must have been the final straw, forcing Castro to reassess. Soon he began to shift his ground, swinging in behind Soviet popular front tactics and moving away from support for guerrillas. To be sure, the shift was not total. Cuba continued to provide some minor assistance to the guerrillas in Guatemala, offered shelter to the *Sandinistas* after their initial defeat in Nicaragua, and then supported them when they returned to the struggle in 1974. With these and one or two other exceptions, however, Cuba for all practical purposes gave up armed struggle as a tactic. Instead it began reaching out to establish diplomatic relations with some Latin American governments it had once vowed to overthrow.

This was the situation in 1979 when suddenly, to the surprise of many, including perhaps Fidel Castro himself, the *Sandinistas* marched triumphantly into Managua, for the first time in twenty years replicating the Cuban revolutionary model.

Return to Armed Struggle?

The victory of the *Sandinistas* inevitably raised questions concerning Cuban and Soviet objectives in Latin America. Now that Cuba's original preference for guerrillas and armed struggle had in a sense been vindicated, might not Havana, and perhaps even Moscow, again embrace such tactics? Might they not resuscitate some of the revolutionary fervor of the 1960s?

At first, the answer to that question seemed to be yes. For one thing, Moscow and the Moscow-line Communist Party in Nicaragua had both been left at the starting blocks and were now scrambling to catch up. Moscow had barely acknowledged the existence of the *Sandinistas* until late in their struggle. The local party, like the Cuban party in 1957 and 1958, had taken the position that armed struggle could not succeed. Thus, it had not supported the *Sandinistas*. Now, in the wake of the latter's victory, and obviously urged on by Moscow as well as by Havana, Communist parties in Guatemala and El Salvador suddenly endorsed armed struggle and went on the offensive. In 1980, Shafik

Handal, the secretary-general of the Salvadoran party, traveled to a number of socialist countries asking for arms. In response, during 1980 and the early part of 1981 both Cuba and the Soviet Union provided some material assistance to the guerrillas of the Farabundo Martí National Liberation Front (FMLN) in El Salvador. Cuba, moreover, trained and possibly armed a group of Colombian M–19 guerrillas who had taken refuge in Cuba after the famous hostage-taking incident at the Dominican embassy in Bogota in 1980. Cuba denied it had armed the guerrillas or facilitated their return to Colombia, but the guerrillas did return and did begin armed actions against the government. The Colombian government drew its own conclusions and severed diplomatic relations with Cuba.

Soviet and Cuban theoreticians for a time openly described the victory of the *Sandinistas* as confirmation of the efficacy of armed struggle. The Cubans pointed to the *Sandinista* experience as the correct model for other Central American revolutionaries. Interestingly, Soviet theoreticians seemed to go even further. In a now famous round table discussion in Moscow organized by the Soviet journal *Latinskaya Amerika,* Soviet participants stated flatly that it now seemed Che Guevara had been right all along. One discussant, Boris Koval, wrote

> the Nicaraguan experience demolishes the previous simplistic interpretation of guerrilla actions, confirms the correctness of Che Guevara's strategic principles, and gives life to his idea of creating a powerful people's guerrilla movement.[1]

Even the normally cautious Sergo Mikoyan, the editor of *Latinskaya Amerika,* acknowledged that

> up to now, the path of armed struggle is the only one that has led to revolutionary victory in Latin America. And the Nicaraguan experience revalidates what had been thought by some to have been refuted by the death of Che Guevara and the defeat of a number of other guerrilla movements.[2]

Nor did Soviet theoreticians believe that armed struggle was the indicated tactic only for Central America. On the contrary, the conclusion of the *Latinskaya Amerika* round table was that "the path of armed struggle...is the most promising, given the specific conditions in most Latin American countries."[3]

It did not take the U.S. observers long to respond to Soviet and Cuban statements suggesting the revival of armed struggle on a large scale. Secretary of State Alexander Haig certainly had such assertions in mind when he charged in early 1981 that in Central America the United

States faced nothing less than Soviet expansionism and aggression articulated through Moscow's Caribbean surrogate, Cuba. Moscow, he said, was operating on the basis of a hit list that leads to the total takeover of Central America.[4]

Supposedly it was the administration's conviction that the Soviets were thrusting aggressively into Latin America in hopes thus of getting at the United States through its soft underbelly that led Washington to launch its *Contra* War in Nicaragua. Conservative think tanks bolstered the administration's cause with analysis of their own. In his book *The Bear in the Backyard*, for example, Timothy Ashby of the Heritage Foundation claimed Moscow's prime strategic goal in Latin America was to "create a threat to the United States along its Southern border." The Kremlin, said Ashby, had "officially stated acknowledgement of the correctness of Guevarist-Castroite armed insurgencies." As evidence, Ashby cited the *Latinskaya Amerika* round table.[5] The venerable Rand Corporation was also obviously referring to the round table when one of its reports stated,

> Cuba, Nicaragua and the Soviet Union view armed struggle as the most promising method by which to undermine U.S. interests in Central America, establish new Marxist-oriented regimes in the region, and ultimately expand the Soviet-Cuban political and military presence in the Caribbean Basin.[6]

Although Soviet and Cuban theoreticians initially reacted to the victory in Nicaragua with warmed-over endorsements of armed struggle, they quickly changed their minds. They expected that the success in Nicaragua would be followed quickly by another in El Salvador and then perhaps one in Guatemala. With one revolution igniting the next, it must have seemed possible that guerrilla fronts might even spring up again all over the hemisphere, as they had during the 1960s.

Such hopes, however, were short lived. The FMLN victory in El Salvador was not to be. When in January of 1981 the FMLN launched what had been billed as its final offensive, it was quickly and easily defeated by the Salvadoran armed forces—without assistance from the United States. In Guatemala disagreements among leftist leaders about the timing and strategy to be pursued following the unsuccessful occupation of the Spanish embassy meant that revolutionary victory would remain no more than a distant dream. The armed forces were far too strong—and ruthless. At that point, Soviet and Cuban analysts took another look and concluded that they had overreacted. Prospects for revolution were not nearly as promising as they had seemed in 1979 and 1980. Now, in the cold light of dawn after January 1981, a far more sober tone began to characterize the ruminations of Soviet area specialists,[7] and increasingly they concluded that "leftist unity," not armed struggle, had been the key ingredient—and lesson—in the *Sandinista* victory.[8] Che Guevara apparently had not been right after all.

To thrash the matter out—and in a sense perhaps to correct the course suggested by the 1980 round table—a major conference of Communist and revolutionary parties was held in Havana in 1982. Strangely, the Cubans had been less bullish than their Soviet colleagues in the wake of the *Sandinistas* triumph. No Cuban analyst, for example, took it to mean that the *Fidelista* line of the 1960s had been right and that all Communist and revolutionary groups should now go back to armed struggle. At the Havana meeting in 1982 they etched their position in stone. Armed struggle was still a valid tactic, Cuban theoreticians asserted, but they then went on to declare that in all of Latin America, the conditions for armed struggle existed in only two countries: El Salvador and Guatemala. Honduras, which by 1982 was on the way to becoming an American aircraft carrier, was cited as a country in which the conditions for revolution were "developing."[9]

Soviet reports on the conclusions of the 1982 Havana meeting were somewhat more circuitous but reflected the same line as that taken by the Cubans. Meeting participants had agreed, said *World Marxist Review,* that the worsening conditions of the masses could only "intensify national liberation and class struggle." Thus the "revolutionary tide" was said to be on the "upswing."[10] These were stirring words. The *World Marxist Review* followed them, however, by noting that conference participants had called not for armed struggle but for "tactical flexibility" because there was no single formula for victory.[11] And participants were reported to have mentioned armed struggle only with reference to El Salvador and Guatemala. More tellingly, the *Review* reported meeting participants to have remembered with great reverence and respect Georgi Dimitrov.[12]

For those who follow Soviet code words, the meaning of the latter statement was clear. Dimitrov had taken over as chief of the Communist International (the Comintern) at its seventh meeting in 1935 and immediately presided over the abandonment of armed struggle (the line favored during the 1928–35 period of militant communism) and the reinstitution of popular front tactics.

Any doubt was dispelled by subsequent articles in Soviet journals. An article in the January 1987 edition of *Latinskaya Amerika,* for example, not only dismissed the efficacy of armed struggle in most Latin American countries, but also scathingly denounced most of its practitioners, both past and present. The actions of Argentine *Montoneros,* Uruguayan *Tupamaros,* and urban guerrillas in Brazil and the M–19's famous

November 1985 attack on the Palace of Justice in Bogota were labeled acts of terrorism. Other revolutionary groups were dismissed with that worst of all Soviet insults: they were called "Trotskyite."[13]

Nor did Soviet and Cuban actions after 1981 contradict their words. El Salvador continued to be described as the one country where armed struggle was called for (Guatemala having been dropped from the list after the 1985 elections there). Yet even in El Salvador there was no credible evidence of significant Soviet or Cuban material support after 1981. Further, both Moscow and Havana indicated their preference for a negotiated settlement and national reconciliation there. The decision on whether to begin such a process rested with the FMLN and the Salvadoran government, but presumably the Soviets and the Cubans, to the extent that they could influence the decision of the guerrillas, were encouraging them in that direction.

The Soviets or the Cubans or both may have been the donors of the large arms cache found in Chile in 1986. But if so, they soon retreated from such activities, principally because President Raúl Alfonsín of Argentina discussed the matter with Fidel Castro and received the latter's promise that Cuba would not meddle in Chile and that its actions there would be guided by the consensus of the democratic presidents of the Southern Cone.[14] That the Soviet Union has also honored Alfonsín's request is suggested by the fact that no more caches were found and that the Chilean Communist Party, doubtless advised by Moscow, soon dropped the idea of going over to armed struggle.

The U.S. government, of course, insisted that Cuba and the Soviet Union were continuing to ship arms to guerrillas in El Salvador, Guatemala, and elsewhere in the region and to stimulate "armed revolutionary violence and subversion." A joint Department of State–Department of Defense blue book issued in March 1985 included a prepared statement by Deputy Assistant Secretary of State James H. Michel on February 28, 1985, and a short policy statement by the Department of State's Bureau of Public Affairs in February 1987. Both sought to prove Cuba and the Soviet Union were pushing armed struggle in Central America and, indeed, were behind the violence there. Yet none of these documents produced evidence to back up the charges. Mention was made, for example, of weapons captured in El Salvador traceable to U.S. stocks left in Vietnam. But these weapons were captured in 1981, when no one denies that Cuba, Nicaragua, and, in a more indirect way, even the Soviet Union were indeed providing material support to the FMLN. There is no evidence that such weapons have come into the country since 1982, that is, since the Cubans and Soviets said they have stopped sending them—or, put another way, since they decided conditions were not right for armed struggle.

Much was also made in the State Department documents of the Soviet provision of military equipment to Nicaragua and Cuba—and to a lesser extent to Grenada before the 1983 invasion. But a government has every right under international law to provide assistance to another. Indeed, the Soviet Union and Cuba had as much right under the U.N. charter and other norms of international law to provide aid to the government of Nicaragua as the United States had to provide it to El Salvador and Honduras. The United States could object to Soviet-Cuban aid to Nicaragua, just as Cuba and Nicaragua objected to U.S. aid to El Salvador and Honduras, but in neither case did such aid violate international accords.

In any event, the matter became moot with regard to the Soviet Union when in February 1989 it suspended all military shipments to Nicaragua. The Soviets called their unilateral suspension an opening gesture and emphasized that a full and lasting solution to the question of outside arms supply can only come about out of negotiations involving all parties, including the United States. The latter rebuffed the call for negotiations and at least initially described the Soviet gesture as meaningless because, it said, Soviet "bloc" (read, Cuban) support for Nicaragua and for the guerrillas in El Salvador continued.

Cuban support to Nicaragua did continue, but, as discussed above, that was assistance Cuba had every right to give. As for Cuba's alleged support for the guerrillas in El Salvador, since 1981 the United States has been unable to produce any hard evidence of it. A few shell casings turned up in 1989 that supposedly had been manufactured in Cuba, but this was hardly definitive evidence because shell casings can be refilled many times over. That they turn up in one country does not mean they were shipped there by the country of manufacture.

Even in the case of the Nicaraguan government, the United States has come up with almost no hard evidence of arms shipments to El Salvador. It captured a few truckloads of arms back in 1981, then, in November of 1989, came up with a small plane that had crash-landed in El Salvador with a load of ground-to-air missiles. In between, there was nothing, and even in the case of the missiles, neither the United States nor El Salvador could establish a link to the Nicaraguan government. Whatever the origin of the missiles, it was neither Cuban nor Soviet. That much was established.

To say that there has been little evidence of Cuban and Nicaraguan support for the FMLN is not to suggest that there was none. Both countries have doubtless given some training to the guerrillas, allowed them safe havens in their national territories, given them moral and political support, and occasionally even small quantities of arms and ammunition. The International Court of Justice reviewed all the evidence in 1986 and concluded that the scope and nature of assistance Nicaragua was providing did not constitute aggression against El Salvador. Nothing has changed between 1986 and December 1989 to alter that assessment. Cuban-Nicaraguan assistance, in short, was never the critical factor in the Salvadoran Civil War the United States portrayed it to be. Further, although halting such assistance was an understandable and legitimate U.S. objective, the United States might have achieved that objective through negotiations. But it eschewed negotiations and pressed on with its *Contra* War.

Clearly then, the victory of the *Sandinistas* in Nicaragua in 1979 did not result in any sustained Soviet or Cuban return to the armed struggle tactics of the 1960s. What Communist parties in almost all Latin American countries have been encouraged to do since 1982 is not to take up arms but to make alliances with other progressive forces. This is simply a slight variation on the popular front tactics long advocated by Moscow; its adoption does not imply any significant change in Soviet-Cuban policy in Latin America.

Guerrilla fronts and armed struggle were hard realities in El Salvador and Guatemala, but these two countries were the exceptions that proved the rule—not because either the Soviet Union or Cuba preferred them but because conditions in the countries themselves so dictated. The level of social injustice and political repression in each—and the inability to do anything about those conditions within the law and the existing system—produced a violent reaction. Opponents of the governments would have taken up arms even if the Soviet Union and Cuba had not existed. And, as one Soviet diplomat put it, "had real democracy existed in either Guatemala or El Salvador, the guerrillas would not have had to take to the hills in the first place."[15] Moreover, both the Soviet Union and Cuba indicated their strong support for negotiated solutions to the conflicts in both El Salvador and Guatemala.

The Objective: Socialism or Democracy?

Do the Soviet Union and Cuba seek to communize the Central American countries, and, therefore, do their policies represent serious obstacles to the process of democratization there? In accordance with Marxist doctrine, the creation of socialist states cannot be the immediate objective of Communists. Socialism can be achieved only after the prior historical stages have been gone through. Capitalism grows out of feudalism; socialism, in turn, follows capitalism. Because all the Central American states save Costa Rica (and of course Nicaragua) are considered to be still in a semifeudal state and because Costa Rica is regarded as a limited democracy, Marxist theoreticians would say that the revolutionary objective in these states must first be the establishment of capitalism and full democracy. Only then might the socialist stage become feasible.

Under Khrushchev, the Soviets did for a time depart from this Marxist law of history because of the Cuban Revolution. Cuba had been a semifeudal country ruled by a dictatorship. Yet without passing through the capitalist phase and with only a brief nod toward bourgeois democracy, it had, by 1962, been recognized by the Soviet Union as a country that was constructing socialism. To accommodate the Cuban phenomenon (and other developing countries that might repeat the Cuban experience) to their doctrinal framework, the Soviets came up with something called the "noncapitalist path to socialism." It was now possible to bypass the capitalist stage, said Soviet theorists, because of the growing strength of the socialist camp and the consequent change in the correlation of forces in the world.

This distortion of Marxism-Leninism was a product of the euphoria of the Khrushchev period over the possibility of socialist gains in the Third World. Like most moments of euphoria, it passed quickly. A number of countries were said to have been on the noncapitalist path to socialism, but, with the exception of Cuba, none got there. Hence, under Brezhnev's more orthodox stewardship, the whole concept of the noncapitalist path was abandoned. Soviet Latin American area specialists returned to the formulas of the past. Boris Koval, for example, emphasized in 1975 that the struggle for democracy would be the determining feature of the Latin American political process for decades to come. The choice faced by Latin Americans, he said, was not between democracy and socialism but, rather, between democracy and fascism.[16]

Did the victory of the *Sandinista* Revolution lead Soviet theorists to revise such conclusions and to resuscitate the idea of moving directly to socialist construction? From a doctrinal point of view, this was an even more important question than that of the tactical efficacy of armed struggle. The answer depended in large part on Soviet perceptions of the Nicaraguan Revolution itself—and of the opportunities in Central America and Latin America as a whole that might flow from that revolutionary experience. Would Nicaragua be seen as on a "noncapitalist path" or as moving to the construction of socialism? Soviet greetings to the Nicaraguan government on the first anniversary of the Great October Revolution following the *Sandinista* victory were, understandably, noncommittal. Nicaragua was said simply to have "set forth on a road of independent development."[17]

Subsequently, there were a number of references to Nicaragua as a "national liberation state" (though notably it was not described as one on the noncapitalist path), and then it was described as a "People's Democracy"[18]—a term implying progress beyond the status of national liberation state. In mid-1983, *Pravda* made one lone reference to Nicaragua's "socialist orientation."[19]

Concomitantly, at least some Soviet area specialists were sufficiently encouraged by events to argue that a speedy transition to socialism in Latin America was indeed possible. Participants at one symposium in 1983, for example, concluded that material conditions in Latin America were such as to make possible the transition to socialism.[20] They did not argue that a capitalist/democratic stage was unnecessary (i.e., they did not resuscitate the concept of the noncapitalist path). Rather, their position was that although the immediate objective was indeed full democracy, changed conditions in Latin America accelerated the process and gave it a scope that went beyond the bourgeois democratic revolution. Indeed it was possible to continue on to socialist revolution in one uninterrupted movement.[21]

By no means did all Soviet area specialists share this optimistic assessment. Most, in fact, continued to insist that full democracy ought to be the goal of revolutionaries in Latin America and sharply criticized those who thought socialist revolution was already on the agenda.[22]

Obviously, the *Sandinista* success in Nicaragua had raised some doubts concerning long-standing conclusions and formulations, thus prompting a debate among Soviet area specialists as to appropriate objectives. This debate, however, like the one over the efficacy of armed struggle, was short-lived. After the one reference in 1983 to Nicaragua's socialist orientation, Soviet definitions of Nicaragua slipped back to "democratic" and even to merely "progressive." Cuba had long been described as an "inseparable part of the socialist community of nations."[23] Clearly, Nicaragua was not considered part of that community or even necessarily on the way to becoming part of it. Soviet ambassador Valery Nikolayenko made that clear in 1988. Nicaragua's revolution, he said, was a pluralist one, as contrasted with Cuba's socialist revolution. And, he went on, Moscow had no interest in drawing Nicaragua closer to the socialist bloc.[24]

Had Moscow had such an interest, if it had seen Nicaragua as an advance base for the communization of Central America, surely the Soviets would have provided Nicaragua with substantial financial assistance. But it consistently refused and in 1987 began cutting back petroleum supplies.

If the transition to socialism is not on the agenda even in Nicaragua, much less could it be described as the objective of revolutionaries elsewhere in Latin America. Hence, by 1985 Soviet area specialists were again virtually unanimous in agreeing that the objective was democracy.

Transition to socialism was relegated to the category of a distant future possibility. Speaking of the Third World in general, for example, a discussion group organized by the *World Marxist Review* concluded, "At the present stage, the peoples of developing countries are not fighting for the immediate advent of socialism, although socialism is often viewed as a *feasible historical prospect* [emphasis mine].... Their goal is democracy."[25] Talk about scaling back expectations! From a historical inevitability, the advent of socialism has become something that is "often" considered to be "feasible" in a future so distant it is referred to in a historical context.

The Cubans had all along been more bearish than their Soviet allies. Fidel Castro himself, for example, urged the *Sandinistas* to maintain a pluralist society and a mixed economy, to have good relations with the church, and to keep lines out to the capitalist West as well as to the socialist East.[26] The *Sandinistas* did not always follow this advice, but it was hardly the advice Castro would have given had he been pushing for an immediate transition to socialism.

Cuban leaders never appear to have been tempted to think such a transition was possible in Central America or in the rest of Latin America. In 1983, for example, Cuban vice president Carlos Rafael Rodriguez stated flatly that "transition to socialism is not today on the agenda in Central America....Objective conditions...do not yet exist."[27]

A comprehensive exposition of the Cuban position was provided in a briefing by Cuban vice minister José R. Viera to a U.S. delegation in October 1987. Asked whether Cuba preferred to see full democracies rather than socialist states in Latin America, Viera responded that it was not a matter of preference. Cuba had chosen the path of Marxism-Leninism, and it, of course, might wish to see the emergence of other socialist states in the region. But the hard fact was, he went on, that the conditions for that simply did not exist in any other Latin American country; hence, there were not likely to be any more Cubas—at least not for a long time to come. Nicaragua was a progressive state that had adapted some socialist ideas and programs to its own environment, but it was not a socialist state.

Meanwhile, Viera went on, conditions did exist for the establishment of full democracy. In fact, that had already been accomplished in a number of countries. What Cuba would like to see at this stage in history—and Viera acknowledged that it might be a stage that would last a long time—was a whole hemisphere of economically developed, flourishing democracies, all providing social justice and dignified lives for their people and all living in peace with one another. For its part, Cuba would remain socialist, but it could gladly and constructively be a part of that kind of family of Latin American nations. That was what

Cuba was working for today. The idea that Cuba was attempting to export communism to the rest of the hemisphere was absurdly wrong. If there were governments that wished to copy Cuba's public health system or the way in which it made education accessible to all, they were welcome to do so, but Cuba had no wish to impose its system, either whole or in part, on anyone, especially because doing so would be out of historical context.[28]

Asked if Cuba had not tried to do just that during the early years of its revolution, Viera answered that it had not tried to export revolution. Cuba had always said that revolution could not be exported. It might, however, have been overly enthusiastic in believing that the conditions for revolution existed and that it could persuade others to that belief. But that was history. He was talking about Cuba's current posture.

With the conversation having come around to the support for armed struggle, Viera was asked if it was not true that Cuba's very Constitution called for the support of national liberation movements. How then could he say that Cuba had no intention of exporting revolution? He responded that Cuba took its internationalist principles seriously and would never abandon them. Cuba, he said,

> Has a duty to express its solidarity with national liberation groups and with peoples struggling for social justice and true freedom....Indeed, however Cuba might choose to express its support for these liberation movements, it would always act within the U.N. charter and the norms of international law. It would never, as the United States had done, defy the World Court.[29]

Soviet/Cuban Preferences for Negotiated Solutions

Viera went on to say categorically that Cuba wanted to see a regional agreement that would end local conflicts, provide mechanisms for the peaceful settlement of disputes, allow the countries of the region to develop economically and to move from limited to full democracies. "We have on several occasions indicated our support for the Arias peace plan," Viera said. "We are prepared to respect its provisions, as long as other extraregional powers respect them as well. We cannot formally commit ourselves to adhere to the plan, however, unless the United States is equally committed."[30]

Cuba's indications of support for the Arias plan are consistent with its earlier expressions of support for the Contadora process, its indications of willingness to discuss the matter with the United States, and its unilateral gestures aimed at improving the atmosphere for constructive dialogue. In 1981, for example, Cuba for a time suspended all military shipments to Nicaragua in an effort to encourage dialogue with the United States and a regional peace process. The United States ignored the gesture.[31] Undaunted, in 1983 Fidel Castro stated that Cuba would be willing to withdraw all its military personnel from Nicaragua and observe an arms embargo applied to Central America if the United States would do the same.[32] This formula may have been unacceptable to the United States, which wanted to continue its military assistance, at least to El Salvador. Still, Castro's overture ought to have opened the door to negotiations. At the very least, the United States should have tested Castro's seriousness of purpose. Instead, it again failed to explore the opening.[33]

These were but a few of Castro's overtures in favor of negotiations. This preference for negotiated solutions did not indicate altruism on Cuba's part; rather, such solutions served Cuba's interests and objectives in the region. Given that Cuba did not believe socialist revolution was possible anyway or that armed struggle was even the appropriate tactic in any country save El Salvador (and even there Cuba is only lukewarm on the idea) and given that its overriding objective until 1990 was the preservation of a *Sandinista* government (an objective that would have been furthered by negotiations), the Cubans naturally preferred to see diplomacy work.

The Soviets also consistently expressed support for the Contadora process and indicated their strong preference for a negotiated solution in Central America, especially in Nicaragua. An official Soviet statement on August 12, 1987, not only welcomed the Esquipulas accords signed by the five Central American presidents, but also emphasized the Soviet government's "determination to respect the decision."[34]

The same Soviet statement emphasized "much [would] depend upon the stand taken by the United States." During the 1987 summit conference between President Reagan and General Secretary Gorbachev, the Soviet leader tested U.S. intentions by suggesting the Soviet Union would be prepared to halt all military shipments to Central America if the United States would do the same. What Gorbachev had in mind was an arrangement that might eventually lead to Central America becoming a demilitarized zone.[35]

As in the case of Castro's overtures, there was no reason to expect the United States would accept this proposal precisely as Gorbachev put it forward. One might, however, have thought the United States would want to explore working out some constructive arrangement. But the Reagan administration simply did not respond.[36]

Some insisted that Soviet military assistance to Nicaragua ought to stop immediately—or, alternatively, that U.S. assistance to the *Contras* should have continued until such aid was terminated. But the two were not analogous. The Arias plan called for an end to assistance of "irregular forces." Under its provisions, the United States should have stopped its aid to the *Contras,* just as the Soviets, Cubans, and Nicaraguans should have halted theirs to the FMLN in El Salvador. But the plan did not demand termination of assistance to established governments. The Soviet Union therefore was free to continue military assistance to Nicaragua, just as the United States was free to aid El Salvador and Honduras. The termination or reduction of such Soviet aid was a legitimate and desirable goal. If the United States expected the Soviets to reduce their military presence in the region, it was unrealistic to expect Moscow to do so unilaterally. Peaceful solutions usually imply reciprocal steps and mutual restraint.

Extraordinary Possibilities Under Gorbachev

In international politics nothing should be taken at face value. Certainly there was a time when Soviet protestations of support for negotiated solutions might have been regarded as little more than tactical jockeying for position—though such assurances should always be carefully examined, whatever one's suspicions. But extraordinary changes are afoot in the Soviet Union and in its foreign policy. Soviet leaders are now indicating a preference for peaceful solutions to regional conflicts and are as much as saying that Soviet foreign policy will no longer be based on assumptions of class conflict[37]—a euphemism for the extension of the revolution and, in the final analysis, for East-West conflict. No less an authority than Politburo member Vadim Medvedev was recently quoted as saying that the old concept of class-oriented foreign policy should be rejected in favor of "common humanity."[38]

For his part, Foreign Minister Eduard Shevardnadze emphasized that Soviet foreign policy will henceforth be based on the interests of the Soviet people and will aim for the universal enhancement of peace. The political systems of other countries are their own affairs. The Soviet Union would remain loyal to the idea of national liberation, but, he seemed to suggest, in today's complicated and dangerous world, there was little the Soviet Union could reasonably do to assist.[39]

What these Soviets seem to be saying is that the Soviet Union's first duty must be to develop its own economy and provide its own people a better way of life. Unless it can make its own economy work, the Soviet Union can be of no use to anyone, certainly not to those who look to it as the hope of and example for a socialist future. Hence, for the foreseeable future, the Soviet Union will concentrate on things at home;

to do that, it wants a relaxation of world tensions, a peaceful settlement of regional disputes, and a muting of the idea of class struggle. Rather than a revolutionary power turning its gaze outward, the Soviet Union is in the process of contraction and introspection. Gorbachev, then, needs the settlement of regional disputes to have the kind of atmosphere in which his domestic reforms have the best chance of working.

Conclusions

The Soviet Union and Cuba are actors in the Central American drama, but actors of secondary importance. They did not create the problem there, nor do they seek to perpetuate the conflict. Neither believes violent revolution has any prospect of success at this point, and both believe it could lead to a widened conflict. Therefore Cuba and the Soviet Union prefer a negotiated settlement, provided such a settlement does not require the capitulation of their friends in the area. The emphasis must be on national reconciliation, not the surrender of one side or the other.

Neither the Soviet Union nor Cuba opposes the development of democratic systems and parties in the region. Indeed, both seem convinced that the historical moment calls for that development. Certainly neither country's policies are based on the hope of communizing Central America—Cuba because it understands that is not possible and the Soviet Union not only because conditions do not favor it, but also because it would imply unwanted costs and risks at a time the Soviets need to concentrate on problems at home.

As of late 1989 both the Soviet Union and Cuba were in a conciliatory mood and wanted an accommodation acceptable to all sides. It would have been possible to engage them in a constructive search for solutions. Their local associates—the FMLN in El Salvador, the guerrillas in Guatemala, and the *Sandinistas* in Nicaragua—were less malleable. In Guatemala, for example, as long as the Guatemalan military remains the real power in that country the guerrillas there are likely to go on fighting—not because the Soviet Union or Cuba want them to, but because that is a realistic response to the situation. The conditions that drove the guerrillas to take up arms in the first place have by no means been remedied. If the Guatemalan military wishes to see the country democratized, it can throw the doors open to such a process. It is not the Soviet Union or Cuba or even the Guatemalan guerrillas that stand in the way of democratization; rather, it is the Guatemalan military itself. Like Pogo, "they had met the enemy, and he is them."

Epilogue

Events since December of 1989 have confirmed all of the conclusions drawn above. If any central lesson was to be learned from the elections in Nicaragua in February of 1990, it was that diplomacy and dialogue can work where force fails. For years the Reagan and Bush administrations insisted the only way to remove the *Sandinistas* was by pressure and force. Thus, these administrations opposed various peace plans and insisted instead on more and more aid to the *Contras*. This achieved nothing. Only when the U.S. Congress, over the administration's objections, halted military aid to the *Contras* and gave the Arias plan a chance to work did an electoral solution became possible. As a direct result of the Arias peace plan, democratic, internationally monitored elections were held in Nicaragua in February 1990. The opposition, led by Violeta Chamorro, won, and the *Sandinistas* stepped down peacefully, something advocates of *Contra* aid said could never happen. The Soviets actually encouraged the *Sandinistas* to hold the elections. The Cubans, although skeptical, posed no objections.

With the *Sandinistas* now out of power, the question of their support for the FMLN in El Salvador has been overtaken by events. To a great extent so has the question of Cuban support. El Salvador does not have a Caribbean coastline. Hence, without the routes across Nicaragua, logistical problems virtually rule out significant Cuban material assistance. Meanwhile, the Soviet Union has abandoned the concept of world revolution. Rather than furthering efforts to extend the socialist system, it says its foreign policy will henceforth be conducted strictly in accordance with the U.N. Charter and will exclude use of force whenever possible. With the Berlin Wall down, Europe reunited, and East-West conflict in the Third World ended, the cold war is over.

The civil war continues in El Salvador, and guerrilla activity is increasing in Guatemala, but in neither case is that because of anything the Cubans or Soviets have said or done. Even less than in the past is Cuban support for the FMLN a significant factor in the Salvadoran situation. The civil war continues in El Salvador because the army refused to accept meaningful reforms. Its repressiveness and unwillingness to abide by the law were among the principal causes of the civil war. Eleven years later, they are among the principal reasons the war continues. After ten years of massive U.S. military assistance and counseling, the Salvadoran army is no more democratically grounded today than it was when the fighting began. In Guatemala also, revolutionary activity is increasing precisely because nothing has changed over the past decade. Guatemala is as far from democracy today as it was in 1980.

The obstacles to democracy in El Salvador and Guatemala today are posed not by Cuba and even less by the Soviet Union. Rather, they are posed by the Salvadoran and Guatemalan armies and by the ultra-conservative forces in those countries who wish to see an unjust status quo preserved forever.

Notes

1. Boris Koval, *Latinskaya Amerika* (March 1980):78.
2. Sergo Mikoyan, *Latinskaya Amerika* (March 1980):102–3.
3. N. Leonov, *Latinskaya Amerika* (March 1980):37.
4. *New York Times*, March 19, 1981.
5. Timothy Ashby, *The Bear in the Backyard* (Lexington, Mass.: Lexington Books, 1987), pp. 153–78.
6. Gordon McCormick et al., *Nicaraguan Security Policy: Trends and Projections* (Santa Monica, Calif.: The Rand Corporation, 1988), p. 12.
7. See N. S. Leonov, *Latinskaya Amerika* (August 1981).
8. *World Marxist Review* (October 1984):68. See also Sergo Mikoyan, "Concerning Particular Aspects of the Nicaraguan Revolution," *Latinskaya Amerika* (July 1982):41.
9. *Prensa Latina* dispatches of April 27 and 28, 1982. For a discussion of the conference and its significance, see Wayne S. Smith, "Castro, Latin America and the United States," in *United States Policy in Latin America*, ed. John Martz (Lincoln: University of Nebraska Press, 1988), pp. 288–305.
10. *World Marxist Review* (September 1983):45.
11. Ibid.
12. Ibid.
13. *Latinskaya Amerika* (January 1987):17–25.
14. As related to the author by an Argentine diplomat who asked to remain anonymous. The account is in a sense verified by the official Cuban position, which is that, in Chile, Cuba will be guided by the consensus of the democratic presidents of the Southern Cone.
15. As indicated by a Soviet embassy officer, who asked to remain anonymous, in a conversation on November 23, 1988.
16. *Latinskaya Amerika* (November–December 1975):37.
17. *Pravda*, November 7, 1979.
18. Morris Rothenberg, *Problems of Communism* (September–October 1983).
19. *Pravda*, June 13, 1983.
20. The symposium was reported in the *World Marxist Review* (October 1984):66.
21. Ibid.
22. See, for example, M. F. Gornov, *Latinskaya Amerika* 7 (1982):10.
23. *Pravda*, April 8, 1981.
24. *Washington Post*, November 6, 1988.
25. *World Marxist Review* (December 1985):71.

26. Wayne Smith, *The Closest of Enemies* (New York: W.W. Norton, 1987), p. 181.

27. *New Times,* January 1984. See also Jesús Montane Oropesa, *World Marxist Review* (November 1985):14.

28. Interview with José R. Viera in October 1987.

29. Ibid.

30. Ibid.

31. Smith, *Closest Of Enemies,* pp. 254–55.

32. Ibid., p. 270–71.

33. Ibid. See my discussion of the role played in this by John Ferch, the chief of the U.S. Interests Section in Havana. Ferch at least tried to get something going in the way of explorations. Unfortunately, he was given no support in Washington.

34. From a Soviet embassy press release dated that same day.

35. Conversation with a Soviet embassy officer, who asked to remain anonymous.

36. Ibid.

37. See, for example, the fascinating article by Y. Plimak in *Pravda,* November 14, 1986, in which he calls for a sweeping review of Soviet thinking and says "the need for profound changes is also applicable to the Marxist theory of class struggle." Plimak goes on to emphasize peaceful means of struggle. Violent revolution, he concludes, entails the risk of wider war—a risk he clearly believes is unacceptable.

38. *Washington Post,* October 6, 1988, p. 41.

39. Based on the Russian text of the Shevardnadze statement of August 12, 1988.

17

The Communist Party of the Soviet Union and the Communist Movement in Central America

Sergo Mikoyan

The Communist Party of the Soviet Union (CPSU) grew out of the Russian Social Democratic Party (RSDP), founded in 1898 at its first congress in the Byelorussian town of Minsk. In 1903 a major split divided the party between the Bolsheviks (majority) and the Mensheviks (minority). That split has been extremely significant for the subsequent nine decades of Russian and world history. No thorough analysis of it has yet been undertaken, nor has it been possible until now to think of reconciling the two schools of thought the two parties represent.

After the October Revolution of 1917, in the beginning of 1918, the VIIth Congress changed the name of the RSDP by adding the words "of Bolsheviks." In connection with the formation of the USSR, the XIVth Congress again, in 1925, changed the name, this time to the All-Union Communist Party of Bolsheviks: VKP(f). This clarification, though with a small "f," was redundant, because three years earlier the Menshevik Party was not only abolished but also severely persecuted, and it ceased to exist inside the country. Finally, after the XIXth Congress of 1952, the ruling party was renamed again. It became the CPSU.

Before 1917 the party's international ties were limited to participation in the Second International, founded by Engels and others in 1889. During World War I, Lenin began to organize separate conferences of leftist elements in the countries of Europe. This helped create the Third, or Communist, International in 1919. Its party members were called "sections" to stress the centralized, antinationalistic, worldwide character of the movement and to reflect the expectations of a world revolution due to come in months or, at worst, a few years. By 1919 sections outside Europe gradually began to appear, including in Latin American countries. The story of these parties' ties with the Third International and the Russian party is largely unknown to historians and other scholars.

When the International was disbanded in May 1943, the international department of the CPSU in Moscow tried to take over its functions. However, this did not work well because, instead of experienced nationals who knew the situations in their countries, the department was staffed with Soviet officials whose main aim was to please their Kremlin bosses. Furthermore, because many old Comintern hands had perished in the purges of 1937–38, many of their substitutes concluded they could only survive by functioning as frightened bureaucrats.

The XXth Congress of the CPSU, with Khrushchev's recognition of the crimes and terror of the Stalin era, transformed the international relations of the Communist parties. For the European parties, so long loyal to the Stalinist version of history, a compensation was arranged. Resolutions were passed that validated the concept of a peaceful transformation of capitalist society into a socialist one.

The "Cominform," created after the war with the nominal goal of mutual information (actually to restore the leadership of the CPSU), became an important arena for measuring loyalty and forming alliances. The Communist parties of Latin America were among the most faithful friends and followers of the CPSU (after, of course, the Eastern European ruling parties.) For them Stalin's crimes did not seem so disgusting. The history of their own countries was often the history of violence without limit; their attitude toward death was relatively accepting. Latin America's geographical distance from Europe also helped. As a result, Latin American Communist parties loudly proclaimed the victories of Stalin's USSR. These parties discussed Stalin's crimes from the point of view of their historical inevitability and downplayed their scale.

Furthermore, nonviolent, parliament-led revolutions were hardly plausible in postwar Latin America, where bloody dictatorships dominated the political scene. The Cuban Revolution of 1959 proved the effectiveness of violent action, although in many countries new radical, leftist movements appeared, pushing the parties loyal to Moscow to accept social democratic reform.

The process helped transform the activity of a number of Latin American Communist parties into a strange amalgam of revolutionary rhetoric and reformist political behavior. In spite of such evident deviation from Leninist theories, Moscow readily accepted these parties as "vanguard." The most important criterion for Moscow's acceptance was the attitude of these other "brotherly" parties toward the CPSU itself, not their faithfulness to communist theory. Moscow demanded acceptance of everything it did, including the invasions of Hungary, Czechoslovakia, and Afghanistan; hysteria about Boris Pasternak; rude intervention in the creative life of intellectuals in the USSR; and shameful repression of so-called dissidents. In all of these difficult situations, most Latin American Communist parties remained loyal to the CPSU. A notable exception, however, was the Communist Party of Mexico, which for a long time irritated the CPSU with its categorical rejection of strangling "socialism with a human face." Another important criterion became the Latin American parties' position vis-à-vis Soviet-Chinese confrontation. Despite several splits, Latin American Communist parties took the Soviet side. They were consequently honored at every international Communist meeting and readily invited to every congress with the understanding that they would give a "dignified" response to unexpected critical words by delegates from the West or East.

The bosses of the CPSU's international department, Suslov and Ponomarev, and some members of the Politburo were only interested in securing the "good behavior" of the leadership of foreign parties. Rare romantics grumbled, but after a time they became cynical about the "leaders" of the world Communist movement. Those "leaders" got accustomed to being met at the airport as VIPs and not having to go through customs or the immigration procedure; to being transported in huge limousines, in their own countries the exclusive privilege of millionaires; to being hosted in the special party hotel, which provided complimentary meals accompanied by caviar and vodka; to using the best available medical care and the best resorts in the USSR; even to "buying" (not paying a penny for) clothes "for the Russian climate" (as well as for all other climates) in a special section of the GUM department store. They liked it; they felt important as soon as they crossed the frontier of the "first socialist state." All of this helped resolve difficult theoretical and political problems.

Such behavior was not characteristic of all Communist leaders coming to Moscow from Latin America. A number felt uneasy and could not understand such "egalitarian" features in the "country of developed socialism." They could not understand why no one in the CPSU wanted to listen to critical remarks or even reasonable proposals. One example was Jorge Shafik Handal, the general secretary of the party in El Salvador, who once visited Moscow just after a new party hotel was built on Dimitrov Street. We stood in the main lobby, which was so huge that we could not recognize the face of a man standing in another part of it. Then we moved to lobbies on the second floor, which had marble floors figured with the Zodiac signs. Gigantic crystal chandeliers hung everywhere. Shafik Handal could not keep silent. He said, "Why all this luxury? Why have they built a Hilton for us? Even Hilton must not waste money so senselessly. Where is Bolshevik modesty? Furthermore, yesterday I asked for a typewriter but was told they didn't have any. Who do they think we are and why do they think we come here?"

Different people came for different reasons. Luis Carlos Prestes of Brazil had an office in the old, modest hotel in the Plotnikov Pereulok and gave interviews. He was extremely serious. I could sense his remorse for his party's unpreparedness for the coup of 1964. "Can you imagine, we [the leadership] even did not know where to meet the next day!" he said. I met at the new hotel the intelligent, modest, friendly Rodney Arismendi of Uruguay, who looked around with mild irony. Narsiso Isa Conde of the Dominican Republic, coming to the premises of *Latinskaya Amerika* in a limousine, made fun of himself: "So small for such a big car," he said, and asked me difficult questions unanswered by those who represented the staff of the Central Committee. Such guests were not liked by that staff. Central Committee staff members did not like, for instance, Shafik Handal's desire to publish an article in *The Communist* (the main theoretical and political magazine of the CPSU) engaging in polemics about strategy and tactics of Communists in Central America. The article was published only after extensive editing. Then he came to the *Latinskaya Amerika* to express what he wanted to say; there his views were virtually unaltered.

At the same time I saw the people the staff of the Central Committee liked. I saw Luis Sanchez and his father from Somoza's Nicaragua spending hours in the restaurant, vodka on their table being constantly resupplied by waitresses, talking with the officials of the international department about their own "revolutionary work" and many other things. I was introduced to each of them, both times believing that they were fearless fighters for a better future for their people, though a bit surprised by the general atmosphere of their "sessions."

There were dignified, experienced, and aged visitors from Argentina, treated with special attention because each of them was entitled to at least one meeting with Ponomarev or perhaps with Ponomarev's Politburo boss, Suslov. (Ponomarev for a long time was a secretary of the Central Committee and the head of the international department. Only in the 1970s was he promoted to a nonvoting member of the Politburo, where Suslov was "responsible" for ideology and international contacts of the party.) Venezuela, Ecuador, Bolivia, Costa Rica, and other countries also had Communist leaders who modeled themselves after the well-known Argentines.

But private behavior, of course, is not what is most important for political analysis. More important were conclusions made by the elite-apparatchiks of the "old guard" of Latin American Communists. They had learned well the "rules of the game," which began to come into play even in Khrushchev's time. Then, however, foreign Communist leaders had more opportunity to see different people from the Soviet leadership, like Krusinen, Mikoyan, and Khrushchev himself, and to discuss issues in a relaxed atmosphere. After Khrushchev's fall, bureaucratic ways took the upper hand. Suslov monopolized that field of the party's activity, granting meetings with Brezhnev as special gifts to the most "dignified" leaders and at the same time turning such meetings solely into matters of protocol and prestige. Brezhnev readily repeated words prepared for him by the international department's staff. He was glad to be free of the responsibility and burden of thinking about foreign leaders' problems.

The rules of the game were simple: leaders of any Communist party had to (1) take the Soviet side against the Chinese or any other opponent, and (2) not criticize (but praise) any actions of the Soviet government or the CPSU. After that, the leaders could do whatever they wanted inside their countries and could even dictate their will to the international department of the CPSU and to the Soviet ambassadors in their countries (if there were any). Splits, expulsions, minicults of personality, departure from Marxist strategy or tactics, any alliance or refusal of alliance, any attitude toward any kind of government were judged in Moscow not for the merit of the action and not on the principle of nonintervention but on the basis of mutual opportunism. No attention whatsoever was given to the principles or morality of the actions.

For any member of the staff of the "third entrance" (the entrance to the building of the Central Committee on Staraya Square, which led to the international department), to work with a foreign Communist meant first of all not irritating a party leader because that leader could express his displeasure to Ponomarev or even to Suslov. For any deviation a reprimand was guaranteed. A strict warning about "political immaturity" could follow, and the potential consequence was not being promoted. For a second deviation, the outcome could be much worse. The cruel and pitiless Suslov could fire the "politically immature" person from the *apparat* and might well add an official party reprimand to the personal dossier of the too-bold staff member. Yet pleasing a leader of a "fraternal" party, being on friendly terms with him, cultivated an excellent reputation for a staff member and could lead to invitations for visits to the country of the leader and other privileges.

Relations between the CPSU and foreign Communist parties differed dramatically from sovietologists' clichés and standard definitions. The CPSU imposed almost nothing on its counterparts. If the rules of the game were maintained, they more often worked in reverse—a foreign party could impose on Moscow a line of behavior for its own country.

In the 1960s, the Cuban Revolution and the independence of the Cuban leadership created a new center of communist thought. Havana was not as prestigious as Moscow, but for more radical elements it became more appealing. Even those who disliked Fidel Castro's radicalism and felt more comfortable in Moscow had to take into account Castro's prestige and make periodic trips to Havana. There they had a much more difficult time than in Moscow. Ignorance of the Latin American reality, which they used in Moscow, was absent in Havana. Of course the Cubans did not pay enough attention to specifics of Latin American countries, but in Havana it was impossible to tell the "old wives' tales" that played so well in Moscow.

After Che Guevara's death it became clear that only violent revolutionary changes could take place in Central America. In the early 1970s, Fidel Castro and Omar Torrijos supported guerrillas in Nicaragua and Guatemala as well as leftist movements in Honduras and El Salvador. Moscow was still unwilling to hear anything that went beyond the reformist, opportunistic approach so comfortable for bureaucrats because it implied minimum risk and minimum trouble. While Western sovietologists wrote about the clever, perfidious efforts of Moscow to use détente for revolutionary expansion, Moscow only did what was necessary not to lose its leadership of "national liberation movements" to Havana. Angola and Ethiopia are good examples of Cuban initiatives reluctantly followed by the Soviet Union.

Its late support for the Nicaraguan Revolution exemplified Moscow's inaction. As late as May 1979, no official body in Moscow wanted to deal with the *Sandinista* "adventurers." Moreover, even the leftist section of the Socialist Party of Nicaragua (the CPSU counterpart), which had some contact with the *Sandinistas*, was not received in Moscow. When an official of that section, flying via Moscow to North Korea in 1978, tried to meet Konstantin Kurin, the Nicaraguan "desk officer" in the CPSU international department, he was only allowed a telephone call from the Moscow airport. He asked for a visa for a few hours to come from the airport to town or for an opportunity to talk at the airport. But Kurin had no instructions to do anything: Luis Sanchez (head of the Nicaraguan Socialist Party) would not be pleased; it would not have been loyal to him. So the telephone call ended with the polite explanation that "this time" nothing else could be done for "technical reasons." In 1978 Moscow knew that Fidel Castro had contacts with the *Sandinistas*. But he also had them with Argentine *Montoneros*, Uruguayan *Tupamaros*, Brazilian "urban guerrillas," Guatemalan Indian peasant guerrillas, and others. The Kremlin was happy to let Castro talk with all those adventurers while Moscow dealt with orthodox Communist parties.

In late April 1979, I accepted an invitation from the World Peace Committee in Helsinki to attend a conference on solidarity with Central American and Caribbean liberation movements, to be held in Panama. On April 30, I arrived in Panama, and from May 1 through May 3, I met representatives of the Nicaraguan left. I was amazed to hear the *Sandinistas*. I checked their information with frank, even indiscreet, questions. I became convinced that they were to begin their final offensive on May 20 and would defeat Somoza. (They began their offensive in June.) On May 4, I was in Moscow and relayed this information, not only to the Soviet Peace Committee, but also to the Central Committee of the CPSU. Only then, when the events unfolding in Nicaragua were explained directly to the decisionmakers, did the apparatus begin to build bridges to the *Sandinistas*. They did so slowly and were careful not to quickly burn bridges with traditional Nicaraguan Communists.

Once the CPSU established contacts with the *Sandinista* Front, it still hesitated to develop these relations too far. It was the *Sandinistas* who insisted on student exchanges, on consultations, and on other matters normal with other parties. For a long time, the *Sandinista* Front was regarded as different from other traditional "fraternal" parties. This was, of course, the case. The FSLN never could turn into just one more traditional counterpart, loyal under any circumstances.

The Soviet refusal in 1989 to give a $200 million credit to help improve the image of the *Sandinistas* before the elections of February 1990 was not simply because of economic difficulties in the USSR itself. The Soviet Union continued to pay many dollars for construction that could have been managed without hard currency. The times of strict economy had not yet come to the Soviet Union.

The Nicaraguan Revolution and the U.S. response brought to life the Central American conflict. The Kremlin decisionmakers never thought to turn Nicaragua into a *place d'arm* for military expansion. The help that was provided could not but have been provided. The political role of the USSR in the world, earlier almost undermined by China, demanded such help be given. And the CPSU as an ideological bulwark of the regime played the most important role in it.

As of summer 1989, the whole context of the role of the CPSU in foreign affairs and with respect to Central America has changed drastically. The leaders of *perestroika* have removed foreign policy from the realm of ideology. This has contributed to a split in the CPSU between "conservatives" and "democratizers." Although the issue of solidarity with liberation movements in the Third World was not mentioned in the early debates of the new, freely elected Supreme Soviet, by 1990 it became impossible not to discuss. True, the domestic democratization process dominates political discourse, and past falsehoods about democracy in the Third World make it difficult for nonspecialists to make informed judgments. Nonetheless, the discussion has begun.

Finally, the very role of the CPSU is changing rapidly. The CPSU can no longer impose its will without discussion and correction by the Supreme Soviet of the USSR and the Russian Federation. The Polit-bureau, that almighty body for decades, has become almost a "club for discussions." Instead, the Presidential Council has taken the power, especially in foreign affairs. Any split within the party would lead to corresponding foreign policy disagreements and lessen the party's role in that sphere. Foreign contacts with Communist parties throughout the world, including in Latin America, will be more or less analogous to those of the Social Democratic International, with the CPSU in the role of the Socintern. With regard to support for national liberation movements, domestic economic difficulties make it all the more difficult for this involvement.

The only chance for the CPSU to retain power is for it to accommodate the Soviet people's demand for democracy. This domestic focus will influence international issues. Any movement that puts greater emphasis on class struggle and class interests than on democracy will not be supported by the CPSU—even less so if the USSR has a ruling coalition or another ruling party. Thus, the CPSU's limited and often misunderstood impact on Central American political parties is likely to be significantly diminished in the future.

18

The Official Party of Mexico and the Country's Diplomacy in Central America

Adolfo Aguilar Zinser

Relations between Mexico and Central America have been characterized by mutual ambivalence and distrust. Central American perceptions of Mexico have in some ways paralleled the apprehension Mexicans have of their own northern neighbor, the United States. Central Americans have admired Mexico's rich and engaging culture, its social history, and its stable political system. Many have seen Mexico's postrevolutionary regime, including its single-party system, as a model of social change and political order. But Central Americans have also resented what they have perceived as Mexico's attempts to establish influence in the region and take advantage of its southern neighbors. As in the case of U.S.-Mexican relations, a knowledge of history enables us to understand this ambivalence.

Mexico's emergence as an independent nation was followed by a short-lived and unsuccessful attempt to integrate Central America into Agustin de Iturbede's empire. In 1823 the self-appointed emperor of Mexico formed what he called the United Provinces of Central America, which included the territories of the Capitania General of Guatemala, once part of the Viceroy of New Spain. In 1824 Central Americans created instead the independent Federation of Central American States, which lasted until 1828. In 1924 the Mexican Congress recognized the independence of these provinces. Yet the status of the province of Chiapas and of the Soconusco region was unresolved for the rest of the century and bitterly disputed by Mexico and Guatemala. The border between the two countries was not settled until 1895.[1]

The dispute over Chiapas—ultimately incorporated into the Mexican territory—left the Guatemalan ruling elites convinced Mexico had unfairly annexed a territory that belonged to their country. This perception has permeated relations between Mexico and Guatemala ever since and has also influenced the view other Central American elites have of Mexico as the big and contemptuous brother to the north.

Mexico has always seen Central America as a potential area of influence, but with a few exceptions, most notably between 1978 and 1986, it has not conducted an active policy in the region. At least two factors have inhibited Mexico's involvement in Central America. First and foremost is the determining role relations with the United States has played in Mexico's diplomatic, political, and economic history. The North has absorbed most of Mexico's attention away from its southern neighbors. Also, the United States has been sensitive to any real or perceived attempt on the part of Mexico to dominate in Central America and the Caribbean.

The Central American ambitions of Emperor Iturbide in 1823, as well as Mexico's support of Cuban independence in 1824, alerted U.S. governing elites to Mexico's potential as a competing influence in this key geopolitical space. Although Mexico has not shown territorial ambitions in Central America or the Caribbean since then, the relative size and power of Mexico and the existence of obvious geographic, cultural, and historic ties between that country and its southern neighbors have kept the United States suspicious of any Mexican presence in the region. Such early awareness of the need to restrict Mexico's presence in the Caribbean and the Central American isthmus was explicitly manifested in the first diplomatic communications Washington addressed to Mexico. In 1825, Henry Clay, secretary of state under John Quincy Adams, instructed Joel R. Poinsett, the first U.S. diplomatic envoy to that country, to warn the Mexican government not to intervene with Colombia on behalf of Cuban independence. That Caribbean island was already regarded as a potential U.S. domain, to be protected from any other country's, but particularly from Mexico's, territorial or political ambitions.[2] The hands-off Central America policy demanded of Mexico since then became a condition, whether implicit or explicit, of cordial treatment to Mexico on the part of the United States.

The Legacy of the Mexican Revolution

The second factor contributing to Mexico's detachment from Central America is the cleavage caused by the uneven political development both Mexico and Central America have experienced, especially after the 1910

Mexican Revolution. With the notable exception of Costa Rica, all other Central American republics have had a slow political evolution. They have been deprived of a sense of national purpose and dominated by a small group of oligarchic elites obsessed with preserving their wealth. This has translated into the entrenchment of resilient military regimes, fiercely antidemocratic and insensitive to the needs of the larger population. These regimes' close identification with the United States has equally contributed to keeping Mexico and Central America at a distance—if not always in a posture of open hostility, at least with an attitude of mutual disgust. For a long time Mexico prided itself on not being akin to the pro-U.S. dictatorships of Central America.

The implicit U.S. ban on Mexico's involvement in Central America, together with underlying antipathy between Central American regimes and the Mexican government, drained for a long time whatever historic motivation Mexico had to become involved in its adjoining region. The clearest manifestation of this mutual detachment is the negligible economic exchanges between Central America and Mexico.[3] Nonetheless, cultural and social contacts between the isthmus and Mexico have always been active. The rich confluence of the two societies is manifest in diverse migrations. For several decades Central Americans have gone to Mexico to be educated in academic disciplines—ranging from the social sciences and the arts to medicine—and to be trained as military officers in Mexico's War College. Central Americans have also traveled to Mexico to escape repression and political persecution. Others have gone to Mexico in search of work or have passed through on their way to the United States.

All of these movements of the Central American population toward Mexico have created a social network and a cultural identity that gives Mexico considerable influence in Central America, an influence closely related to the social ideas, the cultural movements, and the institutions that emerged in Mexico after its social revolution of 1910. Particularly during its initial period of stability and consolidation in the 1930s, the Mexican Revolution became a powerful inspiration to most if not all political and social reform movements of Central America.

Some of the most important decisions of the reformist leadership of Juan José Arevalo and Jacobo Arbenz, who ruled Guatemala between 1944 and 1954, such as agrarian and educational reform, were inspired by the social programs of the Mexican Revolution. As a consequence, after Carlos Castillo Armas overthrew Arbenz in the U.S.-sponsored coup—which was largely a reaction to the expropriation of properties owned by powerful and influential American fruit companies—some of the most prominent supporters of the deposed government went into exile in Mexico. Among them were many of Guatemala's most respected intellectuals, such as Luis Cardoza y Aragon, author of the acclaimed book *Guatemala: The Lines of Its Hands*. Cardoza y Aragon and many other Guatemalan artists, social critics, and political leaders merged easily with the Mexican intellectual community and became household names in Mexico's cultural circles.

The cultural and political appeal of Mexico, particularly strong in Guatemala, is also present in every other Central American country. The Costa Rican Revolution of 1948 lead by José Figueres, the founder of the modern antimilitaristic Costa Rican state, was strongly influenced by the Mexican antiimperialist and pro-self-determination ideas. Figueres himself was forced into exile in Mexico where he met and established strong ties with many other prominent Central American and Spanish exiles. With them, and supported by Mexican sympathizers, he tried to create a regional armed liberation movement, but in 1947 the Mexican police disbanded the group.[4] In El Salvador the timid reform attempted in 1948 after the fall of the cruel dictatorship of General Maximiliano Hernandez Martinez, author of the infamous peasants' massacre of 1932, was influenced by the Mexican revolutionary experience. Evidence of Mexican social ideas in this and other Central American reform movements has predisposed local oligarchies and autocratic regimes against Mexico. Their northern neighbor is perceived as the source of subversive ideas throughout the isthmus.[5]

The PRI: Regional Model of Political Hegemony

Although Central American elites resent Mexico's revolutionary appeal, at the same time they fancy the endurance and power of the official Revolutionary Institutional Party (PRI). The entrenchment of a noncommunist single-party system in Mexico is paradoxically admired by both the reformers and the oligarchies of the region.

The PRI's peculiar brand of authoritarianism, recently described by the Peruvian writer and politician Mario Vargas Llosa as "a perfect dictatorship,"[6] is often perceived by a number of Central American groups of the right and left as a convenient arrangement to establish and assure political and electoral hegemony. Given the endemic instability of all the region's political systems and the precarious consensus most political regimes have enjoyed, the PRI is seen not precisely as a democratic model but as the most successful combination of consensus, political control, and stability ever experienced in Latin America. Until recently some regional political observers, convinced that Latin peoples are not mature enough to be trusted with the responsibility of governing themselves democratically, have viewed the PRI as the best and most benevolent autochthonous alternative to political democracy.

The PRI was born in 1929 as the National Revolutionary Party (PNR), a coalition of regional *caudillos* (military and political bosses) willing to recognize the centralized authority of the new regime in exchange for power-sharing arrangements. Conceived originally as a revolutionary party of the masses led by military chiefs, the party soon became corporatist in structure, subordinated to the state and to the president. When the institutionalization of the army and its removal from politics were complete, the government transformed the PRI's internal structures to include only, as it is today, the official Mexican Confederation of Workers (CTM), the government-sponsored National Confederation of Peasants (CNC), and the so-called popular sector, also a creation of the state to draw in party bureaucrats, the middle classes, and professionals. (The National Confederation of Popular Organizations [CNOP] was renamed UNO in 1990.)[7]

The PRI benefitted from its privileged link to the state apparatus and budgets and established a comprehensive patronage system. At the same time, to assure its electoral supremacy, the official party designed the electoral laws of the country to its own advantage. An intricate system of electoral fraud has also been fixed with full government support. Fraud starts at voter registration and escalates all the way to the confirmation of electoral results.[8] Consequently, since its formation and until 1988 the PRI has never lost or conceded a presidential election. Before 1988 no Senate seat or governor's post of the thirty-two states has gone to the opposition; only a limited number of opposition congressmen were until then admitted to Congress, thereby assuring the PRI's majority, and few municipal governments were left outside the party's control. It is generally accepted that the official results of the 1988 presidential election declaring current President Carlos Salinas de Gortari the winner were false; Salinas may in fact have lost the election to the center-left candidate Cuauhtemoc Cardenas. As a consequence of this controversial election, the PRI has had to recognize opposition parties' control of four Senate seats (1988), one state government (Baja California Norte to the conservative National Action Party in 1989), around 40 percent of the House of Representatives, and several municipal posts. Nevertheless electoral fraud is still rampant in Mexico. The PRI's ability to adapt without losing its authoritarian character and its ability to maintain power while repressing only selectively and in exceptional circumstances have been recognized—and almost admired—by politicians of all creeds in the region. Equally seductive has been the PRI's ability to disguise its antidemocratic and often nasty, repressive character behind a nationalistic rhetoric that emphasizes social justice and national independence. The savvy ways the PRI avoids serious international scrutiny is also one the party's virtues most admired by Latin American autocrats. Yet, despite repeated attempts to reproduce this model, nowhere in the region has a PRI-like party succeeded.

The PRI was the model used in 1949 when members of the Salvadoran oligarchy decided to create a ruling party, the Revolutionary Party of the Democratic Unification (PRUD), transformed in 1961 into the Party of National Conciliation (PCN). To become the official party of El Salvador, the PCN imitated some PRI features such as a multiclass structure with the affiliation of peasants, middle-class organizations, and government-controlled workers.[9] The rigid social structures of El Salvador, the narrow-minded ambitions of the Salvadoran oligarchy and military bosses, and their resistance to meaningful social change and subordination to the United States frustrate attempts to establish a political hegemony like the one enjoyed by the PRI in Mexico. After all, the official party of Mexico is not simply a repressive structure; it is a sophisticated authoritarian arrangement, carefully crafted through a long process of political and military accommodation after a social revolution.

In Costa Rica, José Figueres's own National Liberation Party (PLN) has traditionally professed identification with PRI principles, particularly the doctrinaire postulates that inspire the country's independent and antiinterventionist foreign policy. Yet the PRI's dubious democratic credentials have also been the source of bitter controversy in Costa Rica. In the 1978 campaign, Luis Alberto Monge, presidential candidate of the PLN, received political advice from the PRI. The opposition denounced the presence of Mexican advisers, saying they were in Costa Rica preparing a typical Mexican electoral fraud to assure by any means Monge's victory. Such a scandal might have hurt the PLN's electoral chances and facilitated the victory of Rodrigo Carazo Odio, candidate of the United Opposition Coalition.[10]

In Panama, the Democratic Revolutionary Party (PRD), created in 1979 to consolidate the reform movement led by Omar Torrijos, also reproduced some of the political characteristics of the PRI. In the context of the political opening instituted by Torrijos's signing of the new Panama Canal treaties negotiated with the Carter administration in 1978, the strongman of Panama saw the need to restrict the role of the military in politics and allow parties to compete in elections but at the same time to create new mechanisms to defend his reforms and maintain power. Thus the PRD was organized along the lines of the PRI, as a government party. After the death of Torrijos in 1981, however, a bitter political struggle within Torrijos's camp and a lack of social consensus about the reforms interrupted this incipient political process. The PRD has never consolidated as a hegemonic political force largely because the National

Guard, headed by a sequence of military figures—the last one Gen. Manuel Antonio Noriega—eradicates political competition and erects itself as the guardian of the Torrijista faith (that is, until the American invasion in 1989).[11]

In Nicaragua the PRI was also seen as a role model for the transformation of the *Sandinista* National Liberation Front (FSLN) into a political machine. The structure of the relationship established between the party of the triumphant revolution and the state after 1979 almost mirrors the relationship today between the PRI and the Mexican state.

In general, attempts to reproduce the experience of the PRI in other Central American countries have been made without direct PRI involvement. In fact the ruling party of Mexico has not conducted in Central America a campaign to become the leader of an ideological movement, not as the Communist Party of Cuba did until recently or as Socialist and Christian Democratic parties have done for some time. Encouraged, however, at times by Central Americans' enthusiasm toward the Mexican Revolution, Mexican leaders have been tempted to extend their country's regional influence by encouraging or assisting opposition groups conspiring to depose repressive regimes. With the notable exception of Nicaragua and to some extent El Salvador, the PRI has not been part of those government actions typically implemented by discreet intelligence channels. Since 1979 and through the Confederation of Latin American Political Parties (COPPAL), however, the Mexican government has given the PRI a more active role in Latin American diplomacy and Central American policies.

The pattern of Mexico's political activism in Central America has been particularly evident in the case of the Nicaraguan revolutionary struggles of the 1930s and 1970s. Mexico has also shown sympathy for the Salvadoran and the Guatemalan revolutions, but its attempts to influence political events in Central America have triggered strong responses from conservative governments in the region and opposition from the United States.

The Mexican Political Experience in Central America

Three cases illustrate the complexities of Mexico's political involvement in Central America and of the role the PRI has had in Mexico's Central American diplomacy: Nicaragua both early in this century and in the last two decades and El Salvador after 1980.

In November 1925 a coup overthrew the moderate elected government of President Carlos José Solorzano in Nicaragua. A radical conservative, Emiliano Chamarro, became president. The Mexican government, however, refused to recognize the new regime and withdrew its diplomatic mission from Nicaragua. Chamorro did not last long. He resigned, and Congress, controlled by the conservatives, named Adolfo Diaz, who in turn was recognized as head of state by the United States. In defiance of American policy, in 1926 Mexican president Plutarco Elias Calles extended recognition to the insurgent government of Juan B. Sacasa, leader of a Liberal movement based in Puerto Cabezas. It is believed the Mexican government assisted Sacasa, even militarily. This alleged support was blown out of proportion by the State Department and the Hurst newspapers, which launched a campaign against the Mexican government, then considered in U.S. government circles a "Bolshevist regime." In that climate Diaz formally requested U.S. government assistance to counteract Mexican presence in Nicaragua. On Christmas day 1926, U.S. marines landed in Puerto Cabezas and took control of the city. Eventually the Liberal forces accepted a settlement that included a U.S.-supervised election and the formation of a national guard trained and armed by the United States. Augusto Cesar Sandino, the only Liberal general not to accept the so-called Pact of Espino Negro, retreated to the mountains to resist the U.S. invasion. At the time, relations between Mexico and the United States were strained by the enactment of several Mexican laws restricting the property rights, including mining and oil resources, of foreigners. Events in Nicaragua were used by some Republicans as a pretext to demand military intervention in Mexico to overthrow what they called the "Bolshevik government" of Calles. Commenting on the U.S. government's reaction to the Mexican government's support of Sandino, Robert Pastor stated,

> The United States condemned Mexico for interference and radicalism and increased its support for the incumbent government. This was not the first time that the United States deepened its involvement in Central America due to concern that a foreign rival, even one as weak as Mexico in the 1920s would expand its influence in the region at the expense of that of the United States. And it certainly was not the last time.[12]

Yet in what is already an historic pattern of the bilateral relationship, both countries chose to deescalate the confrontation and compromise. In 1927 Mexico and the United States reached a modus vivendi, and Mexico implicitly agreed to limit its involvement in Nicaragua.

Mexican involvement in Nicaragua was seen in Costa Rica as an expression of expansionist designs. In 1926 the conservative government of President Ricardo Jimenez expressed to the United States its concern that a Liberal victory in Nicaragua might bring about Mexican control of that country's government and eventually of the whole region. Official

Costa Rican hostility toward Mexico increased that year when an aborted revolutionary uprising in the province of Guancaste led by the head of the Reformist Party, Jorge Volio, was linked to Mexico's president Plutarco Elias Calles. In a curious twist of the typical Latin American antiimperialistic argument, President Jimenez abandoned his professed fear of U.S. interventionism in the region and strongly encouraged Washington to intervene in Central America, allegedly to neutralize Mexico's influence.[13]

Mexico's Foreign Policy in Central America

Mexico's second attempt to directly involve itself in a political struggle in Nicaragua occurred in the late 1970s in support of a guerrilla movement inspired by Sandino's anti-American struggle of five decades earlier. This episode constitutes a new chapter in the relationship between Mexico and Central America. Again the U.S. government distrusted Mexico's foreign policy and feared that its southern neighbor might be promoting a political order that would favor the strategic interests of the Soviet Union and Cuba, then the arch-enemies of the United States.

Prior to the fall of Somoza, the Mexican government became one of the strongest supporters of the FSLN and of its unarmed opposition allies. The means by which Mexico extended its support to the foes of Anastasio Somoza, a staunch U.S. ally, introduced a new dimension to Mexico's foreign policy. Instead of establishing open, direct contact with the Nicaraguan insurgents, the Mexican president José Lopez Portillo prudently gave that responsibility to the ruling PRI. The secretary of foreign affairs and the secretary of the interior were involved behind the scenes.

Despite obvious affinities between Mexico's revolutionary regime and the Social Democratic parties in various parts of the world, the government did not encourage contacts between the PRI and those political organizations. Not until the administration of President Luis Echeverria did Mexico's relations with the Social Democratic movement become more active. Such contacts allowed the PRI to develop confidence and expertise in partisan diplomacy. It also helped the government discover the convenience of supporting its foreign policy initiatives with the flexibility of the party's international relations.

Contacts between the PRI and the European and Latin American Socialist International (SI) movement gained momentum during the years the Nicaraguan Revolution was in progress. The Nicaraguan opposition had already become an active international force, seeking political and material support from members of the SI. Mexico became well aware of such moves. This helped the Mexican government build a network of relations and explore new fields of action in Central America.

Until then the PRI had not taken an active role in foreign policy. Mexico's claim of ideological independence and its strict defense of the principle of nonintervention translated into PRI's cautious and reluctant international activity. Until COPPAL was created in Oaxaca, Mexico, in 1979 under the initiative of the PRI, the Mexican government party had always refused to become a member of any political international movement. The idea of forming a regional political organization was first discussed in 1979, on the fiftieth anniversary of the PRI. In an unprecedented move, the ruling party of Mexico invited more than one hundred parties to be present at that celebration. By 1981 COPPAL membership already included twenty-nine parties, most of them also members of the SI. The organization was created in part in response to the activities of the SI in Latin America, but mainly as an attempt to consolidate a Latin American political movement against other regional conservative forces believed to be sponsored and instigated by the Reagan administration. Thus the original COPPAL documents stressed the antiimperialist, nationalistic, and revolutionary character of the organization, captured in its motto: "Latin America for the Latin Americans." Its most prominent members were vocal nationalistic leaders like Jaime Roldos of Ecuador, Omar Torrijos of Panama—both mysteriously killed in airplane accidents—Tomás Borge of Nicaragua and Daniel Oduber and Luis Alberto Monge of Costa Rica.

Based on the foreign policy experience and activism of the Echeverria administration, President Lopez Portillo confidently adopted a risky path in Central America. The Mexican government believed it could play a more assertive and influential role in the region without spoiling relations with the United States. First and foremost was the conviction of many government officials that Somoza's fall was inevitable. They believed that, given the great social injustice and mass repression imposed on the Nicaraguans by Somoza's cruel and long dictatorship, history was on the side of the revolution—a desirable outcome not even Washington could prevent. Second, Mexican officials and foreign policy advisers also believed that the Carter administration was trapped in its own human rights policy and would not move aggressively in Central America to prevent the fall of a discredited ally. Third, Mexico's oil discoveries in the 1970s gave Lopez Portillo confidence in the country's strength and influence internationally. Fourth, the Mexican leaders believed the type of government the FSLN would establish would have great political and ideological affinity with the PRI's regime. Therefore a change of Nicaragua's regime would not only curtail U.S. influence in the region, but it would also provide Mexico with new opportunities to advance its own interests.

On the basis of the prestige of Mexico's social revolutionary tradition, the PRI became the logical instrument to extend Mexico's support to the *Sandinistas* beyond the strict application of the traditional noninterventionist principles of Mexico's foreign policy. By 1987 the PRI had established a close relationship with the Group of Twelve, which provided the channels of communication needed to plan and execute joint diplomatic maneuvers in support of the *Sandinista* cause.

The relationship between Mexico and the Nicaraguan insurgents was not, however, limited to the PRI. It also involved the ministry of the interior and the foreign ministry, especially Mexico's embassy in Managua.[14] The ministry of interior dealt with all matters relating to *Sandinista* activities within Mexico, including the use of the Mexican territory by opposition figures to move out of the region and visit other countries or as a safe base to meet among themselves and consult with representatives of other countries and movements. Mexico's generous understanding with the *Sandinistas* also likely included the use of the Mexican territory to supply their forces with food, medicine, clothing, even munitions, although no evidence exists to prove this. Besides, the *Sandinistas* were authorized to establish discreetly in Mexico some of their propaganda facilities.

The same framework was established to deal with the Democratic Revolutionary Front (FDR), the Farabundo Martí National Liberation Front (FMLN) of El Salvador, and to some extent also with the various revolutionary forces integrated in the National Revolutionary Unity of Guatemala (URNG). The PRI's international relations secretariat was the official conduit Salvadoran rebel leaders used to communicate with the Mexican government. Frequent contacts were also maintained with the Salvadoran opposition representatives attending COPPAL meetings as observers. Mexico's initiative in El Salvador, however, resulted in the French-Mexican declaration of August 1981. It was designed and negotiated directly in the office of the secretary of foreign relations, with little or no participation by PRI officials. The French-Mexican declaration was a de facto recognition of the belligerent status of the FDR-FMLN forces and therefore of their representative in international discussions about peace in El Salvador. Given that recognition, the government of Mexico did not have to communicate with the Salvadoran rebels through PRI channels.[15]

The PRI's role is considerably less prominent in Guatemala. Border relations with that country are so sensitive they are conducted more by the secretary of the interior than by the secretary of foreign relations.

Mexico has been the destiny of most of the Guatemalan opposition's political and intellectual leaders, who in past decades have been forced to leave their country, and, since 1981, the land of refuge for the thousands of Indians and peasants expelled from their lands by the army's counterinsurgency campaign. The presence of Guatemalan opposition figures and refugees in Mexico has created conflicts between the governments of the two countries to the extent of military incursions by the Guatemalan army into Mexico. Given these circumstances, the Mexican government considers relations with Guatemalan opposition forces a sensitive security issue, thus restricted to the initiative and authority of the security apparatus of the country.

The active role of the PRI in Mexico's diplomacy in Central America was interrupted after 1983, with the beginning of the administration of President Miguel de la Madrid. Gustavo Carbajal, president of the PRI in its most active international period, gave no explanation for the PRI's retreat.[16] It is clear, however, that Mexico's political diplomacy in Central America confronted serious U.S. opposition in 1982. The decline in oil prices marked the beginning of a serious financial and economic crisis in Mexico. Needing support from Washington, Mexico gradually abandoned its political commitments in Central America. It first moved away from bilateral relations with the *Sandinistas* and other regional revolutionaries to multilateral diplomacy within the Contadora group. Paradoxically, COPPAL was no longer seen as a useful multilateral instrument to advance Mexico's interests in the region but instead as a dangerous forum closely identified with anti-American forces and postures. The de facto withdrawal of Mexico from COPPAL meant that this political organization came to a virtual standstill. The PRI was not only the leader of the group, but it was also its most generous sponsor. Therefore not until Mexico decided again in 1989 that COPPAL could be a useful instrument did the organization come back again.

In this new phase COPPAL is no longer seen by the PRI as providing an instrument to advance Mexico's foreign policy objectives in Central America but as serving an even more crucial and sensitive role: rebuilding the party's prestige as a respected Latin American political organization and reinforcing the badly damaged image of the Mexican regime in the hemisphere. In this sense, the PRI's new international activity has already become more closely associated with the interests of business than with the demands of its own labor sector.

The revival of COPPAL is thus an attempt to preserve Mexico's credentials as a nationalistic, antiinterventionist, prorevolutionary, avant-garde force in Latin America. The pragmatism shown toward Mexico by most COPPAL members attending that meeting has allowed the PRI to regain support and initiative within the organization. Regardless of its antidemocratic character, Mexico has never been seen as a target for political action by any Latin American democratic, socialist, or revolutionary force, not even Fidel Castro's Communist Party. Indeed, with its progressive traditional rhetoric and its diplomatic, and at times material, support to revolutionary forces, Mexico has immunized itself from interference by others in its political affairs.

The room for maneuver enjoyed internationally by Mexico's one-party system is largely a consequence of the U.S. government's whole-hearted embracing of the Mexican regime. Newborn U.S. sympathy for the PRI originates in the Mexican regime's decision to adopt a probusiness and antinationalistic economic policy. Such is the ironic paradox of today's PRI.

Notes

1. See Adolfo Aguilar Zinser, "Mexico and the Guatemalan Crisis," *The Future for Central America, Policy Choices for the U.S. and Mexico*, ed. Fagen Richard and Pellicer Olga (Stanford, CA: Stanford University Press, 1983), pp. 161–86; and Gilberto Castañeda Sandoval, *Guatemala*, Relaciones Centro America Mexico, eds. Adolfo Aguilar Zinser and Rodrigo Jaubert Rojas (Mexico City: Programa de Estudios Centro Americanos, CIDE, 1987).

2. Jose Fuentes Mares, *Poinsett: História de Una Gran Intriga* (Mexico City: Editorial Oceano, 1985), pp. 69–70.

3. Despite their proximity, economic exchanges between Mexico and Central America have always been relatively small. Mexico's industrial development and Central America's export crop economy have not matched. The creation in the 1960s of the Central American Economic Market and of the Latin American Free Trade Association reinforced Central American exchanges but did not change traditional currents of trade between Central America and Mexico. The war in Central America and the economic and financial crisis of Mexico have widened this economic cleavage. In 1980, Mexico and Venezuela launched the San José Pact to supply oil to Central America in a system of concessions and credits. This program could have become the basis for a new economic relationship among neighbors, but political and economic difficulties have so far frustrated its original intention. No Central American country has been in the position to develop alternative energy programs to take advantage of the loan facilities offered by the San José Pact. For an overview of Mexico-Central America economic relations, see Gabriel Rosenzweig, "La Cooperación Economica de Mexico con Centroamérica a Partir de 1979: Perspectivas Para los Proximos Años," *Politica Exterior de Mexico, 175 Anos de Historia* (Mexico City: Secretaria de Relaciones Exteriores, 1985), 3:351–88; and Raul Benitez Mantu and Cordova Macias, "Mexico and Central America: Percepciones Mutuas y Trayectoria de las Relaciones (1979–1986)," *Mexico en Centro America: Expediente de Documentos Fundamentales 1979–1986*, ed. Benitez Mantu Raul and Cordova Macias Ricardo

(Mexico City: Centro de Investigaciones Interdisciplinarias en Humanidades, UNAM, 1989), pp. 18–21.

4. See Armando Vargas Araya, "Latinoamericanidad de Figueres," *COPPAL* 1 (July–August 1990):44–53.

5. For an overview of mutual perceptions, see Benitez Mantu and Cordova Macias, "Mexico and Central America," pp. 7–32.

6. See Adolfo Aguilar Zinser, "Open to Business—Si; to Dissent—No," *Los Angeles Times* (Commentary), October 5, 1990.

7. For a detailed analysis of the PRI and its origins, see Xavier Garrido Luis, *El Partido de la Revolucion Institucionalizada: La Formacion del Nuevo Estado en Mexico, 1928–1945* (Mexico City: Editorial Siglo, 1989), p. 380.

8. As an illustration of one of the most dramatic electoral frauds of Mexico's modern history, see José Barberan et al., "Radiografía de Un Fraud," *Analisis de los Datos Oficiales del 6 de Julio, Editorial Nuestro Tiempo* (Mexico City: D.F., 1988).

9. The "three sectors" of the PCN were the official General Confederation of Salvadoran Trade Unions (CGSS), the affiliation of public employees, and the Salvadoran Communal Union (UCS), a peasant organization created in 1968 with the support of the American Institute of Free Labor Development (AIFILD). See Benitez Manatu and Cordova Macias, "Mexico and Central America"; and Gordon Rapoport Sarha, *El Salvador*, Relaciones Centro America Mexico, eds. Aguilar Zinser Adolfo and Jaubert Rojas Rodrigo (Mexico City: Programa de Estudios Centro Americanos CIDE, 1987).

10. Several years after the incident, Costa Rican writer Rodrigo Jaubert interviewed then former president Carazo about the PRI's involvement in the presidential election. Carazo said: "Of course the PRI...not only gave material support to the PLN but it was an active partner in the campaign against me. However...at the end of the campaign we joked about it. When President Lopez Portillo asked me how I felt about the help they gave the PLN, I answered him that I was not concerned because I demonstrated in the campaign that I could defeat both." Rodrigo Jaubert Rojas, *Costa Rica-Mexico 1978–1986: De la Concertacion a la Confrontación*, Relaciones Centro America Mexico, ed. Aguilar Zinser and Jauberth Rojas (Mexico City: Programa de Estudios Centro Americanos CIDE, 1987), p. 102.

11. See Anayansi Turner, *Panama*, Relaciones Centro America Mexico, ed. Aguilar Zinser and Jauberth Rojas (Mexico City: Programa de Estudios Centro Americanos CIDE, 1986), pp. 26–27; and Leis Raul, "Panama: Puente de Riqueza Ajena Bajo el Paraguas del Pentagono," *La Crisis Centro Americana*, ed. Daniel Camacho and Manuel Rojas B. (San José: EDUCA y FLACSO, 1984), pp. 180.

12. Robert Pastor, "The United States and Central America After the Cold War: Seal, Peel, or Repeal the Sphere of Influence?" Paper presented at the MacArthur Conference on Superpower Conflict and Cooperation in the Third World, University of California at Berkeley, October 4–6, 1990, first draft, mimeograph. See also Robert A. Pastor, *Condemned to Repetition: The United States and Nicaragua* (Princeton, N.J.: Princeton University Press, 1987); and Robert A. Pastor and Jorge Castañeda G., *Limits to Friendship: The United States and Mexico* (New York: Vintage Books, 1989).

13. Jiménez's anti-Mexican posture is vividly described in Richard Salisbury, "Costa Rica y el Istmo, 1900–1934," *Editorial IV*, San José (1984):105–18.

14. Jorge G. Castañeda, academic specialist on U.S.-Mexican relations, son of the foreign minister of Mexico, and close adviser to the government on Central American issues, has acknowledged that the Mexican embassy in Managua, headed by a highly competent foreign service officer, became a haven for *Sandinista* militants and leaders. Money, messages, people, and other goods entered and left the embassy and traveled to and from Nicaragua on Mexican government aircraft. Pastor and Castañeda, *Limits to Friendship*, p. 179.

15. In their official communiqué, Mexico and France stated that the opposition alliance of the FDR and the FMLN constituted a representative political force ready to assume the obligations and exercise the rights derived from their condition. For a detailed account of the circumstances surrounding this important initiative, see Sarha, *El Salvador*.

16. See Stella Calloni, "COPPAL: Un Foro de Integración Real; Entrevista con el Licenciado Gustavo Carbajal," *COPPAL* 1 (June–August 1990):33–36.

19

Religion and Democratization in Central America

Margaret E. Crahan

Institutional religion, particularly the Roman Catholic Church,[1] has long been regarded as monolithic in its support of the status quo in Central America. Yet churches have traditionally encompassed a broad spectrum of political and ideological positions, and there has always been a variety of opinions and sectors within the church that reflect society as a whole.

Central America was, in fact, the site of Bartolomé de Las Casas's Vera Paz challenge to the political and economic system being implanted by the Spanish in the New World at the outset of the sixteenth century.[2] In the last thirty years, Central America has become the scene of increasing ecclesial challenges to societal structures and patterns of domination. In a region where communities have historically had limited resources to challenge exploitative and nondemocratic structures, the church has facilitated popular organization and mobilization. As a result, the institutional church has been increasingly identified with forces for change, including revolutionary movements on the left. Although some churchpeople support armed struggle, including Marxist-led guerilla movements, the majority continue to promote evolutionary, albeit substantial, change.

This chapter was written while the author was the Will and Ariel Durant Professor at St. Peter's College and fellow at the Institute of Latin American and Iberian Studies at Columbia University. The author wishes to thank Mary DiNardo of St. Peter's and the staff of the institute for their assistance.

Throughout its history in Central America, the Catholic church has periodically challenged the status quo, particularly on issues of socioeconomic justice and political participation. Since the late nineteenth century, Catholic social doctrine has provided the impetus for some churchpeople, who have organized to promote universal suffrage, worker's rights, expansion of access to education, and government-sponsored social welfare programs.

Increased political activism on the part of churchpeople reflected not only the stimulus of Vatican II (1962–65) and the Latin American bishops meeting at Medellín, Columbia, in 1968. It also reflected societal trends, particularly support for reformist developmentalism. Both reinforced each other, and the visible involvement of churchpeople tended to legitimate change-oriented movements. Such activism also made these progressive movements and ecclesial institutions targets of those forces resisting change and contributed to the erosion of the traditionally sacrosanct position of the Catholic church within society. Attacks on churchpeople and institutions tended to reduce divisions within the church and politicize clergy, religious, and laity. The emergence of the Catholic church as a prime defender of human rights in societies increasingly in conflict enlarged its political role.

As Central American societies became more polarized in the 1970s and 1980s and warfare broke out in El Salvador, Guatemala, and Nicaragua, the Catholic church was drawn deeper into political struggle. In each case opinion over the church's actual or alleged political positions was divided. Although the church as an institution claimed political neutrality, it could not maintain that stance given the extent of ecclesiastical involvement in the Central American crisis.

Costa Rica

Over the past century, the Catholic church in Costa Rica has tended to swing between liberal and conservative stances and greater and lesser degrees of political activism. Historically the institutional church has been regarded as conservative, although it took some progressive positions, particularly on socioeconomic issues, even before Vatican II and Medellín.

As early as the late nineteenth century, the bishop of San José, Monsignor Bernardo Augusto Thiel Hoffman (1880–1901), demonstrated concern for injustice, particularly the exploitation of agricultural workers.[3] The government accused Thiel of promoting socialism and the fortunes of the *Union Católica*, which attempted to challenge the anticlerical *Partido Nacional* in congressional and presidential elections in the 1890s. Yet Thiel reflected the upsurge in social concern encouraged by Pope Leo XIII's 1891 encyclical *Rerum Novarum* and a desire to combat the erosion of the church's position in the face of nineteenth-century liberalism.

When *Union Católica* failed to capture the government, the Catholic leadership sought a rapprochement with the Liberals, who dominated Costa Rica into the 1930s. Beginning in the 1920s, this approach was further stimulated by the spread of Marxism in Central America, which was condemned in 1935 by the bishops of Costa Rica, Nicaragua, and Panama. A communist party was founded in Costa Rica in 1931; in response, the church introduced Catholic Action groups to revitalize the laity, particularly the growing middle class.

Within the church, however, some individuals identified themselves with the *Partido Reformista*, which adopted progressive interpretations of Catholic social doctrine. Although the party was not notably successful, it did suggest alternative positions for Catholics and laid the basis for greater Catholic activism in the 1940s. In fact, in his 1940 inaugural address President Rafael Angel Calderón Guardia stated that his administration's programs were rooted in Catholic social doctrine and would attempt to avoid the deficiencies of both capitalism and communism. Social reforms, including social security, a minimum wage, and guarantees of the right to organize labor unions and cooperatives, were instituted and strongly supported by the archbishop of San José, Monsignor Sanabria Martínez (1940–52).

As early as 1938, Sanabria publicly argued that the church was obliged to indicate the causes of societal conflict and propose Christian solutions.[4] Although strongly anticommunist, Sanabria was open to expanding labor rights and increasing state intervention to restrain the excesses of capitalism through the implementation of state-sponsored social welfare programs. Sanabria's positions helped legitimize social and political activism on the part of the laity and generated support for the Calderón government. Sanabria's positions were increasingly supported by the rest of the hierarchy, which distanced the church from the most conservative elements of Costa Rican society.[5]

The church continued to use Catholic Action to limit the appeal of Marxist parties and labor unions. In the late 1940s the church initiated the *Confederación Costarricense de Trabajadores Rerum Novarum* (CCTRN), which challenged the communist-influenced *Confederación de Trabajadores de Costa Rica* (CTCR). As the CCTRN became more aggressive in championing workers' rights via job actions and strikes, Sanabria became preoccupied with its potentially destabilizing effect on the Calderón government. His fears appeared justified when an insurrection broke out in 1948.

Divisions among church leaders over this development were reflected in the support offered the insurrection by Father Benjamin Nuñez, the head of the CCTRN. He subsequently became minister of labor in the Liberationist government.[6] While some clerics collaborated with the new government, Sanabria continued to be critical of it. His opposition was diminished by the 1949 Constitution, which recognized Catholicism as the state religion, allowed religious education in public schools, and permitted priests to hold governmental office.

Thus, well before the 1960s both clergy and laity were politically active. In addition, debate over political and ideological issues within the church increased. The experience of the Costa Rican Catholic church in the pre–Vatican II period appears to have influenced its political behavior in the last twenty-five years as much as the council itself.

In the 1960s, the state improved public welfare, and the church spoke out less on socioeconomic issues. Activism within the church declined, as did its appeal, particularly to the working class. Economic growth in the 1960s, partially as a result of the Central American Common Market, defused some of the pressures on the church to take stands on socioeconomic issues. Not until the economic reverses of the 1970s did the church become more directly involved in poverty issues. Then the critique of capitalism contained in liberation theology, as well as in some secular theories, was debated among the regular clergy and Catholic university students.

During the 1970s differences over the social policies of the church became more apparent. The hierarchy supported such efforts as the *Movimiento Solidarista Costarricense* (MSC), which promoted worker-management cooperation to make capitalist development more efficient,[7] whereas some church leaders, including Monsignor Román Arrieta Villalobos, the bishop of Tilarán, began calling more insistently for land reform.

In 1979 the bishops cited the growing impoverishment of a third of the population in urging the government to undertake socioeconomic changes. The hierarchy suggested that solutions could by found in transcending both capitalism and socialism.[8] They affirmed the church's commitment to a preferential option for the poor and greater activism on their behalf. The prelates also called for agrarian reform. They did not, however, make specific recommendations as to how to achieve greater justice. Their statements were more hortatory than prescriptive and thus reflected a common pattern in the contemporary Catholic church of calling for substantial change without suggesting how it could be accomplished. In this fashion church leaders sought to discharge their moral responsibilities, retain the institution's universal appeal, and maintain a claim to political neutrality. By and large they were not successful with the last two and were criticized by both the right and the left.

The 1980s witnessed continued ecclesiastical preoccupation with the worsening domestic economic situation and the regional crisis, particularly the warfare in Nicaragua and El Salvador. The bishops were increasingly convinced that the way to reduce violence and terror was to deal more effectively with socioeconomic injustice.[9] They urged the rich to agree to higher taxes but were criticized by both conservatives and the left.[10] The left chided the bishops for not going far enough.

After 1982 the Catholic church cooperated with the governments of Luis Alberto Monge (1982–86) and Oscar Arnulfo Arias (1986–90) to ameliorate the impact of economic dislocation and support the latter's Central American peace plan. The church's attitude toward the more conservative government of Rafael Angel Calderón (1990–) is more restrained. Although within the church there continues to be preoccupation over the increasing concentration of land and absence of agrarian reform, the episcopacy, fearing radicalism, has not encouraged peasant mobilization.

Deeming itself politically neutral and centrist, the Catholic hierarchy chose to pursue a cautious strategy of calling for greater efforts on the part of political and economic elites, as well as the general public, to deal with socioeconomic problems through existing structures and programs. This position was challenged by clerical and lay intellectuals within the Catholic church as well as those involved in grass-roots movements, including some base Christian communities (CEBs).[11]

Although this sector enjoys some support, it is not as influential as its counterparts in Nicaragua and El Salvador, in part because political and economic elites have been more responsive to pressures for reforms. But the economic downturns in the 1970s and 1980s have increasingly called into question the capacity of the system to guarantee the basic needs of the majority of Costa Ricans. In the face of this, the Catholic hierarchy has felt more pressure to speak out. It has not, however, emerged as a major voice in political debate. Its critics on the right fear greater activism on the part of the church in favor of more radical reforms. The left would like to see it more aggressively pursue socialism. It is unlikely to do either.

Overall, the Catholic clergy and laity in Costa Rica reflect the political and ideological spectrum of the general populace. Both share a faith in the capacity of the existing system to reverse economic decline. Both also regard Costa Rica as setting a democratic example for the rest of Central America. It is unlikely, however, that Costa Ricans, including churchpeople, will attempt to undertake a role as innovators in any democratization process in the region. Rather, there will continue to be a tendency to legitimize modified reformist developmentalism and liberal democratic structures. Objections that such a strategy is inadequate given the depth of the national and regional crisis have not prompted a major repositioning of the Costa Rican Catholic church.

El Salvador

The political and ecclesial history of El Salvador has been more conflictive than that of Costa Rica, in part, because the oligarchy is stronger and a larger percentage of the population is impoverished. Well before the 1960s a variety of labor, party, and church groups emerged that were preoccupied with political and socioeconomic exploitation in El Salvador.

Although some churchpeople expressed concern as early as the late nineteenth century, suspicion of liberalism and fear of communism prompted the institutional church to take defensive actions, such as ensuring that the Constitution and laws guarantee ecclesial rights. In the 1920s and 1930s, Catholic Action and Christian democracy were introduced from Europe. Both were tinged with anticommunism, which was reinforced by the turmoil surrounding a 1932 peasant uprising led by Agustín Farabundo Martí, a communist.

Suppressed by troops under the direction of Gen. Maximiliano Hernández Martínez, an estimated ten to thirty thousand people were slaughtered. As one commentator noted:

> It is difficult to understate the impact that this event had on the Salvadoran political culture. The specter of 1932 continues to haunt the country to this day. Over the years, an elaborate mythology, replete with stories of blood crazed mobs butchering thousands of well-to-do Salvadorans, has been carefully nurtured to justify the status quo. Even the mildest attempts at reform have invariably been denounced as communist-inspired. By the same token, fear of another uprising helped legitimize the ongoing political hegemony of the Salvadoran military....The memory of 1932, moreover, has justified the resort to unrestrained violence, when necessary, to maintain order.[12]

This encouraged reformist sectors within the church to circumscribe their activities and rhetoric until the 1950s, when escalating pressures for change prompted a greater degree of activism. In the aftermath of Vatican II and Medellín more activity was aimed at achieving ecclesial and societal reforms. This activity was spearheaded not only by clerics, including foreign missionaries, but also by laypeople who had been involved in such groups as the Christian Democratic Party and Salvadoran Social Defense.

The spread of these theological, pastoral, and bureaucratic reforms stimulated experiments that resulted in much greater involvement of clerics, religious, and lay activists with the poor. This tended to politicize churchpeople and stimulate concern about issues such as workers' rights, land reform, and human rights. The Jesuits' work in Aguilares is illustrative.

Beginning in the late 1960s, Jesuits began organizing Christian base communities in the area. By the early 1970s approximately seven hundred Salvadorans out of a population of thirty thousand in the area were actively involved. The CEBs ranged across the spectrum theologically, politically, and ideologically.[13] Some of the more politicized members became involved in organizing rural workers and joined the *Federación Cristiana de Campesinos Salvadoreños* (FECCAS), which in 1973–74 expanded rapidly throughout the country. As it did, it was met with increasing repression by police, military, and landholders. This encouraged some churchpeople to resort to armed struggle and ultimately to join the *Frente Farabundo Martí Para la Liberación Nacional* (FMLN). This peregrination of a minority of church activists was used by some rightists to justify attacks on church institutions and personnel. Between January 1980 and February 1981 paramilitary groups, largely composed of police and soldiers, carried out approximately three hundred attacks.[14] These included the assassinations of the archbishop of San Salvador, Monsignor Oscar Arnulfo Romero (1977–80), and four female missionaries from the United States.

Romero had symbolized the increasing identification of the church with movements for socioeconomic change and the preferential option for the poor enunciated at Medellín and reaffirmed at Puebla in 1979. As early as November 1978 he had supported insurrection in response to the violation of human rights, and on March 23, 1980, a day before his assassination, he also publicly called on members of the armed forces to disobey orders that would cause them to engage in gross violations of human rights.[15]

Other bishops were not as progressive as Archbishop Romero; nor was the bulk of the clergy. After taking office, his successor as archbishop, Monsignor Arturo Rivera y Damas, stated that he would "move toward a neutral, central position, convinced that I have a broad perspective and can play a prophetic role."[16]

Rivera y Damas established sufficient credibility as a nonpartisan actor to serve as a mediator of the sporadic peace talks between the government and the FMLN that have occurred since 1984. In addition, the church attempted to "humanize" the war by negotiating truces, exchanges of prisoners, and the release of the victims of political kidnappings, including the daughter of President José Napoleón Duarte in 1986.

Although some of the more conservative bishops were initially suspicious of peace talks between the government and the Marxist-led FMLN, in late 1986 the hierarchy supported the Esquipulas II process, with Rivera y Damas facilitating talks between the government and the FDR/FMLN. In addition, Rivera y Damas promoted a national debate in 1988 in an effort to mobilize popular pressure on both the government and the FMLN to engage in serious negotiations. On September 3–4, 1988, representatives of some sixty civic organizations gathered in San Salvador under the auspices of the National Debate. Ninety-seven percent indicated the "need for a negotiated, non-military solution to the conflict, for seeking a national consensus and for discovering the role organizations and the people should play in resolving the conflict."[17] Ninety-five percent reflected the U.S. view of the Salvadoran conflict as part of East-West competition. They saw it as "a basic conflict, essentially internal and it is especially due to structural injustice."[18]

The National Debate formally expressed what public opinion polls had long indicated, namely, the overwhelming support for a negotiated settlement to the war. All the participants held that dialogue was "the most rational, just, and Christian way of settling the conflict."[19] All agreed that special attention had to be paid to encouraging disarmament, demilitarization, and respect for human rights; the cultivation of political pluralism; the return and resettlement of refugees; and the ending of foreign aid from all sources.[20]

A permanent mechanism was established to pressure the governments of El Salvador and the United States, together with the FMLN, to agree to a cease-fire and peace talks. Although the far right groups and representatives of the Christian Democratic Party did not participate in the debate, it did include a cross-section of labor unions, peasant organizations, professional associations, and political, religious, and business groups.[21] The debate was clearly a departure from traditional strategies and may serve to stimulate efforts in other countries afflicted with conflict.

The 1989 victory of the rightist *Alianza Republicana Nacionalista* (ARENA) at the polls resulted partially from the erosion of Catholic support for the Christian Democratic Party. A good number of the party faithful were alienated because of corruption in the Duarte government.[22] There is little indication, however, that Catholic activists have incorporated themselves into ARENA. Hence, although some continue to work within the PDC, many appear to be less affiliated with parties than in the past. This suggests that efforts to promote democratization might increasingly be channeled through nonparty mechanisms such as labor and community organizations. A focus on political parties in El Salvador to promote democratization could exclude a substantial proportion of the population that is responsive to Catholic social doctrine and its calls for societal concord based on greater socioeconomic justice and effective political participation.

Guatemala

Support for the Christian Democratic option in Guatemala has also eroded substantially since the outset of the presidency of Vinicio Cerezo in January 1986. The president himself recognized problems, particularly his administration's failure to control the rising cost of living and the increase in violence. Cerezo's government has been criticized by a variety of groups, including representatives of large businesses and labor, peasants, professionals, small farmers, students, and right-wing elements of the military.[23]

The Christian Democratic Party was established in 1957, in part out of fears of communist penetration of the government under President Jacobo Arbenz (1951–54). The archbishop of Guatemala at the time, Monsignor Mariano Rossell (1939–63), supported the overthrow of Arbenz in 1954 in a coup engineered by the CIA.[24] Anticommunism also prompted the strengthening of such groups as the *Juventud Universitária Centroamericana* (JUCA), *Acción Católica Universitaria* (ACU), and the *Cruzada Nacional Contra el Comunismo*.

Within the church there was a sense that, to undercut the appeal of Marxism, churchpeople needed to speak out more in favor of reformist social change. By and large Catholics in the 1950s supported reformism under liberal capitalism. The credibility of this position was increasingly eroded in the 1960s by the economic policies of the military-dominated governments, which widened the gap between the rich and the poor. In addition, the influx of foreign missionaries, together with the impact of Vatican II, prompted greater questioning of the church's positions and activities. Experimentation with pastoral reforms and an expansion of church-supported social programs increased knowledge among church personnel of conditions among the poor. By the end of the 1960s, church activists were beginning to strongly criticize the status quo, thereby prompting repression against priests, brothers, nuns, and lay activists.

In 1980–81 alone six priests and dozens of lay activists were assassinated. Church officials believed most were killed by government security forces. In August 1980 the church pulled all priests and religious from

Quiche Province, where they had served over one million Catholics. In February 1981 four priests, regarded as nonpolitical and relatively conservative, were directed to return by the bishop. Two weeks later one of them, Father Juan Landino Alonzo Fernández, was assassinated. This violence against churchpeople and accusations that the church "stimulates communism" have strengthened the unity of the Guatemalan Catholic church.[25]

The death of Mario Casariego, the archbishop of Guatemala (1963–83), in June 1983 and his succession by Monsignor Prospero Penados del Barrio confirmed the emergence of the church as a critic of the status quo, particularly of military repression.[26] In a 1985 interview, Archbishop Penados indicated that he and his fellow bishops believed the church needed to maintain some distance from the state to ensure the church's independence and freedom "to speak out when it wants to."[27] Chief among those actions was the church hierarchy's denunciation of kidnappings and disappearances. Penados went on to describe Guatemalan society as one in which

> a few people live too well, in great opulence, while the majority live very poorly. National production does not aim at assuring the common good; rather, its goal is the enrichment of a few at the expense of the poor.[28]

This, he believed, increased the appeal of communism, and hence the rich, not the Catholic church, were encouraging Marxist penetration. The Guatemalan bishops, however, continued to criticize Marxists for justifying any means, including violence, to achieve power.[29]

Some prelates and other Catholics see Protestantism as equally subversive as communism, both having their roots in international conspiracies. The bishop of Escuintla, Monsignor Mario Enrique Ríos Montt, asserted in 1982 that "Protestants and Marxists are both against it [the Catholic church]—Protestantism as the arm of conservative capitalism; Marxism as the arm of atheist communism."[30] Monsignor Ríos Montt's own brother Efraín, president of Guatemala in 1982–83, is a leader of *El Verbo*, a fundamentalist sect founded by the U.S.-based Gospel Outreach. Such groups have been growing rapidly in Guatemala in recent years. They generally support conservative political options and have cooperated with the military in rural pacification programs.[31] They have received political and monetary assistance from U.S.-based fundamentalist groups that lobbied the Reagan administration to provide military aid to the government of Ríos Montt and that of his successor as president, Gen. Oscar Mejia Victores (1983–85).[32]

No other Central American country has as strong a Protestant presence as Guatemala. As a result the Catholic church is concerned about its identification with the left, on which fundamentalists can capitalize. In Guatemala, this has inspired the church's caution in taking a position on political and socioeconomic issues, a caution reinforced by the reality of repression.

Under these conditions, the Catholic church welcomed the election of Vinicio Cerezo in 1985, styling it as a return to democracy. In January 1986 Archbishop Penados called on the new government to respect the dignity of the individual by promoting justice and eliminating corruption in the public sector, promoting the common good, ending human rights violations, and initiating investigations into the fate of the disappeared.[33] By the end of Cerezo's term in 1990, church officials were disenchanted. In particular they were dismayed over the government's failure to improve the socioeconomic conditions of the poor majority and to enforce the rule of law. Although the prelates continued to support civilian government and were not convinced of the efficacy of socialist economic models, they did not appear confident that liberalism and capitalism would guarantee democracy in Guatemala. Hence, they criticized the existing system without offering specific alternatives.

At the center of Guatemala's problems, according to the prelates, is the unequitable distribution of land. In 1988 the hierarchy also argued that "the right to private property is not an absolute right; it is conditioned and limited by a broader and more universal principle: God has created all things for the use and benefit of all human beings without distinction of any kind."[34] The episcopacy supported changing societal structures to promote integral development, not merely fostering economic growth. In particular, this development should benefit the indigenous peoples of Guatemala as compensation for their past exploitation. If not, the prelates feared the result might be "even more painful and violent conflicts."[35]

Honduras

The Honduran Catholic church shares with the Guatemalan church a growing concern over socioeconomic disparities and the potential this poses for violence. In a November 11, 1988, communique, the Honduran bishops lamented high inflation, unemployment, underemployment, and the lack of foreign exchange for businesses.[36] The prelates asserted that failure of the government and the elites to deal with the situation could lead to serious instability; they criticized the government and political parties for focusing on partisan politics rather than on the common good. They recommended more attention be paid to reducing the cost of basic foodstuffs and urged business, labor, and the government, as well as other groups, to develop cooperative programs to deal with economic dislocation.[37]

Honduras has the lowest per capita income in the Western Hemisphere except for Haiti, and large increases in U.S. aid and private humanitarian assistance since the early 1980s have not substantially reduced poverty. In fact, income distribution appears to have worsened. Although the Catholic church has demonstrated concern over economic decline, it is also preoccupied by the rapid increase of development and relief organizations linked to evangelical churches. Religiously based and secular private voluntary organizations have tripled in Honduras since 1980.[38] This growth has been stimulated not only by obvious need, but also by the desire of the U.S. government and some U.S. religious groups to make Honduras a bulwark against communism. Similar concern prompted the Catholic church to adopt a reformist developmentalist stance in the 1960s,[39] but progress was limited not only because of resistance from some sectors of the elite, but also because of the limited resources of the Honduran Catholic church.[40]

Despite occasional attempts on the part of the church in the first half of the twentieth century to respond to the socioeconomic and political marginalization of the majority of Hondurans, not until the 1950s did the institutional church begin to involve itself more directly in the daily concerns of the faithful. Vatican II reinforced this impulse, as did the reformism of the presidency of Ramón Villega Morales (1957–63). Anticommunism was a further stimulus, partly as a result of the allegations of Marxist penetration of the Arbenz government in neighboring Guatemala and the coming to power of Fidel Castro in Cuba in 1959.

By the early 1960s, the Catholic church was helping initiate development projects, peasant organizations, cooperatives, and literacy programs. Linked to such efforts was the Social Christian Movement, which received financial assistance from European Christian Socialist organizations.[41] In 1971 this movement helped form a consortium of welfare groups known as CONCORDE *(Consejo Coordinador Para Desarrollo)*, which included some foreign agencies such as Catholic Relief Services. CONCORDE cooperated with the *Central de Trabajadores* (CGT) and the *Unión Nacional de Campesinos* (UNC). As the movement and CONCORDE became more obviously political, the hierarchy began distancing the church from these groups.[42]

A more substantial withdrawal from social activism was occasioned by a massacre at Olancho in 1975, where twelve peasants and two priests were killed by the army and landholders during a demonstration in favor of agrarian reform.[43] Although the hierarchy denounced the massacre and excommunicated those responsible, it also attempted to limit activism within the church. Individuals identified with the theology of liberation and socialism were cautioned, and increased emphasis was placed on spiritual renewal via such groups as the Charismatic Renewal Movement and the Movement of the New Catacombs. This was also part of an effort to compete with evangelical groups, which tended to offer more spiritual and psychological reassurance and release to Hondurans, particularly in the face of rising social tensions. Hence, while the Catholic church maintained its concern for socioeconomic problems, it reduced promotion of community organizing and structural change to achieve justice.

The coming to power of the *Sandinistas* in Nicaragua in 1979, the increased flow of refugees from that country and El Salvador, and the growing militarization of Honduras (in part because of *Contra* and U.S. presence) all exacerbated long-standing Honduran problems in the 1980s and caused the Catholic bishops to speak out. As early as 1982 they warned the government that increasing violence in the country and the actions of the security forces were causing great "uneasiness that, if it continues to grow too much, could finish our democracy."[44] Since then, Catholic leaders have denounced a variety of human rights violations.

The Honduran Catholic church has never had the same connections with political parties that its counterparts in El Salvador and Guatemala have had. The Social Christian Movement has faded, and the church as an institution is not identified with any specific political group. Although individual churchpeople may be active in partisan politics, overall the church has limited itself to attempting to raise consciousness about Honduran problems and encourage lay elites to take the lead in dealing with them. Feeling increasingly pressured by the seriousness of the Honduran situation and evangelical competition, the Catholic church has opted to proceed cautiously in the political arena.

Nor does the church appear to have the convocational potential of the Salvadoran church. The proliferation of both U.S. government and Protestant assistance programs has introduced a variety of institutional competitors. As a result, although the Catholic church supports greater democratization, it is cautious in translating that support into action that might spark losses among the faithful. The church is unlikely, therefore, to assume an active role in politics unless the socioeconomic situation worsens substantially.

Nicaragua

The Nicaraguan Catholic church is perhaps the most political in Central America. It is also deeply riven with internal conflict, which diminishes its capacity to mobilize strong support in favor of specific agendas. Nevertheless, the Nicaraguan church has been an important political actor since well before the *Sandinistas* took power in July 1979. Like the other churches in the region, it has experimented with reformist programs and organizations since the early part of the century. The domination of the Somozas since the 1930s reduced the space available for the church to build alliances with the limited opposition political parties. Nevertheless, in the 1950s and 1960s Catholics in Nicaragua began focusing on the authoritarianism of the government, exploitation of workers, and human rights violations. The Nicaraguan Social Christian Party was established in this period, in part as a result of the efforts of Catholic intellectuals. Subsequently it split and the Popular Social Christian Party was formed, which built links to urban and rural laborers. Neither party developed a substantial mass following.

Other Catholic activists became involved in establishing social programs that expanded greatly in the wake of the devastating 1972 earthquake that killed some ten thousand people. Churchpeople began working in the tent cities that sprang up around the capital, where the poverty of the people and the corruption of the government were clearly evident. This helped politicize and mobilize a considerable number of churchpeople, including Catholic youths from elite schools and their teachers, who included priests, brothers, and nuns.

That same year the Nicaraguan hierarchy issued a pastoral letter calling for a "transformation of structures" to reduce poverty, exploitation, and repression in the country.[45] The letter also called for an expansion of political participation and a more independent judiciary to ensure greater democracy. The government's failure to promote socioeconomic rights was regarded as a prime cause of repression. This argument was a key element in the bishops June 2, 1979, letter, in which they stated that the insurrection then underway was moral and just. Citing the long history of human rights violations by the Somoza regime, the prelates concluded that the government lacked legitimacy.[46] This statement was warmly received by Catholics, who overwhelmingly supported the overthrow of Somoza.

Some interpreted the June declaration as evidence of the church's support for a Marxist revolutionary option. This was not the case. In a July 30, 1979, pastoral letter issued shortly after Somoza's fall, the prelates urged the new Government of National Reconstruction to avoid importing foreign "isms" and political and economic models. Whatever new structures and programs were introduced should be rooted in Nicaraguan realities, including the Catholicism of the vast majority of the people. Furthermore, care should be taken to encourage political pluralism and avoid the "massification" of society.[47] This was a clear reference to communism. Overall, however, the hierarchy was receptive to the new government and did not object when four priests accepted ministerial-level posts.[48] Not until 1981, after a series of disputes between the hierarchy and the *Sandinistas*, did priests holding political office became an issue, not only with the bishops but also with the Vatican.

Church-state tension was generated in part by the prelates' fear that a Marxist regime inimical to the interests of the church was being consolidated. Preoccupations had been aroused by the ideological content of the 1980 literacy campaign (directed by the Jesuit Fernando Cardenal), a proposed national curriculum for public and private schools, and the organization of workers, students, and others into mass organizations. In a November 17, 1979, pastoral letter, the episcopacy indicated a willingness to accept socialism if it did not infringe on the free will of individuals and societies. What the bishops appeared to have in mind was a welfare state based on a multiparty rather than a one-party system. The letter also warned against encouraging class hatred.[49]

The *Sandinistas* responded with an October 1980 statement in which they recognized that the Catholic church had and would continue to have a critical role in Nicaraguan society. They also held that there was no inherent contradiction in being both Christian and revolutionary. The *Sandinistas* proclaimed their respect for religious freedom and traditions but reserved the right to ensure religious activities not be used for political or commercial purposes.[50] This statement reflected the fact that some religious processions had been transformed into antigovernment protests. The prelates were not mollified. Chief among them were the archbishop of Managua, Monsignor Miguel Obando y Bravo, and of the bishop of Juigalpa, Monsignor Pablo Vega. Others, such as Monsignor Ruben López, bishop of Estelí, were less publicly critical of the government.

López's diocese epitomized some of the principal strains within the church. During the insurrection churchpeople in Estelí had strongly supported the guerrillas. By 1980 there was growing debate within Catholic organizations in Estelí, including CEBs, over how to integrate Christian and revolutionary commitments. Catholics were torn not only by the increasing criticism of the government by the bishops, but also by the dilemma of what to do in the face of abuses of power by government officials. With the escalation of *Contra* warfare after 1981, the latter question tended to be submerged by a desire to defend the revolution. This was not without cost; many churchpeople expressed their anguish over moral issues in an increasingly complex conflict.[51] Throughout Nicaragua divisions within the Catholic church developed over the nature and direction of the revolution, as well as the legitimacy of the counterrevolution.

The debate was not simply one between the hierarchy and grass-roots progressives, the so-called popular church. Rather, it cut across class, generational, rural, and urban lines. Major issues included the nature of political pluralism, the role of criticism and critics in a revolutionary society, the ways to encourage popular participation in political and economic decision-making, the legitimacy of universal military service in the party-linked *Sandinista* army, the freedom of the press, as well as the degree to which Marxism and Christianity could coexist. Although the debate was largely dominated by statements of the bishops and the priests in government, it was carried on at all levels within the church. Increasingly the church appeared divided against itself, with vocal pro- and antigovernment sectors.

Repression by the government of some of its more vocal critics such as Bishop Pablo Vega, who was expelled from the country on July 4, 1986, further fueled the debate. To the outside observer it appeared the institutional church strongly opposed the government, whereas the so-called popular church supported it. The situation was eminently more complex, and the majority of Catholics appeared to be uncomfortable with either position. Under such conditions it was unlikely the leadership of either the right or the left within the church could mobilize Catholics behind a specific political or ideological agenda. Even the March 1983 visit of the pope was marred by discord, and efforts by John Paul II to support Obando y Bravo and other critics of the government diminished around 1985. In the late 1980s Vatican diplomats increasingly encouraged the hierarchy to avoid exacerbating tensions with the government, as well as within the church, in order to facilitate the peace process.

Some progress was made when the government in the fall of 1987 urged Monsignor Obando y Bravo to participate in the National Reconciliation Commission established under the Esquipulas II accords. His acceptance was regarded as a step toward defusing tensions. Although there was occasional church-state discord in 1988 and 1989, it did not reach earlier levels.

The major reason was the widespread public desire for an end to war. Facing rampant inflation, unemployment, scarcity, and other problems, Nicaraguans from all sectors were desperate for peace. This prompted increased pragmatism on all sides, including church and state. In March 1989 President Daniel Ortega Saavedra met with Monsignor Obando y Bravo and agreed to news broadcasts on *Radio Católica,* the return of exiled clerical opponents of the government, and the reopening of an archdiocesan social welfare.[52] This did not eliminate all points of contention nor assure support for the government from the hierarchy. Conciliation, if not reconciliation, was encouraged by a pragmatism generated by the need to alleviate the suffering of the Nicaraguan people.

During the 1989–90 presidential campaign, which brought the U.S.-supported UNO coalition of Violeta Barrios de Chamorro to power, some church leaders identified with her whereas others worked for the *Sandinistas*. Since Chamorro took office in April 1990, Archbishop Obando y Bravo has been reported to be playing an unofficial advisory role. Meanwhile, priests who served in the previous government continue to support the *Sandinistas*. Hence, the Catholic church continues to be divided, while the bulk of the faithful seek respite from the ongoing economic crisis. As a consequence, the church in Nicaragua is not sufficiently strong or united to mobilize broad-based Catholic support for a specific political agenda aimed at fortifying democracy.

Panama

Panama has also slipped into a deepening crisis in recent years. The Catholic church in that country, like that in Honduras, has been concerned about worsening socioeconomic conditions, but, largely dependent on foreign personnel and financing, it has had limited resources to combat them. Prior to 1987, superficial prosperity in the urban centers obscured unequal income distribution and the consequent denial of basic socioeconomic rights. Concern over this situation prompted some social welfare efforts by the Catholic church prior to the 1950s and an expansion of them since then. Even before Vatican II and Medellín, community organizations, cooperatives, as well as base Christian communities, had been introduced.

In the 1960s and 1970s such efforts multiplied, in part as a result of an influx of foreign missionaries and foreign assistance. In the Chorrillo neighborhood of Panama City, for example, a CEB founded in the mid-1960s had 200 members by 1971. It sought to provide housing in a barrio where some three thousand families lived in 144 houses, most in one or two rooms. A health center and preschool were also established. By 1973 a housing co-op had been formed to find land to build low-cost houses, partially with volunteer labor. Transportation and consumer co-ops helped provide basic services for the new community.

As such activities expanded, bureaucratization increased and communal decision-making grew less significant. By 1986 the housing co-op was dissolved after only 1,100 houses had been built. Some of the original members of the CEB, as well as outside analysts, have ascribed the outcome to excessively rapid growth and failure to consolidate democratic decision-making and provide education for participation.[53]

Experiences such as Chorrillo have occurred in other areas of Panama and indeed all over Central America. Social welfare projects of the 1950s and 1960s often faded in the 1970s and 1980s, though not without leaving some tangible and intangible benefits. Overall, participants are more willing to organize to make political and economic demands.[54] Such individuals have not been incorporated in great numbers into Panamanian political parties. This was evident in the failure of the anti-Noriega Civic Crusade to consolidate broad-based support among the popular sectors.[55] As in pre-1979 Nicaragua, the long-term existence of an authoritarian government circumscribed the power of political parties to cause the military-dominated government to democratize. A U.S. economic embargo of Panama increased pressures not only on Noriega, but also on the democratic sector and the church. Both urged the United States to lift the embargo, which contributed to 30 percent unemployment, a 40 percent bankruptcy rate, and rising levels of malnutrition and related health problems. The Catholic church became more dependent on foreign assistance, and the crisis substantially diminished its capacity to pursue its pastoral, spiritual, and sacramental activities. Under such conditions it was difficult for the church to take on additional tasks aimed at stimulating democratization.

As a consequence, although the Panamanian Episcopal Conference was active in recommending steps to deal with the Noriega crisis, it did not undertake any major mobilizing activities. It limited itself to urging basic reforms, including the restoration of constitutional guarantees, the withdrawal of the military from politics, the end of government abuse of power, and the building of institutions and mechanisms necessary to ensure democratic elections and an end to state terror.

Since the U.S. invasion in December 1989 and the installation of the government of Guillermo Endara, the Catholic church has been attempting to respond to needs resulting from economic dislocation and ongoing political violence, as well as an upsurge of crime. With close links to the Christian Democratic Party and the current vice president, Ricardo Arias, the hierarchy is seen as supportive of the government. Nevertheless, it has expressed dissatisfaction with the failure of both the Panamanian government and the United States to respond more effectively to socioeconomic needs and to impose civilian control on the military. Although the Catholic church has emerged as a more visible actor in the present crisis, structural impediments within Panamanian society and the church's limited resources make it unlikely the church will play a major role in democratization.

Conclusion

In spite of its official position of political neutrality, the Catholic church in Central America has played an important, although not determining, role in politics. The church, however, cannot be characterized as consistently supporting any particular stance, even though traditionally it has been identified with conservatives. Such identification has flowed, in part, from its criticism of class warfare to achieve change. Only a minority of churchpeople accept armed struggle as necessary, although in exceptional cases even the institutional church has accepted insurrection as legitimate, as in the overthrow of Somoza. In general, however, the church has tended to support reforms of existing Western liberal political structures and capitalism.

As early as the late nineteenth century the Central American Catholic church occasionally allied with political movements and parties when their respective agendas were complementary. Such relationships were not always smooth and usually fell apart under pressure from diverging objectives. Throughout, the church was stimulated in part by a desire to preempt Marxist political and economic options. Although socialism might be accepted by a sector of churchpeople, most continue to regard communism as antithetical to Catholicism.

As conflict resulting from pressure for socioeconomic change escalated in the post–World War II period, the church was drawn into political and ideological struggle. This enlarged its political role and increased debate within the church about the morality and viability of various political and economic options. Although there was not unanimous agreement on any particular partisan agenda, the consistent calls for socioeconomic justice and an end to exploitation and repression made the church the target of increasing violence from sectors opposed to change. This increased politicization within the church. Once repression diminished, however, divisions tended to reemerge and debate became more public. In societies in which there is a high level of political struggle, tensions within the church over its positions reflect and feed general societal tensions.

In pursuit of socioeconomic justice the Catholic church has not only formed alliances with political movements and parties, it has also created a variety of organizations to mobilize the laity to act in support of Catholic social doctrine. They include Catholic Action, student and labor groups, cooperatives, and other community organizations. Beginning in the 1950s the church increasingly set up base Christian communities, literacy campaigns, and human rights organizations. Although the fortunes of such groups waxed and waned, overall these groups increased the organization and mobilization of the popular sectors and aroused the fears of conservative sectors. Such mobilization was not generally sufficient to achieve substantial change.

The enunciation of a preferential option for the poor at Medellín in 1968 stimulated church activism in defense of the impoverished and increasingly led to criticism of the institutional church for allegedly encouraging class conflict. The church's position has been that only through greater socioeconomic justice will the level of societal concord necessary to achieve peace be reached.

The Catholic church in Central America has carved out for itself a controversial position that satisfies neither the extreme right nor the extreme left. As a resource-poor institution dependent on foreign personnel and monies in an increasingly impoverished region, it generally does not have the means to mount major mass mobilization efforts. Nevertheless, it retains considerable powers of moral suasion, which it has lent to such peace efforts as Contadora and Esquipulas. Ecclesial support for such efforts is not likely, however, to determine their ultimate success or failure.

The church has undertaken initiatives, such as the National Debate in El Salvador, that attempt to pressure contending parties to take more conciliatory positions. This is part of a strategy to create more space for the consideration of alternatives to the political and economic models currently in conflict. The likelihood that substantial progress toward the implantation of alternative, more democratic models will be achieved over the short term is not great. Hence, the church also continues to pressure for reforms in existing structures. Given that, and the fact that institutions such as the Catholic church function largely at the level of value formation, the church will most likely contribute more to democratization in Central America over the long term than in the short term.

Notes

1. This chapter focuses primarily on the Catholic church in Central America because the church incorporates well over 80 percent of the population of Costa Rica, El Salvador, Honduras, Nicaragua, and Panama. In Guatemala there is a strong Protestant presence, estimated at between 25 and 28 percent of the population. Although Protestants have played an expanding role in Central America, particularly in the last thirty years, space does not allow an analysis of their part in democratization. *Statistical Abstract of Latin America,* vol. 26, 1988; *World Christian Encyclopedia,* 1982.

2. Between 1537 and 1539 Bartolomé de Las Casas, a former *encomendero* and Dominican friar, worked to reduce conflict in what is today the Vera Paz region of Guatemala. Las Casas lobbied the Spanish monarchy for legislation to decrease exploitation of the Indian and succeeded in convincing Charles I to

issue the New Laws (1542), which sought to protect the Indians. In addition to Las Casas there are other historical precedents for the change-oriented church of today. What is new is that support for broad-based socioeconomic and political change has become the official position of the institutional church.

3. Monseñor Bernardo Augusto Thiel, "Trigésima Carta Pastoral: Sobre el Justo Salario," in *La Palabra Social de los Obispos Costarricenses: Selección de Documentos de la Iglesia Católica Costarricense, 1893–1981*, ed. Miguel Picado (San José: DEI, 1982), pp. 27–36.

4. Monseñor Victor Sanabria Martínez, "Presentación del Programa Pastoral de Mons. Sanabria Como Obispo de la Diócesis de Alajuela (extracto)," in *La Palabra Social*, pp. 45–48.

5. "Cartas Cruzadas Entre el Ex-Presidente Rafael A. Calderón Guardia y los Obispos de Costa Rica," in ibid., pp. 77–79.

6. Ibid., pp. 202-3.

7. Ibid., pp. 224–25.

8. "Evangelización y Realidad Social de Costa Rica: Carta Pastoral Colectiva," in ibid., pp. 159–81.

9. "Iglesia y Momento Actual—Carta Pastoral del Episcopado Costarricense Sobre la Actual Situación del País y la Campaña Electoral," in ibid., pp. 183–94.

10. "Navidad 1981—Unidos en la Esperanza: Carta Pastoral del Episcopado Costarricense Sobre la Crítica Situación Que Vive el País," in ibid., pp. 195–99.

11. For a description of such groups, see Andres Opazo Bernales, *Costa Rica: La Iglesia Católica y el Orden Social Entre el Dios de la Polis y el Dios de los Pobres* (San José: DEI, 1987), pp. 83–115.

12. Donald E. Schulz, "El Salvador: Revolution and Counterrevolution in the Living Museum," in *Revolution and Counterrevolution in Central America and the Caribbean*, ed. Donald E. Schulz and Douglas H. Graham (Boulder, Colo.: Westview Press, 1984), pp. 195–96.

13. Philip Berryman, Lecture, University of California Los Angeles, April 16, 1988.

14. Tommie Sue Montgomery, "The Church and the Salvadoran Revolution," *Latin American Perspectives* 10, 1 (Winter 1983):81.

15. Text of homily of Monsignor Oscar Romero broadcast over YSAX, March, 23, 1980, San Salvador, El Salvador.

16. Monsignor Arturo Rivera y Damas, Speech, April 6. 1981, Washington, D.C.

17. "El Salvador: The 1988 National Debate," *LADOC* 19, 4 (March/April 1989):10.

18. Ibid., p. 11.

19. Ibid., p. 12.

20. Ibid.

21. Joseph P. Fitzpatrick, S.J., "The Church's Great Initiative for Peace in El Salvador," *America* 159, 213 (8 October 1988):213.

22. Lindsey Gruson, "Party's Prayer Is That the Skeptics Come Home," *New York Times*, March 14, 1989.

23. "Guatemala: Christian Democrats Face Mounting Social Tension," *Central American Report* 15, 4 (January 29, 1988):25.

24. José Luis Chea, *Guatemala: La Cruz Fragmentada* (San José: DEI, 1988), p. 77.

25. Warren Hoge, "Guatemalan Clerics Targets of Violence," *New York Times*, May 5, 1981.

26. Americas Watch, *Human Rights in Guatemala During President Cerezo's First Year* (New York: America's Watch, 1987); and Amnesty International, *Guatemala: The Human Rights Record* (London: Amnesty International Publications, 1987).

27. Monsignor Prospero Penados del Barrio, "Church Can Do Very Little," *Latinamerica Press* 17, 43 (November 21, 1985):6.

28. Ibid.

29. William R. Long, "New Guatemalan Archbishop Challenges Government on Human Rights," *Los Angeles Times*, September 14, 1984.

30. Marlise Simons, "Latin America's New Gospel," *New York Times Magazine*, November 7, 1982, p. 47.

31. Raymond Bonner, "Guatemala Enlists Religion in Battle," *New York Times*, July 18, 1982.

32. Ron Howell, "Evangelical Protestants Active in Guatemala," *Los Angeles Times*, September 29, 1984.

33. Foreign Broadcast Information Service (FBIS), "Church Requests Guaranteed Religious Freedom," *Daily Report: Latin America* 6, 11 (January 16, 1986):11.

34. Ibid., p. 18.

35. Ibid., pp. 19–21

36. "Situación Económica Podría Volverse Explosiva, Advierten Obispos del País: Comunicado Especial de los Obispos de Honduras Sobre la Situación Actual," *El Heraldo*, Tegucigalpa, Honduras, November 29, 1988, p. 36.

37. Ibid.

38. Resource Center, "NGOs and Churches: History and Trends," xerox, p. 3.

39. Gustavo Blanco and Jaime Valverde, *Honduras: Iglesia y Cambio Social* (San José: DEI, 1987), pp. 53–61.

40. The Catholic church in Honduras lacks the income and personnel to mount major programs. In Honduras today there are approximately two hundred eighty priests, of whom sixty are native born. There is approximately one cleric for every 15,000 Hondurans. The result is a heavy dependence on lay activists, including Delegates of the Word, who outnumber priests forty to one. This has resulted in the church becoming more responsive to lay concerns, particularly in rural areas where priests are scarce. *Honduras: A Look at the Reality* (Hyattsville, Md.: Quixote Center, 1984), p. 11; Pablo Richard and Guillermo Meléndez, *La Iglesia de los Pobres en América Central* (San José: DEI, 1982), p. 322; Alan Riding, "Honduran Lay Preachers Hear the Pope," *New York Times*, March 9, 1983, p. 4.

41. Resource Center, p. 5.

42. Ibid.

43. Richard and Meléndez, *La Iglesia de los Pobres*, pp. 332–33.

44. "Honduran Bishops Warn Government," *Washington Post*, October 28, 1982.

45. Conferencia Episcopal de Nicaragua (CEN), "El Campo de la Acción Política de la Iglesia," March 19, 1972, Managua, Nicaragua, p. 8.

46. CEN, "Presencia Cristiana en la Revolución: Dos Mensajes—Momento Insurreccional 2 de Junio 1979; Iniciando la Reconstrucción 30 de Julio 1979" (Managua: Cristianos en el Mundo, Comisión Justicia y Paz, 1979), pp. 4–8.

47. CEN, p. 14.

48. Miguel D'Escoto, a Maryknoll priest became foreign minister; Ernesto Cardenal, minister of culture; Fernando Cardenal, director of the National Literacy Campaign and from 1985 to 1990 minister of education; and Eduard Parrales, minister of social welfare and subsequently Nicaraguan ambassador to the Organization of American States. Other priests assumed posts of lesser rank.

49. CEN, "Compromiso Cristiano Para Una Nicaragua Nueva," November 17, 1979, Managua, Nicaragua, pp. 8–9.

50. Dirección Nacional del Frente Sandinista de Liberación Nacional, *Comunicado Oficial de la Dirección Nacional del F.S.L.N. Sobre la Religion* (San José: DEI, 1980), p. 10.

51. Elizabeth Quay Hutchinson, "¡Entre Cristianismo y Revolución, No Hay Contradicción! Catholic Activism in the Insurrection of Estelí, Nicaragua," Ph.D. diss., Harvard and Radcliffe Colleges, March 1986.

52. Mark A. Uhlig, "Ortega Makes Conciliatory Moves to Church," *New York Times*, March 16, 1989.

53. Joan B. Anderson, "From Christian Base Community to Cooperative: The Case of Chorrillo Panama," Paper presented at Pacific Coast Council on Latin American Studies, Tempe, Arizona, October 8–11, 1988.

54. Andres Opazo Bernales, *Panama: La Iglesia y la Lucha de los Pobres* (San José: DEI, 1988), pp. 69–141.

55. John M. Zindar, "Opposition Outflanked," *NACLA* 22, 4 (July/August 1988):31-35.

20

The Party Internationals and Democracy in Central America

Wolf Grabendorff

According to Andreas Kohl, executive secretary of the European Democrat Union, the primary function of international party associations is to provide members with legitimacy.[1] The act of admitting a candidate to the association of democratic parties sanctions the candidate. Thus, the internationals' support for worldwide democracy is reduced to the very act of granting access to the "democratic club." This clinical view of the internationals' function in evolving democratic regimes contrasts sharply with the glimpse provided by scandals that surface from time to time, such as a West German political party foundation being accused of "meddling" in a Latin American country's internal affairs.

The truth about the internationals' support for democracy, however, does not lie in an intermediate position between these contrasting impressions. Rather, it is characterized by extremes and the different forms transnational party contacts can take. Precisely because of the diffuse network of relations in which individual actors, forms, and channels of influence are superimposed on each other, the internationals have become the least understood actors in international relations. This chapter surveys the four main internationals—the Christian Democrat International (CDI), the Socialist International (SI), the Liberal International (LI), and the International Democrat Union (IDU). It examines the way they operate, their common features, and the forms of their influence over (re)democratization and consolidation of nascent democracies in Latin America and in the Central American isthmus in particular.

Political Families

The internationals are less like organizations than families. They have their black sheep, contentious brothers, and forlorn sisters. They do not have strict organizational hierarchies but are loosely structured yet tightly knit groups. They grew out of the postwar experience in Europe, particularly the suffering imposed on political parties by dictatorships and military establishments between the two world wars. They were formed because political parties (1) felt vulnerable in the face of state-sponsored institutions, (2) believed solidarity across borders was necessary for the survival of democratic systems, and (3) thought that transnational integration was essential for operating in a democratic environment.

Within the framework of European-Latin American relations the internationals have come to play a special role only in the last fifteen years. Biregional contacts are relatively recent.[2] Not until the end of the 1970s did the European Community (EC) seek to develop a systematic approach to and regular contacts with Latin America. EC indifference to political developments on and economic relations with the continent was not an isolated phenomenon. Latin America is a latecomer on the international stage. The traditionally preponderant role of the United States in Latin American foreign policy had long impeded attempts within Latin America to diversify external contacts. Moreover, the international community perceived Latin America as a U.S. "protectorate" in which "meddling" would cause friction in the Western hemisphere.

Western Europe has long been particularly respectful of U.S. international interests. Since World War II, Western European foreign policy has been dominated by an East-West approach to world affairs and by a eurocentric concern with prosperous economic and political integration. Accordingly, foreign relations obeyed rules imposed by the East-West division of the world or were governed by interests geared to reinforcing the EC's developing role as an important political and economic actor in the international system. Thus, the EC became inactive in the face of Latin America's economic problems and paid little attention to its political conflicts.

The first response to Latin American demands for closer contact with Europe came from the internationals and from the Socialist International in particular. The "dialogue of the deaf" in biregional governmental relations contrasted with mutual understanding in transnational interparty relations. Acting under fewer constraints than those imposed on official foreign policy, the internationals supported issues relating to parties in Latin America.

Concept of Democracy

Although most recent among the ideologies represented by the internationals,[3] the Christian Democrats alone have created a Latin American school of thought. The Chilean Eduardo Frei and the Venezuelan Rafael Caldera were the protagonists of a Latin American Christian Democratic ideology that developed a political profile largely independent of European influence. Thus, the *Organización Demócrata Cristiana de América* (ODCA), founded at a meeting of the Argentine, Brazilian, Chilean, and Uruguayan Christian Democratic parties on April 23, 1947, in Montevideo, never adhered to the strong anticommunism that so characterized their European counterparts in the cold war period. Neither was the Latin American Christian Democrat movement confessional. "Christian" connoted a moral rather than a religious category, a commitment to the defense of individual rights and collective welfare.[4] In terms of economic policy, the Economic Commission for Latin America (CEPAL) project of autonomous industrialization through import substitution played an important role in the formulation of Christian Democrat economic strategy.

The 1960s were the "Christian Democrat years." On the international level, President John F. Kennedy's concept of communist containment in the aftermath of the Cuban Revolution, embodied in the Alliance for Progress, had prompted good contacts with Latin American Christian Democratic parties. In 1963 Belaunde Terry won the elections in Peru. His victory was followed by that of Frei in Chile in 1964 and, in 1966, by that of Caldera in Venezuela. The early 1970s witnessed an economic reorientation in Latin America as a result of the global economic crisis. The import substitution model proved increasingly unable to cope with Latin America's economic problems.[5] Consequent social unrest threatened structures built on the model of economic and political modernization. The new trend ousted Christian Democrats from power and brought in leftist/Social Democratic governments, as in Chile and Venezuela, or the military, as in Peru. Thus, the United States assisted in toppling the Allende government in Chile.

Indeed, the 1973 coup d'état in Chile was a benchmark in the internationals' involvement in Latin America. For the Latin Americans, the coup fueled doubts as to the viability of reforms without international support and a deep suspicion of the United States. The Europeans, particularly the SI, regarded the rise of what was perceived in Latin America as a new U.S. imperialism as an opportunity to strengthen European influence.[6] Furthermore, the 1970s brought about peaceful transition from authoritarian to democratic rule in three European countries. Successful democratization in Spain, Portugal, and Greece came to symbolize Europe's credibility as a valuable broker in Latin America. It was not by accident that all internationals—except the IDU—attempted to increase influence in Latin America by establishing or strengthening links with their respective Iberian counterparts and by placing Latin American representatives in leading positions within the organizations.[7]

The SI most quickly and coherently reacted to the demand for political and economic alternatives in Latin America. The replacement of socialism by a more flexible concept of social democracy paved the way for the SI to broaden its base in Latin America. International socialism coincided in Latin America with three trends:

1. Political oppression in some countries and the limited opening of military regimes in others gave rise to opposition groups that the SI was quick to recognize and support.
2. Against the backdrop of a widening North-South economic divide, the SI supported the Latin American demand for a new international economic order.
3. Contradictions inherent in U.S. President Jimmy Carter's more liberal approach to U.S. Latin American policy left the SI enough room to broaden its influence in the region and to claim the mantle of human rights advocate.[8]

The LI is a latecomer on the Latin American scene. Not until the early 1980s did Liberals establish contacts with sister parties in Central America. The LI faced the problem of adapting its concept of democracy to Third World needs. The Liberal principle of the indivisibility of freedom, democracy, and human rights lacked the requisite social component with which to recruit counterparts in Latin America. Outside of the industrialized world, liberalism has long been seen as the "ideology of the rich," advocating economic laissez-faire and giving freedom priority over social justice. Thus, the opening of the predominantly European LI to developing countries required respect for different forms of liberalism. Specifically, Liberal reservations about state intervention in the economy and encouragement of private initiative "should not be regarded as a holy writ."[9]

Organizational Structure

The four internationals do not only have large counterpart organizations in Latin America, to a certain extent they are also European–Latin American networks. The CDI branch, ODCA, has twenty-one member-parties and is itself a member of the international.[10] The Federation of

Liberal Parties of Central America and the Caribbean (FELICA), the counterpart organization of the LI, is composed of seven member-parties from Central America and the Caribbean.[11] As in the case of ODCA, FELICA is an autonomous organization that holds observer status before the LI.

Latin American socialist parties are organized in different forums with, in some cases, overlapping membership. The SI Committee for Latin America and the Caribbean (SICLAC) comprises twenty regional member-parties.[12] In addition, Mexico's PRI created in 1979 the Permanent Conference of Latin American Political Parties (COPPAL) as a platform for antiimperialist and democratic forces throughout Latin America.[13] The first meeting was attended by twenty-three parties from the continent, most of which were members of the SI or observers at its congresses.

A third organization was set up on Uruguayan initiative in 1986 in the wake of the First Political Conference of Latin American Socialism which took place in Montevideo in April of the same year. The *Coordinación Socialista Latinoamericana* (CSL) is composed of sixteen South American socialist parties, most of them small splinter groups that do not play a significant role in their respective countries' party spectrums.[14] In contrast to a large coincidence in membership between SICLAC and COPPAL, CSL parties do not generally form part of either organization.[15]

Given their long-standing presence in Latin America, the CDI and SI are quantitatively the most important transnational party organizations. Both count on a solid base in Central America and, to a lesser extent, on similar representation in South America. Not only are the main regional bases of both internationals identical, they also include some of the countries with the longest traditions of democracy: Costa Rica in Central America and Venezuela on the southern part of the continent. Moreover, both the CDI and SI have a member-party in Chile, although neither had significant influence on the Southern Cone parties heading the transition from military to democratic rule in Argentina, Brazil, and Uruguay.

The Internationals and Democracy in Central America

All of the internationals exert considerable influence on the domestic politics of small countries. Thus, it is not surprising that at the beginning of the 1980s—coinciding with the onset of the subregional conflict—all party internationals started to concentrate their activities on Central

America and those countries particularly affected by conflict: Nicaragua, El Salvador, and, more recently, Guatemala.

In April 1984, against a background of the crisis in Central America, the presidents of the SI, CDI, and LI issued the first common declarations on Latin America. The "Common Appeal on Latin America,"[16] though referring to a broad range of economic and political problems on the continent, revealed the overriding concern for the Central American conflict. In spite of their affiliation with different and opposing parties to the conflict, the internationals agreed on essentials that mirrored a critical attitude toward U.S. policy in the region:

- the perception of Latin America's political problems as a result of long-standing economic and social injustice;
- the danger of identifying social and economic strife in Latin America with East-West confrontation;
- the special responsibility of the United States for supporting peace, democracy, and prosperity on the continent; and
- support for the Contadora initiative.

As in the case of EC involvement in Central America, the internationals' attempts to mediate in the conflict came to be the litmus test of European self-assertion vis-à-vis the United States.[17] However, the conservative shift of West European Central American policy and the tightening of the U.S. grip on Nicaragua severely constrained the internationals' room for maneuver. Thus, double pressure, from the U.S. administration and from some Western European governments, eventually led ODCA to abandon positions—such as support for self-determination for the Central American nations and understanding of the causes of armed opposition—and adopt those that more closely aligned themselves with the United States.[18]

The SI, on the other hand, faced an even more difficult situation in Central America. Rhetorical commitment to revolutionary change in El Salvador and Nicaragua drove the SI into a position that left no room for mediation within the region or between Central American parties and the United States. Thus, at the beginning of 1981 several attempts to mediate in the Salvadoran conflict failed because, among other things, full-fledged support for the Democratic Revolutionary Front/Farabundo Martí National Liberation Front (FDR/FMLN) made SI policies appear more directed toward participation in the conflict than mediation of it.[19] In Nicaragua the SI failed to openly express its disagreement with the direction taken by the *Sandinista* regime because it feared being accused of backing the United States in the latter's policy of confrontation. Through its tacit endorsement of developments in Nicaragua, the SI tried to moderate *Sandinista* positions, but in doing so it lost opportunities to influence U.S. policy. Instead, the Reagan administration turned increasingly to the Christian Democratic parties as its interlocutors in the region.

SI influence in the region suffered a further setback as the Contadora group and its peace initiative lost momentum. With affiliates in government in Costa Rica and Venezuela, as well as good relations with Mexico's PRI, the SI had been granted some say in the Contadora process. However, the U.S. administration's decision to boycott the Contadora peace proposal and the presentation of its own plan in April 1985 split the parties involved; moreover, it allowed long-standing disenchantment with the *Sandinistas* within the SI to surface. Harsh criticism of the *Sandinistas* by two regional member-parties, Costa Rica's National Liberation Party (PLN) and Venezuela's Democratic Action (AD), as well as their efforts to distance themselves from the Contadora peace plan, contributed decisively to diminishing SI support for the FSLN.[20]

The Influence of the Internationals
in Central America

Party internationals have two types of influence in Central America, direct and indirect. The most rare is direct influence. The best known case of direct influence was the famous 1:00 A.M. phone call from Willy Brandt to Jimmy Carter in 1978 when he told President Carter, "You had better get the Pentagon people to stop the interruption of elections in Santo Domingo." That is exactly what President Carter did. The elections would not have gone on without that pressure from the Europeans. Another direct intervention, not as well known, was the 1982 intervention of the Italian and German Social Democrats in El Salvador in favor of Napoleón Duarte. It took pressure from the Europeans and the help of the Venezuelans to persuade President Reagan that Duarte should be the candidate.

The second, and most important, type of influence is indirect, through nongovernmental organizations—churches, think tanks, the media, and human rights organizations. Because of coalition politics in Europe, in contrast to the United States, small constituencies are of great importance. They can decide who is going to be in power and who is not. One of those small constituencies, at least in Spain, Holland, Germany, and Italy, is the "Third World constituency," which has particularly strong church ties. It represents between 8 and 15 percent of the respective electorates and votes for candidates on the basis of their

Third World track record. This Third World constituency sometimes even helps decide local elections. Furthermore, most of the some six hundred "private" political organizations in Central America are connected to the internationals' network, largely through partial financing from European countries.

Parties in Government and Opposition

Between the mid-1970s and the present, Social Democrats, Liberals, and Christian Democrats/Conservatives have headed or participated in West European governments. Despite the broad range of countries and parties involved, some assumptions can be made about the transnational party influence on government and opposition parties. From the viewpoint of the (Latin American) counterpart, an international is more attractive the more (European) members it has in government. Alignment with the "strong" is tempting because statements of intent are more likely to be implemented as policy. This may in part explain the growing interest Central American parties have recently shown in joining the IDU. Paralleled by the tendency of the West German Christian Democrat Union (CDU) to increase its weight within the IDU, some ODCA members, such as the Nicaraguan *Partido Social Christiano*, have—thus far in vain—applied for dual membership.

Transnational party associations may be useful in allowing opposition forces to exert international influence and in demonstrating international solidarity in the context of domestic intra- and interparty debate. Official foreign policy, however, has constraints that tend to run counter to transnational party influence. Apart from specific national interests, EC foreign policy coordination and transatlantic relations within the Atlantic Alliance context constitute the primary framework of foreign policy for most West European countries.

A case in point is the Spanish Socialist Party (PSOE). Ever since it took office in 1982, the government under Felipe González has been increasingly careful about open involvement in Central American issues. Furthermore, the inauguration of the socialist term in government coincided with the negotiations on Spanish EC membership and the redefinition of the terms under which the country had joined the Atlantic Alliance. Thus, as an opposition party, in 1980 the PSOE agreed to head the Socialist International's Committee for the Defense of the Nicaraguan Revolution. Once in government, González avoided an assertive posture that would have jeopardized the EC consensus on Central America, even though he has used indirect channels to circumvent constraints put on EC policy in the region by the U.S. administration.

Regional Parliaments

The second channel is the political groups within regional parliaments. In the case of the European Parliament (EP), all of the internationals are represented by political groups whose composition largely reflects its membership in the particular international. Leverage is exerted through coordination with the commission, wherever it comes into play, to jointly influence the council's final decision and by the increasing weight given to the EP's opinion by third parties.[21] In both cases, consensus among the European deputies plays an important role. Issues like the European Common Agricultural Policy have often prompted debates with divisions along national political lines, thus duplicating clashes that take place in the Council of Ministers. Considerably more consensus, however, can be found among members of the EP on a broad range of foreign policy issues. Moreover, the relationship between consensus building and the degree of influence on the council's foreign policy decisions is undoubtedly an important incentive for the EP to set aside national preferences and political differences.

The EC's cooperation agreement with Central America, which was signed in November 1985 and came into force in July 1987, is a case in point supporting policy coordination between the EP and the commission. At all stages of its preparation, the EP endorsed the commission's proposal for a far-reaching cooperation agreement with the countries of the isthmus.[22] The Council of Ministers did not fully adhere to the position of commission and parliament. Yet one of the basic features of the EC-Central American dialogue as such and the cooperation agreement in particular—economic aid as a prerequisite for the promotion of peace and democracy in Central America—came in response to a parliamentary resolution that had been approved in 1982.

The Central American Parliament, which is currently in the process of development, has been largely modeled on the EP. An insight drawn from the European experience is that the Central American Parliament will be able to function only if the Central American parties create political families. Regional parliaments do not function along national voting lines but along transnational ideological lines. Therefore, the Central Americans have to build transnational, ideologically based organizations.

These organizations exist in the case of the Christian Democrats and the Liberals and to a certain extent also in that of the Social Democrats, yet neither the left nor the right count on regionwide organizations and a specific ideological framework in Central America. Once the regional parliament has been set up, however, the political forces represented within it will provide the internationals with an important forum to broaden transnational party contacts.

Political Foundations

The political foundations are often seen as the "executive organs" of their political mother organization, allowing the party to participate in the domestic politics of another country at a nongovernmental level without violating the rule of noninterference in intergovernmental relations. This is no longer true only of the German foundations, which have been involved in Central America for twenty-four years. Today the Spanish, Dutch, and Italian foundations handle at least as much money as do the German foundations, even if their organizational efficiency does not yet match the latter's.

Among the West German foundations, the activities of the *Friedrich-Ebert-Stiftung* (FES) and the *Konrad-Adenauer-Stiftung* (KAS) are particularly impressive. In size alone the international department of the FES matches that of a small foreign ministry. The foundation's international work has traditionally concentrated on Africa and Latin America, the latter being allotted 31 percent of the budget devoted to foreign activities in 1989.[23] Within the KAS's budget for international cooperation, Latin America is assigned over 50 percent of the funds.[24] Broadly speaking, their operations in the Third World are devoted to promoting political pluralism and democratic development. Thus, the foundations have helped fund political, economic, and social development projects[25] and support the development of local media infrastructures,[26] education programs, and research.[27]

The lack of public control occasionally reflects negatively on the activities of the West German foundations abroad. The allegation of meddling in the internal affairs of a country has more than once raised concern in Bonn as well as in the Latin American countries. Yet no direct link has been shown between the foundations' influence on political actors and the size of budget allotted. The foundations' personnel working abroad have demonstrated their competence and motivation. More than money, it is the foundations' ability to contact partners within a particular political, economic, and social environment that makes these foundations efficient tools in transnational party relations.

Phases of Influence

One can identify three phases in the influence of political internationals in Central America. The first came during the dictatorships. At that time public pressure and the financing of exiles' activities, of politicians in exile, and of political training abroad had a limited influence on encouraging democracy in Central America.

The second phase came during the political transitions, when influence consisted of conferring legitimacy on certain parties, giving technical aid, financing elections, and, especially, encouraging the "professionalization" of politicians. Most Central American politicians are not professionals in the sense that they learn to be politicians as a vocation. They are usually politicians because of personality, intellect, and personal ties to certain parties. In creating a professional infrastructure for more politicians, the internationals have had tremendous influence in the transitional period.

The third phase is the consolidation of democracy. Here again the internationals' influence is relatively weak. Once a democratic system is established, political activity normally becomes bilateral and state to state, and transnational politics returns to traditional political relations. Costa Rica as a consolidated democracy is a good case in point. There relations are more traditional—bilateral rather than transnational. This is also true in Nicaragua, where, since the electoral defeat of the *Sandinistas*, transnational politics seems to be on the wane.

The Policy of Good Intentions

The internationals' support for democracy in Latin America is not limited to the simple test of admitting parties to the club of democratic associations. Size alone assigns the major internationals the role of important allies whose support for a specific party might contribute decisively to the political direction of a country involved in a process of profound political and social change. This applied as much to SI support for the *Sandinistas* as to systematic Christian Democratic promotion of the Duarte option in El Salvador.

Yet there is an inherent paradox in transnational party influence. Although parties are sometimes granted more room for maneuver than governments, which allows them to experiment with new policies at a subgovernmental level, that experimentation tends to prompt political statements characterized by rhetorical overcommitment. This may not be a problem as long as member-parties are not in office and are not required to implement the policy they have been endorsing within the internationals. Yet once in government, the emergence of national or international rather than party/ideological priorities usually encourages parties to adopt more pragmatic stances and to become less active in their respective party associations. As a consequence, cooperation between parties of both regions within an international is often reduced to good intentions.

Internationals can become even more constrained by the presence of some members in national governments. The internationals' support for democracy in Central America—the endorsement of the Contadora initiative and, subsequently, the Esquipulas peace process—relied at any given moment on the member-parties involved in conflict settlement. While the CDI and ODCA threw their support behind the Christian Democrat government of Luis Herrera Campins at the onset of the Contadora process, the SI had to withdraw support simultaneous to the abandonment of the Contadora approach by its Venezuelan partner Andrés Pérez. This factor, along with the conservative trend in West European governments' Central American policy and a parallel hardening of the U.S. position, meant that the internationals could not influence crucial stages of democratization in Central America.

As much as the formerly European party associations have been opened up to Latin America, other regions hardly play a role in any of the four internationals. Yet the necessity of supporting regime-allied parties, even when their policies are not congruent with the internationals', the need for inter- and intraparty consensus, as well as the foreign policy constraints imposed on European parties in power, are factors that make long-term policies for the internationals in Latin America difficult. Furthermore, the conflicts that had to be resolved within the respective organizations led to a more limited influence on the outcome of democratization processes in Latin America than is often either suspected by their enemies or assumed by their friends.

Finally, a word about the European-dominated internationals (including the CI) with regard to the U.S. policy during the recent years of democratization in Latin America. Now that the United States is also helping political parties, especially in Nicaragua, the role of the internationals has become less clear. The Latin Americans are now unsure who the "good guys" and the "bad guys" are.

The work of the internationals must always be taken with a grain of salt. Although they can be of some help, the internationals are by no means major international actors and their work is less important than bilateral relationships or, for that matter, even than regional power relations.

Notes

1. Andreas Kohl, "Die Internationale Demokratische Union in Latein-amerika," *Zeitschrift für Latinamerika Wien*, 33 (1987):77–84.

2. For an overview, see my article "European Community Relations with Latin America: Policy Without Illusions," *Journal of Interamerican Studies and World Affairs*, 19, 4 (Winter 1987–1988):69–87. For this particular context, see also "Las Relaciones entre América Latina y Europa Occidental: Actores Nacionales y Transnacionales, Objetivos y Expectativas," *Foro Internacional*, México D.F., 33, 1 (July–September 1982):39–57.

3. Carlota Jackisch, "Las Corrientes Ideológicas Europeas y Su Impacto Sobre América Latina," *Contribuciones* (Dossier '87), Buenos Aires (October–December 1987):27–47.

4. Jackisch, "Corrientes Ideológicas," pp. 44–45.

5. Tomás Amadeo Vasconi, "La Socialdemocracia en América Latina," pp. 2–4. Mimeographed.

6. Felicity Williams, "El Sur de América Latina y las Internacionales Políticas Europeas: La Internacional Socialista y la Internacional Demócrata Cristiana," in *Malvinas Hoy: Herencia de un Conflicto*, ed. Atilio Borón and Julio Faúndez (Buenos Aires: Puntosur, 1989), pp. 365–89.

7. Felipe González (PSOE) has been vice president of SI since 1978, and Adolfo Suárez, leader of the Spanish *Centro Democrático y Social* (CDS), was elected president of the LI at the 1989 LI Congress in Paris, only a year after the CDS had joined the International; Susan Johnson, "LI Congress Bears Witness to Today's Revolutions," *Liberal International Newsletter*, 52 (December 1989):2–4.

8. Uwe Kopsch, "Grenzen und Möglichkeiten Transnationaler Parteienkooperation am Beispiel der Sozialistischen Internationale in Lateinamerika," *Zeitschrift für Lateinamerika Wien*, Wien, 33 (1987):51–64.

9. Urs Schoettli, "New Challenges for the LI in Latin America," *Liberal International Newsletter*, London, 49 (May 1989):12–14.

10. See Ricardo Combellas, "ODCA, América Latina y Europa," *Contribuciones* (Dossier '89), Buenos Aires (October–December 1989):35–37.

11. "FELICA: El Liberalismo Se Organiza en Centroamérica," *Perfiles Liberales*, Bogotá, 1 (April–May–June 1989):12–13.

12. In addition, SICLAC includes two parties from the United States and one Canadian socialist party.

13. See the information about COPPAL provided in *Nueva Sociedad* 89 (May–June 1987):82–86.

14. See the information about the CSL in *Nueva Sociedad* 92 (November–December 1987):95–100.

15. Six socialist parties from Argentina, Brazil, Chile, and Venezuela are members of COPPAL and CSL. Out of these, only the Brazilian PDT is also a member of the SI.

16. "Declaración Conjunta de los Presidentes de la Internacional Demócrata Cristiana, Internacional Liberal e Internacional Socialista Sobre América Latina," *Desarrollo y Cooperación*, Bonn, 3 (1984):3.

17. See, for example, the Final Resolution of the November 1980 Socialist Congress, *Socialist Affairs* (January-February 1981):22.

18. Julio César Santucho, "L'Internazionale Democratico Cristiana in América Latina," in *America Latin, Europa, Italia: Un Rapporto da Rinnovare*, ed. Instituto per le Relazioni tra l'Italia e i Paesi dell'Africa, America Latina e Medio Oriente (IPALMO) (Rome: IPALMO, n.d.), pp. 1–36. See also "La DC Se Define Contra Contadora," *El Día*, México D.F., December 4, 1986.

19. Eusebio Mujal-León, "European Socialism and the Crisis in Central America," *Orbis*, Philadelphia (Spring 1984):53–81, 68–69.

20. See the critical statement by Jürgen Wischnewski, member of a SI delegation that visited Central America in February 1986, in *Frankfurter Allgemeine Zeitung*, February 15, 1986.

21. David Buchan, "A Mandate Which Goes Beyond 1992," *Financial Times*, London, June 30, 1989.

22. See Guido Ashoff, *La Cooperación Para el Desarrollo Entre la Comunidad Europea y América Latina: Experiencias y Desafíos*, Documento de Trabajo, 16 (Madrid: IRELA, 1989), pp. 26–29.

23. Friedrich-Ebert-Stiftung (FES), *Jahresbericht 1989* (Bonn: Presse- und Informationsstelle der FES, 1990), p. 58.

24. See, for example, Konrad-Adenauer-Stiftung (KAS), *Jahresbericht '86* (Bonn: KAS, n.d.), p. 91.

25. In Ecuador, the FES started a project aimed at advising the government on fiscal reform. For several years the KAS has been supporting the Guatemalan association of coffee producers in their attempts to improve their marketing concept.

26. In 1987 the FES, for example, sent an expert to the Caribbean to advise members of the "Caribbean Broadcasting Union" on building a regional news network. FES, *Jahresbericht 1989*, p. 50.

27. This is, among other things, the function of the FES-founded *Instituto Latinoamericano de Investigaciones Sociales* (ILDIS), with branches in Ecuador, Venezuela, and Brazil, and the *Centro Interdisciplinario de Estudios Sobre el Desarrollo Latinamericano* (CIEDLA), set up by the KAS in Buenos Aires, Argentina.

Appendix:
Political Parties and
Elections in Central America

This appendix presents information about elections and parties in the seven countries of Central America. Information on each country is presented in the order the countries appear in the table of contents. The following information is provided for each country: (1) data on chief executive succession, (2) political party names and acronyms, and (3) results of recent legislative elections.

Guatemala

Chief Executive Succession, Guatemala

Year	Presidents	Affiliation
1944	Juan Jose Arevalo Bermejo	(FPL-RN)
1950	Jacobo Arbenz Guzman	(Military)
1954	Coup: Carlos Castillo Armas	(Military)
1958	Miguel Ydigoras Fuentes	(Military)
1966	Julio Cesar Mendez Montenegro	(PR)
1970	Carlos Manuel Arana Osorio	(Military)
1978	Fernando Romeo Lucas Garcia	(Military)
1982	Angel A. Guevara Rodriguez	(Military)[a]
1982	Coup: Efrain Ríos Montt	(Military)
1983	Coup: Oscar Mejia V.	(Military)
1986	Vinicio Cerezo Arevalo	(DCG)
1991	Jorge Serrano Elias	(MAS)

[a]Elections were annulled because no candidate achieved the required majority. The National Congress endorsed General Guevara, who had obtained 38.9 percent of votes (379,051), but he was deposed by a military coup.

Sources: John Booth and Mitchell A. Seligson, *Elections and Democracy in Central America* (Chapel Hill: University of North Carolina Press, 1989), pp. 93–120; and Ronald H. McDonald and J. Mark Ruhl, *Party Politics and Elections in Latin America* (Boulder, Colo.: Westview Press, 1989), pp. 277–89.

Note: In the presidential run-off election of December 8, 1985, Vinicio Cerezo Arevalo received 68 percent of the vote, whereas his opponent, Jorge Carpio Nicolle (UNC), received only 32 percent.

National Political Parties, Guatemala

Acronymn	Political Party
CAN	Authentic Nationalist Center
CAO	Central Organized Aranist
DCG	Christian Democratic Party of Guatemala
FND	Democratic National Front
FNO	National Opposition Front
FPL	Popular Liberator Front
FRG	Guatemalan Republican Front
FUN	National Unity Front
FUR	United Revolutionary Front
FURD	United Democratic Revolutionary Front
MAS	Solidarity Action Movement
MDN	National Democratic Movement
MEC	Emerging Movement of Concord
MLN	National Liberation Movement
PAN	National Advancement Party
PAR	Revolutionary Action Party
PCG	Guatemalan Communist Party
PDC	Democratic Central Party
PDCN	Democratic Party of National Cooperation
PDN	National Democratic Party
PIACO	Independent Anticommunist Party of the West
PID	Institutional Democratic Party
PLA	Authentic Liberal Party
PNR	National Renewal Party
PNV	Plataforma No-Venta (Platform Ninety)
PRA	Authentic Revolutionary Party
PRG	Guatemalan Revolutionary Party
PSD	Democratic Socialist Party
PT	Workers Party
PUA	Anti-Communist Unification Party
RN	National Renovation
UCN	National Center Union
UPA	Anticommunist Patriotic Union
URD	Revolutionary Democratic Unit

Legislative Assembly Elections, Guatemala, 1985

Political Party	Seats in Congress
DCG	51
UNC	22
PDCN/PR	11
MLN/PID	6
PSD	2
CAN	1
PNR	1
PUA/FUN/MEC	0
Total	94

Sources: Central America Report (November 8, 1985), p. 338 and (November 29, 1985), p. 365, taken from Ronald H. McDonald and J. Mark Ruhl, *Party Politics and Elections in Latin America* (Boulder, Colo.: Westview Press, 1989, p. 287). *Note:* Seventy-five of the members were elected democratically, 25 percent were based on proportional representation. Percentage of valid votes in Round 1 of presidential elections; total votes cast were 1,906,952, of which 228,652 (12 percent) were invalid or blank.

Legislative Assembly Elections, Guatemala, 1990

Political Party	Seats in Congress
UNC	41
DCG	27
MAS	13
PAN	12
PNV[a]	12
MLN-FAN	4
PR	1
PSD-APN	1
Total	111

[a]Alliance of PID, FRG, and FAN.

Belize

Chief Executive Succession, Belize

Year	Prime Minister	Party
1961	George Price	PUP[a]
1964	George Price	PUP
1984	Manuel Esquival	UDP
1989	George Price	PUP

[a]PUP dominated the electoral scene from 1961 to 1984. George Price was prime minister from 1961 to 1981, elected again in 1969, 1974, and 1979. On Belizean independence in 1981, Price became prime minister until he was electorally defeated in 1984 by Manuel Esquival.

National Political Parties, Belize

Acronymn	Political Party
PUP	People's United Party
UDP	United Democratic Party

Legislative Assembly Elections, Belize

Year	PUP (seats)	UDP (seats)
1984	7	21
1989[a]	15	13

[a]One UPD member announced that he intended to support the PUP, thus raising the government's legislative majority from 16 to 12.

El Salvador

Chief Executive Succession, El Salvador

Year	Presidents	Affiliation
1944	Maximiliano Hernandez Martinez	(Coup)
1948	Oscar Osorio	(Coup)
1950	Oscar Osorio	(PRUD)
1956	Jose Maria Lemus	(PRUD)
1960	Julio Rivera	(Coup)
1961	Julio Rivera	PCN
1972	Armando Molina	PCN
1977	Humberto Romero	(Coup)
1984	Jose Napoleon Duarte	PDC
1989	Alfredo Cristiani	ARENA

National Political Parties, El Salvador

Acronymn	Political Party
AD	Democratic Action Party
ARENA	Nationalist Republican Alliance
CD	Democratic Convergence
PAISA	Authentic Institutional Salvadoran Party
PAR	Renovated Action Party
PCN	National Conciliation Party
PDC	Christian Democratic Party
PL	Liberation Party
POP	Popular Orientation Party
PPS	Popular Salvadoran Party
PRUD	Revolutionary Party of Democratic Unification (Military-controlled political party that provided regime that backed it. Later renamed PCN.)
PSD	Social Democratic Party
UDN	Nationalist Democratic Union

Legislative Assembly Elections, El Salvador, 1985–91

Party	1985	1988	1991
PDC	33	23	26
ARENA	13	30	39
PCN	12	7	9
CD	–	–	8
UDN	–	–	1
AD	1	0	–
PPS	0	0	0
POP	0	0	–
PAISA	1	0	–
Total[a]	60	60	83

[a]In 1991 the Salvadoran Legislative Assembly was expanded to give smaller political parties greater opportunity to gain formal access to the legislative process.

Honduras

Chief Executive Succession, Honduras

Year	Presidents	Affiliation
1948	Juan Manuel Galvez	PN
1954	Julio Lozano Diaz	PUN
1956	Hector Caraccioli	(Coup)
1957	Jose Ramon Villeda Morales	PL
1963	Oswaldo Lopez Arellano	(Coup)
1965	Oswaldo Lopez Arellano	–
1971	Ramon Ernesto Cruz Ucles	PN
1972	O. Lopez Arellano	(Coup)
1975	Juan Melgar Castro	(Coup)
1978	Policarpo Paz Garcia	(Coup)
1981	Roberto Suazo Cordoba	PL
1986	Jose Azcona Hoyo	PL (51%)
1990	Rafael Leonardo Callejas	PN (52%)

National Political Parties, Honduras

Acronymn	Political Party
ALIPO	Popular Liberal Alliance
FP	Patriotic Honduran Front
MLR	Rodista Liberal Movement
MNR	National Reformist Movement
PC	Communist Party
PDC	Christian Democratic Party
PINU	Innovation and National Unity Party
PL	Liberal Party
PN	National Party
PR	Revolutionary Party
PUN	National Unity Party
URP	Revolutionary Union of the People

Legislative Assembly Elections, Honduras, 1985, 1989

Year	PL	PN	PINU	PDC
1985	67	63	2	2
1989	71	55	2	–

Source: Europa World Year Book 1990 (London: Europa Publications, 1990), p. 1252.

Nicaragua

Chief Executive Succession, Nicaragua

Year	Presidents	Affiliation
1936	Anastasio Somoza Garcia	PLN
1951	Anastasio Somoza Garcia	PLN
1957	Luis Somoza Debayle	PLN
1963	Rene Schick Gutierrez	PLN
1967	Anastasio Somoza Debayle	PLN
1979	Daniel Ortega Saavedra	FSLN
1984	Daniel Ortega Saavedra	FSLN
1990	Violeta Barrios de Chamorro	UNO

National Political Parties, Nicaragua

Acronymn	Political Party
APC	Popular Conservative Alliance
FSLN	Sandinista National Liberation Front
MAP-ML	Marxist-Leninist Popular Action Movement
MUR	Movement of Revolutionary Unity Parties (including PSD, APC, PCN, PSN, among others)
PCD	Democratic Conservative Party
PCN	Conservative Party of Nicaragua
PCN	Nicaraguan Communist Party
PLI	Independent Liberal Party
PLIUN	Independent Liberal Party for National Unity
PLN	Nationalist Liberal Party
PPSC	Popular Social Christian Party
PRT	Workers Revolutionary Party
PSC	Social Conservative Party
PSD	Social Democratic Party
PSN	Nicaraguan Socialist Party
PSN	Nicaraguan Socialist Party
PUCA	Central American Unionist Party
UNO[a]	National Opposition Union (Comprised of 14 different parties, including PSD, APC, PCN, PSN, among others)

[a]The coalition ran a presidential ticket in 1990. Legislative Assembly seats were decided on a party-by-party basis.

Legislative Assembly Elections, Nicaragua, 1984

Party	Number of Seats
FSLN	65
PCD	14
PLI	9
PPSC	6
PCN	2
PSN	2
MAP-ML	2
Total	100

Legislative Assembly Elections, Nicaragua, 1990

Party	Number of Seats
UNO	51
FSLN	39
MUR	1
PSC	2
Total	93

Source: South America, Central America, and the Caribbean, 3rd ed. Europa Publications, 1991.

Costa Rica

Chief Executive Succession, Costa Rica

Year	Presidents	Affiliation
1948	Otilio Ulate Blanco	PUN
1953	Jose Figueres	PLN
1958	Mario Echandi	PUN-PR
1962	Francisco Orlich	PLN
1966	Jose Joaquin Trejos	UN
1970	Jose Figueres	PLN
1974	Daniel Oduber Quiroz	PLN
1978	Rodrigo Carazo Odio	UN
1982	Luis A. Monge Alvarez	PLN
1986	Oscar Arias Sanchez	PLN
1990	Rafael Angelo Calderon	PUSC

National Political Parties, Costa Rica

Acronymn	Political Party
PD	Democratic Party
PDC	Christian Democratic Party
PLN	National Liberation Party
PR	Republican Party
PUN	National Union Party
PUP	Popular Union Party
PURA	Authentic Republican Union
PUSC	Social Christian Unity Party (PUP, PRC, PRD, PDC)
UN	National Unification Coalition (PURA, PUN, PR)

Legislative Assembly Elections, Costa Rica

Years	1953	1958	1962	1966	1970	1974	1978	1982	1986	1990
PLN	30	20	29	29	32	27	25	33	29	25
PD	11									
PUN	1	10	8							
PR		11	19							
UN				27	22	16				
UNIDAD							28	18	25	29
Left			1				4	4	2	

Panama

Chief Executive Succession, Panama

Year	Presidents	Affiliation
1952	Jose Antonio Remon	CPN
1956	Ernesto de la Guardia	CPN
1960	Roberto Chiari	UNO
1964	Marco Aurelio Robles	UNO
1968	Arnulfo Arias Madrid	PRA
	Omar Torrijos	(Coup)
1972	Demetrio Basilio Lakas (President)	PRD
	Omar Torrijos (Chief of State)	
1978	Aristides Royo Sanchez	*
1982	Ricardo de la Espriella	*
1984	Jorge Illueca	*
	Nicolas Ardito Barletta	UNADE
1987	Eric Arturo del Valle	PR
1988	Manuel Solis Palma	a
1989	Guillermo Endara[b]	ADOC[c]

Note: After Noriega was ousted in December 1989, Endara, widely believed to have won the May 1989 elections, was installed in the presidency. See Editors' Update for details.

*Presidents were designated by the "Assembly of Representatives of the Community," later the Legislative Assembly.

[a]When Del Valle was removed from office the Legislative Assembly named former Minister of Education Solis Palma to serve as an interim chief executive with the title "Minister-in-Charge of the Presidency." Solis Palma was never officially president.
[b]After Noriega was ousted, Endara, widely believed to have won the May 1989 elections was installed in the presidency.
[c]The ADOC coalition included the PDC, MOLIRENA, PPA, PAPO, and PNP.

National Political Parties, Panama

Acronymn	Political Party
ADOC	Democratic Alliance of the Opposition (PDC, MOLINERA, PLA, PPA, PAPO, PNP)
COLINA	Coalition for National Liberation (PRD, PALA, PPR, PL, PR, PPP, PDT, PAN)
CPN	National Patriotic Coalition
MOLIRENA	Republican Liberal Movement
PALA	Labor Party
PAN	National Action Party
PAPO	Popular Action Party
PDC	Christian Democratic Party
PDT	Democratic Worker's Party
PL	Liberal Party
PLA	Authentic Liberal Party
PNP	Nationalist People's Party
PPP	Panamanian People's Party
PPR	Revolutionary Panamenista Party
PR	Republican Party
PRA	Authentic Revolutionary Party
PRD	Democratic Revolutionary Party
UNADE	National Democratic Union
UNO	National Opposition Union

Legislative Assembly Elections, Panama, 1989 (Annulled)

Party	Number of Seats
ADOC	**51**
PDC	27
MOLIRENA	15
PCA	9
PRD[a]	**6**

Note: Results of the election were annulled by Noriega. Of the 10 remaining seats, PALA was expected to be allocated 1; 9, allocated by new elections.

[a]This party is headed by COLINA.

Legislative Assembly Elections, Panama, 1989 (Annulled)

Party	Number of Seats
PDC	28
MOLINERA	16
PA	7
PLA	4
Total for Ruling Coalitions	**55**
PRD	10
PL	1
PALA	1
Total for Opposition	**12**

Note: On January 27, 1991, special elections were held for the legislative assembly to fill seats left vacant as a result of the annulled results of the 1989 elections.

About the Book

During the 1980s, superpower rivalry and regional conflicts decimated the Central American economies and eroded political systems within the region. Recent years, however, have witnessed remarkable political change, and since 1990 popularly elected presidents have held office in all seven countries. This book offers a comprehensive analysis of the political party system in each of the Central American states. Contributors present the history of Central American political institutions and examine the domestic and international influences that have shaped the political process, including the church, the military, and the foreign policies of the United States and the former Soviet Union.

About the Editors and Contributors

Adolfo Aguilar Zinser is a senior researcher at the Center for the Study of the United States of America, National Autonomous University of Mexico. He has served in the administration of Mexican president José Echeverria and headed the program on Central America for the Center for Research and Teaching in Economics in Mexico City. Mr. Aguilar Zinser has written widely about Mexican politics and foreign policy.

Cynthia J. Arnson is associate director of Americas Watch, a human rights organization. She has served for five years as senior foreign policy aide to Representative George Miller (D-CA) and is the author of *Crossroads: Congress, the Reagan Administration, and Central America.*

Morris J. Blachman is associate director of the Institute of International Studies at the University of South Carolina. He has written on U.S. foreign policy and Latin America. He is coeditor of *Terms of Conflict: Ideology in Latin American Politics* and coeditor (with William M. Leogrande and Kenneth Sharpe) of *Confronting Revolution: Security Through Diplomacy in Central America.*

Rodolfo Cerdas Cruz is a professor at the School of Political Science of the University of Costa Rica and a senior researcher at the Center of Investigation and Political-Administration Training. Dr. Cerdas Cruz's publications include *The Hammer and the Sickle: The International Communist in Latin America and the Central American Revolution* and *The Crisis of Liberal Democracy in Costa Rica.*

Margaret E. Crahan is the Henry R. Luce Professor of Religion, Power and Political Process at Occidental College. Dr. Crahan's extensive publications on Latin America include *Africa and the Caribbean: The Legacies of a Link* and *Human Rights and Basic Needs in the Americas.* Forthcoming are *Religion, Churches and Change in Contemporary Latin America* and *Debora: Portrait of a Political Prisoner.*

Cristina Eguizábal is a political scientist who teaches at the University of Costa Rica. She is the executive director of *Respuestas*, the Central American Council for International Relations. Dr. Eguizábal is president of the Costa Rican Political Science Association and has served on the Ford-MacArthur Scholarship Selection Committee for Mexico and Central America from 1987 through 1991.

Jorge Mario García Laguardia is a justice on the Supreme Court of Guatemala. An expert on constitutions, he served as director of the *Centro de Asesoria y Promoción Electoral* in Costa Rica. Recently, Mr. García Laguardia served as a professor at the National Autonomous University in Mexico. He has published widely on Central American law and politics.

Virgilio Godoy Reyes is the vice president of Nicaragua, elected as part of the *Unión Nacional Oppositor* (UNO) coalition in 1990. A leader of the Independent Liberal Party, Mr. Godoy served as the national labor minister under the *Sandanista* administration in the early 1980s. He later became a prominent spokesperson in opposition to the *Sandanistas*.

William Goodfellow is executive director of the Center for International Policy, a research institution in Washington, D.C. He is the only American to have attended all six Esquipulas summits dealing with the peace process in Central America. His articles on foreign policy appear regularly in newspapers and journals throughout the United States.

Louis W. Goodman is dean of the School of International Service at The American University in Washington, D.C. Dr. Goodman has written widely on the impact of policies in developed nations and prospects for development in Latin America. He is coeditor (with Johanna Mendelson Forman and Juan Rial) of *The Military and Democracy: The Future of Civil-Military Relations in Latin America* and author of *Small Nations, Giant Firms*.

Wolf Grabendorff is the director of the Madrid-based Institute for European-Latin American Relations. Prior to that, he served as a research associate for Latin American Affairs at the *Stiftung Wissenschaft und Politik* (SWP) in Ebenhausen, Germany, and spent three years as the Latin American correspondent for the German television network ARD in Buenos Aires.

William M. LeoGrande is professor of government in the School of Public Affairs at The American University in Washington, D.C. He is author of *Cuba's Policy in Africa* and coeditor (with Morris J. Blachman and Kenneth Sharpe) of *Confronting Revolution: Security Through Diplomacy in Central America*. He has written widely in the field of Latin American politics and Inter-American relations.

Johanna Mendelson Forman is on the research faculty of the School of International Service at The American University and is the director of the Democracy Projects. She has written about the law and U.S. foreign policy and is coeditor (with Louis W. Goodman and Juan Rial) of *The Military and Democracy: The Future of Civil-Military Relations in Latin America*.

Sergo Mikoyan is a chief researcher at the Institute of Peace (Academy of Sciences, Moscow). Before assuming this post in August 1990, he served as editor-in-chief of the Soviet monthly journal *Latin America*. Mr. Mikoyan has worked as a researcher at the Institute of World Economy–International Relations, and from June 1991 to June 1992 he served as an adjunct professor at Georgetown University.

Richard L. Millett is professor of history at the University of Southern Illinois, Edwardsville. Dr. Millett has published widely on politics and society in Central America, including his *Guardians of the Dynasty: A History of the Nicaraguan Civil Guard*.

James Morrell is the research director of the Center for International Policy. His 1987 report, "Fear of Signing: The Maneuvering Around the Arias Plan," was called the best analysis of the plan to have appeared. Morrell received his Ph.D. in history from Harvard University in 1977.

Ernesto Paz Aguilar is a professor of political science at the National University of Honduras. He is a lawyer and received his Ph.D. in France. He currently serves in the Honduran legislature as a representative of the National Liberal Party.

Héctor Rosada Granados is a professor at Docencia University in Guatemala. Mr. Rosada Granados is the principal investigator, political analyst, and coordinator of the Institute of Investigation and Political "Autoformation." He has written widely on Guatemalan power structure, political parties, and elections.

Kenneth E. Sharpe is a professor of political science at Swarthmore College. He is author of *Peasant Politics: Struggle in a Dominican Village*, coauthor (with Douglas Bennett) of *Transnational Corporations and the Mexican State: The Political Economy of the Mexican Automobile Industry*, and coeditor (with Morris J. Blachman and William M. Leogrande) of *Confronting Revolution: Security Through Diplomacy in Central America*.

Assad Shoman is the executive director of the Society for the Promotion of Education and Research (SPEAR) and the editor of *SPEARHEAD*, a bimonthly journal. An active participant in Belizean national politics, he served as the representative of Belize to the United Nations General Assembly (1975–80). Mr. Shoman has written extensively on the political movements in Belize.

David A. Smith is a professor in the School of Sociology in the National University of Costa Rica. He is also the coordinator of the cultural subprogram of the Central American University Confederation. He has written and lectured widely about Central American education, culture, and politics and about Panama in particular.

Wayne S. Smith is an adjunct professor of Latin American Studies at The Johns Hopkins School of Advanced International Studies (SAIS) in Washington, D.C. A former U.S. Foreign Service officer with assignments in Moscow and Havana, Dr. Smith has published widely on Cuba, Central America, Argentina, and on Soviet policy in Latin America. He recently authored *Portrait of Cuba* and edited *The Russians Aren't Coming: New Soviet Policy in Latin America.*

José Luis Vega Carballo is a professor at the University of Costa Rica. A Costa Rican political sociologist, Mr. Vega Carballo was the coordinator of the *Guide to Central American Political Parties,* a project of the *Centro de Asesoria y Promoción Electoral.*

Index